# *Praise for The Cool Mountain Cookbook...*

"*The Cool Mountain Cookbook* brings the nation's most luxurious ski resorts
to your armchair. Enjoy the breathtaking photographs and vivid descriptions, then move
to the kitchen where you can easily duplicate the resorts' signature dishes by following
Gwen Ashley Walters clear, well-written recipes."

— **Barbara Pool Fenzl,** owner of Les Gourmettes Cooking School,
PBS television host and author of *Southwest the Beautiful Cookbook*
and *Savor the Southwest.*

"An invaluable and well-organized guide for the skier and gourmet alike.
Ms. Walters has brought to life the adventures of a winter sojourn as well as
interpreting chefs' recipes that work for the home cook."

— **Gaye G. Ingram,** author of
*Webster's New World Dictionary of Culinary Arts.*

"Reading a cookbook in its pre-published form puts it to the acid test.
If it can make your mouth water without a single glossy photo, it's a winner,
and when I read *The Cool Mountain Cookbook,* it did just that! I love Gwen's warm approach
to recipes, and her straightforward instructions promise success no matter what level of
experience you have. Her obvious enthusiasm for the food and the resorts where she
tasted it comes across on every page. Within fifteen minutes I not only wanted to eat,
I also wanted to grab my skis and head for the mountains!"

— **Mark Tarbell,** chef/owner of Tarbell's and Barmouche restaurants
in Phoenix, wine columnist and frequent guest of
Food TV Network's Ready-Set-Cook.

"Gwen Ashley Walters has a sensitive approach to food, is a wiz at preparation
and as you will see in reading and using this book, she is both very creative
and thorough — rare combination indeed."

— **Jane Butel,** author of 16 cookbooks, including *Hotter Than Hell,
Southwestern Grill* and *Quick and Easy Southwestern*
(from the foreword of *The Great Ranch Cookbook* also by Gwen Ashley Walters).

# The Cool Mountain
## COOKBOOK

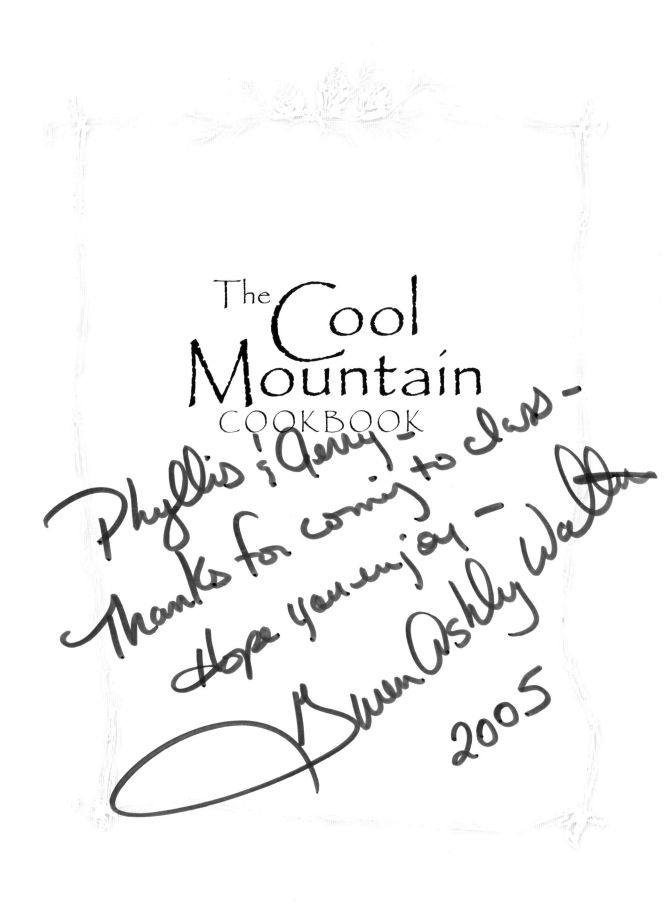

Phyllis & Jerry -
Thanks for coming to class -
Hope you enjoy -

Susan Ashly Walton

2005

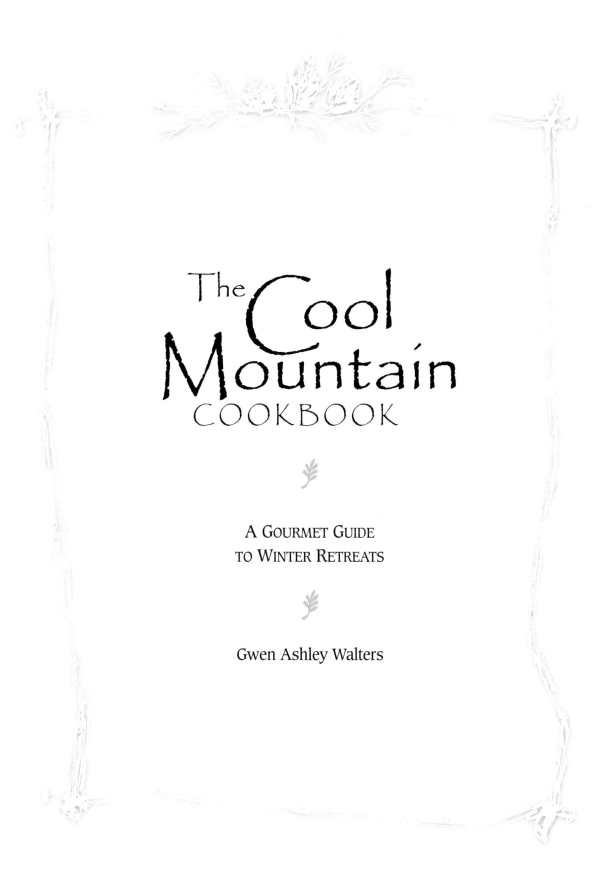

# The Cool Mountain Cookbook

A GOURMET GUIDE
TO WINTER RETREATS

Gwen Ashley Walters

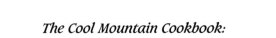

*The Cool Mountain Cookbook:*
*A Gourmet Guide to Winter Retreats*

*Copyright © 2001 by Gwen Ashley Walters, CCP*

Published by
**Pen & Fork**
P.O. Box 5165
Carefree, AZ 85377

Front Cover Photo:
Vista Verde, Steamboat Springs, Colorado

Edited by Olin B. Ashley

Illustrations by Betsy Hillis

Cover by ATG Productions, Inc.,
Christy Moeller-Mosel, Phoenix, Arizona

Interior design by Masterpiece Publishing, LLC
Michele O'Hagan, Phoenix, Arizona

Interior food photography
(except Deer Valley Soy Glazed Sea Bass)
by Jeffrey S. Walters

Library of Congress Control Number: 00-092182

ISBN 0-9663486-1-3

Printed in Hong Kong
First Edition

**www.penandfork.com**

# Dedication

For my incredible husband
Jeffrey Scott Walters

Also by Gwen Ashley Walters
*The Great Ranch Cookbook:*
*Spirited Recipes and Rhetoric from America's Best Guest Ranches*

**Pen & Fork**
Carefree, Arizona

**www.penandfork.com**

# *Table of Contents*

# Content By State

# Content By Recipe Category

*(continued on next page)*

# Content By Recipe Category

(CONTINUED)

*(continued on next page)*

# Content By Recipe Category
## (CONTINUED)

*(continued on next page)*

# Content By Recipe Category
(CONTINUED)

# Introduction

Snow-covered pines whispering in the wind. Ice crunching beneath the cinched ski boots. Breath fogs just outside the mouth, lingering for a moment before blending into the cold, crisp air. Snowflakes fall angelically, covering the tracks of yesterday's skiers. The first run of the day is hauntingly thrilling, swishing through fresh powder, making new tracks. Skiing, either downhill or cross-country, provides a sense of oneness with nature in all her virginal greatness. Wintertime is a peaceful time, with a stillness and serenity unmatched in any other season.

Once upon a time, great skiing meant a trip abroad, to Canada or Europe. Today, some of the top ski mountains are located here in this country, from coast to coast. This book features 20 of the top-rated ski lodges and other glorious winter retreats, located in and around the best ski resorts in America. Even if skiing is not high on your agenda, relaxing in a cool mountain setting is worth its weight in snow. Each lodge selected for this book provides first class amenities, impeccable service, and food that is simply out of this world.

Some of the lodges are located in ski towns, towns renowned for their winter playgrounds, like Aspen and Vail. Others are located off the beaten path, and provide a true winter wonderland escape, offering a harmonious sojourn with nature, far from the hustle and bustle of the resort towns. All of them are the best at what they do. And all of them create incomparable alpine cuisine not likely to be forgotten.

Plan your winter respite using this book as a guide. Travel tips help you decide what vacation destination is best suited to your wants and needs. If you can't break away for a winter recess, then use this book to re-create the fabulous mountain cuisine these lodges have graciously shared. With each bite, close your eyes and transport yourself to another world, one where the snow falls, the air is cool and clean, and peace reigns supreme. Enjoy!

# *Travel Tips*

*I*'ve done my best to accurately present the facts as well as the personal descriptions of each lodge. I hope you enjoy this book and that it will help you find a place that fits your idea of a dream winter vacation. But before you make your plans, I suggest that you read the following points to help you make your decision.

- All rates listed in this book represent the 2001 peak winter season. Unless otherwise noted, the rate represents 1 night's lodging only.

  $ ..........less than $200
  $$ ........$201–300
  $$$ ......$301–400
  $$$$ ....$401 and higher

- Call the lodge to verify the rate and ask if there are other packages you might consider. Most of the lodges have different pricing for different times of the year.

- Ask about arrival and departure times and transportation options.

- If you are going for the skiing, ask about the type of skiing close by. Some are located close to downhill skiing, others offer nearby cross-country and even back country skiing.

- All of the lodges represented are open during the summer and have a whole host of exciting activities and summer fun in store for their guests. Many offer lower rates in the summer, so if you can't get away in the winter, keep them in mind as fantastic summer destinations.

- These tips are only suggestions. I'm sure you will think of other questions to ask as you plan your vacation. The most important thing is to select a destination that offers the activities, food and ambiance you prefer. All of the lodges in this book are destinations worth visiting. Some will appeal to more of your interests than others. My hope is that through this book, you will find vacation destinations that exceed your expectations. Let me know what your experience is, from making a reservation to spending time at the lodge, including the things you like and don't like.

- To e-mail me, visit my website at: ***www.penandfork.com.***
  I will do my best to answer any questions you may have. If I don't know the answer, I'll find someone who does.

# Recipe for Success

Every single recipe in this book was tested in my home kitchen in Scottsdale, Arizona. I also employed two culinary student testers, and a neighbor, Marilyn Robertson, re-tested a number of recipes for me. I know these recipes will work for you in your kitchen. I changed the recipes only when necessary to make them easier, without compromising the integrity of the dish. You will find a good mix of easy and challenging recipes. I want you to have the same success and fun I had re-creating these scrumptious culinary delights. If you run into any problems or have any questions about the recipes, ingredients or procedures, contact me through my Website (*www.penandfork.com*) and I will help you. Read through the points I've outlined below to help ensure your success. But if that doesn't help, I'm only a digital link away.

■ Read the recipe all the way through before you start, even before you go to the grocery store to buy the ingredients. The directions might tell you to start a process the night before.

■ *Mise en Place.* This is the French term for "everything in its place." It means gathering all the ingredients and equipment (and reading the entire recipe) before you begin. This will save you precious time and more than likely determine your success more than any other tip I could give you.

■ Watch for the word "divided" in the ingredient list. It means that ingredient will be used more than once in the recipe. The directions will tell you how to divide the ingredient.

■ Measure ingredients in the appropriate utensils. Use metal measuring cups for dry ingredients, such as flour, sugar, chopped carrots, etc. Level off with a straight edge across the top of the cup for the appropriate measurement. Use glass or plastic measuring cups with spouts for liquid ingredients such as water, milk, honey, etc. Get down to eye level for more accurate measuring.

■ If the preparation method is listed before the ingredient, then you measure it prepared. For example, ½ cup chopped carrot means chop the carrot first, then measure ½ cup. If the preparation is shown after the ingredient, such as ½ cup pecans, chopped, measure first and then chop.

■ *This is very important:* set cooking and baking times for 5 to 10 minutes less than the shortest time given in a recipe. Different ovens cook at different temperatures, and I don't want you to overcook something because your oven cooks hotter than mine does.

# *Recipe for Success*

### (Continued)

■ Across all recipes:
- Flour is unbleached all-purpose
- Eggs are large, about 2 ounces each
- Butter is unsalted
- Milk is whole milk, unless otherwise noted
- Spinach is soaked in cold water to remove dirt, and dried
- Yeast is dry, not quick-acting, unless otherwise noted
- Salt is kosher salt; if you use regular table salt, reduce the quantity by about ¼. Kosher salt crystals are larger than regular table salt, therefore a teaspoon of kosher salt is really less salt than a teaspoon of table salt.

■ Measurement conversions:
- 3 teaspoons   =   1 tablespoon
- 1 cup         =   8 ounces (for milk, water, wine, vinegar, etc.)
- 1 pound       =   16 ounces
- 2 cups        =   1 pint
- 2 pints       =   1 quart
- 4 quarts      =   1 gallon
- 1 cup         =   16 tablespoons

Dry ingredients and some "thick" liquid ingredient weights cannot be converted into cup measurements. For example, 1 cup of flour is 4 ounces, not 8; and 1 cup of sugar is 6 ounces.

**www.penandfork.com**

# Common Procedures

## Demi-glace

Many recipes call for "demi-glace" which, in the traditional French sense, is a highly-reduced, gelatinous sauce of half brown sauce, half veal stock. I use a brand of demi-glace called Custom Master's Touch Sauce Bases. It's easy to prepare, combining 3 tablespoons of the demi-glace per 1 cup of boiling water. I find it in the refrigerated section at A. J.'s Fine Foods. You can order it from A. J.'s if your store doesn't carry it. See Sources, page 192.

There are other sources, however, including a Williams-Sonoma product called "Forgotten Tradition." Another option is the use of homemade beef stock or reduced sodium beef broth or reconstituted beef bouillon, although this option requires either a roux or a slurry to thicken the mixture.

A roux is equal parts (by weight) of fat and flour (for example, ½ an ounce of butter (1 tablespoon) and ½ an ounce of flour (2 tablespoons) which is cooked for a few minutes until it turns golden. Then the cooked roux is mixed into the hot broth and simmered until it thickens and the starch taste disappears, about 15 minutes. Use the ratio of 1 tablespoon of butter and 2 tablespoons of flour per cup of broth. Once thickened, this sauce may be substituted for the demi-glace as you proceed with the recipe.

A slurry is a mixture of equal parts cold water and cornstarch or arrowroot. The boiling broth will thicken immediately when the slurry is added. Remember that it will thicken only if the liquid is boiling. Use 1 tablespoon of cold water and 1 tablespoon of cornstarch per cup of broth.

Both options produce a slightly salty sauce, so do not add any more salt without first tasting. Either method will produce a substitute for demi-glace, though neither will have the depth of flavor of a demi-glace.

# *Common Procedures*

## Hollandaise Sauce

I use a brand of hollandaise called Custom Master's Touch Sauce Bases (same brand as the demi-glace I use). It's easy to prepare; combining 4 tablespoons of the hollandaise mix per 1 cup of boiling water. It needs a little brightening with a tablespoon of lemon juice and dash of cayenne pepper, but it tastes almost fresh with a little doctoring. I find it in the refrigerated section at A. J.'s Fine Foods. You can order it if your store doesn't carry it. See Sources, page 192.

## Roasting Garlic

Preheat oven to 350°F. Cut top ⅓ off, exposing cloves. Brush with olive oil and place in a roasting pan. Roast in the oven for 30 to 40 minutes, or until cloves are golden brown. Cool and remove cloves from papery shell. Will keep, covered, in the refrigerator for 1 week.

## Roasting Hazelnuts

Preheat oven to 350°F. Spread hazelnuts on a sheet pan and roast for 15 to 18 minutes, just until the skins darken and start to crack. Careful or they will burn, but you need to give the as much time as you can to bring out the flavor. Remove from the oven and cool. You will hear a lot of crackling as they cool. Once cooled, place a handful or two in a kitchen towel and rub vigorously. Most of the skins will come off, but don't worry if some don't. Repeat the process until all the nuts have been skinned.

## Toasting other nuts

Preheat oven to 350°F. Spread nuts on a sheet pan and bake for 5 to 7 minutes or until fragrant, stirring occasionally.

## Toasting Coconut

Preheat oven to 350°F. Spread coconut on an ungreased sheet pan and bake for 7 to 10 minutes, or until golden brown, stirring often.

# *California*

## Plumpjack
## Squaw Valley Inn

1920 Squaw Valley Road
P.O. Box 2407
Olympic Valley, CA
96146
**800.323.7666**
**www.plumpjack.com**

**Season:**
Year-round;
peak winter:
January through March

**Guest Capacity:**
140

**Accommodations:**
61 rooms,
6 luxury suites

**Winter Activities:**
Downhill and
cross-country skiing;
snowboarding;
snowmobiling; snowshoeing;
ice skating; sleigh rides

**Peak Winter Rates:**
$$-$$$

**Closest Ski Resort:**
Squaw Valley

The best kept secret among the upper echelon of California skiers? Without a doubt, it's Plumpjack Squaw Valley Inn. Rated "one of the top 101 best hotels in the world" by *Tatler Cunard Travel Guide,* this luxurious resort radiates a small hotel feel with big resort amenities. Originally built as prestigious lodging for the 1960 Winter Olympic athletes, the resort received a complete face-lift in 1995 from one of the most notable national design firms in San Francisco.

Ensconced in the majestic Sierra Nevada Mountains about 200 miles northeast of San Francisco, Plumpjack describes its décor as whimsical and playful. I describe it as comfortable but luxurious, warm and inviting with lots of earth tones and metals. It feels rich but doesn't shout rich.

If you can tear yourself away from the allure of the Inn, the activities that await you after breakfast will justify your decadent breakfast choice, like the Lemon Ricotta Pancakes with Honey-Pecan Butter, served with a side of Applewood Smoked Bacon. Trust me, you'll burn all the calories and then some with a few trips up the ski lift (assuming you actually ski down), or scaling the rock-climbing wall at the center across the street (since it's indoor, it's a year-round activity).

Of course, you could opt for the less filling breakfast, say the Atlantic Smoked Salmon on a Toasted Bagel with Preserved Lemon and Capers, and then feel good about a quick hike through the property's nature trail. Later in the day, you may want an in-room massage before heading to the gorgeous wood, copper and brass bar in the lounge to sip a dry martini. Soon dinner will beckon with wafting smells of roasted garlic and grilled meats. Your taste buds will dance in delight with any of the California-Mediterranean selections, and Plumpjack has graciously shared one of its guests' favorites, Spring Onion Risotto with a lusty tomato and almond sauce.

## Breakfast Menu

SEASONAL FRUIT PLATE

POACHED EGGS WITH SMOKED HAM
ON A TOASTED HERB BISCUIT

✷ COFFEECAKE MUFFINS

## Dinner Menu

BELGIAN ENDIVE & ROQUEFORT SALAD

✷ SPRING ONION RISOTTO
WITH CRUSHED TOMATO AND ALMOND SAUCE

FRUIT & CHEESE PLATE

✷ RECIPE INCLUDED

# Coffeecake Muffins

W hat a great idea, a coffeecake in individual portions! Dense and sweet, these muffins will fill you up in a hurry. The spicy, crunchy topping is terrific. Make the topping first and set it aside while you prepare the muffin batter.

**14 MUFFINS**

**Topping:**
3 tablespoons butter
¼ cup light brown sugar
¼ cup rolled oats
¼ cup flour
¼ cup chopped walnuts
½ teaspoon ground cinnamon

**Batter:**
1½ cups buttermilk
2 eggs
¾ cup (1½ sticks) butter, melted
3¼ cups flour
1 cup light brown sugar
2½ teaspoons baking powder
½ teaspoon baking soda
½ teaspoon ground cinnamon

1. To prepare the topping: place all the ingredients (butter through cinnamon) with the butter on top, in a food processor. Pulse a few times until the mixture is coarse and crumbly. You can do this by hand if you prefer. Set aside.

2. Preheat the oven to 400°F. Spray a muffin pan with nonstick spray.

3. To prepare the batter: Whisk the buttermilk and eggs together. Stir the buttermilk mixture and melted butter until well mixed.

4. Stir together the flour, brown sugar, baking powder, baking soda and cinnamon. Pour the buttermilk/butter mixture over the flour mixture, stirring just to moisten. Scoop ¼ cup of batter into prepared muffin tin (the tin will be almost full). Sprinkle with topping, covering the top of each muffin completely. Bake 15 to 18 minutes, or until a toothpick inserted in the center of a muffin comes out mostly clean, with a few moist crumbs attached.

5. Cool for 3 minutes and turn out onto a cooling rack.

# *Spring Onion Risotto

## WITH CRUSHED TOMATO AND ALMOND SAUCE

A re you a Risotto fan? If not, prepare to become one. The accompanying sauce, a crushed tomato and almond concoction, really cuts through the creaminess of the risotto. The tomatoes take about 45 minutes to roast before you make the sauce so build in some extra time. The risotto may be served without the sauce if you want to save time (don't tell the Chef I said so). Plumpjack uses a special brand of risotto rice called Carnaroli rice, but I was equally successful with the more widely available Arborio rice.

### 6 ENTRÉE SERVINGS

1. Preheat the oven to 350°F. Core the tomatoes and cut crosswise. Season with salt and pepper and place cut-side up on a baking sheet sprayed with nonstick spray. Roast for 45 minutes. Remove and cool.

2. Peel tomatoes once they have cooled. Place tomatoes along with almonds, parsley and marjoram and lemon zest in a food processor and lightly pulse until medium coarse in texture.

3. Place tomato mixture in a saucepan over medium heat. Add stock and bring to a simmer. Add olive oil and swirl pan to form a temporary emulsion. You can do this step 3 after the risotto has cooked and is resting.

**Risotto:**

1. Heat half of the butter (6 tablespoons) in a large saucepan or stockpot (3-quart capacity) over medium heat. Stir in onions and garlic and cook, stirring occasionally for 3 to 4 minutes.

2. Stir in rice, cooking until all grains are coated with butter, about 2 to 3 minutes.

3. Pour in wine and bring to a boil. Reduce to a simmer and cook until the wine has evaporated, about 5 minutes or less.

4. Slowly add 3 cups of stock, stirring frequently over medium heat until most of the stock is absorbed, about 8 minutes. Add another 3 cups of stock and stir, cooking until most of the liquid is absorbed, about 7 to 8 minutes. Pour in the last 2 cups of stock and repeat the process. The rice should be al dente (offers slight resistance when chewed).

5. Fold in whipped cream (optional) and taste for salt and pepper, adjusting if necessary. Stir in remaining 6 tablespoons of butter. Remove from heat and rest, covered, for 5 minutes. Serve on warm plates with the sauce drizzled around the risotto. Top each plate with 1 tablespoon of Parmigiano-Reggiano.

*Photograph on page C-1*

**Tomato Almond Sauce:**

6 Roma tomatoes

¼ cup toasted sliced almonds

¼ cup fresh chopped parsley

2 tablespoons fresh marjoram or oregano

Zest of 2 lemons

½ cup chicken or vegetable stock

2 tablespoons extra virgin olive oil

Kosher salt

Ground white pepper

**Risotto:**

¾ cup (1½ sticks) butter, divided

1 cup roughly chopped spring onions

2 tablespoons finely chopped garlic

3 cups Carnaroli or Arborio rice

1 cup white wine

8 cups hot vegetable or chicken stock

¼ cup heavy cream, whipped to stiff peaks (optional)

Kosher salt

Ground white pepper

½ cup Parmigiano-Reggiano (Parmesan)

## Notes

## Colorado

# THE
# LITTLE
# NELL

## The Little Nell

675 East Durant Street
Aspen, CO 81611
**888.THE-NELL**
**970.920.4600**
www.thelittlenell.com

**Season:**
Year-round; peak winter: late
January through March

**Guest Capacity:**
250

**Accommodations:**
92 rooms, including several
luxury suites

**Winter Activities:**
Downhill and cross-country
skiing; snowboarding;
snowshoeing; spa treatments;
shopping; nightlife

**Peak Winter Rates:**
$$$-$$$$

**Closest Ski Resort:**
Aspen Mountain; Snowmass

isting all of the accolades and awards bestowed upon The Little Nell would fill a book. Suffice it to say that this Relais & Châteaux property has amassed years of AAA Five-Diamond and Mobil Five-Star awards. It's no wonder, really. How many hotel rooms include a garment steamer in the bathroom? For that matter, how many bathrooms are enshrouded in marble and spacious enough for a four-string quartet?

Impeccable decor and ambiance, coupled with stellar dining and service (they even have a "ski-concierge") set The Little Nell apart in the world of luxury mountain resorts. Stay at The Little Nell and revel in the lap of luxury. Try a 4th floor "premium" room, one with vaulted ceilings and 660 square feet of pure opulence. Even the most common rooms are uncommon, with stunning views of either the Aspen Mountain, or the shimmering lights of the quaintly idyllic town. If the mountain was any closer, snow would serve as the floor covering. Instead, plush Belgian-wool carpeting welcomes weary ski feet.

After a day of perusing the shops so unique to Aspen (try Kemo Sabe, Le Chefs D'Aspen and the Cooking School of Aspen), or a full day of gliding up the Silver Queen Gondola then traversing down Aspen Mountain, retire to the bar for a hot apple cider or warm buttered rum. Visions of the coming gastronomical extravaganza are not far behind.

Picture a Gold Beet Soup dotted with Roasted Red Beets followed by a Crispy Seared Sea Bass with Creamed Potato and Lobster Stew, perfumed with a Saffron Fennel Broth. Drooling? Of course. Or perhaps you envision the next morning, starting with Carrot-Ginger Juice, followed by Huevos Rancheros with Ancho Chili and a side of Poblano and White Cheddar Grits. The following Pumpkin Spice Bread recipe is a must to cool the taste sensations awakened by just the thought of another glorious meal in the hands of The Little Nell.

## Breakfast Menu

ASSORTED JUICES

EGGS BENEDICT WITH CHIVE HOLLANDAISE AND SNOW CRAB

❋ PUMPKIN SPICE BREAD

## Dinner Menu

FOIE GRAS SEARED MEDALLION ON A CHESTNUT WAFFLE
WITH PEAR BUTTER AND VANILLA SYRUP

❋ ROAST COLORADO RACK OF LAMB
WITH CHARRED ONION JUS

❋ ZUCCHINI TARTS
STUFFED WITH SPAGHETTI SQUASH AND MASCARPONE

❋ SOUR CREAM APPLE TART
WITH COINTREAU SABAYON

❋ RECIPE INCLUDED

# Pumpkin Spice Bread

D eliciously moist and spicy, this bread will warm any cold morning. The key to moist, tender muffins is to mix as little as possible, just enough to moisten the ingredients. A few lumps are okay. The spice mace is the outer covering of a nutmeg seed. If you don't already have it, you can omit it.

---
**1 LOAF**

1 cup sugar
½ cup vegetable oil
2 eggs
½ cup pumpkin purée
1¼ cups flour
¼ teaspoon kosher salt
1 teaspoon baking soda
¾ teaspoon cinnamon
Pinch nutmeg
Pinch mace
½ cup chopped pecans

1. Preheat oven to 350°F. Beat the sugar and oil for 2 minutes. Add the eggs, one at a time, beating until incorporated. Beat in the pumpkin.

2. Stir together the flour, salt, baking soda, and spices in a large mixing bowl.

3. Pour the egg mixture over the flour mixture and stir just until moistened, folding in the pecans at the end. Do not overmix. Grease and flour a standard 9 X 5-inch loaf pan and fill with the batter.

4. Bake for 35 to 40 minutes, or until a toothpick inserted in the center comes out clean, or with just a few moist crumbs. Cool 5 minutes and turn out onto a cooling rack.

# Roast Colorado Rack of Lamb

## WITH CHARRED ONION JUS

*I*f people knew how easy lamb racks are to prepare, I think lamb would become "the other red meat." This adaptation of the dish they do at The Little Nell is one of my favorite ways to serve it. The recipe calls for roasted garlic, which you can prepare up to a week in advance as long as you keep it refrigerated. I marinated the lamb in the balsamic vinaigrette recipe they supplied for a side of tomatoes and baby greens. The onion jus sauce is dark and intensely flavored. You can make the sauce ahead of time and just reheat to serve.

---

**4 SERVINGS**

1. Whisk together the vinegar, shallots, roasted garlic and thyme. Slowly whisk in the olive oil. Coat the lamb rack with the vinaigrette and marinate for 20 minutes at room temperature, or 1 hour in the refrigerator.

2. Preheat the oven to 425°F. (I cut the 8-bone rack in half for easier handling.) Heat an ovenproof skillet over medium-high heat. When very hot, sear the lamb racks on all sides until brown, about 6 minutes total.

3. Place the pan with the lamb in the oven and finish roasting until desired temperature, about 12 to 15 minutes for medium-rare. Serve with Charred Onion Jus.

**Charred Onion Jus:**

1. Heat the olive oil in a saucepan over medium heat. When hot, add the onions. Cook, stirring frequently for 10 to 12 minutes or until the onions are dark brown. Stir in garlic, thyme and bay leaf and cook 2 minutes.

2. Pour in the wine and cook until the wine is reduced by half, about 8 to 10 minutes. Pour stock and demi-glace and reduce to about 1½ cups, about 20 to 25 minutes.

3. Strain the sauce and return to pan. Season with salt and pepper. This will be a thin sauce; "jus" is French for juice.

1 (8-bone) rack of lamb, trimmed

2 tablespoons balsamic vinegar

1 teaspoon finely chopped shallot

½ teaspoon roasted garlic*

¼ teaspoon fresh thyme leaves

⅓ cup olive oil

**Charred Onion Jus (1½ cups):**

2 tablespoons olive oil

½ cup chopped red onion

1 tablespoon finely chopped garlic

1 sprig fresh thyme

1 bay leaf

1 cup red wine

1 cup chicken or vegetable stock

1 cup demi-glace**

Kosher salt

Ground black pepper

---

*To roast garlic, see Common Procedures, page 20.
**See Demi-glace under Common Procedures, page 19.

# *Zucchini Tarts*
## STUFFED WITH SPAGHETTI SQUASH AND MASCARPONE

*T*his artistic little side dish is served with The Little Nell's lamb dish. The first time you make them is a bit time-consuming, but for the gourmet cook, it's fun to make and oh so delicious — rich and creamy. The next time you make them you will breeze right through the process. It requires special equipment, 3½ or 4-inch English muffin molds. Try muffin tins or be creative like my neighbor Marilyn who used custard ramekins and said that while it made for tall tarts it was still as delicious as the ones I made with the round molds.

### 5 TARTS

1 small spaghetti squash (about 4 cups when cooked)

2 tablespoons butter

3 teaspoons freshly chopped parsley, divided

3 teaspoons freshly chopped thyme, divided

¼ cup Boursin cheese*

⅛ cup Mascarpone cheese

1 egg yolk

¼ teaspoon freshly chopped sage leaves

1 teaspoon finely chopped garlic

1 teaspoon finely chopped shallot

Kosher salt

Ground black pepper

5 small, straight zucchinis

2 tablespoons melted butter

1. Preheat the oven to 350°F. Cut the spaghetti squash in half, scooping out the seeds. To each half, add 1 tablespoon of butter, and 1 teaspoon each of parsley and thyme. Place on a sheet pan, flesh side up, and roast in the oven until tender, about 45 to 55 minutes. Remove and cool slightly. Increase oven temperature to 375°F. Scoop out flesh with a fork and place in a large mixing bowl.

2. In a separate medium mixing bowl, beat Boursin cheese, Mascarpone cheese, and egg yolk. Add cheese mixture to squash flesh and stir in 1 teaspoon parsley, 1 teaspoon of thyme, sage, garlic, shallot and season with salt and pepper to taste. Mix well.

3. Cut off both ends of the zucchini. With a vegetable peeler, shave lengthwise strips from the zucchini. Discard the first few shavings, keeping the wider strips from the center of the zucchini. You want 30 to 35 wide strips, about 5-inches long.

4. Place 5 (3½ or 4-inch) molds on a lightly greased sheet pan. Begin layering the zucchini strips in a circle, overlapping slightly and making sure the bottom is completely covered. About 2 inches of the zucchini strips will hang over the edges. Think of this as a crust, therefore you don't want any gaps on the bottom.

5. Fill the zucchini-lined tarts with ⅓ cup of spaghetti squash filling, smooth the top and begin folding the zucchini pieces over the top, starting with one and moving clock-wise until all flaps have been folded over and tart is completely enclosed. Melt the remaining 1 tablespoon of butter and using a pastry brush, coat the tops with melted butter.

6. Bake tarts at 375°F for 12 to 15 minutes or until heated through. Using a spatula, transfer tart to center of a warm serving plate and then remove the mold.

*Substitute whipped cream cheese if Boursin is not available

※ *Photograph on page C-2*

# Sour Cream Apple Tart

## with Cointreau Sabayon

Plain old apple pie will never grace my lips again after having this marvelous Little Nell creation. The crumb topping is delightful, almost as much as the orange liqueur and nutmeg flavored sauce. Traditional sabayon is actually a French adaptation of an Italian dessert sauce made with egg yolks, wine (Marsala), and sugar. The Little Nell's version is made with Cointreau, an orange-flavored liqueur. I think it tastes best the next day, after the nutmeg has time to flavor the creamy, luscious sauce, though you will need to stir the sauce before serving as it tends to separate over time. The original recipe called for a 12-inch tart. I've scaled the recipe to accommodate a 9-inch tart pan.

-----

**8 SERVINGS**

### Tart Dough:

1. Beat sugar and butter until smooth. Beat in the egg then the vanilla. Stir in the flour until well mixed. The dough will be very soft, sticky and moist.
2. Gather into a ball and flatten into a disk. Wrap with plastic wrap and refrigerate until well-chilled and firm, about 1 hour.

### Filling:

1. Whisk all ingredients (sour cream through salt) until smooth. Refrigerate until needed. Whisk again before using.

### Crumb Topping:

1. Process the first 4 ingredients (flour through cinnamon) in a food processor. Add cold butter chunks and pulse several times, until mixture is coarse and crumbly. Add walnuts or pecans, if using, and pulse 2 or 3 times, enough to mix but not chop too finely. Set aside.

*(continued on next page)*

3 small Granny Smith apples

### Tart Dough:

¼ cup sugar

½ cup (1 stick) butter

1 egg

¼ teaspoon vanilla

1¼ cup plus
2 tablespoons flour

### Filling:

½ cup sour cream

1 egg, lightly beaten

⅛ teaspoon vanilla

½ cup sugar

5 tablespoons flour

Pinch kosher salt

### Crumb Topping:

1 cup flour

½ cup sugar

½ cup light brown sugar

1½ teaspoons
ground cinnamon

9 tablespoons cold butter

½ cup chopped walnuts or pecans (optional)

**Cointreau Sabayon Sauce (2½ cups):**
4 egg yolks
Pinch kosher salt
½ cup sugar, divided
⅓ cup Cointreau, or other orange-flavored liqueur
½ cup whipped cream
Pinch nutmeg

**Sour Cream Apple Tart** *(continued from previous page)*

### Cointreau Sabayon Sauce:

1. Beat egg yolks, salt and ¼ cup of the sugar together with an electric mixer for 1½ minutes, until thick and ribbon-like. Set aside.

2. Boil the remaining ¼ cup of sugar with the Cointreau for 3 minutes, stirring occasionally.

3. Set the egg yolk mixture bowl on a towel for support. While whisking, slowly pour the boiling sugar mixture into the egg yolk mixture. The mixture will thicken quickly.

4. Gently fold in the whipped cream and pinch of nutmeg. Store in the refrigerator until needed. Re-whisk before serving. Will keep overnight, and in fact, I think it tastes better the next day.

### Putting it together:

1. Roll the refrigerated dough to fit a 9-inch tart pan. Press into the bottom and sides. Roll the rolling pin over the top to even the crust with the top, discarding the excess dough. Refrigerate for 15 minutes. Meanwhile, whisk the filling. Set aside. Preheat oven to 350°F.

2. Core, peel and slice the green apples into ½-inch thick slices. Remove the tart pan from the refrigerator.

3. Spread a thin layer of filling (about 1/4 cup) on the bottom of the tart pan. Layer the apple slices in a concentric circle, covering the bottom of the pan. Pour the rest of the filling over the apples. Some of the apples will be exposed, that's okay.

4. Bake until custard is mostly set, about 20 to 25 minutes. Remove from oven and mound the crumb topping over the top. It will be a very thick topping. Return to the oven and bake until the crust is golden brown and the crumb topping is lightly browned, about 20 minutes. Serve with Cointreau Sabayon Sauce.

*T*alk about prime locations. The Lodge at Vail is cozily tucked between the base of Vail Mountain, the largest ski mountain in the country, and Vail Village, a pedestrian-only collage of boutique shops, cafés and nightspots. The lodge itself, the first hotel in Vail, is "Old World charm with Western hospitality." The rooms have everything you would expect from a member of the global Preferred Hotels and Resorts Worldwide, and then some. Antique armoires to house your clothes, high-backed leather chairs to embrace your body, and private balconies to hold your attention as you gaze upon the breathtaking beauty of Gore Valley. The rooms even have humidifiers to help those not accustomed to the dry air cope.

For a private escape, the lodge owns the incredible mountainside Game Creek Chalet, a four bedroom, four bath European-style retreat accessible only by gondola. An exclusive hideaway atop Vail Mountain, the chalet offers a private chef and personal ski guide (and no, they are not the same person, though each probably wouldn't mind trading places with the other once in a while). The chalet is only a few steps away from Game Creek Club, a private club that is now open to the public for dinner.

But don't forget that the lodge at the base of the mountain has two award-winning restaurants, the Wildflower and Cucina Rustica. Zagat has honored the Wildflower with the distinction of the number one restaurant in Vail, and the restaurant has garnered a DiRoNa (Distinguished Restaurants of North American) award annually since 1993.

The Cucina Rustica chef handcrafts his own prosciutto and sausages and makes pasta from scratch — a slice of Italy in the Rocky Mountains. Tearing yourself away from either restaurant is difficult, especially with selections like Texas Wild Boar Cannelloni, Grilled Maple-Marinated Ostrich and Warm Gingerbread with Sautéed Apples from the Wildflower, and Smoked Potato and Parsnip Ravioli and Warm Artichoke Salad from Cucina Rustica. The chef from Wildflower generously shares a four-course dinner menu for you to sample.

### The Lodge at Vail

174 East Gore Creek Drive
Vail, CO 81657
**800.331-LODG**
**970.476.5011**
**www.lodgeatvail.com**

**Season:**
Year-round;
peak winter: January through March

**Guest Capacity:**
280

**Accommodations:**
79 rooms, 44 suites

**Activities:**
Downhill and cross-country skiing; back country (hut to hut) and heli-skiing; sleigh rides; bobsledding; snowmobiling; snowcat dinner tours; snowshoeing; carriage rides, ice skating; hot air ballooning

**Peak winter rates:**
$$$-$$$$

**Closest Ski Resort:**
Vail; Beaver Creek

## Breakfast Menu

FRESH-SQUEEZED CITRUS JUICES

HOUSEMADE GRANOLA

❋ VERY BERRY COFFEECAKE

❋ HAM AND FONTINA CHEESE FRITTATA

## Dinner Menu

PURÉE OF POTATO AND LEEK SOUP

❋ POTATO-CRUSTED HALIBUT WITH MINT GREEN PEA PURÉE
OR
❋ GRILLED COLORADO LAMB CHOPS WITH RED WINE JUS

❋ POTATO GNOCCHI
WITH BUTTERNUT SQUASH AND WILD MUSHROOMS

❋ WARM VAHLRONA CHOCOLATE TART

❋ RECIPE INCLUDED

# Very Berry Coffeecake

J ust bursting with berries, I took the liberty of adding a streusel-like topping (without the fat) to this rich, moist cake. Use a single berry or a mix of berries. I used blackberries and raspberries. This cake is best fresh out of the oven, but I also reheated it the next morning and it was still delicious.

### 1 (8-INCH) SQUARE CAKE

1. Preheat oven to 350°F. Stir together the 3 topping ingredients and set aside.
2. Beat the egg, milk, yogurt, oil and vanilla.
3. In a separate bowl, stir the flour, sugar, baking powder and salt.
4. Pour the egg mixture over the flour mixture and stir just to moisten. Fold in the berries and pour into a greased 8 X 8 baking pan. Sprinkle with the streusel topping and lightly press the topping into the batter.
5. Bake for 30 to 35 minutes, or until a toothpick inserted in the center comes out clean or with just a few moist crumbs attached. Cool 5 minutes, cut and serve.

**Topping:**
½ cup light brown sugar
½ teaspoon cinnamon
¼ cup finely chopped pecans

1 egg
½ cup milk
½ cup plain yogurt
¼ cup vegetable oil
½ teaspoon vanilla
2 cups flour
½ cup sugar
2 teaspoons baking powder
½ teaspoon kosher salt
1½ cup mixed berries (blueberry, blackberry and raspberry)

# Ham and Fontina Cheese Frittata

*A* frittata is an open-faced omelet originally from Spain and Italy. This ham and cheese version is very American and very hearty. You can substitute the fontina cheese (also of Italian heritage) with Gouda, Edam or another semi-soft white cheese.

### 2 TO 4 SERVINGS

6 eggs
2 tablespoons milk
¼ cup chopped ham
¼ cup shredded fontina cheese
2 tablespoons chopped onion
1 tablespoon parsley
Kosher salt
Ground black pepper
1 tablespoon butter

**Garnish (optional):**
¼ cup shredded fontina cheese
1 tablespoon chopped parsley

1. Heat oven to 350°F. Beat the eggs and milk. Add the ham, cheese, onion and parsley and stir. Season with salt and pepper.

2. Melt the butter in a 10-inch ovenproof, nonstick pan over medium heat. Pour the egg mixture into the hot pan and with a rubber heat-resistant spatula, push the eggs from the outside to the center of the pan 3 or 4 times. Then let the eggs cook without stirring for about 3 to 4 minutes. The bottom and edges will begin to set and the top center will not be done.

3. Place the skillet in the oven for 4 to 5 minutes. The frittata should be slightly firm when touched in the middle. Remove from skillet and cut into 4 wedges. Garnish with more grated cheese and chopped parsley (optional).

# Grilled Colorado Lamb Chops
## WITH RED WINE JUS

Aren't little lamb chops cute? And these are so tasty with a luscious red wine sauce. The lodge serves the chops with a side dish of potato gnocchi with butternut squash (recipe follows).

---

**4 SERVINGS**

1. Preheat the grill to medium-high (375°F).
2. Sprinkle the chops with salt and pepper and grill 4 to 5 minutes per side for medium rare. Serve with warm Red Wine Jus.

**Red Wine Jus:**

1. Heat olive oil in a medium saucepan. Add the onion and cook until softened, about 4 to 5 minutes. Add garlic and tomatoes, cooking and stirring occasionally until tomatoes are soft, about 8 minutes. Add the parsley, thyme and red wine.
2. Cook until the wine reduces by half, about 15 minutes. Add the demi-glace and simmer until just 1 cup remains. Strain and either keep warm or cool and refrigerate, re-heating before serving.

---

*See Demi-glace under Common Procedures, page 19.

8 lamb chops (2 each)
Kosher salt
Ground black pepper
Red Wine Jus

**Red Wine Jus (1 cup):**
2 teaspoons olive oil
1 cup chopped onion
1 tablespoon finely chopped garlic
2 Roma tomatoes, cored and chopped
1 sprig parsley
3 sprigs thyme
2 cups red zinfandel wine
1 cup demi-glace*

# Potato Gnocchi
## WITH BUTTERNUT SQUASH AND WILD MUSHROOMS

*R*oast the squash and make the gnocchi a day ahead and then this dish may be put together quickly. It's a colorful and savory side dish complementing the grilled lamb chops nicely. My neighbor Marilyn said she could eat just a plate of this for dinner, and she did.

### 4 SERVINGS

**Potato Gnocchi:**

2 baked russet potatoes, cooled, peeled and grated

1 egg yolk

½ cup flour

¼ teaspoon kosher salt

⅛ teaspoon ground white pepper

**Butternut Squash and Mushrooms:**

1 small butternut squash, roasted and cut into 1-inch cubes*

4 tablespoons butter

1 cup sliced cremini and/or shiitake mushroom caps

2 or 3 tablespoons lemon juice

2 teaspoons sage leaves cut into thin strips

Kosher salt

Ground black pepper

1. Place the grated, cooked potatoes on a work surface in a mound. Make a well in the center and sprinkle with salt and pepper. Add the egg yolk and begin to knead in half the flour. When moistened, add the other half of flour and knead until the dough comes together. Let it rest for 2 minutes.

2. Meanwhile, fill a large pot with cold water, add 1 teaspoon of salt and bring to a boil. Have a bowl of ice water ready.

3. Cut the dough into 4 equal pieces and roll each piece into a ½-inch log. Cut each log into ½-inch pieces. When the water is boiling drop the gnocchi into the water and boil until the pieces float to the surface, about 1 minute.

4. Remove the gnocchi and plunge into the ice water to stop the cooking, then drain. Later, the gnocchi will be pan-sautéed with the roasted butternut squash and mushrooms.

**Butternut Squash and Mushrooms:**

1. Melt butter in a 10-inch skillet, over medium-high heat. Stir in mushrooms and cook until tender, about 5 minutes.

2. Stir in cubed roasted squash and cooked potato gnocchi. Add lemon juice, sage strips and season with salt and pepper.

3. Cook, tossing occasionally, until gnocchi and squash start to brown, about 5 to 8 minutes.

---

* To roast the butternut squash, preheat the oven to 350°F. Cut squash in half and scrape out the seeds. Place flesh-side down on a greased sheet pan and bake for 30 minutes. Remove and cool. Peel and cut squash into 1-inch cubes.

# *Potato-crusted Halibut

### WITH MINT GREEN PEA PUREE

**W**ow! Talk about a vibrant green, this sauce is B-R-I-G-H-T! The hint of mint is a great flavor combination with the crispy potato-covered halibut. One dish and you've got your fish, starch and green vegetable! Add a green salad and bread to complete the meal.

---

**4 SERVINGS**

1. Preheat the oven to 350°F. Season the fish with salt and pepper. Peel and grate the potatoes. Divide the grated potatoes into 4 equal piles and place on a flat skinless side of the halibut.

2. Melt the butter in an ovenproof, nonstick skillet over medium-high heat. When hot, add the fillets with the potato side down. Cook until the potatoes are turning brown on the edges, about 6 to 7 minutes.

3. Place the pan in the preheated oven and cook until fish is firm and the potato crust is golden brown, another 5 to 6 minutes. Remove from oven and turn fish over, potato side facing up. Blot with a paper towel to remove excess butter.

4. Spread ¼ cup of pea purée in a circle on a warm serving plate. Top with the fish, potato side facing up and serve.

**Mint Green Pea Purée:**

1. Have a bowl of ice water ready. Cook the peas in boiling water with ½ teaspoon of salt for 3 to 4 minutes. Plunge the peas into the ice water to stop the cooking. Drain and place in a food processor with ½ cup water. Process until smooth. Strain the purée through a sieve.

2. When ready to serve, reheat the purée in a small saucepan over medium heat. Stir in butter, lemon juice and mint strips. Taste and add salt and white pepper to taste.

❋ *Photograph on page C-3*

4 (6-ounce) halibut fillets
Kosher salt
Ground black pepper
2 russet potatoes
2 tablespoons butter
Mint Pea Purée

**Mint Pea Purée (2 cups):**

2 cups green peas, fresh or frozen
½ cup water
½ teaspoon kosher salt
1 tablespoon butter
1 tablespoon lemon juice
2 fresh mint leaves cut into thin strips
Kosher salt
Ground white pepper

# *Warm Vahlrona Chocolate Tart*

## WITH ROASTED BANANA ICE CREAM AND BANANA COMPOTE

Want a show-stopping dessert to cap off a gourmet dinner? Got some extra time? Then this is your dessert. Vahlrona is a high-end brand of baking chocolate, but I used the widely available Baker's brand. In addition to the recipe components here, you'll need a chocolate sauce and a caramel sauce, which you can purchase or make from other recipes in this book. You'll also need roasted banana ice cream. I used the recipe from Vista Verde (see page 61). Soak the raisins in rum the night before you plan to serve this masterpiece dessert (see Banana Compote). And lastly, you need 6 six-inch tart pans with removable bottoms. It's a lot to do, but aren't your friends worth it?

### 6 SERVINGS

**Sweet Dough:**

½ cup (1 stick) butter, softened

1 cup powdered sugar

3 egg yolks

1 whole egg

½ teaspoon vanilla extract

1⅔ cups flour

**Warm Chocolate Filling:**

9 ounces of bittersweet chocolate, cut into chunks

2 tablespoons butter

½ cup sugar

3 eggs

½ cup cake flour

**Sweet Dough:**

1. Beat the butter and sugar in a stand mixer or with a hand mixer. Beat in the egg yolks, whole egg and vanilla. Slowly add flour until just mixed. Wrap the dough in plastic wrap and let it rest in the refrigerator 15 minutes. Meanwhile, preheat the oven to 350°F.

2. Roll out dough ⅛-inch thick. Cut out 6 circles, using the 6-inch tart shells as a guide, cutting the circle wide enough to cover the bottom and sides of the tart pans. Transfer the dough to the tart shells, pressing the dough firmly on the bottom and up the sides. Trim off the dough even with the top of the sides. Prick the bottom of the shells with a fork several times.

3. Bake for 12 minutes and cool at least 10 minutes before filling. While the tarts are baking, prepare the filling.

**Warm Chocolate Filling:**

1. Turn the oven up to 400°F. Melt the chocolate and butter in a double boiler until melted, stirring occasionally. Remove from heat and set aside. Beat the sugar and eggs. Add the flour, then the melted chocolate/butter mixture. Beat until smooth. Pour ⅓ cup batter into each of the cooled, prebaked tart shells.

2. Bake at 400°F for 12 minutes or until center is set. (Large cracks on the surface is a sign of overbaking.) Finish the banana compote while the tarts are baking.

*(continued on next page)*

**Warm Vahlrona Chocolate Tart**
*(continued from previous page)*

**Banana Compote:**

1. Stir the rum and hot water together then add the raisins. Soak overnight, or at least 6 hours. Strain the raisins and stir with the bananas, walnuts, powdered sugar and lemon juice. Serve immediately. (The bananas will turn brown after a few hours so don't make this too far in advance.)

**Putting it all together:**

1. Re-warm the tarts in a 350°F oven for 10 minutes.
2. Place a warm tart on a serving plate and top with a scoop of roasted banana ice cream.
3. Drizzle with caramel and chocolate sauces and top with a spoonful of Banana Compote.

*To toast nuts, see Common Procedures, page 20.

**Banana Compote:**

¼ cup raisins

⅓ cup dark rum

¼ cup hot water

3 each ripe bananas, peeled and chopped

¼ cup toasted and finely chopped walnuts*

¼ cup powdered sugar

1 tablespoon lemon juice

## Notes

_____

_____

_____

_____

_____

_____

_____

_____

_____

_____

_____

_____

_____

## The Historic Strater Hotel

699 Main Avenue
Durango, CO 81301
**800.247.4431**
**970.247.4431**
**www.strater.com**

**Season:**
Year-round

**Guest Capacity:**
246

**Accommodations:**
93 rooms

**Activities:**
Purgatory Ski Resort
30 minutes north
for downhill and
cross-country skiing,
snowshoeing, horse-drawn
sleigh rides, dog-sledding;
nearby Mesa Verde
National Park;
Durango-Silverton
Narrow Gauge
Railroad tour

**Peak winter rates:**
$

**Closest Ski Resort:**
Purgatory

In 1887, a piece of civilization came to the Wild, Wild West. The Historic Strater Hotel opened its grand doors in the rough and tumble Durango, Colorado, and has been welcoming guests ever since, now more than 100 years. Though completely modern in amenities, nothing else seems changed in this living museum of a hotel. The largest collection of Victorian black walnut antiques graces the lobby and the 93 individually decorated guestrooms. It's a step back in time.

Because the walls can't talk, the rooms have diaries for guests to jot down their thoughts and experiences. Page after page tell of special moments remembered by couples, families and travelers. In another time, you might have spotted Bat Masterson polishing his six-shooter or Louis L'Amour penning a new western novel, as both were guests of the hotel.

The Diamond Belle Saloon, located adjacent to the lobby, is just as authentically preserved as the rest of the hotel. Ragtime piano tunes and waitresses in skimpy fringed saloon costumes provide an old west ambiance fostering frolicsome fun.

Skiing is close by, at Purgatory Ski Resort, just a short 30-minute drive north. Although known for lots of snow and almost as much sunshine to match, Purgatory is a small resort compared to others in Colorado. The locals seem quite happy to keep it that way.

Shopping is a must on the quaint Main Avenue. Gorgeous western wear and home furnishings may be found at Eureka! Dans, and if you are into fly-fishing, take the steps down to the basement-level Duranglers, just a couple of blocks north of the hotel. Durango Coffee Company is a cute shop and they serve a mean latte.

Henry's, the Strater's in-house restaurant, is billed as a Chop House and Italian Bistro. The menu includes Italian-style crab cakes, and Pasta Pescatore, loaded with plump, juicy shrimp and scallops. For meat lovers, try the New York Steak-Tuscan style, or the melt-in-your-mouth Veal Osso Buco. Breakfasts are just as varied and hearty as the dinners. The chef shared a special brandy-tinged oatmeal and a delicious smoked turkey omelet to start off the day.

## *Breakfast Menu*

❄ IRISH OATMEAL
WITH BRANDY-KISSED RAISINS

❄ HUNTER'S RETREAT OMELET

FRESH BAKED MUFFINS

🌿

## *Dinner Menu*

❄ CRAB-STUFFED MUSHROOMS

❄ CHICKEN SALTIMBOCCA
OR
❄ ORANGE MUSTARD GRILLED PORK TENDERLOIN

GRAND MARNIER FROZEN SOUFFLÉS

❄ RECIPE INCLUDED

# Irish Oatmeal

Old-fashioned or rolled oats are not the same as Irish oats. You might be able to find Irish oats or organic steel cut oats (which the Strater Hotel uses) in a health food store. Irish oats take longer to cook and are chewier than the rolled oats. I used regular rolled oats (not quick-cooking) and loved the addition of the brandy and brown sugar. The addition of cold fruit is a perfect contrast to the steaming oats. Use any fresh fruit you like. Blueberries are my favorite. Make sure your guests know to stir up the luscious treasures awaiting them on the bottom of the bowl.

---

**4 SERVINGS**

2 cups water
¼ teaspoon salt
4 tablespoons butter
2 cups oats
⅓ cup light corn syrup
¼ cup brandy
1 cup raisins
8 tablespoons cream
4 tablespoons light brown sugar
1 cup fresh fruit

1. Boil water with salt and add butter and oats when boiling. Reduce to a simmer and cook until tender, about 6 to 10 minutes.

2. Heat syrup and brandy in a saucepan over medium heat, bringing to a simmer. Add raisins and simmer 3 to 5 minutes. Set aside to cool. You could do this step early, even overnight, letting the raisins soak in the brandy syrup.

3. Place 2 tablespoons of cream, 1 tablespoon of brown sugar, 1 tablespoon of drained raisins in each of 4 bowls. Add steaming cooked oats and top with fresh blueberries or other fruit. Let your guests stir the mixture together.

# Hunter's Retreat Omelet

The name conjures up a hardy beefsteak breakfast. This omelet is really quite elegant, and very delicious. It's also fun to make because you flip the omelet halfway through cooking. I used a purchased hollandaise sauce to speed things up. You can double this recipe, and cook it in a 10-inch nonstick skillet, but I wouldn't try flipping it — just stick it in the oven at 350°F for about 3 to 4 minutes to finish it.

---

**1 SERVING**

1. Melt butter in an 8-inch nonstick skillet over medium heat. Add turkey, spinach and cook until hot, about 2 minutes.

2. Stir in eggs, pushing the eggs to the center for about 1 minute. Let brown on the bottom, about 1 or 2 minutes more and then flip the omelet (this is really fun). Sprinkle the cheese evenly over the top and let the omelet finish cooking, about 2 minutes.

3. Fold over onto a warmed plate and top with hollandaise sauce.

1 teaspoon butter

3 eggs, beaten

¼ cup shaved smoked turkey

⅓ cup coarsely chopped fresh spinach leaves

¼ cup grated pepper Jack cheese

¼ cup hollandaise sauce*

*See Hollandaise Sauce under Common Procedures, page 20.

# *Crab-stuffed Mushrooms

The creamy white sauce speckled with green parsley looks beautiful against the earthy brown mushrooms but the flavor is what shines through. These might be the best stuffed mushrooms I've ever eaten. One word about the crab, the better the crabmeat you use, the better these mushrooms will taste. Splurge on fresh crabmeat or buy the very expensive ($10 for 6 ounces) canned lump crabmeat. The plain fancy white crabmeat cans do not do this appetizer justice. We had a little bit of crab stuffing left over so I froze it and used it a couple of weeks later with great results.

### 4 SERVINGS

20 large mushrooms
Olive oil
1 tablespoon chopped garlic
2 tablespoons white wine
6 ounces lump crab meat
¾ cup heavy cream
1 tablespoon butter
½ bunch parsley, chopped
Kosher salt
Ground black pepper

**Sauce:**
1 tablespoon chopped garlic
1 teaspoon olive oil
1½ cups heavy cream
½ teaspoon chopped parsley
1 teaspoon butter
Kosher salt
Ground black pepper

1. Preheat oven to 350°F. Clean mushrooms and remove and reserve stems. Toss the mushroom caps with 2 tablespoons of olive oil and season with salt and pepper. Place cup side of mushroom up on a sheet pan and roast 8 to 10 minutes. Remove from oven, strain off any liquid and set aside until ready to stuff.

2. Finely chop reserved mushroom stems (or pulse in food processor a few times). Sauté garlic in 1 tablespoon of olive oil for 1 minute. Add mushroom stems, cooking 1 to 2 minutes. Pour in white wine and let simmer until the liquid is almost gone. Stir in crabmeat, cream, butter and parsley. Bring to a simmer then reduce heat to medium-low and let cream reduce by about ⅓ (about 8 to 10 minutes) and season with salt and pepper.

3. Spoon crabmeat mixture into mushroom caps, mounding the crabmeat slightly. Return mushroom to a 350°F oven and bake until heated through, about 7 to 10 minutes. Meanwhile, prepare the sauce.

4. Sauté 1 tablespoon of garlic in 1 teaspoon of olive oil for 1 minute. Add 1½ cups heavy cream, and salt and pepper to taste. Cook 4 to 5 minutes, allowing cream to reduce slightly. Stir in chopped parsley and swirl in 1 teaspoon of butter. Drizzle sauce over hot mushrooms and serve.

*Photograph on page C-4*

## Plumpjack Squaw Valley Inn
## California

<hr />

### Spring Onion Rissotto
### with Crushed Tomato and Almond Sauce

## The Little Nell
### Colorado

Zucchini Tarts Stuffed with
Spaghetti Squash and Mascarpone

The Lodge at Vail
Colorado

Potato-crusted Halibut with Mint Green Pea Puree

C-3

The Historic
Strater Hotel
Colorado

Crab-stuffed
Mushrooms

Vista Verde Guest Ranch
Colorado

Chorizo and White Cheddar Breakfast Burrito

Lone Mountain
Ranch
Montana

Tomato, Leek
and Goat Cheese
Brushetta

Triple Creek Ranch
Montana

Vanilla Latte Ice Cream Tart with Fudge Sauce

The Historic Taos Inn, New Mexico

Chile Award (Green Chile Stew)

# Chicken Saltimbocca

I wish my father-in-law had been here to taste this while I was testing. He is the ultimate saltimbocca fan, though when he first introduced me to this "jump mouth" dish (the literal Italian translation), it was made with veal. I really enjoyed this version with chicken and I think you will, too. One note, the sauce can get a little salty, especially if you use canned chicken broth. Try to find a low-sodium broth or even better, use homemade, unsalted chicken stock.

### 4 SERVINGS

1. Cut each chicken breast in half, for 8 total pieces. Cover with plastic wrap and pound until almost ¼-inch thick. Top each breast with a sage leaf and cover with a prosciutto half. Re-cover with plastic and pound to ¼-inch. Sprinkle chicken side with pepper.

2. Preheat the oven to 350°F. Heat a large skillet over medium-high heat. When hot, add 1 teaspoon of olive oil and add 4 chicken pieces, prosciutto side down. Cook about 2 minutes and turn over. Remove chicken to a sheet pan (prosciutto side up) and repeat with the remaining 4 pieces of chicken. Place the chicken breasts in the oven for 3 or 4 minutes or until done. Meanwhile, prepare the sauce.

3. In the same skillet you cooked the chicken, heat 1 tablespoon of olive oil over medium-high heat. Stir in the mushrooms and 1 teaspoon of garlic. Cook 2 minutes. Stir in the chopped sage and pour in the hot chicken stock. Simmer uncovered about 4 minutes. Stir the cornstarch and cold water together and add to the sauce to thicken. Remove sauce from heat and whisk in butter and parsley. Serve over warm chicken.

4 chicken breast halves, boneless and skinless (about 1½ pounds)

8 fresh sage leaves

4 thin slices of prosciutto, cut in half

4 thin mozzarella cheese slices

1 teaspoon olive oil

Ground black pepper

**Sauce:**

1 tablespoon olive oil

½ pound (2 cups) sliced mushrooms

1 teaspoon finely chopped garlic

6 finely chopped fresh sage leaves

1 cup hot chicken stock

1 tablespoon cornstarch

1 tablespoon cold water

1 tablespoon butter

1 tablespoon chopped parsley

# Orange Mustard Pork Tenderloin

*I* could drink this marinade. Luscious undertones of citrus combined with spicy mustard and peppered with red chili flakes, this is the best thing that could happen to a piece of pork. Don't marinate the pork more than 12 hours or the meat will turn mushy from the acid in the marinade. The accompanying sauce adds even more mustard flavor.

---

4 SERVINGS

**Marinade:**
¼ cup Dijon mustard
½ cup olive oil
1 tablespoon finely chopped garlic
1 teaspoon orange zest
1 cup orange juice
½ cup balsamic vinegar
½ cup light brown sugar
2 tablespoons Grand Marnier or other orange-flavored liqueur
1 teaspoon fresh thyme, or ¼ teaspoon dried
½ teaspoon red chili flakes
½ teaspoon kosher salt
¼ teaspoon ground black pepper
2 pounds pork tenderloin
1½ cups sauce

**Orange Mustard Sauce (1½ cups):**
1 teaspoon finely chopped garlic
1 teaspoon chopped shallot
2 teaspoons olive oil
3 tablespoons Grand Marnier or other orange-flavored liqueur
¼ cup orange juice
1½ cups hot beef stock
2 tablespoons Dijon mustard
¼ cup heavy cream
2 tablespoons cornstarch
2 tablespoons cold water
Kosher salt
Ground black pepper
1 teaspoon butter

1. Stir together all the marinade ingredients (Dijon mustard through black pepper). Place pork tenderloin in a shallow pan and pour in the marinade, turning to coat all sides. Cover and refrigerate for 6 to 12 hours, turning occasionally.

2. Preheat the grill to medium-high heat (375°F.). Remove the pork from the marinade and grill for about 25 minutes total (for medium), turning every 5 minutes, grilling all sides. Remove from grill and rest for 5 minutes before slicing. Serve with sauce (recipe follows).

**Orange Mustard Sauce:**

1. Sauté garlic and shallot in olive oil for about 1 minute. Remove the pan from heat and add liqueur. Return pan to heat and add orange juice. Cook for 1 minute over medium heat.

2. Add hot stock, mustard and cream. Bring to a simmer and cook 10 minutes. Thicken with a slurry (stir cornstarch with water and add to the simmering sauce). Bring to a boil to thicken.

3. Remove from heat and taste. Add salt and pepper if desired. Finish by swirling the teaspoon of butter in the sauce until melted.

E scape to the pristine beauty of the high country in north central Colorado at a romantic hideaway called Vista Verde that magically transforms to "Vista Blanca" during the winter months. Though only 25 miles north of Steamboat Springs, it feels like a million miles away from civilization. The 500-acre haven bustles as a sybaritic western guest ranch during the summer months but come winter, the ranch morphs into a serene winterscape offering quiet solitude and deliberate, measured moments, relaxation and rejuvenation.

Be as active as you want to be, with miles of groomed cross-country ski trails and horseback riding through snow-covered pines, or curl up with a good book in front of the crackling fire, sipping rich, hot cocoa. The ranch will be more than happy to shuttle you into Steamboat Springs for a day of downhill skiing or shopping in the quaint downtown. Stop in at Soda Creek for beautiful western wear clothes and rustic western home furnishings, or Off the Beaten Path bookstore for a great selection of regional books.

Back at the ranch, the rustic but elegant log cabins are really like little homes, with one, two or three bedrooms, a cozy mountain-decorated living room, a wood stove and a snack bar. I wonder if the ranch has to worry about squatter's rights. Breakfasts are culinary delights that awaken the senses as well as the taste buds and dinners are gourmet feasts, served by candlelight, with unobtrusive and efficient servers. Children eat early so that adults may relax and savor the quiet moment.

A Mobil Four-Star property, Vista Verde employs talented young chefs professionally trained at the Culinary Institute of America and seasoned at other resorts before applying their creativity at the ranch. Each evening showcases three entrees, two of which the ranch calls the "Lighter Side," that might feature a Grilled Vegetable Napoleon or Free Range Chicken with Fire-roasted Chilies. The chef has shared a chile-dusted pork tenderloin as well as a lighter side entrée of grilled halibut for you to enjoy.

### Vista Verde Guest Ranch

P.O. Box 465
Steamboat Springs, CO 32707
**800.526.7433**
**970.879.3858**
**www.vistaverde.com**

**Season:**
Winter: mid-December
to mid-March;
Summer: June to mid-September

**Guest Capacity:**
35

**Accommodations:**
individual log cabins and lodge rooms with private balconies

**Activities:**
on ranch: cross-country skiing, including skate, telemarking and back country; snowshoeing; horseback riding; sleigh rides; evening entertainment; off-ranch: snowmobiling; dog-sledding; ice climbing; hot air ballooning; downhill skiing at Steamboat

**Peak Winter Rates:**
$$ (includes meals)

**Closest Ski Resort:**
Steamboat Springs

## Breakfast Menu

FRESH FRUIT AND JUICE

❊ BLACKBERRY-STUFFED FRENCH TOAST
OR
❊ CHORIZO AND WHITE CHEDDAR BREAKFAST BURRITO

❊ BANANA CHOCOLATE CHIP BREAD

## Dinner Menu

❊ GRILLED ROSEMARY FLATBREAD

❊ CHILE-ENCRUSTED PORK TENDERLOIN
WITH RED AND YELLOW PEPPER COULIS
OR
❊ PAN-SEARED HALIBUT
WITH A MEDITERRANEAN VINAIGRETTE

❊ BASIL-INFUSED MASHED POTATOES

❊ ROASTED BANANA SPLIT
WITH TRIPLE CHOCOLATE BROWNIE,
STRAWBERRY AND CHOCOLATE SAUCES

❊ RECIPE INCLUDED

# *Blackberry-stuffed French Toast*

*T*he challenge with Vista Verde is that every single recipe the chef sent me is out of this world! And he sent a bunch. He did the same thing for my *Great Ranch Cookbook.* We are just going to have to do a whole separate book on Vista Verde at some point. For this book, I had to select this French Toast recipe because it made my husband beg me to make it again the very next morning. I first tested this with the cinnamon French Toast bread from Spring Creek Ranch (see page 183), but I've since made it with regular store-bought French bread, too.

---

**4 SERVINGS**

1. Beat the cream cheese, powdered sugar and vanilla until light and fluffy. Fold in the berries.

2. Whisk the eggs with the milk and almond extract. Set aside.

3. Cut the bread on the bias about 2 inches thick. Cut a pocket into the bread from the crust top. Be careful not to go all the way through. Carefully, with your finger, open the pocket up so you can insert a spoon.

4. Spoon about 2 to 3 tablespoons of the cheese filling into the pocket, and smooth it out so that it is not bulging.

5. Dip the stuffed bread into the egg mixture and let it sit for a few minutes.

6. Meanwhile, heat a griddle or skillet over medium-low heat. Butter the surface and place a few soaked bread pieces on the hot surface. Cook slowly until golden brown, about 3½ to 4 minutes on the first side and 2½ to 3½ minutes on the other side. Serve with warm maple syrup.

1 cup cream cheese

½ cup powdered sugar

1 teaspoon vanilla extract

1 cup fresh blackberries

4 eggs

½ cup milk

1 teaspoon almond extract

1 loaf soft French bread

2 tablespoons butter

# *Chorizo and White Cheddar
## Breakfast Burrito

horizo is one of my favorite sausages. I love the combination of garlic and chiles this Mexican sausage is laced with. If you cannot locate chorizo, take ¼ pound of pork sausage and add ½ teaspoon garlic powder and 1 teaspoon of hot chile powder. It's not quite the same, but it will do in a pinch. Then set your sights on finding a good future source of this wonderful sausage.

### 4 SERVINGS

4 (12-inch) flour tortillas
8 eggs, lightly beaten
1 tablespoon butter
4 tablespoons chorizo sausage, cooked and drained
8 tablespoons grated white cheddar cheese
½ cup Black Bean Salsa
4 tablespoons sour cream
Cilantro sprigs for garnish

**Black Bean Salsa (2 cups):**
⅔ cup cooked black beans
⅔ cup seeded and chopped tomato
2 tablespoons finely chopped red onion
2 tablespoons chopped cilantro
2 tablespoons spicy V-8 juice
1 teaspoon finely chopped garlic
2 thinly sliced green onions

1. Preheat the oven to 350°F. Scramble the eggs in 1 tablespoon of butter and add the sausage.

2. Wrap the tortillas in foil and warm in the oven for 2 minutes.

3. Spoon about ¼ of the egg and sausage mixture in the lower center of a tortilla. Top with 2 tablespoons of cheese and 2 tablespoons of salsa.

4. Begin to roll the tortilla and after one roll, bring in the sides and continue rolling. Repeat process with the remaining tortillas.

5. Cut the burritos in half on the bias and lay one half over the other on a warmed plate. Top with sour cream and garnish with a cilantro sprig. Spoon another 2 tablespoons of salsa around the plate.

**Black Bean Salsa:**

1. Stir together all ingredients (black beans through green onions). Let rest 30 minutes to blend the flavors. Store covered in the refrigerator.

*❋ Photograph on page C-5*

# Banana Chocolate Chip Bread

Wow! Heavy on the chocolate chips, this is my kind of quick bread. A slice of this and a glass of milk are all I need to make me happy. The pan will be full of batter and the bread rises above the loaf pan almost an inch or two. Be sure to use a toothpick to determine if the bread is done (see step 4).

### 1 LOAF

1. Preheat oven to 350°F. Stir together the flour, baking powder and salt. Set aside.

2. Beat the sugar and butter. Once light and fluffy, add the egg and beat again.

3. Stir in the flour mixture followed by the bananas, zest and milk. Stir just to moisten. Fold in the chocolate chips and nuts.

4. Pour batter into a greased and floured 9 X 5-inch loaf pan. Bake for 55 to 60 minutes, or until a toothpick inserted into the center comes out mostly clean. Remove from oven and cool 5 minutes. Remove from loaf pan and continue cooling.

2½ cups flour

1 tablespoon baking powder

½ teaspoon salt

1 cup sugar

¼ cup (½ stick) butter, softened

1 egg

1 cup ripe mashed bananas

2 tablespoons orange zest

½ cup milk

1 cup chocolate chips

1 cup chopped walnuts (optional)

# Grilled Rosemary Flatbread

How fun! I love making this bread but eating it is even better. Serve this bread warm, with a side bowl of olive oil for dipping. It is best served as soon as you make it, but you can reheat it in a 300° oven, covered with foil, for about 10 minutes, and serve the next day.

### 8 TO 10 ROUND DISKS

1½ cups warm water
2 teaspoons dry yeast
3 to 4 cups flour
1 teaspoon kosher salt
1 tablespoon chopped fresh
Rosemary leaves
Olive oil
Kosher salt and
ground black pepper

1. Stir the warm water and yeast together. Rest five minutes to allow yeast to activate.

2. Stir in 1 cup of the flour and then add the rosemary and salt. Continue kneading in flour, 1 cup at a time until you reach a firm dough consistency. I used 3½ cups in total.

3. Place dough in a bowl, cover and let rise in a warm place until doubled in size. (It took 1 hour in my kitchen.)

4. Punch down and let rise again until almost double in size.

5. Preheat grill to medium-high (375° to 400°F). Divide into 3-ounce balls (about the size of a kiwi). Roll each ball into a flat disk (5 to 7 inches in diameter) and brush with olive oil and sprinkle with salt and pepper.

6. Grill disks about 5 minutes on each side. Serve warm.

# Chile-encrusted Pork Tenderloin
WITH RED AND YELLOW PEPPER COULIS

*T*his dish is a harmonious medley of flavors and colors and textures. The ancho chile is a dried poblano, a broad, dark green mild chile. Drying the poblano intensifies its natural sweetness and earthiness. People who don't like hot, spicy things should start with this ancho chile because it shows the flavor depth of a chile without a lot of heat.

---
### 4 SERVINGS
---

**Ancho Chile Rub:**

1. Preheat the oven to 350°F. Place the chiles on a sheet pan in the oven for 7 to 10 minutes or until very fragrant. Remove and cool. Remove the stems and discard the seeds.

2. Place seeded chiles in a food processor with the cumin, garlic and salt and process until medium coarse in texture. Store up to 2 weeks in an airtight container in the refrigerator. This rub is also delicious on steaks and pork chops.

**Pork Tenderloin:**

1. Preheat oven to 350°F. Trim tenderloins of fat and silverskin. Roll each tenderloin in about ⅓ cup of ancho chile rub, coating completely.

2. Heat vegetable oil in a large ovenproof skillet over medium-high heat. When very hot, add tenderloins, searing all sides, about 6 to 9 minutes total. Place in the oven and roast until medium, about 15 minutes. Remove from oven and rest, covered for 5 minutes.

3. Cut the tapered end off one end of the tenderloin making sure that it has a nice flat cut. Move the knife up about 1½ to 2 inches from the initial cut and make another cut at a 45 degree angle. Move up the pork another 1½ to 2 inches and make a straight cut. (Each piece will have a flat cut to stand on and an angled cut that will be presented up.) You need 12 pieces, three for each plate.

4. Spoon some warm red pepper sauce on the left side of a warmed plate and some yellow pepper sauce on the right side of the plate. When they meet in the middle, they will form a line and won't mix together. This is beautiful! Place the 3 pork pieces, flat sides down, angled sides up in the center of the line formed by the sauces.

*(continued on next page)*

3 pork tenderloins (about 12–14 ounces each)

⅔ cup ancho chile rub

3 to 4 tablespoons vegetable oil

Red and Yellow Pepper Coulis (recipe follows)

**Ancho Chile Rub (1 cup):**

10 each ancho chiles*

2 tablespoons ground cumin

2 tablespoons garlic powder

2 tablespoons kosher salt

---

*Ancho chiles can be found in Mexican or Latin markets and some grocery stores, or through A. J.'s Fine Foods, see Sources page 192. The dried chiles should be soft and pliable, not hard or brittle.

**Red Pepper Coulis (2 cups):**

3 red bell peppers

2 tablespoons finely chopped shallots

1 tablespoon butter

2 cups chicken stock

**Yellow Pepper Coulis (2 cups):**

3 yellow bell peppers

2 tablespoons finely chopped shallots

1 tablespoon butter

2 cups chicken stock

**Chile-Encrusted Pork Tenderloin** *(continued from previous page)*

### Red Pepper Coulis:

1. Chop and seed the bell peppers. Melt the butter in a saucepan over medium-high heat. Stir in the shallots and peppers, cooking 2 to 3 minutes. Pour in stock.

2. Bring to a boil and reduce heat to medium. Simmer until peppers are very soft, about 20 to 25 minutes.

3. Separate the solids from the liquid, placing the solid peppers in a blender. Add just enough liquid to cover the peppers half way. Puree until smooth, adding more liquid to get to a sauce consistency. You may not use all of the liquid. Taste and adjust seasonings, adding pepper and salt if necessary.

### Yellow Pepper Coulis:

1. Chop and seed the bell peppers. Melt the butter in a saucepan over medium-high heat. Stir in the shallots and peppers, cooking 2 to 3 minutes. Pour in stock.

2. Bring to a boil and reduce heat to medium. Simmer until peppers are very soft, about 20 to 25 minutes.

3. Separate the solids from the liquid, placing the solid peppers in a blender. Add just enough liquid to cover the peppers half way. Puree until smooth, adding more liquid to get to a sauce consistency. You may not use all of the liquid. Taste and adjust seasonings, adding pepper and salt if necessary.

# Pan-seared Halibut
## WITH A MEDITERRANEAN VINAIGRETTE

omatoes, artichokes and kalamata olives make this sauce an intensely flavored accompaniment to the mild-flavored halibut. Vista Verde serves this with basil-infused mashed potatoes (next recipe) for a delicious combination.

#### 4 SERVINGS

### Vinaigrette:

1. Bring a pot of water to boil and prepare an ice bath (a big bowl with ice and water). Core the tomatoes and cut an "X" on the bottom of each tomato. Drop into the boiling water for about 30 to 60 seconds and remove with a slotted spoon to the ice bath to stop the cooking. When cool, peel and cut in half lengthwise. Remove the seeds and chop. Set aside.

2. Drain the artichoke hearts, reserving the liquid. Quarter the hearts and set aside.

3. Stir the shallots, garlic, vinegar and V-8 juice in a bowl. Slowly whisk in the olive oil and reserved artichoke liquid. You can do this in a blender for a more stable emulsion.

4. Fold in the chopped tomatoes, quartered artichoke hearts and kalamata olives. Season with salt and pepper to taste. Let rest (at room temperature) for 3 hours to allow the flavors to blend.

### Halibut:

1. Preheat the oven to 350°F. Stir the flour with the salt, garlic powder, thyme and pepper.

2. Heat the olive oil in a large skillet over medium heat. Dredge the halibut in the seasoned flour and add to the hot oil. Cook 2 to 4 minutes or until the fish turns a golden brown. Turn the fish over and place the skillet in the oven to finish cooking, about 5 minutes for medium temperature.

3. To serve, place the fish on a warm plate and spoon the vinaigrette over the top and around the sides.

### Vinaigrette:

4 Roma tomatoes

1 (6-ounce) can marinated artichoke hearts

2 tablespoons finely chopped shallots

1 teaspoon finely chopped garlic

¼ cup red wine vinegar

½ cup V-8 juice

1 cup olive oil

¼ cup pitted kalamata olives, thinly sliced lengthwise

Kosher salt

Ground black pepper

### Halibut:

4 (6-ounce) halibut fillets

¼ cup flour

¾ teaspoon kosher salt

½ teapson garlic powder

¾ teaspoon dried thyme

½ teaspoon ground black pepper

2 to 3 tablespoons olive oil

# Basil-infused Mashed Potatoes

There is not a more perfect vegetable than a potato. I like them fried, baked, steamed, roasted, boiled, mashed and yes, even raw! Basil lovers will flip for this rendition. Try not to eat all of them while tasting for seasonings.

**4 SERVINGS**

3 large baking potatoes
(2 pounds)
2 cups loosely packed
fresh basil leaves
1 cup heavy cream
6 tablespoons butter
Kosher salt
White ground pepper

1. Bring a large pot of salted water to boil. Peel and quarter the potatoes. Boil until tender, about 25 minutes.

2. Meanwhile, stack the basil leaves, a few at a time, and roll like a cigar. Slice very thin crosswise to produce long strips of basil (this cut is called a chiffonade cut). Stir the basil, cream and butter together in a saucepan. Bring to a boil and reduce to a simmer. Simmer for 15 to 20 minutes.

3. Drain and mash the cooked potatoes and add the basil cream, slowly, until you get the right consistency. You may not use all of the cream mixture. Season with salt and pepper.

# *Roasted Banana Split*

WITH TRIPLE CHOCOLATE BROWNIE, STRAWBERRY AND CHOCOLATE SAUCES

This is no drug-store version of a banana split. The brownie base alone is enough to start my toes tingling. Roasting the bananas for the ice cream just intensifies the flavor. This dessert has 4 components: roasted banana ice cream, brownie base, and strawberry and chocolate sauces. The chocolate tart from the Lodge at Vail (see page 42) also calls for roasted banana ice cream. This quart of ice cream is enough to make both desserts. Who needs an entrée anyway?

(see page 42)

---

9 SERVINGS

1. Preheat the oven to 350°F. Place the bananas on a sheet pan and roast in the oven for 15 to 20 minutes or until very soft. Remove and cool. The color will darken but don't be alarmed. It looks good in the finished product.

2. Heat the cream and half-and-half with ½ cup of the sugar and the vanilla (if using a bean, split in half lengthwise and scrape the seeds into the saucepan). Bring to a simmer.

3. Meanwhile, whisk the eggs, egg yolks and remaining ½ cup of sugar.

4. When the cream comes to a boil, remove from heat. Slowly whisk in a ½ cup or so of the hot cream into the egg mixture to warm them. Then whisk the warmed egg mixture into the hot cream mixture and return to the heat, turning the heat to medium-low. Cook, stirring often until the mixture thickens, about 5 to 10 minutes.

5. Puree the cooled bananas in a food processor and stir them into the thickened cream mixture. Strain into a bowl set in ice water. Stir to cool the mixture. When completely cool, pour into an ice cream maker and freeze according to manufacturer's instructions.

## Triple Chocolate Brownie:

1. Preheat oven to 350°F. Line the inside of an 8 X 8-inch baking pan with foil. Spray the foil with nonstick spray.

2. Melt the semi-sweet and unsweetened chocolate with the butter in a double boiler over barely simmering water. Stir occasionally until completely melted and smooth.

3. Stir in the sugar and brown sugar, and continue stirring until the sugars are mostly dissolved, about 10 to 15 minutes. It's okay if the mixture is slightly grainy. Remove from heat.

*(continued on next page)*

### Roasted Banana Ice Cream (1 quart):

4 ripe bananas, peeled

2 cups heavy cream

2 cups half-and-half

1 cup sugar, divided

1 vanilla bean or
1 teaspoon vanilla extract

2 eggs

8 egg yolks

### Triple Chocolate Brownie (9 servings):

9 ounces semi-sweet chocolate, chopped

1 ounce unsweetened chocolate, chopped

½ cup (1 stick) butter

⅓ cup sugar

½ cup light brown sugar

2 eggs

1 egg yolk

1 tablespoon vanilla extract

½ cup flour

1 cup toasted chopped pecans

5 ounces white chocolate, chopped

**Strawberry Sauce (2 cups):**

1 (12-ounce) package frozen strawberries, thawed

1 cup powdered sugar

1 cup water

**Chocolate Sauce (3 cups):**

9 ounces semi-sweet chocolate, chopped

4 tablespoons sugar

2 tablespoons light corn syrup

1 cup heavy cream

4 tablespoons butter

**Vista Verde Banana Split** *(continued from previous page)*

4. Beat in the eggs and egg yolk and then the vanilla. Stir in the flour just until blended. Fold in pecans and white chocolate.

5. Pour into the prepared pan and bake 25 to 30 minutes, or until a toothpick comes out with just a few moist crumbs. Remove to a cooling rack for about 30 minutes. Gently remove brownie from pan and let cool 1 hour. Restrain yourself from eating the brownie until you get the whole dessert put together.

**Strawberry Sauce:**

1. Strain the strawberries, reserving the juice. Place the juice, powdered sugar and water in a saucepan and bring to a boil. Reduce to a simmer and cook until the liquid reduces by half, about 15 to 20 minutes.

2. Stir in the strawberries and cook another 2 to 3 minutes. Cool slightly.

3. Pour the strawberry mixture in a blender and puree until smooth. CAUTION: cover the top of the blender before you blend as hot liquid shoots straight up and can blow the top off. Strain through a sieve and chill.

**Chocolate Sauce:**

1. Place the chocolate, sugar and corn syrup in a bowl and set aside.

2. Heat the cream and butter in a saucepan over medium heat. Bring to a boil and reduce to a simmer. Once the butter is completely melted, pour over the chocolate mixture and whisk until smooth. Serve warm. You can gently reheat in a microwave.

**Putting it all together:**

1. Preheat the oven to 350°F. Cut the brownies into 9 squares and wrap in foil. Reheat in the oven for about 10 minutes.

2. Place a brownie on each plate, top with 1 scoop of roasted banana ice cream. Drizzle with chilled strawberry sauce and warm chocolate sauce.

## Montana

## Lone Mountain Ranch

P.O. Box 160069
Big Sky, MT 59716
**800.514.4644**
**406.995.4644**
www.lonemountainranch.com

**Season:**
Winter: December through
mid-April;
Summer: June through October

**Guest Capacity:**
90

**Accommodations:**
23 individual 1-bedroom
log cabins; 1 3-bedroom log
home; 1 6-guest room lodge

**Activities:**
Cross-country skiing;
ski lessons; guided Yellowstone
Park ski tours; snowshoeing;
guided winter fly-fishing; nearby
downhill skiing at Big Sky

**Peak Winter Rates:**
$$$ (includes all meals,
and there is a minimum
1-week stay)

**Closest Ski Resort:**
Big Sky

W intertime at Lone Mountain Ranch is a lesson in tranquility. Snow-kissed pines whispering in the wind are only disturbed by the call of an elk's bugle, signaling the start the day. A family owned and operated lodge, Lone Mountain offers one of the top cross-country ski resorts in North America. An added bonus is the proximity to Yellowstone Park, and the ski tours the lodge offers into one of our nation's most magnificent parks.

The massive log structure housing the dining room and glass-walled bar is as inviting as it is warm and cozy. It's the perfect retreat after a day traversing deep into the forest, on immaculately groomed ski trails. The terrain is suited for all levels of skiers and lessons are a must for first-timers. Up the road is the Big Sky ski resort for those wishing to downhill ski. If you thought fly-fishing was a summer activity, think again. The lodge offers guided fishing trips and arching a fly line into the Gallatin River, surrounded by snow-shrouded banks is an awesome experience.

If you take a day trip into Bozeman, just 45 minutes north of the ranch, try shopping at T. Charbonneau's for elegant women's western wear and the Country Bookshelf bookstore for a book on Montana life. The bookstore has a rack of local books near the door, most of them signed by the authors. Both shops are located on the old-fashioned main street.

Whichever day trip you decide to do, don't miss a single meal at the lodge. The chef prepares the most fabulous cuisine, fresh and pure mountain-inspired.

## Breakfast Menu

FRESH SQUEEZED CITRUS JUICE

❄ BANANA GRANOLA PANCAKES
OR
❄ SMOKED SALMON STACKED EGGS
WITH HOLLANDAISE

FRESHLY BAKED MUFFINS AND PASTRIES

## Dinner Menu

❄ TOMATO, LEEK AND GOAT CHEESE BRUSCHETTA

❄ PAN-ROASTED BEEF TENDERLOIN
WITH MUSHROOM STUFFING AND PORT WINE SAUCE

❄ HAZELNUT SPAGHETTI SQUASH

❄ ROASTED ROSEMARY RED POTATOES

❄ VANILLA BEAN CRÈME BRÛLÉE

❄ RECIPE INCLUDED

# Banana Granola Pancakes

*T*alk about hearty pancakes! This is a perfect breakfast before hitting the slopes. The flavor is reminiscent of warm banana nut bread. I used the Sundance Nutty Granola (see page 135), but you may use store-bought or your own recipe. Double the recipe for an extra-hungry crowd, or if my husband is one of your breakfast guests. He loves these pancakes! You will, too.

**10 PANCAKES**

1½ cups flour
3 tablespoons sugar
1½ teaspoons baking powder
½ teaspoon baking soda
Pinch kosher salt
1 cup granola
2 eggs
1½ cups buttermilk
2 bananas, sliced very thin
3 tablespoons melted butter

1. Stir the flour, sugar, baking powder, baking soda, salt and granola together.

2. In a separate bowl, beat the eggs with the buttermilk. Pour the egg mixture over the flour mixture and stir just to moisten and fold in the banana slices. Stir in the melted butter.

3. Spray a large skillet or griddle with nonstick spray and heat over medium heat. When hot, ladle ¼ cup batter to form 5-inch cakes.

4. Cook until bubbles form on top and edges start to dry, about 3 to 4 minutes. Flip pancake over and cook the other side for another 2 minutes or until golden brown. Repeat until all batter is used. Serve with warm maple syrup.

# Smoked Salmon Stacked Eggs
### WITH HOLLANDAISE SAUCE

*R*ave reviews from tasters Alex and Rosalie on this one! Rosalie said it was like an Egg McMuffin®, only gourmet. Elegant and easy to prepare if you use a purchased hollandaise sauce. If you are all out of smoked salmon, try smoked turkey or ham. Use an egg poacher if you want really uniform-looking eggs, or follow my directions in step 2. They won't be as pretty, but they will taste just as good.

---

**4 SERVINGS**

1. Beat the cream cheese with the lemon juice thoroughly. Fold in capers and red onion. Split and toast the English muffins.

2. Bring 2 quarts of cold water to a very slight simmer (180°F) in a saucepan. Add 1 teaspoon of vinegar to the water. Crack open an egg on a saucer and slowly slide the egg into the water. Leave it alone for 1 minute, then gently stir the egg white up over the yolk. Cook until desired doneness, about 3 to 4 minutes for a runny yellow center. Remove with slotted spoon and keep warm.

3. Spread the cream cheese mixture on the warm toasted muffin halves. Layer a slice of smoked salmon, then 2 spinach leaves and then a poached egg.

4. Top the stacks with hollandaise and sprinkle with chopped parsley (optional).

8 ounces cream cheese, softened

1 tablespoon lemon juice

1 tablespoon capers

1 tablespoon finely chopped red onion

4 English muffins

1 teaspoon vinegar

8 eggs

8 slices of smoked salmon

1 bunch fresh spinach

1 cup hollandaise sauce*

1 tablespoon chopped parsley (garnish)

---

*See Hollandaise Sauce under Common Procedures, page 20.

# *Tomato, Leek and Goat Cheese Bruschetta

A nice twist on the Italian classic, this appetizer is delicious and garlicky. My brother Steve loves to make bruschetta and this recipe will help keep him from getting bored (not to mention his guests!) A perfect snack to nibble while sipping a good Chianti Riserva.

**8 SERVINGS**

1 leek, white part only

8 Roma tomatoes, cored and chopped

4 tablespoons chopped fresh basil

2 teaspoons finely chopped garlic

1 teaspoon chopped fresh rosemary

2 tablespoons extra virgin olive oil

Kosher salt

Ground black pepper

16 slices crusty French baguette, cut on a bias

½ cup fresh goat cheese

¼ cup grated Parmesan

1. Preheat the broiler. Cut the leek in half lengthwise and run under cold water to remove any residual dirt. Pat dry and cut into long thin strips, about 2 inches long and ⅛-inch wide.

2. Stir the tomatoes, leek strips, basil, garlic, rosemary and olive oil together. Season with salt and pepper and set aside.

3. Place the bread slices on a sheet pan and toast under the preheated broiler until light golden brown. Turn the broiler off and preheat the oven to 400°F.

4. Spread a thin (or thick if you prefer) layer of goat cheese on the freshly toasted bread. Top with a generous tablespoon of the tomato-leek mixture then a teaspoon of Parmesan.

5. Place in a 400°F oven and bake for 7 to 10 minutes, or until Parmesan is melted. Serve warm.

* *Photograph on page C-6*

# *Beef Tenderloin*
## with Mushroom Stuffing and Port Wine Sauce

*I* love this Chef! Every recipe from Lone Mountain is elegant yet easy to prepare and superbly delicious. (Maybe that's why they were in my guest ranch cookbook, too.) The wine sauce is almost drinkable. Serve this with the Hazelnut Spaghetti Squash, a green salad and you've got a romantic meal, or a celebratory meal, or just a fabulous "no special occasion" meal.

---

**4 SERVINGS**

1. Preheat oven to 400°F. Add the bacon to a cold 10-inch skillet and heat over medium-high heat. Cook until bacon is brown. Stir in mushrooms, butter, garlic and rosemary and cook until mushrooms are tender, about 5 minutes. Drain off any liquid and place mushroom mixture into a food processor. Pulse a few times, finely chopping (but not puréeing) the mixture. Remove and season with salt and pepper.

2. Cut a 1-inch incision in the center (from the side, not the top) of the filet from top to bottom. Work the knife from side to side, trying to split the steak in half without actually doing so. You don't want to come through the sides and you don't want your incisions too wide or the stuffing won't stay in.

3. Stuff the pocket from both ends with the mushroom mixture until full, but not bulging, about 2 tablespoons per filet. Season the filet with salt and pepper and lightly dust with flour.

4. Heat a large ovenproof skillet over high heat. Add 2 tablespoons of oil and when hot, add the filets, searing both sides until brown, about 3 minutes per side. Place pan in the preheated oven to finish, about 8 to 10 minutes for medium rare. Let rest 5 minutes before serving.

**Port Wine Sauce:**

1. Boil the port wine with the shallot until liquid is reduced to 1/4 cup. Stir in demi-glace and cook until desired consistency is reached. If you use my demi-glace recommendation, it only takes a few minutes more. Taste, then season with salt and pepper if necessary.

1 slice smoked bacon, finely chopped*

2 portabella mushroom caps, chopped

½ cup sliced white button mushrooms

2 teaspoons butter

1 teaspoon finely chopped garlic

2 teaspoons chopped fresh rosemary

4 (8-ounce) filet mignons

Kosher salt

Ground black pepper

Flour for dusting

**Port Wine Sauce: (1 cup)**

1 cup ruby port wine

1 tablespoon finely chopped shallot

1 cup demi-glace**

Kosher salt and ground black pepper

---

*Bacon is easier to chop if slightly frozen.
**See Demi-glace under Common Procedures, page 19.

# Hazelnut Spaghetti Squash

A clever and creative way to dress up spaghetti squash, this dish is flavorful with a sweet and nutty finish. One of my tasters, June — a great cook herself, thought this would be a fun recipe to add to her collection. If you have some roasted hazelnuts left over from another recipe, finely crush them and sprinkle on this squash before serving as a garnish.

### 6 SERVINGS

1 large spaghetti squash
1 tablespoon hazelnut oil
1 tablespoon butter
2 tablespoons hazelnut liqueur
2 tablespoons light brown sugar

1. Halve and remove the seeds from the squash. Steam the squash until tender, about 30 minutes. Cool and scrape flesh with a fork into a bowl.

2. Heat a 10-inch skillet over medium-high heat and add hazelnut oil and butter. When hot, add squash and cook for 5 minutes, stirring frequently.

3. Pour in hazelnut liqueur and cook until it almost evaporates. Stir in brown sugar and simmer until brown sugar is dissolved, 2 to 3 minutes. Serve warm.

# Roasted Rosemary Red Potatoes

I included this very simple recipe to balance some of the more challenging recipes in the book, and because it's my husband's favorite way to eat potatoes. I've also made this side dish with Yukon Gold potatoes and I have added additional herbs, like fresh chopped oregano and thyme with excellent results. Experiment to create your own favorite.

### 4 SERVINGS

1½ pounds small red potatoes
2 teaspoons chopped fresh rosemary
2 teaspoons finely chopped garlic
2 tablespoons olive oil
Kosher salt
Ground black pepper

1. Bring a pot of salted water to a boil. Quarter the potatoes and boil for 15 minutes.

2. Meanwhile, preheat the oven to 400°F. Drain potatoes, pat dry and place in a large mixing bowl. Stir in rosemary, garlic, oil and salt and pepper to taste and stir, coating each potato in the oil/rosemary mixture.

3. Spread potatoes on a lightly greased sheet pan and bake 20 minutes or until potatoes are golden brown, tossing occasionally.

# Vanilla Bean Crème Brûlée

here are two camps of brûlée lovers. One likes a light, airy cream-tasting brûlée and the other prefers a thick, rich, eggy custard. I fall into the former category while our friend T.J. falls into the latter. Let's just say he was a happy camper tasting this dessert. It's thick, it's rich and it's really quite delicious, even though I prefer the other style. The black specks from the vanilla bean are cool, too, according to T.J. Make the brûlée the day before to completely chill it, but only put the final sugar on top about ½ hour to 1 hour before you serve.

**8** SERVINGS

1. Preheat the oven to 310°F. Scrape the inside of the split vanilla bean and add the seeds (or extract) to a medium saucepan with the cream. Cook over medium heat until just beginning to boil. Remove from heat.

2. Beat the yolks with the sugar in a large bowl. Add some of the hot cream to the yolk mixture whisking constantly. Whisk the warmed yolk mixture into the rest of the hot cream. Skim the foam from the top and strain through a sieve into a pitcher.

3. Place 8 (4-ounce) ramekins in a roasting pan. Pour cream mixture into the ramekins, leaving ½-inch from the top. Place the pan in the oven and pour enough hot water into the roasting pan to come half way up the sides of the ramekins.

4. Cover with foil and bake for 15 to 25 minutes, until the edges are firm and the center only jiggles the size of a nickel when shaken. Remove from the oven and cool, then cover and refrigerate 8 hours or overnight.

5. Sprinkle tops with 1 teaspoon of sugar and place under a preheated broiler for a few minutes (watch carefully) or use a blowtorch to caramelize the sugar. Chill again so that the burnt sugar hardens and the custard is completely chilled again.

2 cups heavy cream

½ vanilla bean split lengthwise, or 1/2 teaspoon vanilla extract

7 egg yolks

½ cup sugar

8 (4-ounce) ramekins

8 teaspoons sugar, regular or superfine

## Triple Creek Ranch

5551 West Fork Stage Route
Darby, MT 59829
406.821.4600
www.triplecreekranch.com

**Season:**
Year-round

**Guest Capacity:**
44

**Accommodations:**
19 individual log and cedar
cabins

**Activities:**
Snowmobiling; snowshoeing;
dog-sledding; winter horseback
riding;
off-property: cross-country and
downhill skiing; flight-seeing;
heli-skiing

**Peak Winter Rates:**
$$$$ (includes all meals,
snacks, wine and cocktails)

**Closest Ski Resort:**
Lost Trail Powder Mountain

Romance is in the air at the enchanting Triple Creek Ranch, in the Bitterroot Valley of Southwestern Montana. Situated on 375 wooded acres and surrounded by national forest on three sides, the picturesque retreat indulges the whims and wishes of couples seeking a winter haven. The adults-only format ensures peaceful, quiet moments for guests to savor. The handsome log cabins with private hot tubs and the world-class cuisine, paired with a vast array of delicious wines, are the perfect prescriptions for jubilant relaxation. This Relais and Châteaux property is also a favorite destination of the exclusive Andrew Harper's Hideaway Report, which recently named the ranch a "favorite discovery of the past 20 years".

Although the ranch offers a plethora of activities, one gets the feeling that just "being" is a favorite pastime among guests. For the more adventurous, there is a "flight-seeing" tour by helicopter (which picks you up at the ranch) to view the snow-blanketed valley and Bitterroot Mountains. Within a 30-minute drive, the Lost Trail Powder Mountain offers downhill and cross-country skiing. Or stay on the ranch and take a winter horseback ride through the unspoiled woods and return for a private massage in your cabin before deciding how to spend the evening.

Dine by candlelight in the intimate dining room or by candlelight in your luxurious cabin. Either location creates an amorous mood, heightened by the serene winterscape. Regardless of where you take your meal, you are bound to enjoy the fruits of labor from the kitchen. Breakfast choices are plentiful and might include thick slices of French bread dipped in an Amaretto-egg batter and griddled to a perfect golden brown. For dinner, would linguine with an orange saffron butter sauce work, or perhaps a charbroiled filet wrapped in crisp bacon and served with mouth-watering Madeira and blue cheese sauce? As with my western guest ranch cookbook, the Triple Creek kitchen has once again shared some wonderfully elegant, but incredibly simple dishes for you to re-create at home.

## Breakfast Menu

✳ **FRESH MELONS**
WITH GINGER HONEY LIME DRESSING

✳ **TRIPLE CREEK GRANOLA**

✳ **THREE CHEESE AND GREEN CHILE FRITTATA**
WITH SALSA FRESCA

✳ **LEMON HUCKLEBERRY SCONES**

## Dinner Menu

CURRIED BUTTERNUT SQUASH SOUP
OR
✳ **SPINACH SALAD**
WITH RASPBERRY VINAIGRETTE

✳ **SEARED VENISON LOIN**
WITH BALSAMIC BLUEBERRY SAUCE

✳ **VANILLA LATTE ICE CREAM TART**
WITH FUDGE SAUCE

✳ RECIPE INCLUDED

# Ginger Honey Lime Dressing

I prepared this super simple dressing at a wine and food festival in Dallas during the recipe testing for this book. The audience was so enamored with the dressing, I promised to e-mail this recipe to anyone who wanted it after I returned home. I didn't realize it would take me almost a week to answer all the e-mail requests I had. Serve it over fresh melons, such as cantaloupe and honeydew. Zest the lime before your squeeze the juice, unless you are steeping the ginger with the lime overnight, in which case you want to use fresh limes to get your zest. Once the zest is removed from the lime, it only remains fresh for a couple of hours.

### 1½ CUPS

1 teaspoon fresh grated ginger

½ cup fresh squeezed lime juice

½ cup honey

2 teaspoons poppy seed

2 teaspoons lime zest

1. Stir the ginger with the lime juice. Set aside for at least 30 minutes (up to overnight).

2. Strain the lime juice and whisk in the honey, poppy seed and lime zest.

3. Drizzle over fresh cut melons.

# Triple Creek Granola

This granola recipe was first printed in my ranch cookbook. The response was so outstanding that I just had to include it in this book (and besides, it is my all-time favorite granola recipe). It can be eaten with cereal or sprinkled over yogurt, or my favorite, just out of the hand. I use a combination of honey and maple syrup, though you could use either one as the recipe states. The granola will keep in an airtight container at room temperature for up to 8 weeks, or frozen for up to 6 months. Try this and you'll be back for more. I guarantee it.

## 16 TO 18 CUPS

1. Preheat oven to 350°F. Toss oats, nuts, coconut, cinnamon and brown sugar until well mixed.

2. Heat the honey and oil just to warm. Pour over dry ingredients and mix until all ingredients are coated with honey mixture.

3. Spread mixture onto lightly greased sheet pans with edges. Bake, stirring frequently to brown evenly (about 17 to 25 minutes, total). Keep a close eye on the granola as toward the end of browning, it turns very quickly.

4. Remove from oven, add dried fruit and stir occasionally to break up clumps, and cool. Store in airtight containers or sealable plastic bags.

1 (18-ounce) container old-fashioned oats

1½ cups sliced almonds

1½ cups pepitas*

1½ cups hazelnuts, roasted, skinned and coarsely chopped**

1½ cups sweetened coconut

1¼ teaspoon cinnamon

½ cup plus 1 tablespoon light brown sugar

1½ cups honey or maple syrup

¾ cup vegetable oil

2 cups chopped dried fruit

*Pepitas (the inner seeds of pumpkin seeds used extensively in southwestern cooking) are available through A.J.'s Fine Foods. See Sources page 192 for details.
**To roast hazelnuts, see Common Procedures, page 20.

# Three Cheese and Green Chile Frittata

*I* adore fresh Anaheim chiles (the mild green chile now widely available in cans, either chopped or whole). With some of my favorite cheeses, including cheddar, and a touch of flour and baking powder to give "rise" to this frittata, you've got the perfect southwestern brunch entrée. The Salsa Fresca that accompanies this recipe is delicious with chips, too.

**4 SERVINGS**

¼ cup flour
½ teaspoon baking powder
⅛ teaspoon kosher salt
⅛ teaspoon toasted cumin seeds*
Pinch cayenne pepper
6 eggs
2 tablespoons butter, melted
1 cup shredded pepper jack cheese
1 cup shredded cheddar cheese
1 cup cottage cheese
½ cup finely chopped red bell pepper
½ cup chopped green chiles
2 tablespoons butter

**Salsa Fresca (2 cups):**
¼ cup chopped red onion
½ teaspoon finely chopped garlic
1 serrano chile, finely chopped**
¼ teaspoon toasted cumin seeds or ¼ teaspoon ground cumin
4 Roma tomatoes, peeled, seeded and roughly chopped
¼ cup chopped cilantro
¼ teaspoon kosher salt
1 tablespoon olive oil
2 tablespoons fresh lime juice

1. Preheat oven to 400°F. Stir the flour, baking powder, salt, cumin and cayenne in a small bowl. Set aside.

2. Whisk the eggs and then stir in the flour mixture. Stir in 2 tablespoons of the melted butter, all 3 cheeses, red pepper and green chiles.

3. Heat the remaining 2 tablespoons of butter in an ovenproof nonstick skillet over medium heat, tipping pan to cover the bottom with the melted butter.

4. Pour egg mixture into skillet and place in the oven. Bake 15 minutes then reduce oven temperature to 350°F and bake another 20 to 25 minutes or until top is golden brown and knife inserted in the center comes out clean. Cool 2 to 3 minutes then transfer frittata to serving platter. Cut into 4 wedges and serve with Salsa Fresca.

**Salsa Fresca:**

1. Process the red onion, garlic, serrano and cumin in a food processor to a "rough chop" consistency, about 10 pulses.

2. Add the tomatoes, cilantro, salt, olive oil and lime juice to the processor and pulse again 3 or 4 times, or until mixture is of a medium consistency. Taste and adjust seasonings.

*To toast cumin seeds, heat a small skillet over medium heat. Add cumin seeds and heat, tossing occasionally for 2 minutes, or until fragrant. Substitute 1/8 teaspoon ground cumin if you can't find the whole seeds.
**Remove the seeds to decrease the "heat". Without the seeds, the serrano is fairly mild. Substitute a jalapeno for the serrano.

# Lemon Huckleberry Scones

I get in trouble with my culinary pals when I say that scones are just a fancy name for sweet biscuits, but to me, that is what they are. The Scottish would beg to differ since they are the originators of this quick bread, and they don't consider our Americanized version of scones in the same league. Call it what you like, Triple Creek adds a nice touch with fresh lemon and blueberries (real huckleberries are not available commercially but are very similar to the widely available blueberry).

---

**8 SCONES**

1. Preheat oven to 400°F. Stir together the flour, ⅓ cup sugar, baking powder, salt and nutmeg. Cut in the butter with pastry blender or by hand until mixture resembles coarse crumbs.

2. Beat the egg with the milk and lemon zest. Pour the egg mixture over the flour mixture and stir once or twice, then add the blueberries and stir just until moist.

3. Gather dough into a ball and place on greased baking sheet. Pat dough into a 9-inch circle, about ¾-inch thick. With a sharp knife, and without cutting all the way through, score the dough into 8 wedges. Do not separate the dough. Brush the tops with melted butter and sprinkle with the remaining 2 tablespoons of sugar.

3. Bake until golden brown, about 20 to 30 minutes. Remove from oven and cool 2 minutes. Separate the scones into 8 pieces and serve.

2 cups flour
⅓ cup sugar
2½ teaspoons baking powder
¼ teaspoon kosher salt
⅛ teaspoon ground nutmeg
½ cup (1 stick) cold butter cut into chunks
1 egg
½ cup milk
2 teaspoons grated lemon zest
¾ cup fresh or frozen blueberries
1 tablespoon melted butter
2 tablespoons sugar

# Raspberry Vinaigrette

The color alone is enough to make me swoon. With the luscious, sweet flavor, this vinaigrette is almost drinkable. It's more a creamy dressing than a traditional vinaigrette, but the tang from the raspberry vinegar is definitely noticeable. Try this on a number of salads, but first treat yourself to a spinach salad with toasted pecans, some crumbled blue cheese and this dressing. I promise you'll never want bottled dressing again.

**1 CUP**

¼ cup fresh or frozen raspberries

1 tablespoon chopped red onion

¼ teaspoon finely chopped garlic

¼ teaspoon pink peppercorns (optional)

¼ teaspoon fresh thyme leaves

2 tablespoons raspberry vinegar

2 tablespoons rice wine vinegar

2 tablespoons red wine vinegar

½ cup olive oil

¼ cup honey

1. Blend raspberries, red onion, garlic, pink peppercorns (optional), thyme and all 3 vinegars in a blender.

2. With the blender on medium speed, slowly drizzle in olive oil then honey, blending until creamy.

3. Strain through a small-holed sieve to trap raspberry seeds. Chill.

# Seared Venison Loin

## WITH BALSAMIC BLUEBERRY SAUCE

If you just poured the blueberry sauce on an old shoe, I think I'd eat it. Fortunately, it's draped over a tender, seared piece of venison and I'm spared the embarrassment of gnawing on a piece of leather. Cook the venison only to medium rare, as most game meats toughen beyond 135°F, and very well might taste like shoe leather. Prepare the sauce first, and re-heat when ready to serve.

---

**8 SERVINGS**

1. Season the venison steaks with salt and pepper. Heat the butter and oil in a large skillet over medium-high heat.

2. Sear the venison, about 2½ to 3 minutes per side for medium rare. Remove to a warm platter and rest 5 minutes before serving.

**Balsamic Blueberry Sauce:**

1. Bring blueberries and beef stock to a boil, reduce heat and simmer vigorously until reduced to 3 cups, about 8 to 10 minutes.

2. While stock is reducing, sauté shallot, garlic and green peppercorns in 1 tablespoon of butter in a small skillet until shallot is translucent, about 3 minutes.

3. Stir in balsamic vinegar and tarragon to the shallot mixture and bring to a boil, stirring occasionally. Simmer until vinegar is reduced to ½ cup, about 8 to 10 minutes.

4. Blend the vinegar reduction and the reduced blueberry/stock mixture in a blender until smooth. (CAUTION: hot liquid in a blender shoots straight up. Cover the blender lid tightly before turning on the blender.)

5. Strain the sauce and keep warm while preparing the venison loin. If necessary, thicken the sauce by stirring together the cornstarch and cold water and stirring this "slurry" mixture into a boiling sauce. (The sauce has to boil for the slurry to thicken.)

3 pounds venison loin, cut into 3-ounce steaks
1½ teaspoons butter
1½ teaspoons vegetable oil
Kosher salt
Ground black pepper
Balsamic Blueberry Sauce

**Balsamic Blueberry Sauce (1½ cups):**

1 cup blueberries, fresh or frozen
4 cups beef stock*
1 tablespoon finely chopped shallot
½ teaspoon finely chopped garlic
1 teaspoon green peppercorns
1 tablespoon butter
1 cup balsamic vinegar
1 tablespoon chopped fresh tarragon
1 tablespoon cornstarch
1 tablespoon cold water

---

*I use a brand called Better Than Bouillon for a quick beef stock, and it comes in a jar. Check with your grocer, or order Better Than Bouillon from A. J.'s (see Sources, page 192).

# *Vanilla Latte Ice Cream Tart

## WITH FUDGE SAUCE

My neighbor Rosalie is a huge coffee ice cream fan, though she usually prefers the frozen yogurt over full-fledged ice cream. I knew that if she liked this dessert I had a winner on my hands (and she did). The meringue topping is not only attractive, it adds another flavor dimension. I even re-froze the dessert after the meringue was added and was very pleased with the result. You can make the ice cream up to 3 days before you finish the tart. You could substitute store-bought coffee ice cream to save some time.

### 8 SERVINGS

**Vanilla Latte Ice Cream:**

1½ cups heavy cream

½ cup whole milk

½ teaspoon vanilla extract

½ cup sugar

2 egg yolks

¼ cup prepared espresso

**Fudge sauce:**

½ cup heavy cream

¼ cup light corn syrup

5 ounces semi-sweet chocolate, chopped

**Vanilla Latte Ice Cream:**

1. Prepare a large bowl of ice water and set aside.

2. Heat cream, milk, vanilla and sugar in a saucepan over medium heat until the sugar is dissolved and the mixture is hot, stirring occasionally.

3. Whisk yolks and slowly pour 1 cup of the hot cream mixture into the yolks, stirring constantly. Pour warmed yolk mixture into the rest of the hot cream mixture and whisk constantly. Cook over medium heat, stirring, until mixture thickens and coats the back of a spoon, about 5 to 7 minutes.

4. Strain the cream mixture through a sieve into a bowl and chill in the ice water.

5. When mixture is chilled, stir in the espresso. Transfer the mixture to an ice cream machine and freeze according to the manufacturer's directions.

**Fudge sauce:**

1. Bring cream and corn syrup to a boil in a heavy saucepan over medium-high heat. Remove from heat and stir in chocolate. Whisk until chocolate is melted and mixture is smooth. Refrigerate for a few minutes until slightly cool, but still pourable, about 30 minutes.

*(continued on next page)*

*❋ Photograph on page C-7*

**Vanilla Latte Ice Cream Tart**
*(continued from previous page)*

**Crust:**

1. Preheat the oven to 350°F. Finely grind the chocolate graham crackers, roasted and skinned hazelnuts and sugar in a food processor. Add the melted butter and process until mixture forms moist crumbs.

2. Press mixture onto the bottom and up the sides of a 9-inch tart pan with a removable bottom. Bake for 10 to 12 minutes. Cool slightly. Pull the ice cream from the freezer to begin softening.

3. Spread a thin layer of fudge sauce (about ½ cup) evenly over the bottom of the crust. Freeze until set, about 15 minutes.

4. Spread the softened ice cream over the fudge-lined tart, smoothing the top. Freeze until set, about 30 to 45 minutes.

**Meringue:**

1. Whip egg whites and cream of tartar until foamy and starting to thicken. Slowly add sugar and continue whipping until stiff peaks form.

**Putting it all together:**

1. Spread another thin layer (about ½ cup) of fudge sauce over the set ice cream and freeze again until fudge sauce is firm, about 20 minutes.

2 Two options for applying the meringue: either place the stiff meringue into a pastry bag fitted with a star tip and cover the tart in stars; or take the easy route, like I did, and spread the meringue over the top and create little peaks all over by lifting up the spatula all over the top. I think it is just as pretty, especially after browning.

3. Preheat the broiler. When hot, place the meringue-topped tart under the broiler until the peaks are toasted, about 1 to 2 minutes. Watch carefully so as not to burn the meringue.

4. Warm the remaining fudge sauce over low heat. Lift tart out of pan, cut into wedges and serve with warm fudge sauce.

*To roast hazelnuts, see Common Procedures, page 20.

**Crust:**
8 chocolate graham crackers (about 2½ cups ground)
½ cup roasted and skinned hazelnuts*
1½ tablespoons sugar
¼ cup (½ stick) butter, melted

**Meringue:**
3 egg whites
Pinch cream of tartar
⅔ cup sugar

**Notes**

## *New Mexico*

## THE HISTORIC
# TAOS INN

### Taos Inn

125 Paseo del Pueblo Norte
Taos, NM 87571
**800.TAOSINN**
**505.758.2233**
**www.taosinn.com**

**Season:**
Year-round

**Guest Capacity:**
80

**Accommodations:**
33 rooms and 3 suites

**Activities:**
Nearby downhill and cross-country skiing; Artist Series and quarterly art exhibitions

**Peak Winter Rates:**
$-$$

**Closest Ski Resort:**
Taos Ski Valley; Angel Fire

Skiers, cowboys and artists alike journey to Taos, New Mexico to embrace the old west small town ambiance. Opened in 1936 as the Martin Hotel, this unique little inn once was home to the town's only physician, "Doc" Martin and his wife. After his passing, Mrs. Martin transformed their residence into what is now known as the Historic Taos Inn. The restaurant in the inn bears the name of Doc Martin and is rated one of the top restaurants in New Mexico by the Zagat Survey, featuring innovative southwestern cuisine.

The Taos Inn is a gathering place for local artists, and holds a semi-annual Artist Series, a tradition started in 1985. Many of the inn's 33 rooms and 3 suites contain hand-painted furniture, including work by local artist Jim Wagner. All the rooms are quite charming, but the courtyard rooms are especially enchanting, circling an authentic northern New Mexico landscaped courtyard.

Taos is laden with unique galleries and southwestern shops. Stop in at Horsefeathers on Kit Carson for vintage cowboy paraphernalia and other western gifts. It's just a short walk from the inn, on the plaza's boardwalk. Nightlife in Taos is exciting and vibrant, but if you stay at the Taos Inn, you don't have to travel much farther than the lobby to the Adobe Bar. The live music varies from top-rated jazz groups to New Mexican native music to southwestern style country/folk. It's a wonderful way to spend an evening unwinding after a day on the slopes.

Dining is always a treat at Doc Martin's, featured not only in Zagat but also in *Bon Appetit* magazine. The menu will always reflect the spirit and fusion of southwestern cuisine with Native American and Mexican influences. You might see homemade chile rellenos on the menu, or Chipotle Shrimp on a Corn Cake. A chile-inspired Southwestern Lacquered Duck or a Smoked Lamb Loin on a Goat Cheese Soufflé might share the menu with a traditional cowboy steak. One thing for sure is that the flavorful food will be remembered long after the meal.

## *Breakfast Menu*

VIRGIN MARY

✻ **BLUE CORNMEAL PANCAKES**
WITH FRESH BLUEBERRIES

FRESH FRUIT

## *Dinner Menu*

WARM FLOUR TORTILLAS

✻ **CHILE AWARD (GREEN CHILE STEW)**

✻ **CAPIROTADA (MEXICAN BREAD PUDDING)**

✻ **TEQUILA CARAMEL SAUCE**

✻ **BISCOCHITOS (SOUTHWESTERN COOKIES)**

✻ **RECIPE INCLUDED**

# Blue Cornmeal Pancakes

WITH FRESH BLUEBERRIES

*D*elicious! I love the texture and the color the blue cornmeal provides. And the blueberries add not only more blue color, but also a nice flavor addition. If you can't find blue cornmeal in your area, I've listed several options on the Sources page for mail ordering (see page 192).

**10 (6-INCH) PANCAKES**

1⅔ cups blue cornmeal
1 cup flour
3 tablespoons sugar
1 teaspoon baking powder
2 eggs
¼ teaspoon vanilla
2 cups half-and-half
4 tablespoons butter, melted
1 cup fresh or frozen blueberries

1. Stir the blue cornmeal, flour, sugar and baking powder together.

2. Beat the eggs with the vanilla and half-and-half. Pour egg mixture over cornmeal mixture and stir just until moistened. Stir in melted butter.

3. Heat a nonstick pan or griddle over medium heat. Spray surface with nonstick spray. Ladle ¼ cup batter onto hot surface. Sprinkle with a few blueberries. Cook until bubbles form on surface and edges start to dry, about 3 to 4 minutes. Turn and cook on the other side for another 2 minutes or until done. Serve with warm maple syrup.

# *Chile Award
## (Green Chile Stew)

O kay, I know the title seems misspelled, that when referring to a bowl of stew the spelling is "chili" and referring to the actual pepper, the spelling is "chile." The inn insists that the official name of their dish is Chile Award. Who am I to argue? If you are lucky enough to get your hands on authentic Hatch green chiles, by all means use them (see Sources, page 192). You'll need 2½ pounds of fresh chiles, and you will need to roast, peel and seed them. With canned chiles, I prefer to buy them whole and chop them myself. Pre-chopped chiles have too many seeds and skin left on. Serve this delicious stew with warm flour tortillas on the side.

### 8 to 10 servings

1. Cook the onions in 2 teaspoons of oil for 2 to 3 minutes over medium-high heat. Stir in garlic, ground beef and pork, and a little bit of salt and pepper to taste. Cook, stirring occasionally until the meat is brown, about 12 minutes. Drain and return to the pot.

2. Stir in the cilantro, cumin, oregano, black pepper, beef base and 1 tablespoon flour and cook 2 minutes, stirring constantly. Pour in water, beer, chiles and tomatoes. Bring to a boil and reduce heat. Simmer for 20 minutes.

3. Melt the 3 tablespoons of butter in a small skillet over medium heat and stir in the flour ½ cup of flour. Cook for 4 to 5 minutes, until the mixture (called a roux) is fragrant and starts turning golden. Stir this roux mixture into the simmering stew mixture, and cook for 20 more minutes or until thickened. Taste and add salt and pepper if necessary.

2 teaspoons vegetable oil

1 cup chopped onions

1 tablespoon finely chopped garlic

½ pound ground beef

½ pound ground pork

⅓ cup lightly packed cilantro leaves, chopped

1 tablespoon ground cumin

2 teaspoons dried Mexican oregano*

1 teaspoon ground black pepper

1½ tablespoons beef base**

1 tablespoon flour

8 cups water

½ cup Tecate or other Mexican beer

2 (27-ounce) cans whole green chiles, chopped

1 (14½-ounce) can chopped tomatoes, drained

3 tablespoons butter

½ cup flour

*Mexican oregano is different from regular or Mediterranean oregano. If you can't find Mexican oregano, you can order it from A. J.'s or Pecos Valley Spice Company, see Sources, page 192.

**Beef base is like beef bouillon, only less salty. I use a brand called Better Than Bouillon, and it comes in a jar. Check with your grocer, or order Better Than Bouillon from A. J.'s (see Sources, page 192).

### * Photograph on page C-8

# Capirotada

A Mexican bread pudding, this is not like any bread pudding you've ever tried — there is no custard. I think it's delicious, and so did my tasters. No, there isn't a typo in the sauce ingredient list. It really does include sugar, onion and tomatoes. I told you it was unique. Make the Capirotada Sauce the day before to speed things up. I've included my own Tequila Caramel sauce recipe because I think it enhances this Mexican jewel (see next page).

---

**8 SERVINGS**

4 cups Capirotada sauce
1 loaf challa or other egg-rich bread
¾ cup (1½ sticks) butter, melted
½ cup pine nuts, toasted
½ cup raisins
1 cup grated Monterey Jack cheese

**Capirotada Sauce (4 cups):**
½ cup sugar
1 cup light brown sugar
⅔ cup chopped tomato
½ cup finely chopped onion
1 cinnamon stick
3 cups water

1. Preheat oven to 350°F. Cut bread into 1-inch cubes and place on an ungreased baking sheet. Place in the oven until toasted to a golden brown, about 7 to 10 minutes.

2 Butter a 13 X 9-inch baking dish and cover the bottom with the toasted bread cubes. Drizzle with melted butter. Sprinkle with toasted pine nuts, raisins and cheese. Pour Capirotada sauce all over the bread, making sure most of the cubes are soaked. Rest for 15 minutes for the liquid to absorb into the bread.

3. Cover with foil and bake for 45 minutes. Cool 10 minutes and cut into squares. Serve with Tequila Caramel Sauce.

**Capirotada Sauce:**

1. Stir together all the ingredients and bring to a boil in a medium saucepan over medium-high heat. Reduce to a simmer and cook for 1 hour.

2. Strain and use immediately or cool and place in an airtight container in the refrigerator for up to 3 days.

# Tequila Caramel Sauce

*D*on't tell my husband, but I used his high-dollar sipping tequila for this recipe. I suppose you could use any old tequila, but I'm sticking to my story that the better the tequila, the better the sauce. This sauce will keep in the refrigerator for a week.

### 1½ CUPS

1. Heat the sugar and water over medium heat in a tall saucepan. Cook until the sugar liquifies and turns golden brown, about 12 to 14 minutes.
2. Remove from heat and carefully and SLOWLY add the heavy cream (CAUTION: the mixture will bubble up violently, which is why you need a tall pan.)
3. Return to the heat and stir until the mixture is smooth.
4. Remove from heat and stir in tequila then the butter until it melts. Serve warm or at room temperature. Store any leftover sauce, covered, in the refrigerator for up to 2 weeks.

1 cup sugar
2 tablespoons water
1 cup heavy cream
2 tablespoons tequila
¼ cup (½ stick) butter, cut into chunks

# *Biscochitos*

These Mexican shortbread cookies are delicious. Traditionally made with lard, I've used a combination of butter and shortening to get flavor and tenderness. It's best to make the dough the day before so that it hardens properly in the refrigerator for the best rolling. You can re-roll the scraps after the first cutting, but only once. A third rolling makes the cookies too tough. I used my southwestern cookie cutouts: a cowboy, a cactus, a chile and a coyote. This recipe easily doubles for a crowd.

---

### 15 TO 20 COOKIES, DEPENDING ON CUTTER SIZE

½ cup sugar
¼ cup butter
¼ cup shortening
1 egg yolk
¼ cup milk
¼ cup brandy
¼ teaspoon vanilla
2 cups flour
½ teaspoon baking powder
Pinch salt
1½ teaspoons anise seeds
Cinnamon-sugar
for sprinkling

1. Beat the sugar, butter and shortening until light and fluffy. Beat in the egg yolk, then the milk, brandy and vanilla. The mixture will look curdled.

2. Stir together the flour, baking powder, salt and anise seeds. Fold the flour mixture into the butter mixture until well mixed.

3. Divide the dough in half and roll into two logs. Wrap each log in plastic wrap and refrigerate overnight.

4. Preheat the oven to 375°. Lightly flour a work surface and remove 1 log from the refrigerator. Pat or roll dough to about ½-inch thickness. Cut with cookie cutters and sprinkle with cinnamon-sugar. Place on an ungreased sheet pan. Gather up the scraps and roll again to ½-inch thickness and cut more cookies. Repeat the process with the other refrigerated dough, rolling and cutting twice.

5. Bake for 8 to 10 minutes, or until puffy and turning golden on the bottom. Remove and cool 2 minutes. Remove with a spatula to a cooling rack and cool completely.

## New York

### Lake Placid Lodge

P.O. Box 550
Lake Placid, NY 12946
**518.523.2700**
www.lakeplacidlodge.com

**Season:**
Year-round

**Guest Capacity:**
80

**Accommodations:**
34 lodge rooms,
suites and cabins

**Activities:**
Cross-country skiing
on property; downhill skiing
nearby at Whiteface Mountain;
nearby village offers
ice-skating, shopping and
an Olympic Museum

**Peak Winter Rates:**
$$$-$$$$

**Closest Ski Resort:**
Whiteface Mountain

If you had a little cabin up in the mountains, you'd want it to look just like Lake Placid Lodge (or at least you will want to hire their decorator). Think Ralph Lauren. Think warm cozy rooms with rock fireplaces, log and twig bed frames, Indian blankets and red-checked curtains framing gorgeous views of a peaceful lake. This prestigious Relais & Châteaux luxury lodge is nestled against the pristine Lake Placid, surrounded by millions of acres of the Adirondack North Woods.

There isn't a publication that hasn't sung Lake Placid Lodge's praises — magazines *Travel and Leisure, Conde Nast Traveler, Outside, Fortune* and a host of other publications, including *Wall Street Journal.* All the accolades may be summed up in one sentence: Lake Placid Lodge is a rustically romantic retreat with stunning views, immaculate service and world-class cuisine.

The solitude of the lodge will beg you to relax and do nothing during your holiday, but only steps away a trail leads to groomed cross-country trails, beckoning you to come glide through the pine-scented forest. If the skiing doesn't get you, the village of Lake Placid, just minutes away, will. Dotted with shops and galleries filled with Adirondack artists' wares, the village recently opened a new Olympic Museum. Both the 1932 and 1980 winter Olympics were held in Lake Placid, and Olympic wannabes can watch ski-jumping, or try their own skills on the bobsled or luge track for the thrill of a lifetime.

Back at the lodge, snuggle up in an overstuffed chair with a good book and a glass of wine in front of a roaring fire. Just don't fall asleep and miss dinner. The seasons dictate the menus at Lake Placid Lodge and wintertime brings a whole bounty of game and pumpkins and squashes to the table. Perhaps a Toasted Confit Duck and Sweet Potato Ravioli will start your meal, followed by Cider Peppercorn Glazed Venison with a grand finale of a Warm Mandarin Cake with Campari Orange Sorbet. The chefs at Lake Placid Lodge have created a special menu for this book, inspired by the winter harvest.

## *Breakfast Menu*

FRESH SQUEEZED JUICE

❊ LEMON POPPY SEED WAFFLES
WITH LEMON CURD AND STRAWBERRY MINT COMPOTE
OR
❊ BRIOCHE FRENCH TOAST
WITH APPLE CRANBERRY COMPOTE AND MAPLE WALNUT BUTTER

❊ PUMPKIN WALNUT MUFFINS
WITH STREUSEL TOPPING

## *Dinner Menu*

ROAST SPICED QUAIL
WITH BLACKBERRY AND APPLE JUS

❊ HOME-SMOKED SALMON
WITH A SPICED BUTTERNUT SQUASH AND WILD MUSHROOM CHOWDER

❊ LIMA BEAN ROSEMARY RISOTTO

❊ ROASTED BABY TURNIPS
WITH HONEY AND THYME

❊ COCONUT MOUSSE
WITH ORANGE VANILLA COMPOTE

❊ RECIPE INCLUDED

# Lemon Poppy Seed Waffles

## WITH LEMON CURD AND STRAWBERRY MINT COMPOTE

*T*his is it. This is THE killer breakfast recipe in this book — a flavor explosion! My tasters were beside themselves, cooing about how wonderful this dish is. And one was a teenager, Mark Passovoy. He was visiting his grandparents for a week and often had to trudge over to my kitchen for a tasting. He said with a sigh, "Life as a food taster … our work is never done!" Well said, Mark.

### 10 WAFFLES

2 cups flour

Pinch of kosher salt

1 tablespoon baking powder

4 lemons (zest only, but save the juice for the lemon curd)

2 teaspoons poppy seeds

1 egg, separated

2 cups milk

1 teaspoon vanilla extract

4 tablespoons melted butter

Lemon Curd

Strawberry Mint Compote

**Lemon Curd (2½ cups):**

1½ cups water

Juice of 3 lemons (just shy of ⅔ cup)

¾ cup sugar

2 egg yolks

¼ cup cornstarch

2 tablespoons butter

**Strawberry Mint Compote (3 cups):**

4 cups sugar

2 cups water

2 vanilla beans split lengthwise

6 cups strawberries, hulled and halved

6 tablespoons chopped fresh mint

**Lemon Poppy Seed Waffles:**

1. Spray a waffle maker with nonstick spray and preheat. Stir the flour, salt, baking powder, lemon zest and poppy seeds.

2. Beat the egg yolk with the milk and vanilla in another bowl.

3. Whip the egg white to soft peaks in a third bowl.

4. Pour the milk mixture over the flour mixture and stir just to moisten. Gently fold the whipped egg white into the batter. Gently stir in the melted butter.

5. Pour a generous ¼ cup batter into preheated waffle maker. Cook according to manufacturer's directions or until light golden brown.

**Lemon Curd:**

1. Bring the water and lemon juice to a boil. Meanwhile, beat the sugar, egg yolks and cornstarch together. Add a few tablespoons of the hot water/lemon mixture to the egg mixture to warm it without cooking the eggs.

2. Pour the warmed egg mixture into the saucepan with the water/lemon mixture and stir. Cook over medium heat until thick (just a few minutes).

3. Remove from heat and stir in butter until melted. Strain through a sieve and keep warm for serving.

**Strawberry Mint Compote:**

1. Heat the sugar and water. Add the split vanilla beans and heat gently. Stir in strawberries and simmer for 5 minutes.

2. Remove from heat. Remove vanilla beans and stir in mint just before serving.

# *Brioche French Toast*

## WITH APPLE CRANBERRY COMPOTE AND MAPLE WALNUT BUTTER

**D**id I say the last recipe was the killer one? I might have meant this one. Oh, they are both fabulous. My kitchen assistant Scott and I both sat down to eat this one (normally we taste while standing, ready to move onto the next recipe.) It definitely got our attention. If you can't locate brioche bread, then substitute challa, or another egg-rich bread.

---

**4 SERVINGS**

**French Toast:**

1. Whisk the eggs and the egg yolks with the milk, cinnamon, vanilla and sugar. Lay the bread slices in a large shallow pan and pour the egg mixture over the top, turning to coat both sides.

2. Spray a large, nonstick skillet or griddle with nonstick spray and heat over medium-low heat. (It's best to cook French toast slowly, more slowly than pancakes so that the middle is cooked through.) Cook the toast until golden brown, about 5 minutes, turn over and cook other side until golden brown. Top with the Maple Walnut Butter and Apple Cranberry Compote and serve.

**Maple Walnut Butter:**

1. Place all ingredients in a food processor and process until blended. Remove to a serving ramekin or bowl and chill slightly. Will keep, covered, in the refrigerator for up to 3 weeks.

**Apple Cranberry Compote:**

1. Place all the ingredients, including the ½ cup of water, in a medium sauce pan and cook over medium heat for 15 to 20 minutes or until apples are soft. Add a little more water if necessary to thin.

---

*This delightfully sweet-tart version is the creation of my kitchen assistant, Scott Clapp. Enjoy.

3 eggs
2 egg yolks
2 cups milk
½ teaspoon cinnamon
¼ teaspoon vanilla extract
2 tablespoons sugar
8 thick slices brioche bread
Maple Walnut Butter
Apple Cranberry Compote

**Maple Walnut Butter (1 cup):**
½ cup (1 stick) butter, softened
½ cup toasted walnuts
2 tablespoons maple syrup

**Apple Cranberry Compote* (1½ cups)**
4 cups chopped peeled, cored apples
1 cup apple sauce
¾ cup sugar
1 cup dried cranberries
3 tablespoons raspberry vinegar
¼ teaspoon cinnamon
Pinch ground nutmeg
½ cup or more water (to thin)

# Pumpkin Walnut Muffins
## WITH STREUSEL TOPPING

P umpkin and spices smell wonderful when baking. The payoff, though, is in the taste. Just don't forget to add the pumpkin before you bake the muffins, like I did the first time. Oh, like you've never done anything like that before? No snickering. Just enjoy a warm, spicy, moist muffin.

### 12 TO 14 MUFFINS

1½ cups plus
2 tablespoons flour
1¼ cups sugar
1 teaspoon salt
1½ teaspoons baking powder
1 teaspoon cinnamon
¾ teaspoon ground nutmeg
¾ teaspoon ground cloves
¾ teaspoon ground allspice
3 eggs
½ cup vegetable oil
1½ cups plus 2 tablespoons
pumpkin purée
1 cup chopped walnuts
½ cup golden raisins

**Streusel topping:**
¼ cup light brown sugar
2 tablespoons flour
1 teaspoon cinnamon
2 tablespoons cold butter
½ cup finely
chopped walnuts

1. To prepare streusel topping: Stir together the brown sugar, flour and cinnamon. Cut in cold butter by hand or with a pastry blender until mixture is crumbly. Stir in walnuts and set aside.

2. Preheat oven to 350°F. Stir together the flour, sugar, salt, baking powder, cinnamon, nutmeg, cloves and allspice.

3. Lightly whisk the eggs with the oil and pumpkin purée. Pour the egg mixture over the flour mixture and stir just to moisten. Fold in walnuts and raisins. Do not overmix.

4. Spray muffin tins with a nonstick cooking spray. Spoon muffin mix into each cup, ¾ full. Top with a generous tablespoon of streusel topping. Bake 20 to 25 minutes, or until a toothpick inserted in the center comes out clean or with just a few moist crumbs attached.

# *Home-smoked Salmon

## WITH SPICED BUTTERNUT SQUASH CHOWDER AND SCALLOP VERMOUTH FROTH

The title is long and so is the flavor of this marvelous dish. Don't be intimidated by the name or the procedure. It's really simple, but I admit, the whole dish takes about 3 hours to prepare. You could just smoke and grill the salmon and serve it with a steamed vegetable and mashed potatoes for a quicker dish. But I don't want you to miss the colorful chowder and foamy scallop broth — delicious! So make this on the weekend when you have a little more time. One note of caution, the heating of the chips will turn the inside of your pan black. I used a throwaway aluminum-roasting pan.

------
**6 SERVINGS**

**Home-smoked Salmon:**

1. Soak the wood chips in water for 30 minutes. Drain and place wood chips in an aluminum-roasting pan. Put sprigs of herbs over the top then place a greased wire rack (like a roasting rack) over the chips.

2. Cover the pan with a sheet of foil and heat for 10 to 15 minutes on top of the stove over medium heat until the chips are heated and smoking. Carefully fold back the foil and place the salmon on the greased wire rack spacing evenly. Replace the foil and seal tightly. Return to the stove for 5 minutes, then take off the heat. Stand in a cool place for 10 minutes.

3. Remove the salmon and place in a covered container in the refrigerator until needed. The salmon is not quite cooked through at this point.

4. If you are making the chowder and froth, start now while salmon chills in the refrigerator. If you are just making the salmon, to finish, preheat the grill to medium-high, (375°F). Grill salmon, about 3 minutes on each side for medium.

**Spiced Butternut Squash, Fennel and Wild Mushroom Chowder:**

1. Have a large bowl of ice water ready, with a strainer set in it. Cook the squash, potatoes and fennel briefly in boiling salted water (about 3 minutes). Drain and plunge into the strainer in the ice cold water to stop the cooking. Drain and set aside.

2. Heat 2 teaspoons of oil in a large skillet. Stir in mushrooms and cook, stirring occasionally for 5 minutes. Add shallots, garlic and thyme. Cook for another 2 minutes, stirring often.

3. Stir in the squash, potatoes, fennel, salt, white pepper, five-spice powder and cayenne pepper. Cook for 3 more minutes or until thoroughly heated. Taste and adjust seasonings and add the chopped chives just before serving.

*(continued on next page)*

**The Smoked Salmon:**

6 (6-ounce) salmon fillets or steaks, 1-inch thick
2 cups hickory or applewood chips
(or substitute your favorite)
3 sprigs of rosemary
3 sprigs of thyme

**Chowder (6 servings):**

2 cups finely chopped peeled butternut squash*

1 cup finely chopped Yukon gold potatoes

1 cup finely chopped fennel bulb

2 teaspoons olive oil

2 cups chopped wild mushrooms (cremini, oyster, shiitake, etc.)

2 tablespoons finely chopped shallots

½ teaspoon finely chopped garlic

1 teaspoon fresh thyme leaves

¼ teaspoon kosher salt

¼ teaspoon white pepper

1 teaspoon Chinese five-spice powder

⅛ teaspoon cayenne pepper

1 tablespoon finely chopped chives

* **Photograph on page C-10**

**Scallop Vermouth Froth
(6 servings):**
1 tablespoon butter
1 cup chopped scallops
½ cup sliced shallots
1 cup finely chopped white
button mushrooms
½ teaspoon finely
chopped garlic
1 cup dry vermouth
3 cups heavy cream
Kosher salt
Ground white pepper

**Home-smoked Salmon** *(continued from previous page)*

4. To serve, mound ⅔ cup of chowder mixture in a shallow
   serving bowl. Ladle Scallop Vermouth Froth (recipe follows)
   around chowder and top with grilled smoked salmon.
   Beautiful!

**Scallop Vermouth Froth:**\*\*

1. Heat the butter over medium heat in an ovenproof sauté pan
   and add the scallops and shallots. Cook for 7 to 8 minutes, or
   until most of the liquid has evaporated.

2. Stir in the mushrooms and garlic and continue cooking until
   the mushrooms have cooked down (about 10 minutes).

3. Pour in the vermouth and reduce until only ⅓ cup is left, about
   10 minutes. Pour in the cream and salt and white pepper.
   Bring to a slow simmer and cook, stirring frequently for about
   10 minutes.

4. Strain the sauce through a sieve and place back on the stove
   to reduce further if necessary. Consistency should be that of
   heavy cream. Taste and adjust seasonings as necessary. To
   make it frothy, use a hand mixer or hand blender and blend
   for a minute or two.

5. Ladle sauce around the chowder in a shallow serving bowl
   and top with grilled smoked salmon.

---

\*Try to chop the squash, potatoes and fennel all about the same size, a ¼-inch cube.
Not only will they cook more evenly, the final dish will look uniform and professional.
I've found that a sturdy vegetable peeler is the easiest way to peel the tough skin off
the squash, and I wear disposable latex gloves to keep my hands from getting sticky
and turning orange.
\*\*If you don't like or can't eat scallops, don't just skip this recipe. Substitute an
additional cup of mushrooms for the 1 cup of scallops.

## Notes

_____

_____

_____

_____

_____

_____

_____

_____

# Lima Bean Rosemary Risotto

W ant me to eat a lima bean? Either pay me a million bucks, or put it in this creamy, rich rice dish. I'm not kidding; this is divine. Before you Lima lovers send me hate mail, just know that I have a new respect and outlook for this Peruvian legume.

### 4 HEARTY SERVINGS

1. Cook the onions, celery, carrots and garlic in 2 tablespoons of butter over medium heat for 7 to 10 minutes, or until onions are translucent.

2. Stir in the rice and rosemary and cook for 3 minutes. Pour in one cup of the heated stock and cook, stirring until the rice has absorbed most of the liquid, about 10 minutes. Add another cup of stock and keep stirring, cooking until the rice absorbs the liquid. Add the last cup of the stock and continue cooking until the liquid is absorbed. The rice should be creamy but should still have a slight "bite" when chewed.

3. Stir in the lima beans, remaining 4 tablespoons of butter and Parmesan. Taste and add salt and white pepper if necessary.

¾ cup finely chopped onion

¾ cup finely chopped celery

¾ cup finely chopped carrots

½ teaspoon garlic

6 tablespoons butter, divided

1 cup arborio (or other risotto-style) rice

1 tablespoon finely chopped fresh rosemary

3 cups vegetable or chicken stock, heated

1 cup cooked lima beans

4 tablespoons freshly grated Parmesan

Kosher salt

Ground white pepper

# Roasted Baby Turnips
## WITH HONEY AND THYME

*I* rank turnips right up there with lima beans on the yuck scale. But once again, my tune changed after tasting this scrumptious rendition. I love good recipes for bad vegetables! Even if you don't like turnips, you will love this sweet, caramel-tinged roasted root. The recipe calls for a small amount of lavender, which you can find in the spice section in your grocery store. It is optional, however, so don't fret if you can't find it.

### 4 SERVINGS

16 (1-inch) baby turnips or 4 small regular purple-topped turnips

3 tablespoons finely chopped shallots

4 tablespoons butter

8 tablespoons honey

⅛ teaspoon lavender (optional)

1 tablespoon finely chopped garlic

1 tablespoon fresh thyme leaves

1. If using baby turnips, peel, leaving a little of the green tops intact. If using regular turnips, peel and cut into quarters, or 1-inch chunks. Bring a pot of salted water to a boil.

2. Drop turnips in boiling water for about 6 minutes and drain.

3. Meanwhile, cook the shallots in the butter over medium heat in a large skillet.

4. Add the turnips when the butter just starts to turn brown and cook, stirring constantly for 2 to 3 minutes.

5. Add honey, lavender (optional), garlic and thyme. Keep stirring the turnips to prevent burning. Cook 4 to 5 minutes until the sauce thickens and the turnips have turned a caramel color. Serve immediately.

# Coconut Mousse

## WITH ORANGE VANILLA COMPOTE

*L*ight. Fluffy. Exquisite. I increased the coconut just a bit because I love coconut. If you want only a "hint" of coconut, omit the coconut extract. This is an elegant dessert that looks beautiful in a small crystal dessert cup. The lodge tops this dessert with a thin wafer coconut cookie. You could add a thin wafer if you'd like. Choose one of those fancy wafers dipped in dark chocolate.

### 10 TO 12 SERVINGS

1. From the ⅓ cup of coconut milk, remove 4 tablespoons and place in a small saucepan with the 2 packages of gelatin.

2. Heat over low heat, just until gelatin dissolves, stirring constantly (about 1 minute). Remove from heat and set aside to cool.

3. Meanwhile, whip the heavy cream to soft peaks and fold in the rest of the coconut milk. Add the coconut extract, if using.

4. Whip the egg whites to soft peaks in another bowl, slowly adding the ½ cup sugar toward the end of the process.

5. Fold the gelatin mixture into the egg white meringue and then fold in the whipped cream. Place in a covered container and refrigerate for 3 to 4 hours or overnight.

6. To serve, scoop the mousse with an ice cream scoop into a small decorative bowl. Ladle with 3 or 4 tablespoons of the Orange Vanilla Compote (recipe follows) and top with a wafer cookie or toasted coconut (optional).

### Orange Vanilla Compote:

1. Remove the peel and white pith from the oranges. Cut out the segments and set aside. Squeeze the juice from the remaining pulp to equal ½ cup.

2. Boil the juice, sugar, vanilla bean and liqueur in a small saucepan over medium-high heat. Stir the cornstarch with the tablespoon of cold water to make a very thin paste. As the juice mixture is boiling, whisk the cornstarch paste into the juice. Reduce to a simmer and cook gently for five minutes.

3. Remove from heat and add the reserved orange segments. Chill before using. Remove the vanilla bean just before serving.

⅓ cup sweetened coconut milk, divided

2 (¼-ounce) packages unflavored gelatin

2 cups heavy cream

¼ teaspoon coconut extract (optional)

4 egg whites

½ cup sugar

1 cup toasted coconut (optional garnish)*

### Orange Vanilla Compote (2 cups):

8 oranges

½ cup orange juice

¾ cup sugar

1 vanilla bean split lengthwise

2 tablespoons Cointreau or other orange-flavored liqueur

1 tablespoon cornstarch

1 tablespoon cold water

---

*To toast coconut, see Common Procedures, page 20.

# Mirror Lake Inn

## Mirror Lake Inn

5 Mirror Lake Drive
Lake Placid, NY 12946
**518.523.2544**
www.mirrorlakeinn.com

**Season:**
Year-round

**Guest Capacity:**
300

**Accommodations:**
128 rooms and suites

**Activities:**
Cross-country skiing;
snowshoeing; ice skating;
toboggan riding;
nearby downhill skiing;
ice-climbing; scenic flights

**Peak Winter Rates:**
$-$$$$

**Closest Ski Resort:**
Whiteface Mountain

Mirror Lake Inn is more than just a luxury hotel, it's a world-class spa and resort, garnering awards like the AAA Four-Diamond award and reader poll awards from *Conde Nast Traveler* magazine, including "#1 in service" and one of the "top 6 for food and accommodations." Blending Adirondack charm with New World elegance, Mirror Lake Inn provides a civilized setting for a winter vacation. Located on the edge of the sleepy Lake Placid village, the inn provides easy access to a multitude of winter activities, including ice skating, cross-country skiing and glorious shopping at the 100-plus quaint shops.

The rooms and suites are elegant and spacious, with some having 2 stories, a lower level as a living area plus the bedroom upstairs. Several of the suites are large enough for five or six-member families. While the suites are luxurious and large, the inn offers smaller, but cozy Colonial rooms at a much lower rate, making the inn affordable to anyone.

But who wants to stay in the room when there is a spa to indulge? How about a four layer facial using seaweed and salt, or a full-body seaweed wrap to purge the body's impurities? Massages run the gamut of Swedish, Shiatsu, reflexology, sports and deep tissue. Unwind in a whirlpool in one of the private sanctuaries, lavishly appointed with marble and mahogany.

All that relaxing is sure to work up an appetite and the Mirror Lake Inn presents a bounty of healthful spa cuisine, as well as less spa-oriented gourmet fare. Fine dining awaits you in the Averil Conwell dining room, with delicacies such as Pan-seared Venison with Pancetta and Blackberry Rhubarb Jam. For a more casual setting try the Cottage overlooking Mirror Lake, with dressed up pub-style food. Either dining choice translates into a pleasurable, memorable meal.

## *Dinner Menu*

❋ THREE ONION TART

❋ SHRIMP WHITEFACE
OR
❋ PORK TENDERLOIN SADDLEBACK
WITH APPLE CRANBERRY CHUTNEY

MIRROR LAKE INN BUTTERNUT SQUASH

MAPLE CRÈME BRÛLÉE

❋ RECIPE INCLUDED

# *Three Onion Tart

**R**ich and decadent, this recipe was one of my neighbor Marilyn's favorite dishes. It takes some time to properly caramelize the onions because you have to cook them over a low heat to fully develop the caramel flavor — we're talking over an hour. The slicer disc on your food processor or a mandoline will come in handy to prepare the onions. So will a gas mask. If you don't have a gas mask, then put your onions and shallots in the freezer for about 30 minutes before you slice them to help reduce the fumes. A 10-inch tart pan works best, but you could squeeze the filling into a 9-inch pan if you don't have the 10-inch size, although it will be very full.

---

8 SERVINGS

3 white onions, peeled and sliced (about 8 cups)

8 shallots, peeled and sliced (about 2 cups)

2 leeks, white part only*

2 tablespoons sugar

6 tablespoons butter

½ cup sherry

2 tablespoons chopped fresh sage leaves

Kosher salt and pepper

1 sheet frozen puff pastry dough, thawed

3 eggs, lightly beaten

½ cup milk

1 cup crumbled blue cheese

1. Slowly cook the onions, shallots, leeks and sugar in the butter in a 12-inch nonstick skillet over medium-low heat, stirring occasionally until all the onions are dark caramel brown, about 70 to 90 minutes. You need to stir less in the beginning, and a little more once they start to turn golden. Stir in sherry and turn the heat to high. Cook another 2 minutes, or until most of the sherry has evaporated. Stir in sage and salt and pepper to taste.

2. Preheat the oven to 325°F. Roll out a puff pastry sheet just large enough to cover the bottom and sides of a 10-inch tart pan. Spray the tart pan with nonstick spray, then line the tart pan with the pastry dough pressing into the bottom and sides and trimming the edges.

3. Place tart pan on a lightly greased sheet pan. Spread the onion mixture evenly over the bottom of the tart pan.

4. Beat the eggs with the ½ cup milk. Slowly pour over the onion mixture.

5. Bake in a preheated oven until the center is firm and the crust is golden, about 30 to 35minutes.

6. If you are making the tart the day before you plan to serve it, cool and slice into individual portions. Before serving, crumble blue cheese over the top and re-heat in a 350°F oven until cheese is melted and tart is thoroughly heated, about 15 minutes.

7. If you serve it the same day you make it, after baking for 30 minutes, remove tart from oven and sprinkle with the blue cheese. Return to the oven until the cheese melts, about 3 minutes. Remove and cool slightly before cutting and serving.

---

*Leeks hold on to dirt extremely well. After you cut the white part off, cut it again in half, lengthwise. Hold the leek under running cool water, fanning the leek to open it up and rinse out the dirt. Then you can slice the leeks crosswise, into half moons. Two leeks, white part only, should yield about 1 cup sliced.

*✲ Photograph on page C-11*

# Pork Tenderloin Saddleback

## WITH APPLE CRANBERRY CHUTNEY

*M*irror Lake Inn prepares the pork by pan-searing and finishing in the oven. I grilled it because I love the extra flavor grilling provides. The Apple Cranberry Chutney is sweet and tart, and tastes scrumptious with the pork.

---

4 SERVINGS

**Pork Tenderloin:**

1. Preheat the grill to medium-high (375°–400°F). Smear the olive oil all over the pork tenderloin. Sprinkle with salt and pepper.

2. Grill the pork for about 25 minutes in total for medium, rotating and turning about every 5 minutes to grill all sides. Place on a cutting board and rest for 5 minutes, covered, before slicing on the bias. Cut slices about 1-inch thick, giving each person 3 or 4 pieces. Serve with the chutney.

**Apple Cranberry Chutney:**

1. Bring the apples, apple juice, vinegar and both sugars to a boil over medium-high heat. Reduce to a simmer and cook 8 to 10 minutes. Stir in cinnamon, cloves and cranberries. Cook another 5 minutes or until apples are tender.

2. If necessary, thicken with a slurry by stirring together the cornstarch and cold water and adding this mixture to the apple mixture. Bring to a boil to thicken. Remove from heat and serve.

2 pounds pork tenderloin
1 teaspoon olive oil
Kosher salt
Ground black pepper
1 cup Apple Cranberry Chutney

**Apple Cranberry Chutney (2 cups):**
2 large Granny Smith apples, peeled, cored and chopped
1 cup apple juice
½ cup cider vinegar
½ cup sugar
½ cup light brown sugar
⅛ teaspoon ground cinnamon
Pinch ground cloves
1 cup dried cranberries
1 tablespoon cornstarch
1 tablespoon cold water

# Shrimp Whiteface

T he inn prepares this dish "to order", meaning they prepare one at a time, as a guest orders it. I increased the quantities and tested it as a four-serving recipe. What this means is that you can play with the quantities and make it for any number of servings. It is really delicious, creamy but with a nice tang from the feta. I also tested it with chicken breasts and loved the result. If you use chicken, cut 4 boneless, skinless breast halves into thin strips so that they cook quickly. Increase the cooking time from 2 minutes for the shrimp, to 4 minutes for the chicken strips in step one. By the way, this dish is named after the Olympic Mount Whiteface, the lone mountain of the Whiteface Ski Resort.

**4 SERVINGS**

24 large shrimp, shelled and deveined

2 tablespoons olive oil, divided

2 tablespoons finely chopped garlic

1 pound dried linguine

2 Roma tomatoes, cored, seeded and cut into 1/2-inch strips

6 shiitake mushroom caps, sliced

6 white button mushrooms, sliced

6 oyster mushrooms, sliced

1 cup feta cheese, cubed

1 cup chopped fresh spinach leaves

½ cup white wine

½ cup chicken stock, heated

¼ cup chopped fresh herbs (like rosemary, sage, parsley and thyme)

Kosher salt

Ground black pepper

1 tablespoon chopped parsley (garnish)

1. Have all your ingredients prepared and ready. Bring a large pot of salted water to a boil to cook the pasta. Just before the water comes to a full boil, heat 1 tablespoon of oil in a 12-inch skillet over medium-high heat. When oil is hot, add the shrimp and garlic. Cook 2 minutes, stirring constantly. (Shrimp won't be quite done.) Remove the shrimp with a slotted spoon and cover with foil to keep warm.

2. Add the linguine to the boiling water and cook according to package directions.

3. Meanwhile, add the other tablespoon of olive oil to the skillet over medium-high heat and then add the tomatoes, mushrooms, feta cheese and spinach. Cook 2 minutes. Stir in the white wine and cook 2 minutes. Stir in hot chicken stock, the reserved shrimp and the fresh herbs. Cook until the shrimp is done, about 2 more minutes. Season with salt and pepper.

4. Drain the pasta when done, and toss with the shrimp and sauce. Divide the pasta into 4 heated pasta bowls, making sure each bowl receives 6 shrimp. Garnish with chopped parsley.

# *Utah*

# DEER VALLEY® RESORT

## Deer Valley Resort

P.O. Box 1525
Park City, UT 84060
**800.424.DEER**
**435.649.1000**
www.deervalley.com

**Season:**
Winter: December through early
April; Summer: mid-June
through Labor Day

**Guest Capacity:**
N/A

**Accommodations:**
No overnight accommodations,
day lodge only

**Activities:**
Downhill and cross-country
skiing; racing course;
snowmobiling; sleigh rides; heli-
skiing; hot air ballooning

**Peak Winter Rates:**
N/A

**Closest Ski Resort:**
Deer Valley

It's too bad that the only thing spending the night at Deer Valley are your skis. You see, Deer Valley is a day lodge with no guestrooms. Then why include it in this book? Food, glorious food, that's why. You won't find finer cuisine than what Deer Valley creates daily through its seven restaurants, including the award-winning Mariposa.

Deer Valley cuisine is divided between two locations. The base location of Snow Park Lodge is home to the Snow Park Restaurant, featuring made-to-order breakfasts and lunch, Snowpark Lounge and the Seafood Buffet, an award-winning collection of chilled shellfish and sizzling seafood entrees.

Silver Lake Lodge, located mid-mountain, is home to Mariposa, a consistently #1 rated fine dining restaurant, Silver Lake Restaurant, serving breakfast and lunch, McHenry's, home of the award-winning "Best Burger" and Bald Mountain Pizza featuring gourmet pizzas, salads and pasta.

The culinary team at Deer Valley is impressive; many have been cooking at the resort for 20 years or more. One long-timer is Executive Pastry Chef Letty Flatt, a petite brunette with a gargantuan appetite for skiing and baking. Letty's first book, *Chocolate Snowball and Other Fabulous Pastries from Deer Valley Bakery* (Three Forks) hit the bookshelves in the fall of 1999. Letty thoughtfully marked each recipe for degree of difficulty, using the same system used to rate ski trails, a green circle for easy, a blue square for intermediate and black and double black diamonds for advanced. But even the black diamond recipes are doable for the average cook, thanks to Letty's simplistic approach and carefully worded instructions.

Deer Valley's online store (www.deervalley.com) is the perfect place to order Letty's book, or other gifts from the resort, including the delicious turkey chili mix, based on the same recipe McHenry's uses everyday. It will be difficult to tear yourself away from one of the unique dining spots at Deer Valley. You might even have to make two trips, one for the food and one for the skiing.

## *Breakfast Menu*

FRESH SQUEEZED ORANGE AND GRAPEFRUIT JUICE

SPINACH, MUSHROOM AND GRUYÈRE EGG CUSTARD

MAPLE PEPPERED BACON

❄ APPLE CINNAMON MUFFINS

❄ BANANA COCONUT BREAD

## *Dinner Menu*

❄ SUN-DRIED TOMATO PESTO MASCARPONE

❄ MUSHROOM AND WILD RICE SOUP

❄ HONEY SOY-GLAZED CHILEAN SEA BASS
WITH GINGER BUTTER SAUCE

❄ GREEN ONION MASHED POTATOES

❄ APPLE BERRY COBBLER

❄ RECIPE INCLUDED

# Apple Cinnamon Muffins

B ursting with moist apples, warmed by a generous dose of cinnamon and finished with the crunch of toasted walnuts, this muffin is one of my all-time favorite recipes. The resort adapted this muffin mix from a recipe by Marion Cunningham, but they have thoroughly made it their own.

---

**14 MUFFINS**

4 cups chopped apples (peeled or unpeeled)

1 cup sugar

2 cups flour

2 teaspoons baking soda

2 teaspoons cinnamon

1 teaspoon kosher salt

2 eggs, lightly beaten

½ cup vegetable oil

2 teaspoons vanilla

1 cup raisins

1 cup chopped walnuts

1. Preheat the oven to 325°F. Grease and flour a muffin pan. Use three bowls for this recipe.

2. Stir the apples with the sugar in a large bowl.

3. Sift flour, baking soda, cinnamon and salt in a medium bowl.

4. Whisk eggs, oil and vanilla in a third bowl. Stir this egg mixture into the apple/sugar mixture.

5. Sprinkle the flour mixture over the apple/egg mixture and stir until just moistened. Stir in raisins.

6. Scoop ¼ cup of batter into prepared muffin pan (cup will be full).

7. Chop the chopped walnuts even more finely and sprinkle on top of each muffin.

8. Bake for 25 to 30 minutes, or until a toothpick inserted in the center of a muffin comes out clean or with just a few moist crumbs attached.

# Banana Coconut Bread

I thought I had tried all the great banana bread recipes until I had this one. Wow! The coconut is such a sweet addition. The bread is big, moist and delicious. You'd better pour a tall glass of milk to go with this one.

### 1 LOAF

1. Preheat oven to 350°F. Grease and flour a 9 X 5-inch loaf pan. Use 3 bowls for this recipe.

2. Beat the butter and sugar until light and fluffy (I used an electric mixer). Add bananas and beat, scraping sides of the bowl. Add eggs, beat and scrape bowl again. Set aside.

3. Stir milk, lemon juice and almond extract in a small bowl. Set aside.

4. Stir flour, baking powder, baking soda, salt and coconut together in a third bowl.

5. Alternate adding the flour mixture with the milk mixture to the egg mixture, beginning and ending with the flour mixture. Scrape bowl in between additions, stirring just to moisten.

6. Pour into prepared loaf pan. The pan will be full of batter. Bake for 50 to 65 minutes, or until a toothpick inserted in the center of the bread comes out clean or with just a few moist crumbs.

⅔ cup butter, softened

1 cup sugar

4 bananas
(very ripe, mashed)

3 eggs

¼ cup milk

2 teaspoons lemon juice

¾ teaspoon almond extract

2½ cups flour

1¼ teaspoons baking powder

½ teaspoon baking soda

½ teaspoon kosher salt

1¼ cups sweetened, grated coconut

# Sun-dried Tomato Pesto Mascarpone

**B**eautiful! Three distinct layers of red, green and white make this an attractive as well as delicious appetizer. The flavor is creamy, herbaceous and earthy sweet. Warm garlic toast is the perfect accouterment to deliver a stunning flavor explosion to your guests. Make this the day before or at least 3 hours before you intend to serve it so that it can chill properly.

---

**6 TO 8 SERVINGS**

---

**Cream cheese layer:**

½ cup (1 stick) butter, softened

½ cup (4 ounces) cream cheese, softened

¼ teaspoon kosher salt

¼ teaspoon ground black pepper

**Pesto layer:**

2 cups lightly packed fresh basil leaves

1 teaspoon chopped garlic

2 teaspoons olive oil

2 tablespoons grated Parmesan

2 tablespoons toasted sliced almonds

**Sun-dried Tomato Layer:**

¼ cup sun-dried tomatoes packed in oil, drained and lightly packed

½ teaspoon chopped garlic

½ teaspoon chopped shallot

¼ teaspoon ground black pepper

**Cream cheese layer:**

1. Process butter and cream cheese in a food processor until smooth. Add salt and pepper and process again until thoroughly mixed. Set aside.

**Pesto layer:**

1. Process all the pesto ingredients (basil leaves through almonds) in a food processor until almost smooth. The consistency should be paste-like but you should still see texture. Set aside.

**Sun-dried Tomato Layer:**

1. Process all sun-dried tomato layer ingredients (tomatoes through pepper) in a food processor until paste-like but you still see some texture. Set aside.

**Putting it all together:**

1. Line 2 (6-ounce) ramekins with plastic wrap with at least 1 inch extra over the sides. Beginning with the cream cheese mixture, spread about ½-inch thick on the bottom. Chill for 5 minutes in the freezer. (Freezing helps harden the cheese so that your next layer spreads easier.)

2. Remove from freezer and add a thin (½-inch) layer of pesto, smoothing with a spoon. Freeze 5 more minutes and then remove and add another layer of cream cheese. Freeze again for 5 minutes and add a thin (½-inch) layer of sun-dried tomato.

3. Finish with another layer of cream cheese. Refrigerate ramekins for 3 hours or overnight.

4. To serve, invert ramekins onto a serving plate, remove mold and plastic and serve with warm garlic toasts or crackers.

Experience winter in
a variety of ways....

Top Left: Vista Verde, CO
Top right: The Equinox, VT
Bottom: The Little Nell, CO

## Lake Placid Lodge
### New York

Home-smoked Salmon with a Spiced Butternut, Fennel and Wild Mushroom Chowder in a Scallop Vermouth Froth

Mirror Lake Inn
New York

Three Onion Tart

Deer Valley Resort, Utah

Honey Soy-glazed Chilean Sea Bass with Ginger Butter Sauce

The Homestead Resort, Utah

Oven-roasted Tomato and Avocado Soup

# Stein Eriksen Lodge, Utah

## Chocolate Volcano with Raspberry Coulis

Sundance
Utah

Joe's Special on
Homemade Cheese Biscuits

Gift Baskets

Wine Cellar

Fresh Roasted
Coffee Beans

Southwest
Cookbooks

# PAUL'S PANTRY INC.

Gourmet Foods, Wine Cellar & Housewares

www.paulspantry.com
480-488-4300
El Pedregal Marketplace
Carefree, Arizona

Gourmet
Southwest Foods

Unique
Housewares
& Kitchen
Gadgets

Truffles &
Chocolates

# Mushroom and Wild Rice Soup

I love thick, earthy soups, just like this one. And it doesn't rely on cream to make it rich. Generally I prefer fresh mushrooms to dried mushrooms, but this recipe calls for a combination of both and it works. The recipe calls for fresh chanterelles and shiitakes. Shiitakes are widely available but if you can't find any, substitute a fresh portabella cap. If you can't find chanterelles, substitute with oyster or hedgehog mushrooms. Use cremini (common brown Italian mushroom) if all else fails.

### 6 SERVINGS

1. Reconstitute the dried porcini mushrooms in just enough boiling water to cover them and set aside for at least 30 minutes. Remove, reserving the liquid, and rinse and chop the porcinis. Strain the liquid through cheesecloth to remove any grit and set aside to use later.

2. Meanwhile, heat the 2 tablespoons of butter in a 4-quart soup pot and cook the onion until transparent. Add the garlic and fresh mushrooms and cook over medium heat until soft, about 5 minutes. Sprinkle in the flour and cook, stirring frequently for about 10 minutes.

3. Whisk the heated chicken stock into the mushroom mixture. Stir in the white wine, the soaked, rinsed and chopped porcini mushrooms, and the strained liquid used to soak the porcinis. Simmer for 1 hour.

4. Strain the soup and purée the solids with a little of the soup liquid in a blender. Working in batches, fill the blender to only half full. CAUTION: hot liquid in a blender shoots straight up so cover top with a kitchen towel and apply pressure before turning on the blender. Add the purée back into the soup. Season with lemon juice, dry sherry, thyme and salt and pepper. Keep warm.

5. Prepare the garnish by cooking the shiitakes and chanterelles in 1 teaspoon of butter over medium heat until tender, about 10 minutes.

6. Place about ¼ cup cooked wild rice in each bowl, ladle soup over rice and top with 1 each shiitake and chanterelle.

2 cups dried porcini mushrooms

Cheesecloth (for straining)

2 tablespoons butter

¾ cup chopped onion

1½ teaspoons finely chopped garlic

1 cup chopped fresh chanterelle mushrooms

1½ cups sliced fresh shiitake mushrooms caps

2 tablespoons flour

7 cups chicken stock, heated

¼ cup white wine

2 tablespoons lemon juice

2 tablespoons dry sherry

1 teaspoon fresh thyme leaves

Kosher salt and black pepper to taste

**Garnish:**

4 shiitake mushroom caps, sliced

4 chanterelles, halved

1 teaspoon butter

1½ cups cooked wild rice

# *Honey Soy-glazed Chilean Sea Bass

## WITH GINGER BUTTER SAUCE

Rich, rich, rich! The glaze is dark and sweet and when paired with the rich, buttery taste of Chilean sea bass, you have a wonderfully succulent meal. The Ginger Butter sauce is creamy white and adds another rich flavor dimension. Sea bass is a wonderful fish to cook because its high moisture content ensures that you won't overcook it — my kind of fish!

---

### 4 SERVINGS

4 (6-ounce) Chilean Sea Bass fillets
Honey Soy Glaze
Ginger Butter Sauce

**Honey Soy Glaze (1½ cups):**
1 cup soy sauce
2 tablespoons rice wine vinegar
6 tablespoons honey
¼ cup cold water
¼ cup cornstarch

**Ginger Butter Sauce (1¼ cups):**
½ cup peeled, thinly sliced ginger
4 tablespoons finely chopped shallots
1 cup white wine
½ cup heavy cream
¾ cup (1½ sticks) cold butter, cut into chunks
½ teaspoon kosher salt
¼ teaspoon ground white pepper

**Chilean Sea Bass:**

1. Preheat oven to 350°F. Coat the sea bass lightly with the Honey Soy Glaze.

2. Place in a greased shallow baking dish and bake for 20 minutes or until done.

**Honey Soy Glaze:**

1. Preheat a saucepan over medium-high heat. When very hot, slowly add soy sauce to the pan. (It should really sizzle.)

2. Stir in rice wine vinegar and honey.

3. Stir cold water and cornstarch together, then stir into sauce.

4. Reduce heat to medium-low and stir sauce until thickened, about 1 or 2 minutes. Cool slightly before coating sea bass.

**Ginger Butter Sauce:**

1. Cut the ginger slices into thin strips. Cook the ginger, shallots and white wine in a small saucepan over medium-high heat, reducing by three quarters, about 5 to 10 minutes.

2. Pour in heavy cream and reduce by half, about 5 minutes. Remove mixture from heat. Whisk in butter chunks, a few at a time, until melted. Keep adding butter chunks, stirring until melted, returning to a very low heat if necessary (too much heat and your sauce will separate). Add salt and white pepper and strain through a sieve before serving.

### ❊ *Photograph on page C-12*

# Green Onion Mashed Potatoes

I sat down and ate the whole pot of these mashed potatoes as soon as they were done. I was supposed to save them for the sea bass dish, but how could I resist? The crunch of the green onion is perfect against the soft, moist potato. Roast the garlic in advance to save time.

### 6 SERVINGS

1. Peel and chop potatoes into 2-inch chunks. Boil potatoes in salted water until soft, about 25 to 30 minutes.

2. Heat the butter and cream.

3. Strain hot water from potatoes, stir in roasted garlic and just enough of the warm butter/cream mixture to make the right consistency.

4. Stir in green onions and salt and pepper.

*To roast garlic, see Common Procedures, page 20.

4 large baking potatoes (2½ to 3 pounds)

½ cup (1 stick) butter

2 cups heavy cream

1 head of roasted garlic, peeled*

½ cup thinly sliced green onions

1 teaspoon kosher salt

½ teaspoon ground black pepper

# Apple Berry Cobbler

This is a perfect dessert for a crowd — a hungry crowd. The apples and berries are a great combination though you could use just the apples. I added a frozen mixture of raspberries and blueberries to my apples. This dessert is just as good at room temperature as it is warm, with whipped cream or ice cream (well, almost).

**12 SERVINGS**

5 pounds Golden Delicious apples, peeled, cored and thinly sliced

½ cup berries (optional)

1 cup sugar

¼ cup flour

2 cups flour

1½ cups sugar

1 cup (2 sticks) cold butter, cut into chunks

1. Preheat oven to 350°F. Butter a 9 X 13-inch baking pan. Stir apples, berries, 1 cup sugar and ¼ cup flour in a large mixing bowl. Spread into buttered pan.

2. Stir together the 2 cups flour and the 1½ cups sugar. Cut in the cold butter chunks. Work the mixture through your fingers until it resembles coarse meal. (You could use a food processor to do this, pulsing until the mixture looks like coarse meal, but it's really fun to get your hands into your work.)

3. Press flour/butter mixture into apple mixture (your pan will be very full).

4. Bake for 1 hour or until top is golden brown and fruit is bubbling.

Is it Western, Southern, New England-ish or European? The answer is a little bit of each. Originally the home of a Swiss-born farmer, the discovery of a hot mineral spring turned the farmer into entrepreneur and the home into a resort. The Homestead, endowed with 12 consecutive AAA Four-Diamond awards, is also a top-rated ski lodge.

While cross-country skiing and snowshoeing are offered on property, the Homestead is only 25 minutes away from famed downhill skiing at Park City and Deer Valley. The Homestead also offers romantic horse-drawn sleigh rides for couples, finishing with a classic Chateaubriand dinner in the fine dining restaurant or group sleigh rides finishing with perhaps a slow-roasted prime rib served in the more casual grill room.

The resort is a distinct collection of buildings, including the original farmer's home, a New England-styled Victorian bed and breakfast called The Virginia House. Guestrooms, cottages and condominiums round out the room choices, all with private entrances. Country inn ambiance abounds throughout the property, extending to the Homestead's two restaurants.

Simon's Restaurant (named after the farmer), serves haute cuisine in a romantic, elegant setting. Fanny's Grill (named after the farmer's wife), offers a slightly more casual scene, serving breakfast, lunch and dinner. Start your day with a plate of Strawberry Pancakes or the Hot Pot, a hearty corned beef hash drizzled with hollandaise sauce. After a bit of skiing to work off the scrumptious breakfast, relax with a spa treatment, soaking in pure, warm mineral spring water and anticipate the evening meal at Simon's. Envision a plate with a Sautéed Crab Cake with Grilled Avocado and Tobiko Caviar on a Pesto of Watercress followed by Steamed Lobster smothered in a Grapefruit Butter Sauce with Spiced Orzo. Is your mouth watering yet? Just wait until you sample the recipes the Homestead has generously shared. Dreams will become reality.

## HOMESTEAD

### The Homestead Resort

P.O. Box 99
Midway, UT 84049
**800.327.7220**
**435.654.1102**
**www.homesteadresort.com**

**Season:**
Year-round

**Guest Capacity:**
625

**Accommodations:**
150 rooms/suites

**Activities:**
Cross-country skiing; snowshoeing; snowmobiling; sleigh rides; nearby downhill skiing; natural mineral springs/spa

**Peak Winter Rates:**
$-$$$$

**Closest Ski Resort:**
Park City; Deer Valley

## Breakfast Menu

FRESH-SQUEEZED JUICE

BOWL OF BERRIES

✳ CRANBERRY SCONES

FRESH SCRAMBLED EGGS WITH SAGE SAUSAGE

## Dinner Menu

✳ OVEN-ROASTED TOMATO AND AVOCADO SOUP

✳ WILD MUSHROOM AND CORN PANCAKES
WITH ASIAGO CHEESE

✳ PECAN-CRUSTED PORK TENDERLOIN
WITH MAPLE BARBECUE SAUCE

✳ CORN BREAD PUDDING

✳ CARAMEL PECAN CHEESECAKE

✳ RECIPE INCLUDED

# *Cranberry Scones*

These cream-based scones are rustic and delicious. Exploding with dried cranberries, the top and bottom are crunchy while the middle remains moist and tender. The Homestead rolls this dough out and cuts it with cookie cutters for individual biscuit-like scones. I prefer leaving the dough whole and scoring it into wedges. Either way, it's important to line your pan with parchment paper so that the scones don't brown too much on the bottom before the top is done.

**8 GENEROUS SCONES**

1. Preheat oven to 400°F and line a baking sheet with parchment paper.

2. Stir together the flour, sugar (less the 2 tablespoons reserved for the top), baking powder, salt and cranberries.

3. Make a well in the center and pour all but the 3 reserved tablespoons of cream in the center and stir just to moisten.

4. Gather the dough up and place it on a lightly floured surface. Pat into a circle about 7 inches in diameter and about 1 inch high. With a long knife, cut the dough into 8 equal wedges, but don't separate the wedges.

5. Brush the tops with the reserved 3 tablespoons of cream and sprinkle with the 2 remaining tablespoons of sugar. Carefully lift the circle and place on the parchment-lined baking sheet. I used two large spatulas to lift the dough.

6. Bake for 20 to 25 minutes, or until a toothpick inserted in the center comes out with just a few moist crumbs attached. The top and sides will be lightly golden.

2¾ cups flour

½ cup sugar
(reserve 2 tablespoons)

1½ tablespoons baking powder

½ teaspoon kosher salt

½ cup dried cranberries or other dried fruit

1¾ cups heavy cream
(reserve 3 tablespoons)

# *Oven-roasted Tomato and Avocado Soup

D ivine! My neighbor, Marilyn Robertson, thinks this soup is better cold, like a gazpacho. Truth is, I ate my portion all at once, hot, and thought I was in heaven. I trust Marilyn's judgment, so next time I make this I'll set some aside to try cold before I devour the whole thing. It takes 2 hours to oven-roast the tomatoes and about 20 minutes to make the soup. The Homestead purées the avocado to serve on top, but I just cut mine into chunks, which immediately sunk to the bottom. Oh well, either way, after one taste, you'll never eat tomato soup out of the can again.

### 4 TO 6 SERVINGS

20 Roma tomatoes, cored, halved and scored*

4 tablespoons vegetable oil

2 tablespoons chopped fresh basil leaves

2 tablespoons chopped fresh tarragon leaves

2 tablespoons chopped fresh parsley

3 cups chicken stock

1 teaspoon ground coriander

1 teaspoon ground cumin

Kosher salt and ground black pepper

2 tablespoons chopped fresh cilantro (garnish)

### Avocado Purée:

2 avocados

2 teaspoons lime juice

4 tablespoons half-and-half

Kosher salt

Ground black pepper

1. Preheat oven to 250°F. Rub tomatoes with the oil and sprinkle with basil, tarragon and parsley. Roast in the oven for 2 hours. Remove the tomatoes from the oven and purée in a food processor then strain through a large holed sieve. (Alternatively you can run through a food mill.)

2. Place the purée in a soup pan, add the chicken stock and bring to a boil. Reduce heat and simmer 10 minutes, occasionally skimming the foam that surfaces. Season with the coriander, cumin and salt and pepper.

### Avocado Purée:

1. Peel and chop the avocado. Beat with lime juice, half-and-half and salt and pepper until smooth.

2. To serve, ladle 6 to 8 ounces in a bowl, top with ½ teaspoon chopped cilantro and a dollop of Avocado Purée (or avocado chunks). Alternatively, you may put the purée in a squirt bottle and decorate the top with a swirl.

---

*Lay the cut tomatoes cut side down on a large, greased sheet pan. Cut an "X" on the skin side to score them.

❋ *Photograph on page C-13*

# Wild Mushroom and Corn Pancakes

WITH ASIAGO CHEESE

This is an elegant appetizer or a really nice brunch entrée. You can make the pancakes the day before and store them in the refrigerator to finish later. I used a wild mushroom mixture of a chopped portabella cap, oyster and shiitake mushrooms. I had so much fun making them, and flipping them in the pan. I only left one on my ceiling (kidding).

---

**10 PANCAKES**

1. Gradually whisk milk into flour in a medium bowl. Whisk in eggs, egg yolks, sugar and then melted butter. Strain through a sieve, pressing with a spatula. Cover the batter and let it rest 30 minutes.

2. Heat a 10-inch nonstick skillet over medium-high heat. Add the cold butter and when melted, stir in the mushrooms and garlic and cook until softened, about 5 minutes. Stir in the corn and remove from heat, but keep warm.

3. Heat an 8-inch nonstick skillet over medium heat. When hot, remove from heat and spray with a nonstick spray and return pan to heat. Slowly ladle a scant ¼ cup pancake batter into the pan and sprinkle about 3 tablespoons of the mushroom/corn mixture all over the top. Cook the pancake until the bottom is golden brown, about 1½ minutes. Turn (or flip!) the pancake over and cook for another minute. Remove pancake and cool slightly.

4. Repeat until all the batter is used, and store the pancakes stacked with parchment or wax paper in between. You can do this much the day before. Cover in an airtight container and keep in the refrigerator.

5. When ready to serve, bring pancakes to room temperature (about 15 to 20 minutes). Meanwhile, preheat the broiler. Heat an 8-inch nonstick skillet over medium-high heat. Add a scant tablespoon of cream and swirl the pan. Cook for 30 seconds or until the cream reduces slightly, then add a pancake, cooking only 1 minute or less to heat through. Flip over and heat the other side for another minute.

6. Top with 2 tablespoons of grated Asiago cheese and place on a sheet pan while you repeat the process a few more times to fill up the sheet pan (I was able to fit 6 pancakes on my standard cookie sheet). Place the sheet pan with the pancakes under the broiler until the cheese melts (about 2 minutes or so). Transfer pancakes to serving plates and sprinkle with chopped tomato and basil.

1 cup milk
¾ cup flour
2 eggs
2 egg yolks
2 tablespoons sugar
2 tablespoons butter, melted
4 tablespoons cold butter
3 cups chopped wild mushrooms
1 teaspoon finely chopped garlic
1½ cups corn kernels, fresh or frozen
8 tablespoons heavy cream
1 cup grated Asiago (or Parmesan) cheese

**Garnish:**
1 cup chopped seeded tomato
2 tablespoons chopped fresh basil

# *Pecan-crusted Pork Tenderloin*
## WITH MAPLE BARBECUE SAUCE

'm reminded of my southern roots with this dish. We used to roll everything in pecans. Interestingly, you first cook the tenderloin, then slather on the smoky sweet sauce and finally roll it in the chopped pecans — it's a little messy but I guarantee you'll be licking your fingers.

**6 SERVINGS**

2 pork tenderloins
(about 2 pounds)

Kosher salt and
ground black pepper

1½ cups maple
barbecue sauce, divided

1½ cups finely chopped
toasted pecans*

**Maple Barbecue
Sauce (2½ cups)**

1 cup ketchup

1 small yellow onion,
peeled and quartered

½ cup Worcestershire sauce

½ cup light brown sugar

½ cup white wine vinegar

2 teaspoons dry mustard

¾ teaspoon Tabasco

2 tablespoons maple syrup

**Pork Tenderloin:**

1. Preheat the grill to medium-high heat (375° to 400°F). Season the tenderloins with salt and pepper and brush with ½ cup of barbecue sauce. (The Homestead directions say to grill the tenderloin for a few minutes to get grill marks and then finish in a 375°F oven for about 12 to 15 minutes, but I just grilled the tenderloins until they were done, about 25 minutes for medium, turning occasionally.)

2. When cooked, roll the tenderloins in the remaining 1 cup of barbecue sauce and then roll in the chopped pecans. Slice into medallions before serving.

**Maple Barbecue Sauce:**

1. Put all ingredients (ketchup through syrup) in a food processor and process until mostly smooth. Cover and refrigerate until needed. You can make this up to 3 days before.

*To toast pecans, see Common Procedures, page 20.

# Corn Bread Pudding

The Homestead serves this with the Pecan-crusted Pork Tenderloin. Sweet enough to eat as a dessert, it's the perfect side dish for the southern-influenced entrée. I used a country white bread for the cubes, and lightly toasted them in a 300°F oven for 10 minutes before I made the dish.

**6 SERVINGS**

1. Preheat oven to 400°F. Grease an 8 X 8-inch glass baking pan. Layer dry bread cubes in the bottom.

2. Bring the milk and butter just a boil. Pour the hot milk mixture over the bread cubes and let soak for 5 minutes.

3. Meanwhile, stir the corn, eggs, sugar, salt, dry sherry, vanilla and spices together. Pour the corn mixture over bread/milk mixture.

4. Set the dish in a large roasting pan and put in the oven. Add enough hot water to the roasting pan to come half way up the sides of the 8 X 8-inch pan.

5. Bake until a knife inserted in the center comes out clean, about 60 to 75 minutes.

5 cups dry bread cubes (1-inch)

3½ cups milk

¼ cup (½ stick) butter

2 cups corn kernels, fresh or frozen

2 eggs, lightly beaten

⅓ cup sugar

¼ teaspoon kosher salt

1 tablespoon dry sherry

¼ teaspoon vanilla extract

⅛ teaspoon cinnamon

Pinch ground nutmeg

# Caramel Pecan Cheesecake

How do you define ecstasy? For me it's this Caramel Pecan Cheesecake. I prefer light creamy cheesecakes over the thick, dense cheesecakes. Even our friend Walter, a confirmed New York-style cheesecake lover from way back enjoyed this fluffy version. And the crust? It's just like a candy bar, with pecans and gooey caramel. I made my own caramel sauce (see page 157, and chill before using) but you can use a store-bought version, too. All of my tasters gave this the best dessert award. Have all the ingredients at room temperature before you start and make the cheesecake the day before so it has enough time to properly chill and set.

---

**12 SERVINGS**

**Crust:**
2 cups chopped pecans, crushed
½ cup sugar
½ cup (1 stick) melted butter
½ cup caramel sauce

**Filling:**
3 pounds cream cheese, softened
1 cup sugar
4 eggs
1 teaspoon vanilla

1. Preheat the oven to 350°F. Place a roasting pan on the lowest rack of the oven, and then pour very hot water into the pan. Set the next rack just above the water bath.

2. The easiest way to crush the pecans is to pulse them for a minute or two in a food processor. To finish the crust, stir the crushed pecans, sugar and melted butter together until moistened. It will look a little wet. Press this mixture into the bottom of a 10-inch springform pan. (I wrap the bottom of my springform pan in heavy-duty foil in case it leaks during cooking, which it usually does). Pour ½ cup cooled caramel over pecan mixture and spread evenly with a spatula. Set aside.

3. Beat the cream cheese in a mixer for 2 to 3 minutes, until light and fluffy, stopping occasionally to scrape the sides and bottom. Add the cup of sugar and beat for 2 to 3 minutes. Beat in the eggs, one at a time, stopping to scrape the sides and bottom after the last egg, then add the vanilla and beat 1 more minute. (All this beating helps make it fluffy.)

4. Pour the filling over the crust and bake on a sheet pan in the oven for 60 to 75 minutes, or until the top is dark golden brown and a toothpick inserted in the center comes out mostly clean (just not wet). The cake will rise about ½ inch above the top of the pan during cooking, but will settle during cooling. Remove from the oven and cool on a wire rack for 2 hours. Refrigerate, covered, overnight. Remove the outer form and cut the cake with a serrated knife, cleaning the knife in between each cut. Serve with left over caramel sauce.

**STEIN ERIKSEN LODGE**

*He* is an Olympic Gold Medalist and the famed Director of Skiing at Deer Valley Ski Resort. And he has a lodge named after him. He is Stein Eriksen, and it is not just any lodge. A world-class Norwegian style luxury hotel, Stein Eriksen Lodge is the recipient of numerous awards, including the Mobil Four-Star, AAA's Four-Diamond, and a host of others too copious to name in this tiny space.

Located mid-mountain just above Silver Lake Village with ski-in/ski-out privileges, the lodge exudes old-world charm with the charisma of the American West. A recent expansion and renovation brought even more notoriety to the lodge, as if it were needed. Its reputation precedes itself among the upper tier of skiers and discerning winter travelers. In preparing for this book, I was asked time after time, "Oh, you are including Stein Eriksen, aren't you?" Of course, how could I not?

The rooms are a mixture of condominium suites, deluxe and luxury rooms. Many have fireplaces and all are decorated with imported European fabrics and heavy brushed pine from Spain. Add Italian hand painted chandeliers and handcrafted Portuguese tiles, and suddenly the lodge becomes an old-world refuge nestled in the Wasatch Mountains just 45 minutes from Salt Lake City.

Easy access to the lodge from the slopes means you can return to the lodge for lunch, or stay out on the slopes longer and not miss an early apres-ski cocktail. Open only during the ski season, the Valhalla Restaurant features wild game and succulent seafood served in a romantic alpine setting. Open all year, the Glitretind offers breakfast, lunch and dinner, and in winter, a fabulous skier's gourmet luncheon buffet. For the true foodie, the lodge offers monthly cooking classes such as a wild game grilling class or one that explores the foods of Italy. Until you make the trip to Stein Eriksen yourself, enjoy these delicious dishes shared by the chef from Glitretind.

## Stein Eriksen Lodge

P.O. Box 3177
Park City, UT 84060
**800.453.1302**
**435.649.3700**
**www.steinlodge.com**

**Season:**
Year-round;
peak winter: mid-December
through early April

**Guest Capacity:**
125

**Accommodations:**
170 rooms and suites

**Activities:**
Downhill skiing, cross-country
and back country skiing;
snowmobiling; nearby winter
sports park

**Peak Winter Rates:**
$$-$$$$

**Closest Ski Resort:**
Deer Valley

## Breakfast Menu

❉ GRAVLAX CURED SALMON
WITH BAGEL CHIPS

❉ GRAND MARNIER FRENCH TOAST
WITH ORANGE CINNAMON BUTTER

❉ BANANA WALNUT MUFFINS

## Dinner Menu

MARINATED SHRIMP
WITH SOUTHWESTERN POSOLE AND TOMATILLO SALSA

❉ HERB-CRUSTED ELK LOIN
WITH A PORT WINE SAUCE

❉ GREEN ONION SPAETZLE

❉ CHOCOLATE VOLCANO
WITH RASPBERRY COULIS

❉ RECIPE INCLUDED

# Gravlax Cured Salmon

## WITH BAGEL CHIPS

S tein Eriksen serves this at breakfast, seriously. I think it works anytime of day, and I first served it as an appetizer while my neighbors uncorked a bottle of Chardonnay. Originating in Sweden, this paper-thin, sugar-salt cured salmon is so simple to prepare you won't believe it. The vodka curing removes the fishy taste from this strong-tasting fish. You can find the juniper berries in the spice section of your larger grocery stores, or order it from A.J.'s, (see Sources, page 192). The salmon only takes a few minutes to prepare, but it takes 2 days to cure, and it's worth it. Try it, you'll love it.

---

**6 SERVINGS**

1. Stir the brown sugar, salt, juniper berries, vodka and chopped dill together until the sugar dissolves. (The kosher salt will not dissolve.) Pour mixture into a container that will hold the salmon fillet. Place the salmon fillet, skin side up in the mixture.

2. Cover tightly and place in the refrigerator. Cure for 48 hours total, turning the fillet over about every 12 hours.

3. After 2 days, rinse the stiff salmon quickly under cold running water. Pat dry and on a 45° angle, slice as thin as possible.

4. Toast the bagel halves and cut into bite-size pieces. Arrange the salmon and bagels on a platter with small bowls of the onions, capers and cream cheese. Garnish with dill sprigs.

1 cup light brown sugar

1 cup kosher salt

8 juniper berries (crushed)

1 cup vodka

1 bunch chopped dill leaves

1 (12-ounce) salmon fillet, with skin on

**Garnish:**

2 plain bagels, split

½ small red onion, thinly sliced

3 tablespoons capers

6 ounces cream cheese, softened

Dill sprigs

# *Grand Marnier French Toast*

### WITH ORANGE CINNAMON BUTTER

I can't think of a better way to get vitamin C. (Okay, I'm not claiming nutritional benefits here, I'm writing a book!) I love French toast and this is absolutely divine and should be lavished on someone special. I also tested this with a multi-grain bread and loved the result. You can make the butter up to a week in advance. You'll find lots of uses for this butter if you don't use it all on the French toast, like spreading on bagels, muffins or just plain toast. Let the butter soften before you serve it.

**6 SERVINGS**

6 eggs

2 cups half-and-half

¼ cup orange juice

¼ cup Grand Marnier
(or orange-flavored liqueur)

1 tablespoon cinnamon

12 (1-inch thick) slices
of French bread

Fresh mixed berries
for garnish (optional)

**Orange Cinnamon
Butter (⅔ cup):**

2 tablespoons orange juice

1 tablespoon Grand Marnier

½ cup (1 stick)
butter, softened

1 teaspoon orange zest

¾ teaspoon cinnamon

1. To prepare the Orange Cinnamon Butter: heat the orange juice and Grand Marnier in a small saucepan over medium-high heat. Reduce by half, about 5 minutes, and cool. Beat the softened butter with the reduced orange juice mixture, orange zest and cinnamon until light and fluffy. Place in a serving container and chill until needed, but leave out at room temperature at least 30 minutes before serving.

2. To prepare the French toast: beat the eggs, half-and-half, orange juice, Grand Marnier and 1 tablespoon of cinnamon. Dip the bread in the egg mixture and place in a shallow pan to soak for a few minutes.

3. Meanwhile, heat a large nonstick skillet or griddle over medium-low heat. Spray with nonstick spray and cook toast until golden brown on each side, about 3 to 4 minutes on the first side, and 2 to 3 minutes on the other side. Don't cook too fast or the outside will brown before the inside is done. Serve toast on a warm plate with mixed berries (optional) and a dollop of the Orange Cinnamon Butter.

# Banana Walnut Muffins

Sign me up! These moist, dense banana muffins are best just out of the oven, but I also enjoyed them the next morning, reheated for just a few minutes in the toaster oven. Yummy! If you don't have walnuts, just substitute pecans.

### 16 MUFFINS

1. Preheat oven to 350°F. Grease a muffin pan and set aside.
2. Beat bananas, eggs, oil, vanilla and chopped walnuts together.
3. Stir the flour, sugar, baking soda, salt and mace (or ground nutmeg) together in a large mixing bowl.
4. Pour the banana mixture over the flour mixture and stir just to moisten.
5. Fill greased muffin pans ¾ full and bake for 20 to 25 minutes or until a toothpick inserted in the center comes out clean or with just a few moist crumbs attached.

2 cups mashed ripe bananas (3 to 4 medium-size)

3 eggs

1 cup vegetable oil

1 teaspoon vanilla

¼ cup chopped walnuts

2 cups flour

1 cup sugar

1 teaspoon baking soda

¼ teaspoon kosher salt

⅛ teaspoon ground mace (or nutmeg)

# Herb-crusted Elk Loin

## WITH A PORT WINE SAUCE

Elk meat is very similar to deer meat in taste and texture. It also shares the same lean-meat qualities. It's no wonder, really. Elk and deer meat are both classified as venison, coming from the same "deer" family. Game meat is best served medium-rare. Overcooking the elk will result in a dry, gamy taste. If your loin has thin ends and a thick middle, cut off the ends and cook separately to avoid overcooking. If you can't locate elk loin, try beef tenderloin. The Port Wine Sauce is sweet and rich, tinted with a touch of pineapple juice. The wine sauce can be made ahead and reheated.

### 8 SERVINGS

2½ pounds elk loin
1 tablespoon finely chopped fresh rosemary
1 tablespoon finely chopped fresh oregano
1 tablespoon finely chopped fresh thyme
1 tablespoon finely chopped fresh sage
2 teaspoons finely chopped garlic
¼ cup plus 1 teaspoon olive oil
1 teaspoon kosher salt
½ teaspoon ground black pepper

**Port Wine Sauce (1¼ cups):**
2 cups cabernet sauvignon wine
1 bottle ruby port wine (750ml)
¾ cup sugar
½ cup Demi-glace*
1½ cups pineapple juice

**Elk Loin:**

1. Preheat the oven to 350°F. Mix the herbs (rosemary through sage) with the garlic, ¼ cup olive oil and salt and pepper and set aside.

2. In an ovenproof skillet over medium-high heat, add 1 teaspoon of olive oil. When pan is very hot, add the elk loin and sear on all sides until brown, about 6 minutes total.

3. Remove from pan and carefully roll the loin in the herb mixture. Place the loin back in the pan and put in the preheated oven and cook until medium-rare (130°F), about 13 to 15 minutes.

4. Remove from oven and let rest, covered with foil for about 5 minutes before slicing. This allows the juices to re-distribute throughout the meat, and the temperature will rise to 135°F.

**Port Wine Sauce:**

1. Pour all ingredients in a 2½ or 3-quart saucepan and stir.

2. Vigorously simmer over medium-high heat until the mixture reduces to about 1¼ cups and is thick and syrupy, about 40 minutes.

*See Demi-glace under Common Procedures, page 19.

# *Green Onion Spaetzle*

I
f you like to really get your hands in your food while cooking then this is the dish for you. Spaetzle is a German side dish of dumplings. Believe it or not, there is a kitchen tool specifically for making spaetzle, but I used my hand-held grater, forcing the dough through the largest holes. The dish is prepared in two stages, first boiling the dough, which can be done a day in advance, and then pan-frying to brown. If you are bored with potatoes, this is a delicious alternative.

### 8 SERVINGS

**First stage:**

1. Stir the flour, baking powder, salt, white pepper, nutmeg and green onions together.

2. Beat the eggs with the milk or water in a separate bowl. Pour the egg mixture over the flour mixture, stirring thoroughly. The dough should be very sticky. If not, add more liquid.

3. Bring a large pot of salted water to a boil. Prepare a large bowl of ice water. Using a grater or colander with big holes, scoop up a handful of dough and over the boiling water force the dough through the holes. The dough will drop into the water in little short tube shapes. When the dough floats to the surface, about 1 minute, the spaetzle is cooked.

4. Remove with a slotted spoon to an ice water to stop the cooking. Repeat the process until all the dough is cooked. Drain the spaetzle from the ice water, pat dry and store in an airtight container in the refrigerator or proceed to the second cooking stage.

**Second stage:**

1. Melt the butter in a large nonstick skillet over medium-high heat, then add the oil.

2. Working in batches, add the spaetzle when the pan is hot, cooking and stirring until they turn golden brown, about 6 to 10 minutes. Season with salt and pepper if desired.

**First stage:**

3 cups flour

½ teaspoon baking powder

1 teaspoon kosher salt

½ teaspoon ground white pepper

⅛ teaspoon ground nutmeg

1 bunch green onions, finely chopped

3 eggs, lightly beaten

⅔ cup milk or water

**Second stage:**

1 tablespoon butter

1 tablespoon vegetable oil

Boiled spaetzle

Kosher salt

Ground black pepper

# *Chocolate Volcano

## WITH RASPBERRY COULIS

To me, there is nothing more sensual than a warm chocolate cake, oozing with dark, gooey chocolate. Kindred chocolate lovers know exactly what I'm talking about. Coulis is a French term for a thick purée or sauce. The lodge serves this with an optional scoop of vanilla ice cream, but do you really want to dilute the dark, rich chocolate flavor? Me neither.

### 5 SERVINGS

14 tablespoons butter
(1 stick plus 6 tablespoons)
1 cup semi-sweet
chocolate morsels
4 eggs
4 egg yolks
1½ cups powdered
sugar, sifted
¾ cup flour
1 tablespoon of butter
5 (8-ounce) ramekins

**Garnish (optional):**
Fresh raspberries
Mint sprigs
Vanilla ice cream

**Raspberry Coulis (2 cups):**
1 (12-ounce) package
frozen raspberries, thawed
2 tablespoons sugar
½ cup orange juice

1. Preheat oven to 450°F. Butter 5 (8-ounce) ramekins. Set aside.

2. Melt the 14 tablespoons of butter and chocolate in a double boiler over simmering water. Stir until melted, remove from heat and cool slightly.

3. Beat eggs and egg yolks in a large mixing bowl until thick and lemon-colored (I used an electric mixer but you may do this by hand). Add powdered sugar to eggs and beat. Add flour and beat again until smooth. Beat in chocolate mixture. Divide mixture evenly among the 5 buttered ramekins.

4. Bake for 10 to 12 minutes or until the tops just start to crack (too much cracking is a sign of overcooking). It should be slightly undercooked in the middle. Let stand for exactly 8 minutes. Turn upside down on a serving plate and remove mold. Serve immediately with Raspberry Coulis. Garnish with fresh raspberries and, if you wish, a scoop of vanilla ice cream (optional).

**Raspberry Coulis:**

1. Place thawed raspberries, sugar and orange juice in a blender and blend until mixture is puréed.

2. Remove and strain through a sieve to remove seeds. I put it in a squeeze bottle to squirt designs on the plate. Store in the refrigerator for up to 1 week.

### * Photograph on page C-14

The craggy cliffs atop Mount Timpanogos glisten pink, reflecting the spectacular sunset, while the silvery snow glitters just below. Breathtakingly beautiful is the only way to describe Robert Redford's Sundance. "One of the best lesser-known ski resorts" (read: less crowded) is how the editors of *Ski* magazine describe this little slice of heaven, just an hour to the south of Salt Lake City. Skiers who travel to partake in Sundance's grandeur seem just as eco-minded as its famous founder. There is an unmistakable balance between nature and humans within the confines of this 6,000-acre wilderness, thanks to Redford's vision and the thoughtful caretakers of this precious habitat.

Lodging at the base of the mountain are The Pine and River Run cottages, tucked between the white barked Aspens and old-growth pines and encircled by a crystal-clear stream. Inside, the homey rooms are dressed in Native American fabrics and patterns, with warm wood furniture, and most with rock fireplaces waiting to crackle and pop and heat your soul. The cottages are steps away from the Sundance Village, with access to the ski lifts, the old-fashioned Sundance General Store (the inspiration for the Sundance catalog), and the Art Shack Studios, with daily art and craft workshops.

Dining options are as bountiful as the pristine woods surrounding the resort. Skiers will want to stop in the mountaintop Bearclaw's Cabin for a cup of hot soup and a warm chocolate chip cookie. Back at the base, the Foundry Grill offers breakfast, lunch and dinner in a casual atmosphere and serves hearty New West cuisine, like Smoked Trout Hash for breakfast and Oven-roasted Salmon for dinner. The recipes presented here are from the Foundry Grill, and offer you a taste of the robust cuisine of this rustic resort. For a more intimate, candlelit dinner, dine in the enchanting Tree Room, cloaked in authentic Native American art and artifacts from Redford's personal collection and featuring seasonal mountain cuisine. But don't be disappointed if you don't see Mr. Redford. Maybe he didn't know you were coming.

# sundance

## Sundance

RR 3 Box A-1
Sundance, UT 84604
**800.982.1600**
**801.225.4107**
**www.sundance-utah.com**

**Season:**
Year-round; peak winter:
December through early April

**Guest Capacity:**
250

**Accommodations:**
95 rooms and
12 mountain homes

**Activities:**
Downhill and cross-country skiing; snowshoeing; Artisan Center with classes and exhibits; state-of-the-art screening room with library of films

**Peak Winter Rates:**
$$-$$$$

**Closest Ski Resort:**
Sundance

## *Breakfast Menu*

SELECTION OF FRESH JUICES

❄ **SUNDANCE NUTTY GRANOLA**

❄ **BROWN SUGAR OATMEAL**

❄ **JOE'S SPECIAL**
ON HOMEMADE CHEESE BISCUITS

## *Dinner Menu*

CAULIFLOWER SOUP WITH TOASTED ALMONDS

❄ **SPICY MEATLOAF**
WITH CARAMELIZED ONIONS

ROASTED GARLIC MASHED POTATOES

❄ **WARM CHOCOLATE CAKE**

❄ **RECIPE INCLUDED**

# Sundance Nutty Granola

M olasses gives this cereal a dark color and a deep, sweet flavor. I like the combination of almond chunks and pecans, but you could add or substitute just about any nut you like. You also have freedom in the dried fruit selection. I used equal parts of dried cherries, cranberries and golden raisins.

### 18 CUPS

1. Preheat the oven to 350°F. Spread the oven racks to accommodate 2 large sheet pans, avoiding the very top and very bottom of the oven. If you have a tiny oven, like I do, cook the sheet pans one at a time. It takes a little longer, but the granola cooks more evenly. Spray 2 large sheet pans with nonstick spray and set aside.

2. Stir the first 7 ingredients, (almonds through cinnamon) together in a very large bowl or a big stockpot.

3. Heat the honey, maple syrup, molasses and oil in a saucepan until warm. Pour the honey mixture over the almond mixture and stir well.

4. Divide the mixture evenly between the 2 sheet pans (use more and cook in batches if necessary) and bake for 30 to 40 minutes, stirring every 15 minutes and rotating the pans between the 2 racks for even baking. Remove from oven when golden brown and stir in dried fruit. Stir occasionally while cooling to break up clumps. Store in airtight container for up to 8 weeks, or freeze up to 6 months.

2 cups chopped almonds
2 cups chopped pecans
1 cup sunflower seeds
1 cup sesame seeds
1 cup wheat germ
5 cups old-fashioned oats
1½ tablespoons ground cinnamon
½ cup honey
½ cup maple syrup
¾ cup molasses
¾ cup vegetable oil
3 cups chopped dried fruit

# Brown Sugar Oatmeal

Mmmmm. Filled with crunchy toasted walnuts, plump, juicy raisins and sweetened with brown sugar, this oatmeal is far superior to anything that comes out of a box. Perfect for a cold morning, this breakfast starter is rich, delicious, thick and creamy.

**4 SERVINGS**

2 cups old-fashioned oats
½ teaspoon kosher salt
2 cups water
1½ cups heavy cream
¼ cup light brown sugar
¼ cup assorted dried fruits (raisins, currants, apricots, etc.)
¼ cup toasted chopped walnuts*

1. Stir the oats, salt and water together in a saucepan over medium-high heat. Bring to a boil then reduce heat and simmer until oats are tender, about 3 to 4 minutes.

2. Stir in the cream and simmer until the mixture is thick and creamy, about 5 to 6 minutes.

3. Stir in the brown sugar and dried fruits and heat through. Ladle into bowls and top with toasted walnuts.

*To toast walnuts, see Common Procedures, page 20.

# Homemade Cheese Biscuits

*T*wo keys to making flavorful tender biscuits, in my opinion, are 1) using a blend of butter and shortening (the butter adds the flavor but the shortening helps make the biscuit tender) and 2) barely mixing the dough. To help biscuits rise, after cutting the biscuit, I flip it over before placing on the baking sheet so that the cut bottom is now on top for baking.

**8 BISCUITS**

1. Preheat the oven to 425°F. Stir together the flour, sugar, baking powder, baking soda and salt. Cut in the cold butter and shortening with a pastry blender or by hand.
2. Stir in buttermilk and cheese, just until moistened. Do not overmix. The less you mix the dough, the more tender the biscuits. The dough will be a little sticky.
3. Turn dough out onto a lightly floured work surface and flour your hands. Lightly pat the dough to about 1-inch thickness. Cut 8 circles with a 3-inch biscuit or cookie cutter. Turn biscuit upside down and place on a greased sheet pan.
4. Beat the egg with the milk or cream, and brush the tops with this egg wash. Bake for 10 to 12 minutes, until golden brown.

2½ cups flour
1 teaspoon sugar
1 teaspoon baking powder
¾ teaspoon baking soda
½ teaspoon salt
¼ cup (½ stick) cold butter, cut into chunks
¼ cup (4 tablespoons) vegetable shortening
1 cup buttermilk
1 cup grated cheddar cheese
1 egg, lightly beaten
2 tablespoons milk or cream

# *Joe's Special

When I told my neighbor Alex that I was testing a recipe called Joe's Special, his eyes lit up and his mouth started watering. I was intrigued by his response. I had never heard of the dish, but then again, I, unlike Alex, never lived in San Francisco, home to this marvelous breakfast feast. Alex loves this dish, even if it is a "gourmet" adaptation of the real thing. That, my friend, is a real compliment.

---

**4 SERVINGS**

1 tablespoon vegetable oil

1 cup sliced red onion

1 cup sliced fresh mushrooms

2 cups shredded fresh spinach

1 cup cooked chopped Italian sausage

6 eggs, beaten

1 cup shredded pepper Jack cheese

Kosher salt and pepper to taste

4 cheese biscuits, cut in half

1. Heat oil in a large skillet over medium heat. Stir in red onion and cook 3 to 4 minutes.

2. Stir in mushrooms, spinach and cooked sausage, stirring and cooking for 2 more minutes.

3. Stir in beaten eggs and cook, pushing the eggs to the center of the pan with a heat-resistant spatula for about a minute.

4. Stir in cheese and cook until eggs are done, but not dry. Salt and pepper to taste. Spoon egg mixture over warm open-faced biscuits and serve.

* *Photograph on page C-15*

# Spicy Meatloaf

## WITH CARAMELIZED ONIONS

Comfort food, like meatloaf, will always be in style. Sundance adds its own twist to Mom's classic, with a smoky chipotle pepper, sweet caramelized onions and homemade ketchup. The chipotle (a dried, smoked jalapeno) is noticeable, but not too hot, so you can kick it up a notch by doubling the amount listed in the ingredients. Remember to include time to slowly caramelize the onions, about 50 to 60 minutes. You may even do the onions the day before. Try the homemade Hickory Bell Pepper Ketchup recipe from the Equinox on page 154 instead of store-bought ketchup for a fabulous taste sensation.

---

### 4 SERVINGS

1. Caramelize onions in 1 tablespoon of butter over low heat, about 50 to 60 minutes. Set aside to cool and divide in half.

2. Preheat oven to 350°F. Stir together ½ of the caramelized onions and the rest of the ingredients (red bell pepper through salt and pepper), except the ¼ cup of ketchup and form into a loaf. Place in a standard loaf pan and bake for 20 minutes.

3. Top with the ketchup and then the rest of the caramelized onions and bake for another 10 to 15 minutes, or until done.

---

*Chipotles canned in adobo (vinegar and spices) sauce can be found in Mexican markets and some grocery stores. A. J.'s always carries it, so if you can't find it in your area, give them a call and they will ship it to you. See Sources, page 192.

1 tablespoon butter

2 large yellow onions (about 5 cups) sliced

½ cup chopped red bell pepper

½ cup green bell pepper

1 tablespoon chopped canned chipotle (in adobo sauce)*

2 teaspoons finely chopped garlic

1¼ pounds ground beef

2 eggs

½ cup seasoned bread crumbs

Kosher salt and pepper to taste

¼ cup ketchup

# Warm Chocolate Cake

We need to add the words "light and airy" to the title to distinguish this cake from others in this book. Don't get me wrong, it is still very, very chocolaty. Some tasters liked this better; others liked the heavier, richer chocolate cakes. I have a solution — make both and invite me over.

**8** SERVINGS

8 (4-ounce) ramekins
1 tablespoon butter
¼ cup flour
¾ cup (1½ sticks) butter
4½ ounces good quality chocolate, chopped
4 egg yolks
4 egg whites
2 tablespoons sugar
1 tablespoon flour

1. Preheat oven to 325°F. Butter and flour the ramekins with the 1 tablespoon of butter and ¼ cup of flour. Set aside.

2. Melt the ¾ cup butter and chocolate in a double boiler over simmering water.

3. Whisk the yolks and add a small amount of the warm butter/chocolate mixture to the eggs then add the warmed eggs to the butter/chocolate mixture and stir well.

4. Beat the egg whites to the soft peak stage, then sprinkle with the 2 tablespoons of sugar and continue beating until the whites are stiff. Fold the whipped whites into the chocolate mixture. Sprinkle with the 1 tablespoon of flour and gently stir.

5. Fill the prepared ramekins ¾ full. Bake in a preheated oven for 10 to 12 minutes, or until just set.

6. Remove from oven and let stand for 8 minutes before unmolding onto a plate. Serve by itself, or with a scoop of ice cream and/or fudge sauce.

## Vermont

## Cortina Inn and Resort

103 U.S. Route 4
Killington, VT 05751
**800.451.6108**
**802.773.3333**
www.cortinainn.com

**Season:**
Year-round

**Guest Capacity:**
250

**Accommodations:**
96 guestrooms and suites

**Activities:**
Snowshoeing; sleigh rides;
snowmobiling; nearby downhill
and cross-country skiing

**Peak Winter Rates:**
$-$$ (includes hearty country
breakfast buffet with
minimum stay)

**Closest Ski Resort:**
Killington

*C*entral Vermont is absolutely gorgeous anytime of year, but especially through the fall foliage and, of course, the snow-blanketed winter. Located near Killington, the Cortina Inn and Resort is the epitome of country inn charm. Old-fashioned hospitality sets the inn apart from other lodging near the largest Vermont ski area. The two-story brick, wood and stucco inn has charming canopied terraces and the inside lobby is large, bright and filled with cozy sitting areas and local art.

The rooms are spacious and individually decorated, with antiques, country quilts and other knickknacks that give the rooms a comfortable, homey feel. The superior rooms have access to a terrace or balcony, and the deluxe rooms have views of either the mountains or gardens. Many rooms have fireplaces and sitting areas, a place to curl up with a good book. There are wonderful accommodations for large families, including a mountain suite with a loft with four twin beds and a king-size bed on the ground level master bedroom.

The inn boasts two outstanding restaurants, including the award-winning Zola's Grille. On Sunday, Zola's provides an outlandish buffet that grabbed the attention of the *New England Travel Guide,* that labeled it best overwhelmingly massive brunch. Zola's is a blending of New England and Northern Italian with a little French Bistro thrown in. Dishes such as Maryland Crab Soup, Pan-roasted Rainbow Trout and specials like Mako Grilled Shark with Maple Mashed Potatoes will delight ravenous skiers and non-skiers alike. For casual fare, check out Theodore's for cocktails, pizza and burgers, with the occasional Vegetable Quesadilla for variety. The cozy pub is a great place to meet after skiing for food, fun and conversation. The chef at Zola's graciously shared a delicious breakfast entrée as well as an intriguing wild game dinner menu.

## Breakfast Menu

ASSORTMENT OF JUICES

❋ POACHED EGGS OVER BLACK BEAN SALSA
WITH SMOKED MOZZARELLA CREAM

BLUEBERRY BLINTZES
WITH PEACH AND RASPBERRY CHUTNEY

COFFEE CAKE

## Dinner Menu

❋ CRAB CROSTINI OVER FIELD GREENS

WARM SPINACH SALAD
WITH PECANS AND LEMON SHERRY VINAIGRETTE

❋ PAN-SEARED VENISON MEDALLIONS
WITH APPLE BRANDY PEAR SAUCE

❋ WILD MUSHROOM BREAD PUDDING

❋ CAPE COD CRANBERRY PIE


❋ RECIPE INCLUDED

# Poached Eggs over Black Bean Salsa

## WITH SMOKED MOZZARELLA CREAM

The first time I tried this, the salsa was very tangy because of the balsamic vinegar. I then tried it with lime juice in place of the balsamic and I liked it better. You can even use a combination of balsamic and lime juice. Whichever way you decide, you will absolutely love the creamy cheese sauce that accompanies this great little breakfast or brunch dish. And if you can't find smoked Mozzarella, then see Sources, page 192, or just substitute smoked Gouda or even smoked Cheddar.

---

**4 SERVINGS**

8 eggs (2 per person)
Black Bean Salsa
Smoked Mozzarella Cream
2 tablespoons roughly chopped cilantro (garnish)

**Black Bean Salsa (4 cups):**

1 (15 ounce) can black beans, drained
2 teaspoons vegetable oil
1 cup chopped red bell pepper
1 cup chopped green bell pepper
1 cup chopped red onion
1 tablespoon chopped garlic
1 tablespoon roughly chopped cilantro
¼ cup balsamic vinegar or lime juice
Kosher salt
Ground black pepper

**Smoked Mozzarella Cream:**

1 teaspoon vegetable oil
1 tablespoon finely chopped shallot
1/4 cup white wine
2 cups heavy cream
1/2 cup shredded smoked Mozzarella or smoked Gouda
Kosher salt
White pepper

1. Use an egg poacher or bring 2 quarts of cold water to a very slight simmer (180°F) in a saucepan. Add 1 teaspoon of vinegar to the water. Crack open an egg on a saucer and slowly slide the egg into the water. Leave it alone for 1 minute, then gently stir the egg white up over the yolk. Cook until desired doneness, about 3 minutes for a runny yellow center.

2. Remove egg with a slotted spoon and place on a mound of black bean salsa on a warm plate. Top the egg with the Smoked Mozzarella Sauce and garnish with chopped cilantro.

**Black Bean Salsa:**

1. Stir all ingredients (black beans through black pepper) together and let rest 20 minutes to blend flavors.

**Smoked Mozzarella Cream:**

1. Heat oil in a saucepan over medium heat. Stir in shallot and cook 1 minute. Add white wine and cook another minute.

2. Pour in heavy cream and bring to a simmer. Cook until reduced by half, about 20 to 30 minutes.

3. Remove from heat and stir in cheese. Season with salt and white pepper.

# Crab Crostini

*I* have to rank this up there with the Lobster Cakes from Alpenhof. My neighbors Liz and Larry gave it a "10." (Okay, so they've given lots of "10's" in this book, but do you think I would give you less than stellar dishes to prepare?) This is a delicious, elegant appetizer and the better your crabmeat, the better your dish. I bought my cooked crabmeat fresh from my butcher. It really tastes better than canned crabmeat. Pick through the meat to make sure all the shells have been removed.

### 4 SERVINGS

1. Heat olive oil in small saucepan over medium heat. Stir in the shallot and garlic and cook 1 minute.

2. Pour in cream and reduce by half, about 10 minutes. Remove from heat and stir in cream cheese, stirring until cheese is blended.

3. Preheat oven to 400°F. Spread garlic butter on baguette slices and top with 1 tablespoon or so of the cooled cream cheese mixture. Top with 2 tablespoons of crabmeat and sprinkle with chopped tomato and parsley.

4. Place on a sheet pan and bake for 7 to 10 minutes or until cheese is hot and bread is crispy. Watch the bottom of the bread carefully so that it doesn't burn. Serve immediately.

1 teaspoon olive oil

2 teaspoons finely chopped shallot

2 teaspoons finely chopped garlic

½ cup heavy cream

8 ounces cream cheese, softened

4 tablespoons softened butter mixed with 1 teaspoon garlic salt

12 (¾ inch thick) slices of French baguette

1 cup picked, cleaned lump crab meat

½ cup finely chopped tomato

2 tablespoons chopped parsley

# *Pan-seared Venison Medallions*
## WITH APPLE BRANDY PEAR SAUCE

*T*he sauce is dark, sweet and fruity — a perfect accompaniment for the venison. You can use the less expensive loin cut instead of the tenderloin, or you can substitute a beef or pork tenderloin. The Cortina Inn serves this luscious entrée with the equally delicious Wild Mushroom Bread Pudding (see next recipe).

---

4 SERVINGS

1½ pounds venison tenderloin

Apple Brandy Pear Sauce

**Marinade:**

1 cup olive oil

½ cup red wine

1 tablespoon finely chopped garlic

1 tablespoon finely chopped shallot

1 teaspoon dried thyme

1 teaspoon kosher salt

½ teaspoon ground black pepper

**Apple Brandy Pear Sauce (2 cups):**

2 cups apple brandy

1 sprig fresh rosemary

1 sprig fresh thyme

1 tablespoon finely chopped shallot

1 cup peeled, cored and chopped pear

3 cups apple cider or juice

1 cup demi-glace*

1. Whisk together all marinade ingredients (olive oil through black pepper).

2. Cut venison tenderloins into 8 equal steaks. Lay steaks flat in a shallow baking dish and pour marinade over the pieces, turning to coat both sides. Marinate 20 minutes at room temperature, or up to 1 hour in the refrigerator. Meanwhile, make the Apple Brandy Pear Sauce.

3. Preheat the grill to medium-high heat (375° to 400°F). Remove steaks from marinade and place on the grill. Grill 3 to 4 minutes per side for medium rare, longer if steaks are thicker than 1 inch. Let the meat rest 5 minutes before serving.

**Apple Brandy Pear Sauce:**

1. Stir brandy, herbs, shallot and pear in a 2½ or 3-quart saucepan over medium-high heat. Be careful with the brandy, as it is highly flammable.

2. Cook until most of the liquid has evaporated, about 25 minutes. Pour in apple cider and bring to a boil. Reduce by half, about 20 minutes, and add demi-glace. If demi-glace is not available, you can substitute 1 cup of beef stock, thickened with a slurry (1 tablespoon of cornstarch that has been mixed with 1 tablespoon of cold water). Bring the stock to a boil; it must be boiling for the slurry to work.

---

*See Demi-glace under Common Procedures, page 19.

# *Wild Mushroom Bread Pudding

B read puddings aren't limited to the dessert table, as evidenced by this savory, mushroom version. This is a perfect side dish to the wild game recipes that the Cortina Inn serves. If you are using dry, day old bread cubes, you can skip the oven-toasting in the first step.

### 4 SERVINGS

1. Preheat oven to 350°F. Place the bread cubes on an ungreased sheet pan and lightly toast in the oven for about 10 minutes, remove and cool.

3. Butter an 8 X 8-inch glass baking dish and layer bottom with the toasted bread cubes and set aside.

4. Heat olive oil over medium-high heat in a large skillet. Stir in portabella and shiitake mushrooms and cook 3 minutes. Add garlic, thyme and salt and pepper and cook another 3 minutes, or until mushrooms are just tender. Remove from heat and cool slightly, then if there is any residual liquid, drain the mushroom mixture in a colander.

5. Beat eggs and whisk in cream. Stir cooled, drained mushroom mixture with the egg mixture and pour over bread, making sure each cube is soaked. Set aside for 5 minutes.

6. Bake for 20 to 25 minutes, or until mixture is set and the bread cubes are golden brown. Cool for 5 minutes then cut into squares.

*Photograph on page C-17*

2½ cups French bread cubes (1-inch)

1 teaspoon butter, softened

1 tablespoon olive oil

1 cup sliced (¼-inch thick) portabella mushroom cap

1 cup sliced (¼-inch thick) shiitake mushroom caps

1 teaspoon finely chopped garlic

½ teaspoon fresh thyme leaves

½ teaspoon kosher salt

¼ teaspoon ground black pepper

4 eggs

1 cup heavy cream

# Cape Cod Cranberry Pie

This sweet/tart pie is simple to make, especially for those pie crust-challenged people because the crust is really a batter that's just poured on top before it's baked. This pie received a big thumbs-up from one of my teenage testers, Kate Dobrin, who normally doesn't like pie. Go figure.

**6 TO 8 SERVINGS**

2½ cups cranberries
(fresh or frozen and thawed)
½ cup sugar
¾ cup chopped pecans
2 eggs
1 cup sugar
1 cup flour
½ cup butter, melted
¼ cup shortening, melted

1. Preheat oven to 325°F. Grease a 10-inch pie pan. Spread cranberries over the bottom. Top with ½ cup sugar and pecans.

2. Beat eggs and gradually beat in 1 cup of sugar. Stir in flour, butter and shortening and beat until just smooth. Pour batter over cranberries.

3. Bake for 1 hour or more until top is golden brown. Serve cold or warm with vanilla ice cream.

The history of the Equinox, a AAA Four-Diamond resort, is truly fascinating. Once a gathering place for American Revolutionaries, then known as the Marsh Tavern, it was the first British property seized by the revolutionaries to fund their war effort. Founded in 1769, the Equinox has gone through several owners, each leaving a profound mark in the form of expansion. Today, the Equinox sits on 2,300 acres between the Green and Taconic Mountain ranges, in picturesque southern Vermont.

In addition to the spacious rooms and elegant suites, the property offers the Charles Orvis Inn that operates almost like an "inn-within-an-inn." Once owned by the famous fishing Orvis founder, the "cottage" is four levels (including a finished basement) and offers 10,000 square feet of lovely bedrooms, a library, a billiards room, a sitting room and a fly-tying room.

Unique to this resort is the British School of Falconry, a program designed to teach the ancient art of hunting with hawks, that are so amicable to humans. It's hard to describe the feeling of the first landing of one of these predators on your gloved hand. It's awesome and breathtaking. Not that you need anything more thrilling, but the resort is also home to the Land Rover Driving School, which offers excitement of its own through off-road obstacle courses.

Don't forget about the skiing, though. The resort has on-premise cross-country skiing, snowshoeing and snowmobiling. Nearby Stratton Mountain provides the downhill skiing. After any of these activities, indulge in a spa treatment or take a fitness class at the resort. Or perhaps relaxing in your room or suite is what you need to energize yourself for the coming feast in the fine dining Colonnade, an elegant room where classical dishes are prepared with New England flavor. The cornerstone of the resort dining, the historic Marsh Tavern, offers scrumptious breakfasts and lovely, traditional New England fare for dinner, like Devonshire Shepherd's Pie and Pan-seared Turkey with a pine nut and herb crust. The executive chef has generously shared a few of the favorite dishes from the historic Equinox resort for you to enjoy.

## The Equinox

P.O. Box 46
Historic Route 7A
Manchester Village, VT 05254
**800.362.4747**
**802.362.4700**
**www.equinoxresort.com**

**Season:**
Year-round

**Guest Capacity:**
400

**Accommodations:**
183 rooms and suites

**Activities:**
Off-road driving at Land Rover Driving School; British School of Falconry; snowmobiling; cross-country skiing; snowshoeing; ice skating; spa treatments and fitness classes; nearby downhill skiing

**Peak Winter Rates:**
$-$$$$

**Closest Ski Resort:**
Stratton Mountain

## *Breakfast Menu*

STRAWBERRY SMOOTHIES

❊ EQUINOX SCOTTISH BLUEBERRY FLAPJACKS
OR
YANKEE RED FLANNEL HASH AND EGGS

❊ LEMON BLUEBERRY BREAD

## *Dinner Menu*

❊ MAINE SHRIMP FRITTERS
WITH HICKORY BELL PEPPER KETCHUP

❊ VERMONT VENISON CHILI

❊ APPLE CRANBERRY STRUDEL

❊ WARM BANANA BETTY

❊ RECIPE INCLUDED

# Equinox Scottish Blueberry Flapjacks

M aybe it's a Scot thing, but these flapjacks are square, not round. You bake these "pancakes" in the oven in a sheet pan and then cut them into squares to serve — totally cool. They are light, delicious and actually fun to make.

### 6 TO 8 SERVINGS

1. Preheat oven to 325°F. Grease and flour a jelly roll pan (17½ X 11½ X 1).
2. Stir oats, flour, sugar, baking powder and salt in a large mixing bowl and set aside.
3. Beat eggs and milk together and set aside.
4. In another small bowl, toss the blueberries with the ¼ cup of flour and set aside.
5. Melt the butter, brown sugar, honey and maple syrup in a small saucepan over low heat. Pour warm syrup mixture over the oats mixture and stir just until moistened.
6. Add egg mixture and stir again.
7. Fold in blueberry/flour mixture and lightly stir.
8. Pour into prepared pan and bake for 30 to 35 minutes, until golden brown. Cool a couple of minutes then cut into squares and serve with warm maple or blueberry syrup.

2¼ cups old-fashioned oats

2 cups flour

¾ cup plus
1 tablespoon sugar

2½ tablespoons
baking powder

⅛ teaspoon kosher salt

3 eggs, lightly beaten

2 cups milk

1½ cups blueberries,
fresh or frozen

¼ cup flour

½ cup (1 stick) butter

¼ cup light brown sugar

¼ cup honey

¼ cup maple syrup

# Lemon Blueberry Bread

I want some more of this. I love lemon quick breads that you can actually taste the lemon (you know what I'm talking about). The texture of this batter is very cake-like, due to the "creaming" method of the butter, sugar and eggs. Double this recipe and you'll have 2 lemony loaves, one to keep and one to, uh, keep, too.

### 1 LOAF

6 tablespoons butter, softened

1½ cups sugar

1 tablespoon grated lemon zest

2 eggs

2⅓ cups bread flour*

½ teaspoon kosher salt

1 teaspoon baking powder

¾ cup milk

½ cup fresh or frozen blueberries

Lemon Glaze

1. Preheat oven to 350°F. Grease and flour a 9 X 5-inch loaf pan.
2. Beat the butter, sugar and lemon zest together in a mixer until light and fluffy. Beat in the eggs, scraping the bowl.
3. Stir the bread flour, salt, and baking powder in a separate bowl. Alternately mix the dry ingredients and the milk into the butter mixture, scraping the bowl.
4. Fold in the blueberries and pour into the prepared loaf pan.
5. Bake for 50 to 60 minutes, or until a toothpick inserted in the center comes out clean.
6. After bread comes out of the oven, poke holes all over the top with a skewer or toothpick and slowly pour the lemon glaze over the top. Cool a few more minutes then remove from pan and cool on a rack.

**Lemon Glaze:**

½ cup sugar

¼ cup lemon juice

**Lemon Glaze:**

1. Heat sugar and lemon in a small saucepan over medium-low heat until the sugar has dissolved. Follow step six above.

*You can substitute regular all-purpose flour, but add an extra tablespoon.

# *Maine Shrimp Fritters*

## WITH HICKORY BELL PEPPER KETCHUP

D id I mention that I love my job? I also love anything fried. But this recipe is the crème de la crème of all things fried. If you normally don't like to fry things at home, I think this recipe might change your mind. For more shapely fritters, make the batter 3 to 4 hours ahead of time and chill before frying. The ketchup is great to have on hand for all sorts of things, like smeared on french fries, hot dogs and hamburgers, or as a straight cocktail sauce or a topping for meatloaf. Try it with the Spicy Meatloaf recipe from Sundance (see page 139).

### 35 FRITTERS (8 TO 10 APPETIZER SERVINGS)

1. Heat olive oil in a large skillet over medium-high heat. Sauté garlic, green onion, corn and red bell pepper for 1 minute. Remove from heat and cool 2 to 3 minutes.

2. Toss cooled corn mixture with flour, cilantro, salt and pepper.

3. Beat the milk and eggs together. Pour egg mixture over corn mixture and stir lightly. Fold in chopped shrimp. Place shrimp batter into the refrigerator for 10 to 15 minutes while frying oil is heating. (Or, refrigerate batter for 3 to 4 hours for more shapely, round fritters.)

4. In a deep frying vessel (a deep pot or pan specifically for deep-frying), heat enough oil to come to a 3 to 4 inch depth. When temperature reaches 350°F, you are ready to begin. Using a scant ⅛ cup measure, scoop batter and drop into hot oil. Only add 5 or 6 pieces at a time, so that the temperature of the oil doesn't drop.

5. Cook 1 to 1 ½ minutes, or until deep golden brown. Remove to a paper towel-lined plate to drain, and keep warm while you fry the rest of the batter. Let oil return to 350°F before adding the next batch. Repeat until all batter has been fried. Serve warm with the Hickory Bell Pepper Ketchup (recipe follows).

*(continued on next page)*

2 teaspoons olive oil

1 teaspoon finely chopped garlic

¼ cup finely chopped green onions

3 cups corn kernels (fresh or frozen)

½ cup chopped red pepper

1 cup flour

3 tablespoons roughly chopped cilantro

1 teaspoon kosher salt

½ teaspoon ground black pepper

½ cup milk

3 eggs

12 medium-sized shrimp (26/30 count), peeled, deveined and roughly chopped

4 or more cups of vegetable oil, for frying

**Hickory Bell Pepper Ketchup (3½ cups — enough to share with neighbors):**

½ cup golden raisins

½ cup apple juice

2 teaspoons roasted garlic*

¼ cup chopped roasted, peeled red pepper

1 ½ teaspoons liquid hickory smoke

1 cup chili sauce

¼ cup light brown sugar

2 teaspoons kosher salt

⅛ teaspoon cinnamon

⅛ teaspoon ground red (cayenne) pepper

*(continued from previous page)*

### Hickory Bell Pepper Ketchup:

1. Cook the raisins and apple juice in a small saucepan over medium-high heat until most of the liquid has evaporated, about 15 minutes. Add the roasted garlic, roasted red pepper and liquid smoke. Remove from heat and transfer to a food processor. Pulse until mixture resembles a paste, scraping bowl in between pulsing.

2. Stir the chili sauce, brown sugar, salt, cinnamon and red pepper in a large mixing bowl until brown sugar dissolves. Add chili sauce mixture to raisin paste and pulse a few more times. Transfer mixture to a container and chill until needed. Delicious!

*To roast garlic, see Common Procedures, page 20.

### Notes

# *Vermont Venison Chili

Okay, I'm from Texas and we Texans think we are the only ones who know how to make chili. I stand corrected, after testing this recipe, except for the beans — we don't put beans in chili. This is a marvelous, dark, rich chili — smoky, slightly sweet and throat-warming. Don't let the ingredient list fool you. This is easy to put together.

---

### 4 HEARTY SERVINGS

1. Sear the venison cubes until dark brown in a stockpot over medium-high heat, working in batches so you don't overcrowd the pan. Remove meat and set aside.

2. In the same pot, heat 2 teaspoons of oil over medium heat and add the onions, garlic and both bell peppers. Cook for 3 to 4 minutes or until the onions are translucent. Add the chipotle and tomato paste and cook until the tomato paste turns a rust color, about 3 minutes.

3. Return the seared venison to the pan and pour in the maple syrup, dark beer and Worcestershire sauce, stirring and scraping the bottom of the pot to remove any brown bits.

4. Stir in the brewed coffee and beef or venison stock, bay leaf, thyme, oregano, chili powder, cumin and red pepper. Bring to a boil. Reduce heat and simmer for 3 hours or until meat is very tender, adding more beef stock or water if necessary.

5. To thicken the chili, remove about 2 cups of the solids and purée in a blender with a bit of the liquid. Stir this back into the pot. Stir in the kidney beans, if using, and taste. Season with salt and pepper if needed. Garnish with a dollop of sour cream and cheddar cheese.

---

*It's important to use leg meat. I have found that other "stew" cuts of venison are too gristly and result in unpleasantly chewy chili.

**Chipotles (smoked jalapenos) are available dried or canned in adobo sauce (preferred), which I buy from A. J.'s. See Sources, page 192.

### ✳ *Photograph on page C-18*

2½ pounds venison leg meat, cubed (thank goodness for butchers!)*

2 teaspoons vegetable oil

1¼ cups chopped onion

2 teaspoons finely chopped garlic

1¼ cups chopped red bell pepper

1¼ cups chopped green bell pepper

1 chipotle pepper in adobo sauce,** chopped

2 tablespoons tomato paste

2 tablespoons maple syrup

1 cup dark beer

2 tablespoons Worcestershire sauce

¼ cup brewed coffee

5½ cups beef or venison stock

1 bay leaf

½ teaspoon dried thyme

1 teaspoon dried oregano

1 tablespoon chili powder

2½ teaspoons ground cumin

¼ teaspoon ground red (cayenne) pepper

2 cups cooked kidney beans (if you must)

Kosher salt

Ground black pepper

**Optional garnish:**

½ cup sour cream

½ cup cheddar cheese, grated

# *Apple Cranberry Strudel*

L uscious warm apples bathed in cinnamon and sugar, dotted with cranberries, all wrapped up in crispy phyllo layers — a delightful dessert. Who said working with phyllo dough was hard? I think I did, once. It's really not — but sometimes you get a temperamental box. This dessert is so delicious you'll have the art of phyllo dough mastered in no time. I've learned to buy 2 boxes at a time in case one is just too dry to start with. The key is to work quickly and keep the dough covered with plastic wrap or a slightly damp dishtowel. The Equinox serves this with a vanilla sauce, but I prefer a caramel sauce. I've included my own recipe for you on the next page. Read through this recipe completely before starting so that you understand my instructions about how to lay out and roll up the phyllo dough.

---

**8** SERVINGS

1 cup sugar
1 tablespoon cinnamon
1 cup graham cracker crumbs
Parchment paper
6 sheets phyllo dough, room temperature
¼ cup (½ stick) melted butter
Pastry brush
2 cups sliced, peeled Granny Smith apples
½ cup dried cranberries
Cinnamon/sugar mixture (1 teaspoon cinnamon plus 3 tablespoons sugar)

1. Preheat the oven to 350°F. Stir the 1 cup of sugar, 1 tablespoon of cinnamon and graham cracker crumbs in a small mixing bowl. Set aside.

2. Place a couple of pieces of parchment paper on a work surface large enough to hold the phyllo sheets. Take 2 sheets of phyllo dough and place on top of the parchment, keeping the other 4 phyllo sheets covered. With a pastry brush lightly coat the 2 sheets completely with melted butter. Sprinkle the buttered phyllo sheets with about ½ cup of the sugar/graham cracker mixture.

3. Top with 2 more phyllo sheets, brush with melted butter and top with another ½ cup of sugar/graham cracker mixture. Repeat process with remaining 2 phyllo sheets, topping with another ½ cup of the sugar/graham cracker mixture.

4. Turn the parchment paper so that one of the shorter ends of the phyllo is facing you. (Think of the phyllo sheet as a rectangular picture and you want it vertical, not horizontal, in front of you.) Place the 2 cups of sliced apples mounded on the end closest to you, leaving a 2-inch border on both sides and and on the bottom. Sprinkle with the remaining ½ cup sugar/graham cracker mixture then top with the dried cranberries. Fold in the 2-inch margin on the long sides and on the bottom, and start rolling up the pastry, tucking and rolling as you go. (It's like rolling a jumbo burrito.)

5. With the seam side down, you should now have a log about 12 to 14 inches long and 5 inches tall. Place the log on a parchment paper-lined baking sheet with shallow sides (like a jelly roll pan). Butter the phyllo log and sprinkle with the cinnamon/sugar mixture.

*(continued on next page)*

156

## Apple Cranberry Strudel
*(continued from previous page)*

6. Bake the strudel for 1 hour, or until dark golden brown. Cool at least 10 minutes and cut on the bias, 1-inch thick slices. Serve with vanilla sauce, caramel sauce or whipped cream.

### Easy Caramel Sauce:

1. Heat the sugar and water over medium heat in a tall saucepan. Cook until the sugar liquifies and turns golden brown, about 10 to 12 minutes.

2. Remove from heat and carefully and SLOWLY add the heavy cream (CAUTION: the mixture will bubble up violently, which is why you need a tall pan.)

3. Return to the heat and stir until the mixture is smooth. Remove from heat and stir in butter until it melts.

### Easy Caramel Sauce
**(1½ cups):**

1 cup sugar

2 tablespoons water

1 cup heavy cream

¼ cup (½ stick) butter, cut into chunks

## Notes

_____

_____

_____

_____

_____

_____

_____

_____

_____

_____

_____

_____

_____

_____

_____

_____

# Warm Banana Betty

This is a twist on the traditional colonial Apple Brown Betty, layering bananas instead of apples. It's quite delicious — creamy, smooth and reminiscent of a warm banana pudding. I like this dish because you can make it in advance and store in the refrigerator, heating quickly in the microwave just before serving. Just be sure to cool for a couple of minutes after heating in the microwave or you'll burn your tongue. I know this from personal experience.

### 5 SERVINGS

2 cups milk

½ cup and 4 teaspoons sugar, divided in half

1 egg

3 tablespoons cornstarch

2 tablespoons cold butter

½ teaspoon vanilla

⅓ cup gingersnap cookie crumbs

¼ cup graham cracker crumbs

2 tablespoons melted butter

4 bananas, peeled and sliced

5 (8-ounce) ramekins

1. Prepare a large bowl of ice water and set aside.

2. Heat the milk and ½ of the sugar (¼ cup plus 2 teaspoons) in a medium saucepan over medium heat.

3. Beat the remaining ¼ cup plus 2 teaspoons of sugar with the egg and cornstarch in a separate bowl.

4. When the milk and sugar come to a simmer, slowly pour a small amount into the egg mixture, whisking constantly. Return this egg mixture to the hot milk mixture on the stove and cook until it thickens, stirring constantly (about 4 to 5 minutes). When the mixture coats the back of a spoon, remove it from the heat and add the cold butter and vanilla. Stir until the butter is melted. Strain into a bowl that will fit into the ice water bath. Cool, stirring occasionally.

5. Stir the gingersnap and graham cracker crumbs together in a small bowl. Knead in the melted butter.

6. Ladle the cooled custard mix equally among 5 (8-ounce) ramekins. Divide the sliced bananas between the 5 ramekins. Top with the crumb mixture and heat in microwave for 1 ½ to 2 minutes. Cool 1 or 2 minutes and serve.

Stowe is one of those postcard-perfect New England towns, with a gently rolling landscape, white steeples, and quaint, tree-lined streets. Just as picture-perfect is the Topnotch Resort and Spa, five minutes from Stowe, nestled in the quiet countryside of north central Vermont in the Green Mountains. As Stowe's only AAA Four-Diamond and Mobil's Four-Star resort, Topnotch provides an exclusive winter escape for the body and soul, all on 120 acres of woods and streams. This member of the Preferred Hotels and Resorts Worldwide organization is also a *Conde Nast Traveler* reader-ranked top spa and resort.

The décor is earthy, with lots of stone and wood accents, along with traditional colonial furniture. The rooms vary from a spacious but cozy bedroom to a luxurious multi-bedroom condominium, with several choices in between. But with the abundance of winter outdoor activities, not to mention the Spa, who plans on staying in their room? Cross-country skiing is available on property, and downhill skiing is just minutes away at the Stowe ski resort.

Step into the 23,000 square foot Spa, and you'll feel as if you have stepped across the Atlantic and into a famous European day spa. Enjoy the vast array of massage and spa treatment choices, like a Cranio-Sacral session to help reduce stress, or a Vermont Wildflower Herbal Wrap to relax and sooth tired muscles. The Spa also features a 60-foot indoor lap pool and a whirlpool with a hydromassage waterfall. It might be tough to get in a day of skiing with all the spa choices awaiting you.

It won't be hard to tear yourself away from any activity to sample the delicious cuisine at any of Topnotch's restaurants. Try Maxwell's, the fine dining restaurant for steaks, seafood and game, and sample Buttertub Bistro for casual lunches and dinners. Both restaurants offer Spa cuisine with plenty of choices low in fat and calories but high in flavor and creativity. The chef at Maxwell's has included a sampling of both the Spa cuisine and regular menu choices for you to enjoy.

## Topnotch At Stowe

P.O. Box 1458
Stowe, VT 05672
**800.451.8686**
**802.253.8585**
**www.topnotch-resort.com**

**Season:**
Year-round

**Guest Capacity:**
325

**Accommodations:**
110 luxury rooms, suites
and condominiums

**Activities:**
Downhill and cross-country skiing; snowshoeing; sledding; full European health spa

**Peak Winter Rates:**
$$-$$$$

**Closest Ski Resort:**
Stowe

## Breakfast Menu

SEASONAL FRUIT JUICES

❋ CHILLED MELON SOUP

❋ WARM BLUEBERRY CRÊPES
WITH VERMONT MAPLE CREAM

CARROT BRAN MUFFINS

## Dinner Menu

❋ TOPNOTCH SPA CAESAR SALAD

❋ SMOKED BREAST OF DUCK
WITH DRIED CRANBERRY RED WINE SAUCE

❋ CHESTNUT GNOCCHI

CHOCOLATE SPA MADELEINES

❋ RECIPE INCLUDED

# Chilled Melon Soup

**L**ight, refreshing and lowfat, this soup is a great starter for the blueberry crêpes (next recipe). The recipe calls for the summer cantaloupe but is equally delicious with the winter honeydew melon. This dish could change your opinion about Spa cuisine.

**6 SERVINGS**

1. Place all ingredients (cantaloupe through cinnamon) in a large bowl and stir. Working in two batches, place half the mixture in a blender and purée until smooth.
2. Finish puréeing the other half of the ingredients and combine both puréed batches. Taste and add more cinnamon if desired. Chill. Can be made the night before.

6 cups chopped, peeled, seeded cantaloupe
1½ cups fresh orange juice
¼ cup fresh lemon juice
¼ cup fresh lime juice
1 tablespoon honey
¼ teaspoon ground cinnamon

# *Warm Blueberry Crêpes

## WITH VERMONT MAPLE CREAM

*I*f I didn't tell you this was a spa dish and only 72 calories/2 grams fat per crêpe, you'd never know it. This is one of those few low calorie/low fat dishes that tastes great and you don't feel you've given up anything. Making crêpes is fun, and after you get the hang of it with one pan, try adding a second pan to speed things up. I remember unofficial competitions in culinary school, each student trying to see how many pans we could get going at once without under or over cooking any of the crêpes. I made it to 5 pans successfully, but I remember one guy who made it to 7! The whole key to good crêpes is a good, sturdy nonstick pan. I love my nonstick All-Clad pans for making beautiful, golden crêpes.

### 10 SERVINGS

**Maple Cream (1 cup):**

1 cup lowfat cottage cheese

2 tablespoons maple syrup

½ teaspoon orange zest

⅛ teaspoon vanilla extract

Pinch cinnamon

**Blueberry Filling (2½ cups):**

2 cups fresh or frozen blueberries (more for garnish)

½ cup orange juice

1 tablespoon cornstarch

1 tablespoon cold water

**Lowfat Crêpes (30 crêpes):**

¾ cup flour

¾ cup whole-wheat flour

3 tablespoons sugar

2 teaspoons baking powder

6 egg whites, slightly whipped (foamy)

2 cups 2% milk

3 tablespoons vegetable oil

1 teaspoon vanilla extract

**Maple Cream:**

1. Combine all ingredients (cottage cheese through cinnamon) in a blender and purée until smooth and creamy. Chill before using. Store in the refrigerator for up to 1 week.

**Blueberry Filling:**

1. Place blueberries and orange juice in a saucepan and bring to a boil over medium-high heat.

2. Stir together the cornstarch and 1 tablespoon of cold water and pour into boiling blueberries, stirring constantly. The mixture will thicken quickly.

3. Lower the heat and simmer for 2 to 3 minutes. Keep warm.

**Lowfat Crêpes:**

1. Stir together the flour, whole-wheat flour, sugar and baking powder and set aside.

2. Whisk together the foamy egg whites, milk, oil, and vanilla. Pour the milk mixture over the flour mixture and whisk just until smooth. Set aside for 20 to 30 minutes to allow the batter to rest.

3. Heat a nonstick 8-inch skillet over medium heat. Spray with nonstick spray and pour in ⅛ cup of batter, quickly lifting and swirling the pan to coat the bottom with a thin layer. Return pan to heat and cook until edges start to brown, about 1½ minutes. Shake the pan to loosen the crêpe and flip it with a spatula to brown on the other side, about 30 to 45 seconds. You will probably have to throw out the first crêpe or two. The first side you cook is the presentation side. Make 2 crêpes for each person.

*(continued on next page)*

**❋ *Photograph on page C-19***

**Warm Blueberry Crêpes**
*(continued from previous page)*

4. You can finish cooking the crêpes now or within a day and store in the freezer, tightly wrapped. Place a piece of parchment paper or wax paper in between each one before wrapping and freezing.

5. To serve, place a crêpe flat on a small plate, presentation side down. Spoon 2 tablespoons of the warm filling just below the center of the crêpe. Roll the crêpe into a tube shape, seam side down. Repeat process, making 2 crêpes per person. Place 2 crêpes on a warm serving plate and drizzle with 1 tablespoon of Maple Cream and garnish with fresh blueberries and a mint sprig (optional).

**Notes**

_____

_____

_____

_____

_____

_____

_____

_____

_____

_____

_____

_____

_____

_____

_____

_____

_____

# Topnotch Spa Caesar Salad

T he dressing is similar to a creamy ranch/Italian blend. The addition of anchovies makes it taste authentic and utterly delicious. I don't think you can tell that it is low fat. One serving of salad with 2 tablespoons of dressing is about 120 calories and 4 grams of fat.

**4 Servings**

### Dressing (2¼ cups):

2 cups lowfat cottage cheese

¼ cup buttermilk (1% fat)

1 tablespoon champagne or white wine vinegar

2 teaspoons lemon juice

1 teaspoon finely chopped garlic

3 anchovies, rinsed in warm water

¼ cup grated Parmesan cheese

½ teaspoon dry mustard

¼ teaspoon ground black pepper

Kosher salt

### Salad:

12 cups romaine lettuce, washed, dried, cut into bite size pieces

1 cup spa Caesar salad dressing

1 teaspoon grated Parmesan cheese

4 teaspoons sliced scallions

Fresh cracked black pepper to taste

**Dressing:**

1. Place all ingredients except salt (cottage cheese through black pepper) in a blender or food processor and process until smooth. Taste and add salt if desired. Chill before serving. Dressing may be refrigerated for up to 2 weeks.

**Salad:**

1. Toss lettuce with dressing and cheese. Sprinkle with cracked black pepper. Divide salad onto 4 chilled plates and garnish each with a teaspoon of scallions. Add croutons if desired.

# Smoked Breast of Duck

### WITH DRIED CRANBERRY RED WINE SAUCE

The resort actually cold-smokes this duck before finishing on the grill. To simplify the procedure, I've created a smoky marinade that takes the place of cold-smoking and speeds up the process significantly. The smoke flavor comes from a product called liquid smoke. Look for it on the same aisle as the barbecue sauces. The wonderful flavor of the smoke-drenched duck plays nicely with the sweet cranberry-wine sauce. The resort serves this dish with a fabulous chestnut gnocchi (next recipe).

---

#### 4 SERVINGS

**Marinade:**

1. Whisk the oil, vinegar, liquid smoke and black pepper together. Place duck breast, skin side up, in a shallow baking dish. Pour the marinade over the breast and turn to coat, and turn again, so that the skin side is still up. Cover and marinate in the refrigerator for 4 to 8 hours, turning occasionally.

2. Soak the cranberries in the wine and brandy. Set aside for later. Proceed with red wine sauce.

**Red Wine Sauce:**

1. Bring all the ingredients except the demi-glace (red wine through ginger) to a boil in a saucepan. Vigorously simmer until the liquid is reduced to 1 cup, about 20 minutes.

2. Stir demi-glace into reduced wine mixture and simmer for 5 minutes. Set aside and proceed with duck preparation.

**Duck preparation:**

1. Preheat oven to 400°F. Remove duck from marinade and discard marinade. Heat a skillet over medium-high heat. When very hot, place duck, skin-side down in pan (it will splatter so if you have one of those pan screens to cut down grease splatters, use it.) Sear duck until skin is golden brown, about 2½ minutes then turn and sear the other side another 2 minutes.

2. Remove duck to a roasting pan and place in the oven to finish cooking. Cook to an internal temperature of 165°F, about 15 minutes. Let rest 5 minutes, covered to keep warm, before slicing.

3. Meanwhile, drain duck fat from searing skillet and add the dried cranberries (including wine and brandy). Cook 3 to 4 minutes and add the red wine sauce. Simmer 10 minutes, until slightly thickened. Remove from heat and whisk in 1 tablespoon of butter until melted.

4. Slice duck on a bias and serve with the cranberry red wine sauce.

**Marinade:**

¼ cup olive oil

2 tablespoons red wine vinegar

1 teaspoon liquid smoke

¼ teaspoon ground black pepper

4 (6 or 8-ounce) duck breasts

1 cup dried cranberries

½ cup sweet Muscat wine or port wine

¼ cup brandy

1 tablespoon butter

**Dried Cranberry Red Wine Sauce:**

1 (750 ml) bottle pinot noir or merlot wine

3 tablespoons chopped shallots

6 shiitake mushroom caps, sliced

½ teaspoon whole black peppercorns

2 bay leaves

1½ teaspoons chopped fresh ginger

1 cup demi-glace*

---

*See Demi-glace under Common Procedures, page 19.

# Chestnut Gnocchi

As attractive as it is delicious, this gnocchi is the perfect accouterment to the wine-drenched smoky duck breasts (previous recipe). The traditional shape is barrel-like, and can be achieved by rolling a small piece of dough with a fork and your thumb. Hold your hand in front of you with your palm facing down. Place a fork in this hand, parallel to the ground with the fork tines at your thumb. Place a ¾-inch piece of dough between the fork and your thumb. Begin to roll the dough with your thumb, against the fork tines with an up-and-down motion. If this doesn't make any sense, then just pinch the dough in the center and go with that. If you can't locate fresh chestnuts, then see my note at the bottom of the page. If you roast your own, do so in a 350°F oven for about 20 minutes. Be sure to cut a slit on the flat side or the nuts will explode in the oven. After roasting and cooling, peel and remove the skin.

### 4 TO 6 SERVINGS

½ pound sweet potatoes
1 egg
1 egg yolk
¼ teaspoon ground clove
⅛ teaspoon ground nutmeg
1 teaspoon ground black pepper
1½ teaspoons kosher salt
½ pound roasted chestnuts, finely ground*
1½ cups flour
1 teaspoon of butter

1. Preheat oven to 350°F. Bake sweet potatoes for 35 to 40 minutes until soft. Cool and peel and mash.
2. Beat egg, egg yolk, clove, nutmeg and salt and pepper together. Stir in mashed sweet potato. Fold in ground chestnuts.
3. Stir in flour and gently, lightly knead until combined. If too sticky, add more flour. Try not to overwork the dough or the gnocchi will be tough.
4. Divide dough into 3 equal pieces. Roll in a cigar shape, about ¾-inch in diameter. Cut cigar-rolls into ¾-inch pieces. Roll with a fork as described in the introduction, or pinch with your thumb and forefinger to shape.
5. Bring a large pot of salted water to a boil.
6. Drop the gnocchi pieces in the boiling water and cook until they rise to the surface, about 1 minute. Remove with a slotted spoon and place in a pan to cool. The gnocchi may be made up to 1 day in advance up to this point, stored covered, in the refrigerator.
7. To serve, heat a skillet over medium heat and add a teaspoon of butter. Cooking in batches, add the gnocchi and toss, cooking until lightly browned. Add more butter as necessary.

---

*I used a 10-ounce can of chestnuts, drained, chopped and dried in a 350°F oven for 30 minutes. Then I pulsed the mostly dried chestnuts in a food processor for a few seconds.

# Wyoming

## The Alpenhof Lodge

P.O. Box 288
Teton Village, WY 83025
**800.732.3244**
**307.733.3242**
www.alpenhoflodge.com

**Season:**
Mid-May through mid-October
and early December through
early April

**Guest Capacity:**
125

**Accommodations:**
43 rooms and junior suites

**Activities:**
Downhill and cross-country
skiing; snowmobiling;
snowshoeing; sleigh rides; dog-
sledding; hot air ballooning

**Peak Winter Rates:**
$-$$$$

**Closest Ski Resort:**
Jackson Hole

The rugged, eclipsing Grand Tetons must resemble the jagged silhouette of the magnificent Bavarian Alps in southern Germany. Perhaps that is why the Alpenhof Lodge is a near replica of a Bavarian country inn, complete with German antiques and woodworks, and a dark wood beam and white stucco exterior.

Tucked at the base of Rendezvous Peak (an incredible monster of a mountain), the Alpenhof radiates European country charm with Western friendliness and service. A relatively small resort, the lodge offers 43 rooms and junior suites (with sitting areas) all decorated with both modern American and traditional Bavarian furniture. The rooms are spacious, bright and impeccably clean. Some have fireplaces, some have balconies where you can view the majestic grand mountains, and some have both. Each will have a welcoming basket upon your arrival.

Compared to other ski resorts, Jackson Hole attracts the best, most expert skiers. It's really not for novice alpine skiers. That said, the Alpenhof offers a myriad of other wonderful winter activities, including snowmobiling, beautiful sleigh rides and breathtaking hot air balloon rides. And then there is shopping in Jackson, a two-day affair at least. On the east side of the square, an adorable little kitchen shop called Good Goods is a must stop. Just off the square on King Street is a wonderful "old west mercantile" called Jackson Hole Emporium, with lots of local gifts and treats. Worth seeking out is a friendly, comfortable bookstore called, appropriately, the Valley Bookstore, sequestered in a board-planked shopping nook to the west of the square on Cache Street.

Returning to the lodge after a full day of winter playing, you might want to stop in at the casual Bistro for a micro-brew and great big juicy burger, or a hearty pasta dish. For something more elegant, the Alpenhof Dining Room, awarded with Mobil's Four-Star award, is sure to delight your senses with outstanding mountain-fresh cuisine. Game is frequently on the menu, and the chef has graciously shared a delicious venison dish paired with a sweet and spicy marmalade as well as a hearty breakfast menu.

## *Breakfast Menu*

STRAWBERRY BANANA SMOOTHIES

❄ SMOKED SALMON OMELET

❄ ALPENHOF BREAKFAST POTATOES

❄ CINNAMON SOUR CREAM COFFEECAKE

## *Dinner Menu*

❄ LOBSTER CAKES

❄ HERBED VENISON MEDALLIONS
WITH RED CURRANT CINNAMON MARMALADE

SAUTÉED SPAGHETTI SQUASH

CHOCOLATE BRIOCHE BREAD PUDDING

❄ RECIPE INCLUDED

# *Smoked Salmon Omelet*

L ots of flavor and color in this dish from the tomato, chile and spinach, not to mention the smoked salmon. Although the recipe makes one 8-inch omelet, I think it's enough for 2 servings if you are serving a side dish (like the filling Alpenhof Breakfast Potatoes).

**1 SERVING (A 3-EGG OMELET)**

3 eggs

1 tablespoon butter

1 ounce smoked salmon, cut into thin strips (about ¼ cup)

3 leaves baby spinach cut into thin long strips (about ⅛ cup)

2 tablespoons diced Roma tomato (extra for garnish)

1 tablespoon finely chopped Anaheim pepper (green chile)

¼ cup grated Gruyère cheese (or Swiss cheese), divided

1 teaspoon finely chopped parsley (garnish)

Kosher salt and ground black pepper to taste

1. Have all ingredients prepared and ready. Preheat oven to broil.

2. Vigorously whip the eggs in a mixing bowl.

3. Heat the butter in an 8-inch nonstick skillet on medium heat. Pour the beaten eggs into the heated butter and with a wooden spoon not touching the bottom, gently stir. (This creates a smooth bottom surface that will show). Cook, shaking the pan until the eggs are almost cooked, about 3 minutes. The eggs will still be soft.

4. Layer the salmon, spinach, tomato, green chile, salt and pepper (to taste) and 2 tablespoons of the cheese on one half of the eggs. Quickly place under the preheated broiler. Cook until the cheese is melted, about 1 minute.

5. Remove from oven and gently slide the omelet onto a serving plate, folding over ½ of the omelet to make a half-moon. Top with the remaining 2 tablespoons of cheese. Sprinkle with a garnish of finely chopped tomatoes and parsley and serve.

# Alpenhof Breakfast Potatoes

I've yet to meet a bad potato dish and this one is colorful, tasty and easy. You can easily double this recipe. If you can't find Yukon Gold potatoes, use all red potatoes or you can even use a regular baking potato instead. Paprika adds a nice color, but no heat. If you want a little kick, add a pinch (or more) of cayenne.

---

**4 SERVINGS**

1. Boil the unpeeled potatoes until almost cooked, about 20 minutes. Cool and cut into ½ inch cubes.

2. Melt the butter in a large skillet over medium heat. Add cubed potatoes, onion, garlic, bell peppers and paprika. Cook, stirring occasionally, until potatoes are browned, about 20 to 25 minutes. Season with salt and pepper and serve immediately.

2 red potatoes, unpeeled

2 Yukon Gold potatoes, unpeeled

4 tablespoons butter

½ cup chopped yellow onion

2 tablespoons finely chopped garlic

2 tablespoons chopped red bell pepper

2 tablespoons chopped green bell pepper

2 teaspoons paprika

Kosher salt and pepper to taste

# Cinnamon Sour Cream Coffeecake

*T*his cake is moist and heavy on the cinnamon side. Interestingly, it is also a dark cake, which is surprising when you cut it open and expect to see a pale cake, like other sour cream coffeecakes. The wheat germ is responsible for the darker color, and it adds a little bit of vitamin E and folic acid, too.

### A 10-INCH BUNDT CAKE

1 cup (2 sticks) butter, softened
1¼ cups light brown sugar
2 eggs
1½ teaspoons vanilla
2 cups flour
¼ cup wheat germ
1¼ teaspoons baking soda
1 teaspoon baking powder
1 teaspoon cinnamon
1 cup sour cream, room temperature

**Topping:**
½ cup light brown sugar
1½ teaspoons cinnamon
¾ cup chopped pecans

1. Grease and flour a 10-inch Bundt pan. Preheat oven to 350°F. Prepare the topping by stirring the ½ cup brown sugar, 1½ teaspoons cinnamon and chopped pecans in a small bowl. Set aside.

2. Beat butter and 1¼ cups brown sugar until light and fluffy, about 3 minutes. Beat in eggs, one at a time until smooth, then add vanilla and stir.

3. Stir the flour, wheat germ, baking soda, baking powder and cinnamon in a separate bowl. Add this flour mixture alternately with sour cream to egg mixture, beginning and ending with the flour mixture. Stir just to moisten, and do not overmix.

4. Pour ⅓ of the batter into the prepared pan. Top with ½ the topping, then add the remaining ⅔'s batter. Top with the remaining ½ topping and run a knife through the topping and batter in order to incorporate some of the topping into the batter. Bake in a preheated oven for 50 to 55 minutes, until a toothpick comes out clean, or with just a few moist crumbs attached.

Cortina Inn and Resort, Vermont

Wild Mushroom Bread Pudding

The Equinox
Vermont

Vermont Venison Chili

Topnotch at Stowe Spa and Resort
Vermont

Warm Blueberry Crepes with Vermont
Maple Cream

Alpenhof Lodge
Wyoming

Lobster Cakes

Rusty Parrot Lodge
Wyoming

Raspberry Cream French Toast

Spring Creek Ranch, Wyoming

Huckleberry Crème Brûlée

Cross-country or downhill –
Skiing at its best

Top: Vista Verde, CO
Middle: Sundance, UT
Bottom: Deer Valley Resort, UT

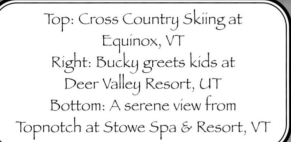

Top: Cross Country Skiing at
Equinox, VT
Right: Bucky greets kids at
Deer Valley Resort, UT
Bottom: A serene view from
Topnotch at Stowe Spa & Resort, VT

# *Lobster Cakes

Incredible! I sampled this appetizer among two sets of native East Coast neighbors who know how good lobster should taste. The verdict — a perfect "10." Not the prettiest cakes you've seen because they are so chunky with luscious lobster meat but they might be the tastiest. Serve with your favorite tartar or cocktail sauce. I personally like to mix one part tartar sauce to two parts cocktail sauce.

### 14 (3-INCH) CAKES

1. Melt the butter in a large heavy skillet over medium-high heat and add the onion, garlic and carrot and stir. When onions are soft, about 3 minutes, add the bell peppers and cook another 2 minutes.

2. Add the cooked lobster meat and cook for 1 minute, or until lobster is gently heated through. Set mixture aside to cool for about 10 to 15 minutes. When cool, transfer lobster mixture to a large bowl and stir in beaten eggs, mayonnaise and parsley and salt and pepper.

3. Sprinkle 1 cup of bread crumbs over lobster mixture and toss. Add just enough bread crumbs for mixture to barely hold its shape. Form cakes by hand, using ¼ cup of lobster mixture.

4. Pour enough oil to come to ¼-inch depth in a large, nonstick skillet over medium heat. When very hot, add lobster patties. Cook until brown on both sides, about 3 minutes per side for a 1-inch thick cake. Remove from skillet and drain on a plate lined with paper towels. Serve warm with your favorite sauce.

*** Photograph on page C-20**

4 tablespoons butter

1 cup chopped yellow onion

1 teaspoon finely chopped garlic

¼ cup peeled, chopped carrot

½ cup chopped red bell pepper

½ cup chopped green bell pepper

2½ pounds cooked lobster tail meat, cut into chunks

2 eggs, beaten

2 tablespoons mayonnaise

¼ cup fresh chopped parsley

Kosher salt and ground black pepper to taste

1½ cups bread crumbs (or less)

Vegetable oil to fry

# Herbed Venison Medallions
### WITH RED CURRANT CINNAMON MARMALADE

D oesn't this sound delicious? It is — and simple, too. The marmalade is a sweet, thick sauce that accents the mild gaminess of the venison, and it can be made in advance. The recipe calls for loin meat, which is not quite as tender as the tenderloin cut, but it is also not as expensive. My butcher says the difference between the venison tenderloin and the venison loin is like the difference between the beef filet mignon and the New York strip in terms of texture and taste.

---

### 5 SERVINGS

2 pounds venison loin cut into 10 (3-ounce) medallions

Kosher salt and ground black pepper

Red Currant Cinnamon Marmalade

#### Marinade:

1 cup olive oil

½ cup red wine

¼ cup fresh chopped thyme

¼ cup fresh chopped rosemary

¼ cup fresh chopped sage leaves

¼ cup fresh chopped parsley

1½ teaspoons kosher salt

¾ teaspoon fresh ground black pepper

#### Red Currant Cinnamon Marmalade (2 cups):

1 teaspoon olive oil

2 tablespoons finely chopped shallots

4 cups currants

1 cup red currant jelly

1 stick of cinnamon

1. Whisk all of the marinade ingredients together. Cut the venison loin into 10 medallions, about ½ inch thick (if you didn't already have your butcher do this for you). Place the medallions in a large, shallow pan and cover with the marinade, turning to coat both sides. Marinate for 10 to 20 minutes at room temperature or for 1 hour in the refrigerator, turning occasionally.

2. Preheat the grill to medium-high (375°–400°F). Remove medallions from marinade and season with salt and pepper. Place on the hot grill, cooking 4 minutes per side for medium rare, longer if your cut is thicker than ½ inch. Serve with the Red Currant Marmalade.

#### Red Currant Cinnamon Marmalade:

1. Heat the olive oil in a small saucepan, over medium heat. Add shallots and cook 1 minute. Stir in currants, jelly, and cinnamon stick.

2. Reduce heat to low and simmer until most of the liquid has evaporated, about 25 to 30 minutes. Remove cinnamon stick and cool.

3. Place a dollop of marmalade over the grilled venison or any other game dish. Will keep, covered, for 3 weeks in the refrigerator. Bring to room temperature before using.

S tone and timber drenched, the Rusty Parrot is more than an elegantly rustic bed and breakfast masquerading as a splendid Western log mansion. On the edge of town, just a few blocks from the antler-framed square in the center of Jackson, Wyoming, the Rusty Parrot is a vision of winter bliss. A Mobil Four-Star and AAA Four-Diamond property, the lodge is a welcome respite after a grueling day on the most vertical ski drop in the country, Rendezvous Peak at the Jackson Hole ski resort. Tired bones are rejuvenated at the in-house day spa, the Body Sage.

The spa is noted for its sports therapies, catering to the athletic Jackson crowd, including a hot arnica wrap, using the mountain daisy-like herb arnica, reputed to help heal bruising and soreness. But even if you're not a tip-top athlete, the spa offers a multitude of massages, facials and other body-purifying treatments including a special "Moor" mud wrap using imported Austrian mud laden with earthy botanicals. The spa has its own website, www.bodysage.com, where you can check out all the other goodies that this award-winning spa has to offer.

After a salt glow scrub or an aromatherapy steam bath, retire to your snug, comfy room and cuddle under the down comforter. The rooms are decorated with wrought-iron beds and honey-pine furniture with lots of homey touches, including a stuffed teddy bear. Sweet dreams are the only thing between you and the next morning's bountiful feast, served in the Great Room, just off the cozy cabin-like lobby.

Phenomenal breakfasts such as House-cured Pork Tenderloin Hash and Crab Cakes Benedict share the menu with house-made granola and fresh, seasonal fruit. Sumptuous afternoon treats await ravenous guests upon their return from an action-packed day of skiing or shopping. It's the attentive staff that elevates this romantic lodge to its lofty status, and that includes the talented kitchen staff, who generously shared some special recipes for you to sample.

### Rusty Parrot Lodge
P.O. Box 1657
Jackson, WY 83001
**800.458.2004**
**307.733.2000**
**www.rustyparrot.com**

**Season:**
Year-round; peak winter:
January through March

**Guest Capacity:**
70

**Accommodations:**
32 rooms

**Activities:**
nearby downhill and
cross-country skiing;
day spa; shopping

**Peak Winter Rates:**
$$-$$$$

**Closest Ski Resort:**
Jackson Hole; Snow King

## Breakfast Menu

❄ RASPBERRY CREAM FRENCH TOAST
OR
❄ ITALIAN SCRAMBLE
WITH GORGONZOLA CHEESE

## Afternoon Delights

❄ ASPARAGUS SALAD
WITH BALSAMIC CRANBERRY VINAIGRETTE

❄ PINEAPPLE COCONUT CAKE

❄ RECIPE INCLUDED

# *Raspberry Cream French Toast

**S**imply delicious! And such a unique color, too, after it's cooked, kind of a dark mauve. I think a raspberry sauce would be divine with this dish, (see recipe for Raspberry Coulis on page 132), but the lodge serves this crunchy French toast with warm maple syrup which is also delicious. Garnishing with fresh raspberries is an extra special touch, if you can get them. Remember to cook the toast slowly to produce a crunchy exterior and a moist (but done) interior.

### 4 TO 5 SERVINGS

1. Preheat oven to 400°F. Place the powdered sugar, vanilla, milk, heavy cream and raspberries in a blender and blend until smooth. Pour mixture into a large bowl and whisk in beaten eggs.

2. Place bread slices in a large shallow pan. Pour egg mixture over the bread and turn to coat both sides. Let sit 5 minutes.

3. Meanwhile, heat a nonstick skillet or griddle over medium-low heat. When hot, add 1 tablespoon of oil and heat for 1 minute. Add several soaked bread slices and cook for 5 to 6 minutes, until golden brown then flip and cook on the other side until golden brown, about 4 to 5 minutes more.

4. Remove bread from skillet and place on a baking sheet in the preheated oven for 3 to 5 minutes, or until crisp. While the first batch is crisping in the oven, cook the next batch of bread in the same manner, 5 to 6 minutes on the first side and 4 or more minutes on the other side. Finish in the oven for an additional 3 to 5 minutes.

5. Sprinkle with powdered sugar and fresh raspberries (optional). Serve with warm maple syrup.

½ cup powdered sugar

2 teaspoons vanilla extract

½ cup milk

1 cup heavy cream

2 cups raspberries (fresh or frozen)

6 eggs, beaten

12 slices day-old French bread (1-inch thick)

Vegetable oil as needed

Sifted powder sugar (optional garnish)

Fresh raspberries (optional garnish)

* *Photograph on page C-21*

# *Italian Scramble*

## WITH GORGONZOLA CHEESE

To all my vegetarian friends, this dish is for you. To all you carnivores, (me included) dress this up with a bit of hot Italian sausage and we're right back where we want to be. Either way, I love this dish (always the diplomat). The key to soft, melt-in-your-mouth scrambled eggs, in my opinion, is a lot less scrambling. After I pour the eggs into the hot pan, I gently push the eggs to the center a few times with a heat-resistant spatula. Then, over the course of the next 3 or 4 minutes as the eggs cook, I gently stir, only a couple of times, to break up the billowy curds.

### 4 SERVINGS

1 link (about ½ cup) hot Italian sausage (optional)

3 Roma tomatoes

1 medium zucchini, rough chopped

½ cup chopped onion

1 garlic clove, chopped

2 tablespoons chopped fresh basil

3 teaspoons olive oil, divided

6 eggs

3 tablespoons milk

Kosher salt

Ground black pepper

¼ cup crumbled Gorgonzola or other blue cheese

Fresh basil leaves (garnish)

Purchased pesto sauce (garnish)

1. (Vegetarians: skip to step 2.) If using Italian sausage, remove casing and cook in a small skillet over medium-high heat until browned. Drain and set aside.

2. Core tomatoes, cut in half lengthwise and removed seeds.

3. Chop finely by hand, or pulse a few times in a food processor the tomatoes, zucchini, onion, garlic and basil. Add 1 teaspoon of olive oil and stir or pulse again once or twice.

4. Heat a nonstick skillet over medium heat and add the remaining 2 teaspoons of olive oil. When hot, add the vegetable mixture and cook, stirring for 1 minute. (Carnivores: add the cooked sausage at this point.)

5. Beat the eggs with the milk and salt and pepper to taste. Pour egg mixture into the pan with the vegetables. Using a heat-resistant spatula, gently push the eggs and vegetables from the outer edge to the center a few times working around the pan.

6. Cook, with minimal stirring for 2 to 3 minutes. Add the crumbled blue cheese and cook until melted. Divide among 4 heated plates and garnish with fresh basil leaves and a few drops of pesto (optional).

# Asparagus Salad

## WITH BALSAMIC CRANBERRY VINAIGRETTE

Salad might be a misnomer here, but because the asparagus spears are drizzled with a luscious, tangy-sweet vinaigrette, I've classified this as a salad. It could be an appetizer or a side dish, too. One thing for sure, it is a delicious way to serve my favorite green vegetable. Blanching (quickly cooking then quickly stopping the cooking) is a great technique for all kinds of vegetables, and it helps keep this asparagus bright green while providing a tender-crisp texture. The vinaigrette recipe makes 1½ cups, so you will have plenty to slather on your salad greens during the following week.

### 4 SERVINGS

1. Place the first 7 ingredients (balsamic vinegar through white pepper) in a blender and blend for 10 seconds. With the blender running, slowly pour in the ½ cup olive oil. The cranberries will still be a little chunky and that is okay. Set aside.

2. Bring a large pot of salted water to boil. Prepare a large bowl of ice water. Trim the asparagus. (I take a spear and bend it in half. Where it snaps is where the tender part ends and the tough part begins. Discard the tough ends or save for a vegetable stock.)

3. When the water comes to a boil, drop the trimmed asparagus in the water and boil for 1 to 2 minutes, depending upon the thickness of the asparagus. Immediately remove the asparagus from the boiling water and plunge into the ice water to stop the cooking process. When the asparagus is cool, about 3 or 4 minutes, drain and pat dry.

4. Toss the asparagus and tomato strips with about ¼ cup or more of the vinaigrette. Line 4 plates with lettuce leaves (optional) and divide the asparagus among the 4 plates.

**Vinaigrette:**

½ cup balsamic vinegar

⅓ cup honey

¼ cup dried cranberries

¼ cup chopped yellow onion

½ teaspoon finely chopped garlic

½ teaspoon kosher salt

½ teaspoon white pepper

½ cup olive oil

**Asparagus:**

1 bunch (about 30 spears) asparagus

3 Roma tomatoes, cut into thin strips, seeds removed

8 green leaf or other lettuce leaves (optional garnish)

# Pineapple Coconut Cake

Coconut lovers will go ape over this moist, dense cake. I proudly gave this to my lovely neighbor Rosalie and a few days later I asked her what she thought. And she said, "Well, I'm sure if I liked coconut, it would be a lovely cake." Oops. I made it in a Bundt pan, but you could use a 10-inch springform pan. I didn't test it this way, but the lodge says to line the bottom of a springform pan with pineapple rings and place a maraschino cherry in the center of each ring, then top with the batter (only fill two-thirds full) and bake about 45 minutes.

### A 10-inch Bundt cake

2 cups sugar
1 cup vegetable oil
3 eggs
2 cups shredded coconut
1 (14-ounce) can coconut milk
1 (8-ounce) can crushed pineapple with syrup
1 teaspoon vanilla extract
4 cups flour
1 tablespoon baking powder

1. Preheat oven to 350°F. Spray a Bundt pan with nonstick cooking spray and set aside.

2. Beat the first 7 ingredients (sugar through vanilla) together. (I used my stand mixer, though you may do this by hand.)

3. Stir the flour and baking powder into the pineapple mixture just to moisten. Pour the batter into the prepared pan.

4. Bake for 55 to 60 minutes, or until a toothpick inserted into the center comes out clean or with just a few moist crumbs attached. The top of the cake will be dark golden brown.

5. Remove from the oven and cool 10 minutes, then turn out onto a cooling rack and cool completely.

Few places on this earth are as strikingly beautiful as the Grand Teton Mountains in northwestern Wyoming. And what better place to view them than snuggled in your lodgepole pine bed in your toasty, fireplace-warmed room at Spring Creek Ranch, a AAA Four-Diamond resort. Every room has a view. The authentically western ranch proclaims "A view with a room," and they're not kidding. A rambling spread just a few minutes drive, north of Jackson, Wyoming, Spring Creek Ranch offers a cowboy-style experience with citified flare.

Even though Jackson is just moments away, you might not make it into town because the ranch has a considerable line-up of activities to keep you occupied for weeks. In addition to cross-country skiing and sleigh rides, the ranch's mountaineers will teach you the fine art of ice-climbing. If you do venture off property, there is nearby downhill skiing at the Jackson Hole ski resort, or a snowcat trip through Yellowstone Park or even a sleigh ride through the pristine Elk Refuge. These are just a few of the activities available. It would take the rest of this book to list them all.

The ranch's fine dining restaurant, The Granary, also offers a view of the Tetons through its floor-to-ceiling picture windows. If you can take your eyes off the gorgeous mountain scenery, you'll see another sight to behold — four-star cuisine from an award-winning chef. The chef was honored with an invitation to re-create his alpine gastronomy at the James Beard House in New York City, as part of a Best Hotel Chefs celebration. After a taste of the menu the chef kindly shared, you might just find yourself booked on a flight to Jackson for more mountain cuisine and a chance to see "a view with a room."

### Spring Creek Ranch

P.O. Box 4780
Jackson, WY 83001
800.443.6139
307.733.8833
www.springcreekranch.com

**Season:**
Year-round

**Guest Capacity:**
120

**Accommodations:**
36 luxury rooms,
25 suites and
25 studio apartments

**Activities:**
Cross-country skiing; snowmobiling; dog-sledding; sleigh rides; ice-skating; heli-skiing; nearby downhill skiing;

**Peak Winter Rates:**
$$-$$$$

**Closest Ski Resort:**
Jackson Hole

## Breakfast Menu

✳ FRENCH TOAST BREAD

SPRING CREEK GRANOLA

✳ BUTTERMILK WAFFLES
WITH HUCKLEBERRY COMPOTE

✳ COCOA-KISSED SOUR CREAM COFFEECAKE

## Dinner Menu

ROASTED WINTER SQUASH SOUP

✳ ROAST TENDERLOIN OF ELK
WITH BLACKBERRY SAUCE AND
GREEN PEPPERCORN ORANGE MARMALADE

✳ FIVE GRAIN PILAF

✳ HUCKLEBERRY CRÈME BRÛLÉE

✳ RECIPE INCLUDED

# French Toast Bread

You know that Martha makes her own bread for her French toast, right? Now you can, too! The lodge bakes its bread in coffee cans and the resulting round loaves just add another gourmet touch. I tried both the coffee can and a loaf pan with equally successful results. After you bake this bread, try it with Vista Verde's Blackberry Stuffed French Toast Recipe on page 53. Martha would be proud.

### 2 ROUND (OR RECTANGULAR) LOAVES

1. Stir the lukewarm water with the yeast and 2 tablespoons of sugar in a large mixing bowl and set aside for 5 minutes.

2. Meanwhile, melt the butter with the milk in a small saucepan over medium heat. Remove from heat when the butter is melted.

3. Stir the warm butter mixture into the yeast mixture. Stir in the honey and eggs. Sprinkle 3¼ cups of flour over the yeast mixture then sprinkle the salt over the flour and stir. The dough should be slightly sticky, but add more flour, ¼ cup at a time if the dough is too wet. Cover the bowl with a kitchen towel and allow the dough to double in size in a warm spot. (It took me just over an hour, but it depends on the warmness of your kitchen, the freshness of your yeast, etc.)

4. Remove the dough to a lightly floured work surface. Stir together the 4½ teaspoons of cinnamon and sugar and sprinkle over the dough. Flatten out the dough, turning it over onto itself a few times to work in the cinnamon and sugar. Divide the dough in half and place into greased coffee cans (only one end removed), or place in two standard greased loaf pans. Allow the dough to rise to about 1 inch from the top of the can or loaf pan.

5. Preheat the oven to 375°F. Bake until top is golden brown, about 20 to 25 minutes. Remove and cool 5 minutes before removing from cans. Cool completely before slicing.

¼ cup lukewarm water
2¼ teaspoons dry yeast
2 tablespoons sugar
4 tablespoons butter
½ cup milk
1 teaspoon honey
2 eggs, lightly beaten
3¼ cups (or more) flour
1 tablespoon kosher salt
4½ teaspoons cinnamon
4½ teaspoons sugar

# Buttermilk Waffles

### WITH HUCKLEBERRY COMPOTE

This is just a good basic buttermilk batter that can be used for pancakes or waffles, though I prefer it as a waffle batter. The huckleberry is similar to the blueberry but is rarely cultivated and is usually found in the wild. There are lots of huckleberry bushes in Wyoming, close to Yellowstone Park — for the bears and for this Spring Creek Ranch waffle dish. Substitute the readily available blueberry if you're not in their neck of the woods.

**10 WAFFLES**

2⅓ cups flour
4 teaspoons baking powder
2 teaspoons baking soda
¼ teaspoon kosher salt
2 tablespoons powdered sugar
3 eggs, separated
3 cups buttermilk
1 tablespoon vegetable oil

**Huckleberry Compote (2½ cups):**
¼ cup light corn syrup
¼ cup finely chopped red onion
3 cups frozen, thawed blueberries
¼ cup Cassis (black currant liqueur)
¼ cup orange marmalade
1 tablespoon chopped fresh mint

**Waffles:**

1. Stir the flour, baking powder, baking soda, salt and powdered sugar in a large mixing bowl.

2. Beat the egg yolks with the buttermilk and oil.

3. Whip the egg whites to the soft peak stage, about 2 to 3 minutes.

4. Pour the buttermilk mixture over the flour mixture and stir just to moisten. Fold in the beaten egg whites just until you no longer see white streaks.

5. Heat a waffle maker and spray with a nonstick spray. Add a generous ¼ cup of batter to the preheated waffle maker and cook until golden brown. Serve with Huckleberry Compote or warm maple syrup.

**Huckleberry Compote:**

1. Heat the corn syrup in a medium saucepan over medium-low heat. When heated, stir in onion and cook 2 minutes. Add blueberries and increase heat to medium-high.

2. Bring to a boil and reduce to a simmer, cooking 5 minutes.

3. Add the liqueur and marmalade and simmer an additional 5 minutes, stirring frequently.

4. Remove from heat and stir in mint. Serve warm.

# Cocoa-kissed Sour Cream Coffeecake

There is cocoa in the crumb topping, but it's subtle (so add a little more if you'd like). This cake is moist and almost dessert-like instead of a breakfast bread. I've eaten it at all times of the day. As a dessert, I added a scoop of chocolate ice cream to a warm slice of cake and drizzled the whole thing with chocolate sauce. Yep, I'm still smiling.

**9 SERVINGS**

1. Preheat oven to 350°F. To prepare the topping: stir together all the topping ingredients (brown sugar through cinnamon) in a small bowl and set aside.
2. To prepare the batter: stir the flour, baking soda, baking powder and salt together and set aside.
3. Beat the butter with the sugar until light and fluffy. Add the eggs, one at a time to the sugar mixture, beating to incorporate. Stir in the vanilla.
4. Alternately, stir in the flour mixture and sour cream to the butter mixture, starting and ending with the flour mixture. The batter will be very thick.
5. Spray an 8 X 8-inch baking pan with nonstick spray. Spread half the batter on the bottom of the prepared pan. Sprinkle with ¼ cup of topping. Spread the remaining half of batter on top, and top with remaining topping.
6. Bake for 40 to 50 minutes or until a toothpick inserted in the center comes out clean or with just a few moist crumbs attached.

**Batter:**
2 cups flour
1 teaspoon baking soda
½ teaspoon baking powder
½ teaspoon kosher salt
½ cup (1 stick) butter, softened
1 cup sugar
2 eggs
¾ teaspoon vanilla
1 cup sour cream

**Topping:**
¼ cup light brown sugar
½ cup finely chopped walnuts
1½ teaspoons cocoa
½ teaspoon ground cinnamon

# Roast Tenderloin of Elk

WITH BLACKBERRY SAUCE AND GREEN PEPPERCORN ORANGE MARMALADE

*T*he marmalade is just a garnish on this dish but it adds a sweet-hot dimension. The elk is marinated for at least an hour with a wet rub mixture that contains juniper berries. Juniper berries can be found in the spice section of your grocery store, and their flavor, reminiscent of pine, really complements wild game. The lodge serves this with a delicious Five Grain Pilaf (next recipe).

---

**4 SERVINGS**

1½ to 2 pounds elk tenderloin

**Wet rub:**

2 tablespoons vegetable oil

4 teaspoons finely chopped shallot

4 teaspoons juniper berries, crushed

4 teaspoons dried parsley

2 teaspoons ground black pepper

Pinch ground cloves

**Blackberry Sauce (2 cups):**

1 cup frozen blackberries

1 tablespoon light corn syrup

¼ cup black currant liqueur or blackberry brandy

2 cups demi-glace*

1 bay leaf

1 fresh thyme sprig

1 teaspoon lemon juice

Kosher salt

White pepper

**Roast Tenderloin of Elk:**

1. Stir together all the wet rub ingredients. Coat the tenderloin completely with the rub. Place in a container, cover and marinate in the refrigerator for at least an hour, or up to 8 hours, turning occasionally.

2. Preheat oven to 375°F. Elk tenderloins really taper on the ends, with a much thicker middle section. To ensure even cooking, cut the ends of the tenderloin off so that the whole section of the middle section will be the same thickness. The ends will cook much quicker, so you want to have the 2 ends roughly the same thickness and then the middle will be thicker.

3. Heat an ovenproof skillet on high heat. Once hot, quickly sear the elk on all sides, about 5 minutes total. Place a roasting rack on a sheet pan and place the middle section of the elk on the rack (this allows heat to circulate around the meat while roasting).

4. Place the thick middle section of the elk in the oven and roast for 8 minutes. Add the end pieces to the rack and cook all the pieces for another 5 to 7 minutes for medium rare. (Elk is extremely lean and tends to dry out if cooked much beyond medium rare.) Remove elk from oven and rest 2 to 3 minutes. Slice the elk on the bias into ½-inch thick medallions, serving 3 per person. Drizzle with Blackberry Sauce and a dollop of Green Peppercorn Orange Marmalade.

**Blackberry Sauce:**

1. Heat the blackberries, corn syrup, liqueur, demi-glace and herbs in a saucepan over medium-high heat. Bring to a boil, then reduce to a simmer. Cook 30 minutes, or until ¾ of the liquid remains. Remove herbs and place sauce in a blender, working in batches to purée.

2. CAUTION: cover the top of the blender before you blend as hot liquid shoots straight up and can blow the top off.

*(continued on next page)*

**Roast Tenderloin of Elk**
*(continued from previous page)*

3. After puréeing all the sauce, strain through a sieve. Sauce should be velvety smooth and shine with a luster. Stir in lemon juice, salt and pepper to taste. Keep warm until you serve, or cool, cover and refrigerate for up to 2 days, re-heating before serving.

**Green Peppercorn Orange Marmalade:**

1. Stir together all 3 ingredients. Serve at room temperature. Will keep in the refrigerator, covered, up to 1 month.

---

*See Demi-glace under Common Procedures, page 19.

**Green Peppercorn Orange Marmalade (½ cup):**

4 tablespoons orange marmalade

2 tablespoons green peppercorns, with juice, finely chopped

1 teaspoon dried parsley

# *Five Grain Pilaf*

M ake a big batch of the five grain mixture to keep on hand because this is a great side dish. The texture is interesting, combining soft basmati rice with the chewiness of wild rice. I'm not a big fan of barley by itself, but I love it in this dish. This is a good way to get a nutritious dose of grains, and the different colors and textures look great on the plate.

---
**4 SERVINGS**

1. Bring the water to a rapid boil. Add the rice mixture, pecans, butter, salt and pepper.
2. Reduce heat, cover and simmer on low for 25 to 30 minutes. (It's okay to lift the lid and peek. All of the water should be absorbed before you turn off the heat.) Let stand 5 minutes. Pilaf should be fully cooked and soft in texture with some resistance from the wild rice. Fluff with a fork and serve hot.

2¾ cups water

1 cup five grain mix *

¼ cup chopped pecans

2 tablespoons butter

1 teaspoon kosher salt

½ teaspoon white pepper

**\*Five Grain Mix:**

1 cup each for a 5 cup yield:

• white basmati rice
• brown basmati rice
• bulgar wheat
• wild rice and
• barley

# *Huckleberry Crème Brûlée

Now this is my kind of crème brûlée! I like the light, airy texture. If you prefer a thicker, more custard-like crème brûlée, check out the Lone Mountain version on page 71. Make this the day before you plan to serve to allow enough time to chill before you add the burnt sugar top, but don't put the burnt topping on too soon or it will turn watery. After you burn the sugar on the top, you'll need about ½ an hour to 1 hour to re-chill the dessert for serving.

### 8 SERVINGS

2 cups heavy cream
½ cup sugar
plus 1 tablespoon
½ vanilla bean, split, or ½
teaspoon vanilla extract
Pinch kosher salt
6 egg yolks
¾ cup huckleberries
(blueberries) fresh or frozen
8 (4-ounce) ramekins
8 teaspoons sugar,
regular or superfine

1. Preheat oven to 325°F. Heat the cream, 1 tablespoon of sugar, the vanilla bean (or extract) and salt in a saucepan over medium heat. Bring just to a boil and remove from heat.

2. Meanwhile, beat egg yolks with remaining ½ cup sugar until lemon colored and thick, about 3 to 5 minutes by hand or 1 minute with an electric mixer. Add some of the hot cream into the yolk mixture whisking constantly. Whisk the warmed yolk mixture into the rest of the hot cream. Skim the foam from the top and strain through a sieve into a pitcher.

3. Place the ramekins in shallow roasting pan and fill evenly with the strained cream and yolk mixture. Sprinkle each with a handful of blueberries. Place in the preheated oven. Pour enough hot tap water into the roasting pan to come up half way up the sides of the ramekins.

4. Cover roasting pan with foil and bake 15 to 20 minutes, or until the edges of the ramekins are firm and the center only jiggles about the size of a nickel when shaken. Remove, cool for an hour then cover each ramekin with plastic wrap and refrigerate for 8 hours or overnight.

5. To serve, sprinkle tops with 1 teaspoon of sugar and place under a preheated broiler or use a blowtorch to caramelize the sugar. Chill again so that the burnt sugar hardens and the custard is completely chilled again.

*※ Photograph on page C-22*

# *Acknowledgements*

Once again, my book is a collaborative effort by an extremely talented group of individuals. Without these gifted souls, I would be just a writer in search of a topic. My gratitude and admiration for these friends, family and associates will be lasting evidence of the debt I owe each of them.

- To my husband, Jeff, my inspiration and soul mate. He is gifted in so many ways and I am constantly amazed at his ability to quickly learn and master new skills. I asked him if he would take some food shots for this book and even though he had no formal training in photography, he agreed. It was a wild experience working together again and we once more learned a tremendous amount about the art of patience. I'm so grateful he took the time to produce these beautiful shots, and I couldn't be prouder of the results.

- To my editor, Olin Ashley. What a thrill it was to work with him again on this book. He polished my sentences and caught my mistakes, all with a loving hand and incredible support (with just the right amount of affectionate sarcasm thrown in to keep me on my toes). Thank you, Dad. I wouldn't want to do a book without you.

- To my beautiful mother, who endured a painful but successful year of chemotherapy with grace, humility and faith. She was so supportive of my efforts and let me take over her kitchen on several occasions to cook for television shows and other cooking demonstrations I lined up in the Dallas/Ft. Worth area. I know some days she would have rather had a quiet house, but she never complained about my productions.

- To my illustrator, Betsy Hillis. She illustrated my ranch book and I wanted her to do this book as well. She is in such demand that I wasn't sure she could squeeze in some original art for me. But she did and all the little snow scenes and pine boughs in this book are the result of her talented hand. And, for those of you wondering, yes, she did graduate from White Zinfandel to Cabernet Sauvignon. Thank goodness!

- To Christy Moeller-Mosel at ATG Productions. She took my rough concept for a book cover and turned it into a work of art. She was so easy to work with, so accommodating and always gave me her opinion and lots of options from which to choose.

- To Michele O'Hagan at Masterpiece Publishing. The interior design of the book is the result of her efforts and I love how she transformed Betsy's illustrations into cool, frosty scenes.

- To Tom Hummel at Toppan Printing. I could not have asked for a more helpful, kind, supporting partner in printing. Tom was calm, cool and collected at every stage of the process, and played the mentor/educator role for me, demystifying the complicated world of printing.

# Acknowledgements
(CONTINUED)

- To Donna Bachman, friend, former award-winning chef and teacher. Donna was invaluable in helping me translate the unique language of corporate chefs, as well as testing some of the recipes herself. I can always count on Donna as a solid springboard for my ideas.

- To Gaye Ingram, CCP. Gaye's book, *Webster's New World Dictionary of Culinary Arts* was opened beside my computer during the entire writing process, and often, Gaye was on the other end of the phone with me, helping me decide how to describe a technique or style a particular phrase. She is a wonderful friend and an extraordinarily talented food professional.

- To Susan Prieskorn and Letty Flatt. There are no better bakers than these two ladies as far as I'm concerned. Both were incredibly helpful and generous in sharing their knowledge and expertise.

- To the staff at Paul's Pantry, a delightful gourmet shop at El Pedregal in Carefree, Arizona — Lorna, Rita, Erma, Nancy, Kathleen, and Cindy. Our food shots are beautiful because we used housewares from Paul's Pantry. I really appreciate how helpful and supportive all the ladies have been on this book.

- To Carol Swinton for locating a Maytag blue cheese source as well as finding the Ideal Cheese Shop for me.

- To Chef Cathy Rosenberg for her sharp eye and thoughtful comments. Who knew that fillet versus filet had so much meaning to the French?

- To my Scottsdale Culinary Institute student testers, Scott Clapp and Leon Mathis. Both men made being in the kitchen all day and night for months fun and productive.

Scott was near the end of his schooling during our recipe testing and therefore was adventurous and constructively critical. He was a tremendous help and I really enjoyed his culinary creativity. He's on to a food writing career now and I wish him the best of luck. Perhaps someday we will collaborate on another project.

Leon had just begun his culinary schooling when we started testing, so he was wide-eyed, curious, and eager to learn new and exciting ingredients and techniques. He has a whole new respect for hot liquid in the blender, too. Leon is a hard worker, a good man and will be an asset to our field.

# *Acknowledgements*
## (CONTINUED)

- To my tasters I owe many thanks. The critiques were extremely helpful but the best part was listening to each of my tasters really give me their most thoughtful opinions of each dish they tasted. We both benefited from the experience.

Marilyn Robertson is a dream come true. Not only was she one of my most important tasters, she was actually one of my testers, too. Marilyn is a fabulous cook and loves nothing better than to spend a day in the kitchen. She spent many days in her kitchen re-testing recipes and helping me tweak and ease instructions and ingredients. She was a lifesaver and I can't tell you how much I love having her near.

Rosalie and Alex Passovoy were critical tasters with the ranch cookbook as well as this book. I could always count on them to come at a moment's notice and taste a dish. They also provided some special tasters for me this time, their grandchildren Mark and Emily Passovoy. Mark and Emmy each spent a separate week with their grandparents and often came to taste my dishes. For a couple of young teenagers, I was impressed with their adventurous palates, willing to try anything new and to share their honest opinions.

Liz, Larry and Kate Dobrin also were very helpful during the recipe testing, willing to take the extra food and share their opinions. Liz and Larry love good food so I trusted their comments and insights.

Pat and Jan Johnston win the prize for best note taking. I could always count on a detailed report after leaving a dish with them and I really appreciate the seriousness in which they undertook their task.

Pete and Malen Eyerly were always willing to try something, even if they really were not hungry. I think they didn't want to hurt my feelings. Malen, who really doesn't like salmon, boldly tried the Gravlax, and I think I actually heard an "mmmm" from her.

I also want to thank my other tasters, including Al and Kathy Keir, T. J. McCue, Walter Krauss, Jim MacKenzie, and Orson Kinney.

- Last, but certainly not least, I want to thank all the properties and their staff who helped me gather the information for this book. I thoroughly enjoyed working with each and every one of them. In alphabetical order, they are: Lisa-Marie Allendorf, Brian Aspell, Matt Baldwin, David Barrocas, Beth Bartlett, Pam Blanton, Laurie Bott, Jim Bray, Robert Breyette, Gerard Brunett, Nancy Cooke, Reggie Cooper, Robert Corliss, Randy Cysck, Kent Elliott, John Ellsworth, Letty Flatt, Steve Fralin, Thomas Gay, Jonathon (you're the man) Gillespie, Christa Thompson Graff, Jennifer Hawkins, Tricia Hayes, Marcia Hara, Heidi Jeromin, Mark Johnson, Karen Kelly, Roxanna Kestner, Wayne and Judy Kilpatrick, Kathryn Kincannon, Jason Knibb, Jennifer Kohler, Missy Larsen, Mary Jane Lawrence, Keith Luce, Tanya Mark, Laura Messina, Bryan Moscatello, John and Suzanne Munn, Rustin Newton, Clark Norris, Jim Norton, Tom Romagnuolo, Jason Sharp, Coni Thornburg, Annie Wallis, and Julie Wilson.

# Sources

## ■ Anything and everything:

### A.J.'s Fine Foods

23251 N. Pima Rd.
Scottsdale, AZ 85255
480.563.5070

7141 E. Lincoln Dr.
Scottsdale, AZ 85253
480.998.0052

10105 E. Via Linda #110
Scottsdale, AZ 85258
480.391.9863

13226 N. 7th St.
Phoenix, AZ 85022
602.863.3500

5017 N. Central Ave.
Phoenix, AZ 85012
602.230.7015

7131 W. Ray Road #37
Chandler, AZ 85226
480.705.0011

Think of A. J.'s as a fresh farmers market, a wine cellar, a fishmonger, a local butcher, a bakery and a specialty gourmet foods purveyor. Everything I needed for the recipes in this book I found at A. J.'s. Even if you don't live near an A. J.'s you can still enjoy their products and services. Visit their website at **www.ajsfinefoods.com** or call any one of the stores.

## ■ Blue Corn Meal:

### Jane Butel's Pecos Valley Spice Company

P.O. Box 964
Albuquerque, NM 87103
800.473.8226
**www.pecosvalley.com**
Extensive collection of southwestern ingredients including blue cornmeal and authentic masa. Also carry large selection of dried chile pods and ground chiles, as well as mixes and cookbooks/videos by noted southwestern author Jane Butel.

## ■ Cheese:

### Ideal Cheese Shop, Ltd.

1205 Second Avenue
(at 63rd St.)
New York, NY 10021
800.382.0109
**www.idealcheese.com**
Incredible selection of Old World and New World cheeses. Nice gift selections, too. I found smoked Mozzarella (for the Poached Eggs over Black Bean Salsa recipe) on their site.

## ■ Chiles:

### Jane Butel's Pecos Valley Spice Company

P.O. Box 964
Albuquerque, NM 87103
800.473.8226
**www.pecosvalley.com**
Large selection of dried chiles both pods and ground.

### Southwest Chile Company
**www.southwestchile.com**
Authentic Hatch New Mexican green chiles (roasted, peeled and frozen), and other dried chiles.

## ■ Chocolate:

### Only Gourmet

P.O. Box 2214
Orinda, CA 94563
**www.onlygourmet.com**
High quality couverture (chocolate) from Bernard Callebaut.

### The Chocolate Source
800.214.4926
**www.chocolatesource.com**
Vahlrona brand couverture, for the Vahlrona Chocolate Tart recipe from The Lodge at Vail.

## ■ Coffee:

**Cave Creek Coffee Company**
P.O. Box 4390
Cave Creek, AZ 85327
480.499.0603
www.cavecreekcoffee.com
Way cool beans, like the robust Cowboy Beans, smooth Spur Cross blend and a host of other delicious, fresh-roasted Arabica beans. Owners Dave and Anita Anderson have created a java shop with ambiance and style, and they will ship their custom-blended beans to you.

**Little City Roasting Company**
3403 Guadalupe
Austin, TX 78705
512.467.2326
512.459.9670 (fax)
www.littlecity.com
Fresh-roasted coffee blends, including custom blends. Try Top Shelf Blend and the Little City special blend. Owner Donna Taylor-DiFrank has kept Austin buzzing since 1993. Little City gladly ships.

**Only Gourmet**
P.O. Box 2214
Orinda, CA 94563
www.onlygourmet.com
Only Gourmet carries several coffee manufacturer lines, including award-winning Oren's Daily Roast from New York City.

## ■ Gourmet Foods and Housewares:

**Paul's Pantry at El Pedregal**
P.O. Box 2207
Carefree, AZ 85377
480.488.4300
www.paulspantry.com
Fabulous gourmet shop! Lots of beautiful place settings, napkins, cookware, gadgets and nice selection of wine, handcrafted candies and specialty foods. All the food shots inside this book were styled using housewares from Paul's Pantry (except the Deer Valley shot). Get your hands on their catalog and visit when you're in the Phoenix area.

**Only Gourmet**
P.O. Box 2214
Orinda, CA 94563
www.onlygourmet.com
Find smoked salmon, caviar, pate, champagne, chocolates and more at this e-retailer.

**Sur La Table**
www.surlatable.com
If you have a store nearby then you know what a great store this is. I love the original shop across from Pike Place Market in Seattle. I found the ring molds needed for The Little Nell's Zucchini Tarts while surfing on this site.

## ■ Honey:

**Robson's Old West Honey Company**
P.O. Box 428
Aguila, AZ 85320
520.685.2439
520.685.2343 (fax)
Sonoran Desert Mesquite Honey is delicious, and I used it for all the recipes calling for honey in this book. They also sell under the brand name Silver Meadow. The owner, Charles H. Robson, has written an informative book called *Seven Health Secrets from the Hive,* now in its fourth edition.

## ■ Nuts:

**J. J. Hull's**
4649 N. Detroit
Toledo, OH 43612
www.jjhulls.com
Good selection of both snacking and baking nuts, look for pepitas and hazel-nuts (also called filberts), both of which are needed for the Triple Creek Granola.

*(continued on next page)*

### ■ Sauces:

I used a brand from Custom Foods called Custom Master's Touch Sauce Bases for the demi-glace and hollandaise sauces in this book. (www. customfoods.com) They don't sell directly to consumers, so check with your grocery store to see if they carry it or if they can order it for you. If you can't locate this product in your area, call A. J.'s Fine Foods (see previous page).

### ■ Spices:

**Penzeys Spices**
P.O. Box 933
Muskego, WI 53150
800.741.7787
**www.penzeys.com**
Serious spices for serious cooks. All kinds of custom blended spices, too. Try the Juniper Berries (for the Gravlax) and Chinese Five-Spice Powder (for the Butternut Squash Chowder), and also stock up on black and white peppercorns for everyday use.

**Jane Butel's Pecos Valley Spice Company**
P.O. Box 964
Albuquerque, NM 87103
800.473.8226
**www.pecosvalley.com**
One of the best collections of southwestern spices, look for Mexican Oregano and the freshest ground cumin I've ever tasted. They have a nice collection of BBQ mixes, too.

# Bibliography

*Cross-Country Ski Vacations,*
by Jonathan Wiesel,
Sante Fe: John Muir Publications, 1997.

*Food Photography and Styling,*
by John F. Carafoil,
New York: Amphoto, 1992.

*The Great Ranch Cookbook: Spirited Recipes
and Rhetoric from America's Best Guest Ranches,*
by Gwen Ashley Walters,
Carefree, Arizona: Guest Ranch Link, 1998.

*The Recipe Writer's Handbook,*
by Barbara Gibbs Ostmann and Jane L. Baker,
New York: John Wiley & Sons, Inc., 1997.

*Rocky Mountain Skiing,* by Claire Walter, Rev. Ed.,
Golden, Colorado: Fulcrum Publishing, 1996.

*Skiing USA: The Guide For Skiers and Snowboarders,*
by Clive Hobson, 2nd Ed.,
New York: Fodor's Travel Publications, Inc. 1997.

*Webster's New World Dictionary of Culinary Arts,*
by Steven Labensky, Gaye G. Ingram
and Sarah R. Labensky,
New York: Prentice Hall, 1997.

# Glossary

**Adobo sauce:** a Mexican sauce of chiles, spices and vinegar. Canned chipotles are generally seasoned with this spicy sauce.

**Ancho Chile:** the dried form of a poblano chile, which is relatively wide at the stem end, thus indicating it is a mild chile on the heat scale, with a rating of about 3 on a 10 point scale (jalapeno is rated 5).

**Asiago:** a hard grating cheese made from cow's milk and originally from Northern Italy. A great substitute for Parmesan cheese.

**Barley:** an ancient grain used mostly for animal feed and in alcohol production. Most commonly known brand for the dinner table is pearled barley, though it is not the most nutritious barley because the bran has been removed.

**Basmati:** a specific long-grain rice from the Himalayas. Known for its sweet fragrance and delicate flavor. Basmati is a staple of Indian and Middle Eastern markets, but is also widely available in the U.S.

**Beef Base:** a product made from dehydrating beef stock, making a paste-like substance that may be reconstituted (with water) back into a liquid stock. It is similar to bouillon, but contains more stock and fewer additives than bouillon. There are many brands on the market, including *Better Than Bouillon* that comes in beef, chicken, ham, lobster, vegetable or clam flavors.

**Betty:** baked pudding dating back to Colonial times. Most commonly known is Apple Brown Betty with apples and brown sugar, while this book has a banana version, Warm Banana Betty, with gingersnap cookie crumbs.

**Blanch:** quick-cooking technique used to set color or to partially cook a vegetable to be finished later (or frozen) that involves boiling water and an ice bath. For example, green peas may be blanched in boiling water (usually salted) for 1 or 2 minutes, then plunged into ice water to stop the cooking process. The bright green color is set and the peas are partially cooked, ready for a salad or a sauce, such as the Mint Green Pea Purée for the Potato-crusted Halibut from The Lodge at Vail.

**Brioche:** butter and egg-rich yeast bread from France. Sometimes it is baked in a special pan called Brioche pan, with fluted sides, a narrow bottom and wide top.

**Capirotada:** a Mexican bread pudding baked with a sugar syrup of sugar, onions, tomatoes and cinnamon instead of the traditional egg custard. The dish also contains pine nuts and raisins.

**Challa:** traditional Jewish yeast bread made with lots of eggs and usually honey or sugar. The most common form is a braided loaf.

**Chiffonade:** a specific knife cut that shreds green vegetables and herbs into long strips. Basil leaves, for example, are rolled crosswise into tight "cigars" and sliced crosswise into thin strips, less than $\frac{1}{8}$ of an inch.

**Chutney:** originally an Indian condiment. Contains fruit, spices, sugar and vinegar.

# Glossary

(CONTINUED)

**Cold-smoking:** a method to cure or preserve foods (usually meats) using a very low temperature (55–80°F) over a long period of time. The food is generally not fully cooked after cold-smoking and must be cooked further before consumption. Cold-smoking is a way to add a smoke flavor to foods. Most cold-smoked foods are first soaked in a salt brine and the end result is a much more concentrated flavor than smoking at a higher temperature.

**Compote:** fruit, either fresh or dried, cooked in sugar and water then mixed with spices and sometimes nuts. Used as a condiment or sauce.

**Coulis:** French term for puréed sauce, generally fruit but may also be a vegetable, like the Red and Yellow Pepper Coulis for Vista Verde's Chile-encrusted Pork Tenderloin.

**Crostini:** thin small toast rounds that serve as a base for an appetizer like the Crab Crostini from the Cortina Inn and Resort. Crostini is "little toasts" in Italian.

**Flapjack:** another word for an American pancake.

**Fontina:** if the cheese is labeled Fontina Val d'Aosta, it is an Italian semi-soft to firm cheese made from a female sheep (ewe). There is an American version of fontina that is similar, but made from cow's milk. Substitute Swiss, Edam or Gouda.

**Frittata:** open-faced omelet of either Spanish or Italian heritage, or both.

**Fritters:** deep-fried cake, either sweet or savory. Most commonly known is an Apple Fritter dusted with powdered sugar, although this book has a shrimp appetizer called Maine Shrimp Fritters with Hickory Bell Pepper Ketchup.

**Gnocchi:** Italian for dumplings. Made with regular flour, semolina flour (pasta flour), potatoes or other grains, and either boiled or baked.

**Huckleberry:** similar to a blueberry in taste and appearance. Grown only in the wild, the huckleberry has a slightly thicker skin than the blueberry and only 10 tiny hard seeds in the center (the blueberry has many more seeds).

**Jus:** French term for "juice," usually referring to the natural juices released from meats and poultry as they cook, and served as sauce for the dish.

**Medallions:** cut of meat that is usually small and round, such as a slice of a beef, pork or venison tenderloin.

**Pepitas:** the inner seed of a pumpkin seed. Green, long and narrow, the seed may be eaten raw or toasted and salted. Used extensively in southwestern cooking.

**Poach:** liquid cooking method where the item to be cooked is submerged into a barely simmering liquid (about 180°F). The liquid may be water (generally used for poached eggs) or a flavorful broth or wine used for poaching fish or chicken.

# Glossary
## (CONTINUED)

**Roux:** a mixture of fat and flour for the purpose of thickening sauces and soups and adding extra flavor. A roux is cooked first to various degrees of brown (blonde, pale, brown). After adding a cooked roux to sauce or soup, it must be cooked for 15 to 20 minutes to cook out the starch.

**Sabayon:** French version of the Italian zabaglione sauce. This rich dessert sauce is cooked, using whipped egg yolks, sugar and wine (generally Chablis or Champagne, though the Italians would only consider Marsala).

**Saltimbocca:** traditionally made with veal, this Italian dish consists of veal medallions, pounded thin and sautéed in butter then braised in white wine. Sage and prosciutto are standard ingredients. The Strater Hotel presents a different twist with a chicken Saltimbocca.

**Sauté:** One of the most misused terms in cooking. To sauté is to cook quickly in a small amount of fat (oil, butter, etc.). If you are "sautéing" for more than a few minutes, then you're really not sautéing, but more likely pan-frying.

**Slurry:** a mixture of a starch (cornstarch, arrowroot) and water used to thicken sauces and soups without adding extra fat. Use 1 tablespoon of starch and 1 tablespoon of cold water per 1 cup of liquid to be thickened and mix thoroughly. Liquid must be boiling before slurry is added to thicken.

**Streusel:** a topping for baked goods containing butter, sugar, nuts and spices that is placed on top of muffins, cakes, etc., before baking.

**Strudel:** German pastry consisting of many layers of thin dough wrapped around a filling (sweet or savory) and baked until golden brown.

**Vahlrona:** a high-end brand of baking chocolate known as couverture. To be classified as couverture chocolate, it must contain at least 32% cocoa butter. The Vahlrona brand contains anywhere from 56% to 70+%, and is a preferred brand among top pastry chefs.

# Index

# *Index*
## (CONTINUED)

# Index

(CONTINUED)

THE COOL MOUNTAIN COOKBOOK

# *Index*

(CONTINUED)

# *Index*

## (CONTINUED)

# *Index*
(CONTINUED)

# *Index*

## (CONTINUED)

# Index

(CONTINUED)

# Index

(CONTINUED)

# *Index*

## (CONTINUED)

# Index

(CONTINUED)

# *Index*

## (CONTINUED)

# *Index*

(CONTINUED)

## The Cool Mountain Cookbook

**Pen & Fork**
P.O. Box 5165
Carefree, AZ 85377
**480.595.0890 (fax)**
*www. penandfork.com*

■ **Please send:**

___ Copies of *The Cool Mountain Cookbook*
   @ $19.95 each .............................................................$_____

___ Copies of *The Great Ranch Cookbook*
   @ $19.95 each .............................................................$_____

■ **Shipping and Handling:**

$3.50 for 1st book ...........................................................$_____

$2.00 for each additional book .......................................$_____

Subtotal ......................................................$_____

AZ residents ad 7.1% tax.............$_____

**Total**...........................................$_____

*Enclose a check made payable to Pen & Fork*

■ **Shipping Information** (please print):

Name _____

Address _____

City, State, Zip_____

Phone _____

Email_____

Visit *www. penandfork.com* for bonus recipes.

## The Cool Mountain Cookbook

**Pen & Fork**
P.O. Box 5165
Carefree, AZ 85377
**480.595.0890 (fax)**
*www. penandfork.com*

■ **Please send:**

___ Copies of *The Cool Mountain Cookbook*
@ $19.95 each ...............................................$_____

___ Copies of *The Great Ranch Cookbook*
@ $19.95 each ...............................................$_____

■ **Shipping and Handling:**

$3.50 for 1st book ..........................................$_____

$2.00 for each additional book ......................$_____

Subtotal ....................................$_____

AZ residents ad 7.1% tax.............$_____

**Total**..........................................$_____

*Enclose a check made payable to Pen & Fork*

■ **Shipping Information** (please print):

Name _____

Address _____

City, State, Zip_____

Phone _____

Email_____

Visit *www. penandfork.com* for bonus recipes.

A Popular Science Book

# BUILD YOUR OWN
# Wood Toys, Gifts & Furniture

# R. J. De Cristoforo

**Popular Science Books**
New York

 **Van Nostrand Reinhold Company**
New York  Cincinnati  Toronto
London  Melbourne

*Published by*

**Popular Science Books**
Times Mirror Magazines, Inc.
380 Madison Avenue
New York, NY 10017

*Distributed to the trade by*

Van Nostrand Reinhold Company
135 West 50th Street
New York, NY 10020

Library of Congress Catalog Card Number: 80–5885
ISBN 0-442-21883-0

MANUFACTURED IN THE UNITED STATES OF AMERICA

For all the children—
and the grownups too

# Contents

## Trucks and Cars

## On-Track Train

## The Train

## Games

## Wagons

## Riding Toys

## Odds and Ends

# III. Mainly for Adults: Gifts and Furniture

## Lathe Projects

## A Collection of Tables

## Trio of Campy Table Lamps

## More Furniture

## Outdoor Plant Containers

## Found Whimseys

# Preface

This is a book of toy, gift, and furniture projects. Some can be completed in an evening; others require more time. Some projects are comparatively *easy* to build. But if you want the easier projects to show good craftsmanship, they will need the same attention and care as the *harder* projects.

The first section in this book has information on materials such as lumber, lumber products, and fastening hardware; information on dowels; tool techniques; and so on. Next come the toy projects. This section is introduced by a chapter showing the secrets for making a variety of wheels and axles—needed for most of the toys. After that come the many projects mainly for adults.

All drawings show full details and recommended measurements. You can transfer patterns to wood by using the enlarging-by-squares method. This method also allows you to change sizes of projects. For example, if the drawing recommends $\frac{1}{2}$-inch squares, you can always opt for a larger version, using $\frac{3}{4}$- or 1-inch squares. Then too, it's not critical that a toy car be a certain length if you prefer a different length.

I've had each of the toys and games in this book child tested. Adults have tested the household furnishings. And many items have also been market tested. That is, they would likely sell if you made them for extra income.

The essential materials are wood and wood products. All projects can be made either with hand or power tools, which really only determine production time, not quality. After all, a carefully cut curve looks the same whether cut with a jigsaw or a coping saw. The occasional plastics included are items such as recycled caps from bottles and pens, and some decorative tapes. Nothing here needs a battery.

You can enjoy using some of the toy projects *with* children. There's a tick-tack-toe game with some extra functions. There's a spiral game that will test your coordination as well as a child's. There's a wagon for the child to pull and tote things in. And there's a wagon for *you* to pull when toting the child. A no-gas car will give you exercise, since you push it up a gentle slope after the child drives it down. Yet this car will be strong enough for *you* to ride in too—provided the child lets you.

Because children don't object to the natural look of wood, I gave the toy and game projects natural finishes. But that shouldn't stop you from substituting bright colors. If you do, be sure to work with non-toxic sealers and finishes.

In these days of save-a-dollar do-it-yourselfing, it's easy to forget the plain old fun that should be part of home workshop tasks. Of course, there's great satisfaction to be had in doing home chores you'd otherwise hire out for. But it's also smart to tackle projects just for the fun of doing them—and then perhaps for the added joy of giving the finished projects as gifts.

Since all projects in this book are for home and family, they'll offer you opportunities for family activities that can substitute for passive diversions such as television. I can vouch for the interest the toy and game projects arouse in children. In fact, kids seem *determined* to help build them.

You may be surprised at the tasks children can do if you offer encouragement and instruction. Here's a good opportunity to teach the use of a tool or to demonstrate, for example, the different results from sandpapering with and across wood grain. Kids don't need kids' tools, which are generally useless anyway and can lead to discouragement. Of course, you should adjust your expectations to the child's readiness. Some children learn quicker and handle tools better than other children of the same age. So you'll have to chose tools and determine your supervision accordingly. Yet it's common that a four- or five-year old can use a hand saw correctly. Not a full-size saw! A 12- to 14-inch saw will serve well. Such "short" saws are available individually, or they can be found in a "Nest of Saws" package. For kids, avoid use of a keyhole or compass type saw since these usually have dangerously sharp points.

Whatever the tool, kids can learn only what you teach. If you want them to help, want them to enjoy what they are doing, and want to enjoy them while they are doing it, remind yourself to be a patient teacher. Otherwise the whole proposition might be a mistake. Be sure that you and your helpers have fun. That's important.

I'd like to thank Georgia-Pacific Corporation for permission to reuse texts which I earlier contributed to their book *Great Possibilities for the Home.* Those texts and project ideas make up principal parts of projects 54, 55, 56, 57, 61, 62, 64, 66, 67, 68, and 69.

R.J. De Cristoforo

# I.
# PROJECT ESSENTIALS

1

# MATERIALS AND TOOLS

## LUMBER

The materials used for the majority of the projects in this book, especially those in the toys and games section, are pine and fir lumber, good grades of plywood, some pieces of hardwood, and occasionally some hardboard. The materials lists that accompany many of the drawings do not always specify the wood species to use. They simply state "lumber" or "plywood." This allows you options.

Usually, birch can be used—in place of maple, for example, because they are both hardwoods. But a hardwood can't be substituted for a softwood.

And you shouldn't substitute lumber for plywood. Because you can make many of the projects in this book from small pieces, having a choice allows the use of suitable "scrap," that is, leftovers you previously couldn't bring yourself to discard or burn.

Wood is classified as *hardwood* or *softwood,* but the terms are not truly adequate since they are just forestry designations that tell whether the wood came from a broad-leaved, deciduous tree (hardwood) or a needle-bearing, evergreen tree (softwood). In each category the actual *working* hardness or softness of some particular species confutes the classification. For example, fir is a "softwood" that is quite hard. Poplar is a "hardwood" that is relatively soft and easy to work.

Pine, cedar, redwood, and fir are all softwoods. Mahogany and walnut (both easy to cut) and maple, birch, cherry, and oak are common hardwoods. Here are some factors that can influence your selection of wood.

**Appearance.** An elaborate, heirloom-type project, where material cost is not a factor, justifies an exotic species with an attractive grain and painstaking finishing that enhances the design. If your project were a grandfather's clock, you might select traditional clock woods such as mahogany, walnut, or cherry.

**Use.** There is little point in using fine cabinet woods to make garage storage shelves. This principle also applies to particular components in a project. If the part isn't visible (such as a reinforcement piece), you can make it from a more economical grade of wood.

**Part Size.** When the width of a project part is greater than 11 inches, you may want to choose between gluing up slabs of lumber or working with plywood. Your choice can also be influenced by your tools. It's not difficult to cut and assemble lumber slabs if you have a table saw, a jointer, and plenty of clamps. Yet even if you have an elaborate shop, you may opt for plywood. There are plenty of good grades of plywood that won't make you feel you've compromised on the project's ultimate appearance.

**Wear and Tear.** Wooden wheels on a project like a wagon that will be used outdoors and may bear the weight of a passenger should be made of a tough wood such as maple, birch, or fir. The wheels on light-weight pull toys, of course, can be made of tough woods too, but pine and even some grades of plywood will do.

**Personal Taste.**   Then too you might choose one wood species over others because you like its natural finish, or because its natural finish may match your home decor. A kitchen towel rack and shelf can receive a natural or a painted finish. So if I recommend fine lumber and you decide to use plywood, that's your privilege.

## BUYING LUMBER

Lumber grades indicate quality and tell you roughly the kind and number of blemishes and defects a board may contain.

**Softwood Grades.**   Although there are some differences in grading procedures, the three basic classifications for softwoods are *select, common,* and *structural.* Each classification has subgroups that indicate quality.

• In the *select* group, which is kiln dried, the A-clear is top of the line, being wood that is practically defect-free. The B-select will have some blemishes, but can still be used for a natural finish. C and D grades have defects that can be concealed with paint.

• In the *common* group, classes are by number, with number 1 being free of decay, splits, and warp. But number 1 is allowed to have blemishes and tight knots. Numbers 2, 3, 4, and 5 decrease in quality. Number 5 isn't good for much other than filler in rough construction.

• The *structural* group doesn't include lumber of use for projects in this book. Its grades include *construction, standard, utility,* and *economy.* Quality declines rapidly from *construction* grade to *economy.*

It's convenient that most lumberyards allow you to select your own wood. Often, you may decide upon a lesser, more economical grade because you can see the salvageable material in it. A lumberyard "shelving bin" may contain scraps and odd pieces of various grades at discount prices.

It pays to browse and then inspect for grain, knots, blemishes, and weight. For example, the heavier of two similar B- or C-grade pieces may contain more moisture. The moist, heavier piece would be less desirable. Yet if B- or C-grade pieces have no other defects, you may be able to cut A-select pieces from them.

As **Figure 1** shows, actual wood dimensions are less than the dimensions you order. That's because sizes are labeled in the *rough* dimensions rather than in actual *dressed* dimensions. Remember this when reading a materials list. If the part is listed as $1\frac{1}{2} \times 3\frac{1}{2}$ inches, what you need is a 2 × 4. This does not apply to lengths. If you order a board 6 or 8 or 10 feet long, that's what you will get.

**Hardwood Grades.**    Hardwood grading differs from softwood grading. A piece of softwood is usually judged and graded as a whole after it has been dressed. Hardwood is examined in the rough and graded on the basis of the clear wood it contains, rather than on its store of defects.

• *Firsts* and *Seconds* in hardwood grades are commonly combined and labeled as FAS. The material is judged from the poor side—which should allow you to get clear cuttings most of the way through. Technically, you should be able to get clear wood that is a minimum of 6 inches wide and 8 feet long.

• *Selects* are the next step down. While defects are allowed on the back side, the good or "face" side should be clear in pieces measuring not less than 4 inches wide and 6 feet long.

• Two other grades that might be worth considering are number 1 and number 2 common. They usually contain so much waste that they are cut up to remove bad parts and sold as "shorts." But such small pieces can be utilized as small parts for projects.

Hardwood thicknesses are often labeled in quarter inches. For example, 4/4 (four-quarter stock) means 1 inch thick. 6/4 (six-quarter stock) means

**Fig. 1.** This chart shows the nominal and actual sizes of softwood lumber. The text explains hardwood dimensions.

| End Sections | Nominal Size (what you order) | Actual Size (what you get in inches) |
|---|---|---|
| ▭ | 1 X 2 | $\frac{3}{4} \times 1\frac{1}{2}$ |
| ▭ | 1 X 3 | $\frac{3}{4} \times 2\frac{1}{2}$ |
| ▭ | 1 X 4 | $\frac{3}{4} \times 3\frac{1}{2}$ |
| ▭ | 1 X 5 | $\frac{3}{4} \times 4\frac{1}{2}$ |
| ▭ | 1 X 6 | $\frac{3}{4} \times 5\frac{1}{2}$ |
| ▭ | 1 X 8 | $\frac{3}{4} \times 7\frac{1}{4}$ |
| ▭ | 1 X 10 | $\frac{3}{4} \times 9\frac{1}{4}$ |
| ▭ | 1 X 12 | $\frac{3}{4} \times 11\frac{1}{4}$ |
| ▫ | 2 X 2 | $1\frac{1}{2} \times 1\frac{1}{2}$ |
| ▭ | 2 X 3 | $1\frac{1}{2} \times 2\frac{1}{2}$ |
| ▭ | 2 X 4 | $1\frac{1}{2} \times 3\frac{1}{2}$ |
| ▭ | 2 X 6 | $1\frac{1}{2} \times 5\frac{1}{2}$ |
| ▭ | 2 X 8 | $1\frac{1}{2} \times 7\frac{1}{4}$ |
| ▭ | 2 X 10 | $1\frac{1}{2} \times 9\frac{1}{4}$ |
| ▭ | 2 X 12 | $1\frac{1}{2} \times 11\frac{1}{4}$ |
| ▫ | 3 X 4 | $2\frac{1}{2} \times 3\frac{1}{2}$ |
| ▫ | 4 X 4 | $3\frac{1}{2} \times 3\frac{1}{2}$ |
| ▭ | 4 X 6 | $3\frac{1}{2} \times 5\frac{1}{2}$ |
| ▫ | 6 X 6 | $5\frac{1}{2} \times 5\frac{1}{2}$ |
| ▫ | 8 X 8 | $7\frac{1}{2} \times 7\frac{1}{2}$ |

$1\frac{1}{2}$ inches. 12/4 (twelve-quarter stock) means 3 inches. These dimensions refer to the wood in the *rough* state. The material loses thickness when dried and dressed. In a local lumberyard that stocks hardwoods you'll be able to see and measure what you are buying. If you order through a catalog, the thicknesses of dressed hardwood will run approximately as follows: 1 inch (4/4) will be $\frac{3}{4}$ to $\frac{13}{16}$ inch. $1\frac{1}{2}$ inches (6/4) will be $1\frac{1}{4}$ to $1\frac{3}{8}$ inches, and so on. If your needs are specific, be sure to state that you are listing *finished* sizes.

## PLYWOOD

As in lumber, these man-made panels can be either *hardwood* or *softwood*. The terms tell what materials were used as the surface veneers. Common softwood plywoods are Douglas fir, pine, redwood, and cedar. The variety of hardwoods is vast, ranging from mahogany and walnut to rosewood and teak.

The face veneer has everything to do with appearance, but the workability of the panel is determined chiefly by the panel's core. The cut edges on veneer-core plywood, especially the economical shop-grade panels, are difficult to finish. They will often have voids which should be filled if the edge is left exposed. Cabinet-grade, veneer-core plywoods have tighter cores, and voids are rare. After a good sanding and finishing job, an exposed edge-ply can serve as an element of design rather than an eyesore.

Lumber-core panels work almost like solid wood. The core is actually a slab of solid boards that are edge-glued and run parallel to the grain of the surface veneers. A second layer of veneer (called crossbanding) runs at right angles between the face veneers and the core. Because lumber-core panels essentially have a lumber edge, you should have little trouble smoothing and finishing, drilling for dowels, and shaping.

Whatever plywood you use and no matter whether you finish naturally or paint, be careful when handling plywood edges. They're a great source of splinters.

## TOOLS AND TOOL HINTS

**Measuring and Marking Devices.** "Measure twice, cut once"—that's good advice. No matter how good your cut is, the joint or part won't be right if you're not accurate and if you haven't carefully marked the dimension point or line. People often place the measuring device flat on the work and mark by making a short, heavy line. A better way is to make a dot with the point of a sharp, hard pencil. Many rules have incised lines that make fine grooves for the point of the marker to slide in **(Figure 2).** Use the dot system even if the instrument does not have grooves—it's more accurate.

Measurement points and lines can be drawn with a sharp pencil, but often when marking cut-lines you can be more accurate if you scribe with a knife **(Figure 3).** A bonus feature here, if you score carefully a few times, is that the knife severs the surface fibers, and this results in a smoother edge when you saw. If the knife line is difficult to see, simply mark over it with a sharp pencil.

**Fig. 2.** Use a sharp, hard pencil to mark dimension points. A dot, rather than a short, heavy line, is more accurate.

**Fig. 3.** A knife makes a finer line than a pencil and, because it severs surface fibers, it invites smoother saw cuts.

One of the more convenient measuring tools is a flexible *tape,* a palm-size instrument with a metal band that springs back into its small case when it is released. There are many types and sizes; some are very bulky, with tapes that stretch out to a hundred feet. In the shop, you'll want one that's easy to handle and read and measures at least 8 feet **(Figure 4).** That's the length of a standard plywood panel.

The *folding* or *zigzag* rule used to be the standby of the carpenter, and it's still popular, especially for short measurements. Most rules extend to 6 feet and are about 8 inches long when folded. Their stiff blades are an advantage. For example, they make a rigid span between the blade and rip fence on a table saw. Good ones have an extension, usually made of brass, that slides in a groove in the first blade **(Figure 5).** This makes it possible to use the rule for inside measurements. Because the sliding extension is removable, it can be used on its own as a small rule.

**Fig. 4.** A flexible tape is a convenient measuring device. Blades on shop types should be at least 8-feet long.

**Fig. 5.** The folding or *zig-zag* rule is still popular. The sliding extension can be removed and used as a short rule.

**Fig. 6.** Bench rules come in 1-, 2-, and 3-foot lengths. Good wooden ones have ends reinforced with metal.

A *bench rule* (**Figure 6**) is handy. It can be metal or hardwood, and is available in one-, two-, and three-foot lengths. It's a good measuring device and has an extra feature—it serves nicely as a straightedge.

A square is essential; the most useful one is the *combination square* (**Figure 7**). It has a removable, one-foot blade that can serve as a bench rule, and its head permits drawing lines square to an edge or at a 45-degree angle. The head can be locked at any point on the blade, which makes the combination square a good edge-marking gauge.

A pencil *compass* or wing *dividers* can be used to draw circles and arcs. Wing dividers are made with a removable steel point, so you can substitute a pencil when you need to. Tools of this type are limited in the radii they can

**Fig. 7.** The combination square has a 12-inch blade and a head that allows marking square across stock or at a 45-degree angle.

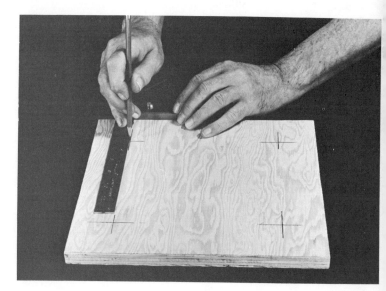

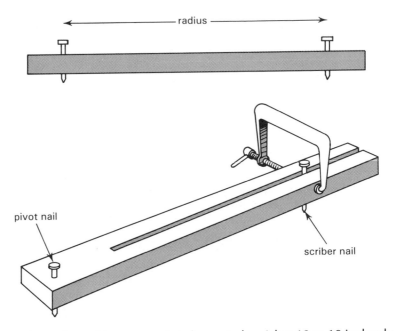

**Fig. 8.** A design for making trammels to large circles. A bar 12 to 18 inches long will do for most work.

span; 6 inches is usually their limit. To draw larger circles you need special *trammels,* or you can work as shown in **Figure 8.** This trammel is an adjustable type—the scriber point can be locked with a small C-clamp at any point in the slot.

**Saws.** Hand saws **(Figure 9)** are designed either for *crosscutting* (cutting a board to length) or *ripping* (cutting a board to width). The major differences between the two types are the shape of the teeth and the number of them per inch on the blade. Rip saws have fewer, larger teeth with deep gullets between them for easy removal of large waste chips. Each tooth works like a tiny chisel, chipping out its own bit of wood.

**Fig. 9.** The teeth on hand saws are designed either for ripping or for crosscutting. The crosscut design is the better first saw to own.

Crosscut teeth cut with a shearing action; they cut across wood grain like so many small, sharp knives. The more teeth-per-inch on the blade, the smoother the cut will be. A good crosscut saw is a logical beginning for a hobbyist. It does a more respectable job of ripping than a rip saw does of crosscutting, and it is the saw to use for cutting plywood. Normally, a crosscut saw is stroked at about a 45-degree angle. Decrease the angle when you are sawing plywood.

In all cases, you will saw more accurately if you clamp or tack-nail a guide strip to the work as shown in **Figure 10.** The strip will help you to cut straight and to hold the saw vertical, creating an edge that will be square to adjacent surfaces.

A *backsaw* is very handy, especially when you are sawing small pieces and use the saw with a miter box such as the one shown in **Figure 11.** Common backsaws run about 12 to 14 inches long with many small teeth and a blade that is stiffened by a "spine" along the top edge. A good one is ideal for precise, straight or angled cuts. Construction details of a miter box you can make for yourself are shown in **Figure 12.**

Not all cuts are straight. Therefore, saws that can follow curved lines are essential, especially in toy-making. The *coping saw* **(Figure 13)** is a versatile saw designed for curve-cutting. Its U-shape frame has a chuck at each end for gripping blades that, on the average, are about 6 inches long. There are various blade widths with a wide assortment of teeth-per-inch specifications to match the work on hand. Choose a wide blade with large teeth for heavy stock; a narrow blade with many teeth is best for smoother cuts and intricate forms.

Because the coping saw's blades are gripped at each end, the saw can be used for "piercing" cuts—cuts made without need of a lead-in cut from the

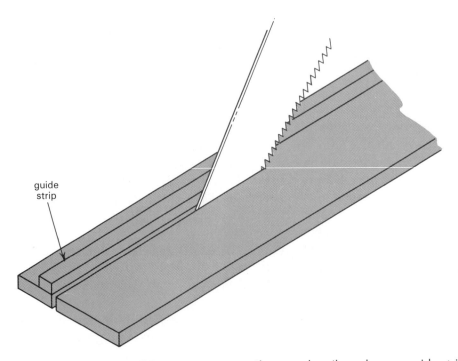

guide
strip

**Fig. 10.**   Straight cuts will be more accurate if you tack-nail or clamp a guide strip to the work.

**Fig. 11.**   A miter box helps you produce accurate straight or angular cuts. You can buy or make one.

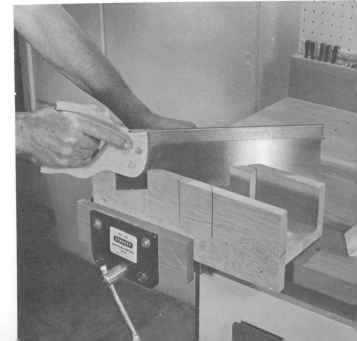

**Fig. 12.** How to make a miter box: Use well-seasoned hardwood. Width of the box should suit the scope of work; minimum is about 4 inches. Assemble with glue and flathead screws. Mark cutlines accurately on edges and vertical surfaces before you saw. The accuracy of the box depends on how well you make the guide marks.

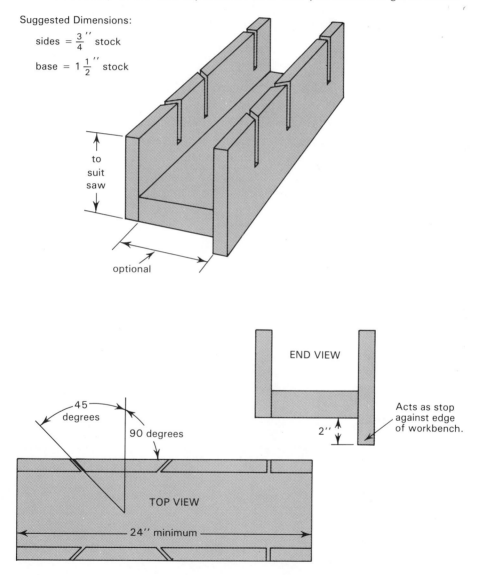

Suggested Dimensions:

sides $= \frac{3}{4}''$ stock

base $= 1\frac{1}{2}''$ stock

to suit saw

optional

END VIEW

Acts as stop against edge of workbench.

2''

45 degrees

90 degrees

TOP VIEW

24'' minimum

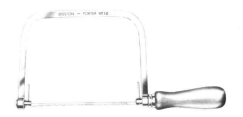

**Fig. 13.** A typical coping saw. Some have deeper throats, but all have blade mounts that permit inside as well as outside cutting.

edge of the stock. To make a pierced cut, you first drill a hole in a waste area and pass the blade through before locking it in the chucks. The blades can be rotated in the frame, so the cutting direction can be adjusted to any line. Also, the blades can be installed so that the teeth point either toward or away from the handle. Thus you can conveniently saw on either the push or the pull stroke—handy for many types of work.

When you saw, the work itself should be firmly gripped, either in a vise **(Figure 14)** or on a special V-block holder that you can make for yourself **(Figure 15).** The holder can be clamped to a bench or gripped in a vise. It's a handy jig for holding work flat when you have a lot of coping work to do.

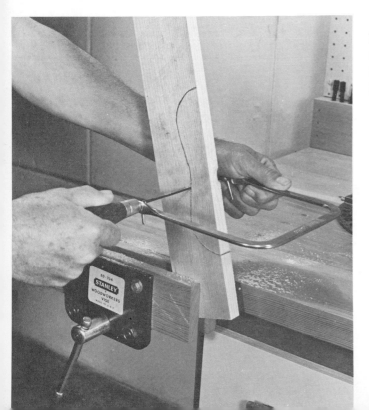

**Fig. 14.** Coping-saw blades can be rotated in the frame. They can also be mounted to cut on either the push or the pull stroke. The choice is often handy.

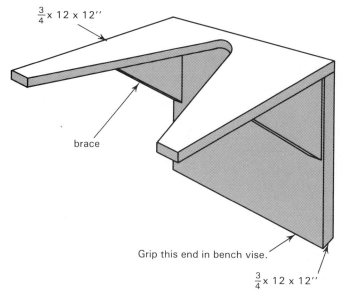

$\frac{3}{4}$ x 12 x 12″

brace

Grip this end in bench vise.

$\frac{3}{4}$ x 12 x 12″

**Fig. 15.** The V-block holder (details at left, supporting work below) is gripped in a vise. The work is clamped to its surface so the saw has freedom in the "V." Here, mount the blade so its teeth point toward the handle. Cut on the down stroke.

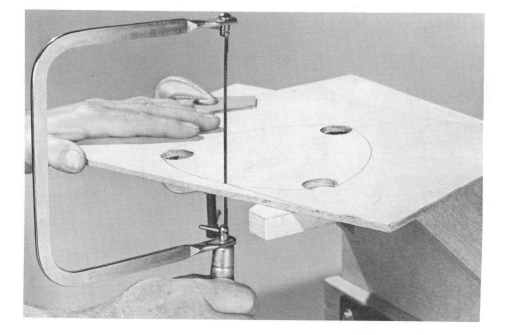

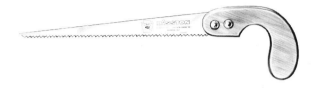

**Fig. 16.** The keyhole saw has a sharp point that allows you to start inside cuts by drilling a small hole in a waste area.

The *keyhole* saw **(Figure 16)** is also used for making external or internal curved cuts, but it can't do the fine work that is possible with a coping saw. An advantage of the keyhole saw is that the blade is "free." Thus you can make an internal cut much further away from an edge than with a framed saw.

The electric *saber saw* **(Figure 17)** is the tool to think about for easy curve cutting. It can do all the work of a keyhole saw and most of the work of a coping saw but much faster and with considerably less effort. Today's models have variable speeds and a large variety of blades, so tool applications can range from scrollwork to heavy-duty cutting.

Saber-saw blades are gripped only at one end. So, as shown in **Figure 18,** you can make internal cuts without a lead-in cut. The blade can be poked

**Fig. 17.** The electric saber saw allows faster, easier cutting of curved lines. Modern ones have several or continuously variable speeds.

through a hole drilled in waste areas or it can penetrate the stock on its own with the following technique. Rest the saw on the front edge of the base so that the blade is parallel to the work surface. Hold the saw very firmly and slowly tilt it back until the blade makes contact and starts to cut a groove. Continue to tilt backwards until the blade has pierced the stock. Then you can set the tool firmly on its base and finish cutting.

Among stationary tools, the *jigsaw* **(Figure 19)** is the king of intricate curve-cutting. Like the coping saw, it has chucks that grip the blades at each end; piercing is possible when you pass the blade through a hole in the work and then lock the blade in place. The jigsaw handles well in delicate fretwork, but it's no sissy. Maximum depth-of-cut is usually about 2 inches,

**Fig. 18.** Shown below, inside cutting is easy with a saber saw. Just start the cut at a hole as explained in the text.

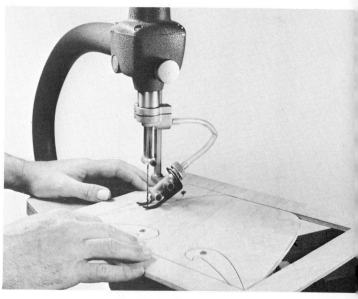

**Fig. 19.** Shown above, the stationary jigsaw is good for sawing all types of internal and external curves. A 2-inch depth-of-cut allows you to "pad," or stack, parts when you need similar pieces.

| Blade | Blade Dimensions | | | | Operation Facts | | |
|---|---|---|---|---|---|---|---|
| | Thickness (Inches) | Width (Inches) | Teeth Per Inch | Stock Thickness (Inches) | Cut Radius | Kerf | Best for |
| 5 | .028 | .250 | 7 | $\frac{1}{4}$ and up | large | coarse | soft and hard wood, pressed wood |
| 3 | .020 | .110 | 15 | $\frac{1}{8}$ to $\frac{1}{2}$ in metal $\frac{1}{8}$ and up in other material | medium | medium | metal, wood, bone, felt, paper |
| 1 | .010 | .040 | 18 | $\frac{1}{16}$ to $\frac{1}{8}$ | small | very fine | wood, bone, plastics |
| 6 | .012 | .023 | 20 | up to $\frac{1}{8}$ | very small | fine | plastics, bone, fiber, comp. board |
| 7 | .020 | .070 | 7 | up to $\frac{1}{4}$ | medium | medium | plastics, bone, hard rubber |
| 8 | .010 | .070 | 14 | $\frac{1}{8}$ to $\frac{1}{2}$ | medium | very fine | wood, plastics, bone, hard rubber |
| 2 | .020 | .110 | 20 | $\frac{1}{16}$ to $\frac{1}{8}$ | medium | medium | aluminum, copper, mild steel |
| 4 | .028 | .250 | 20 | $\frac{3}{32}$ to $\frac{1}{2}$ ($\frac{1}{4}$ max. in steel) | large | coarse | aluminum, copper, mild steel |

**Fig. 20.** Common blades used in a jigsaw cut a variety of materials.

and it can accommodate blades as wide as $\frac{1}{4}$ inch for heavy-duty work. One advantage of the jigsaw is that you can get duplicate pieces. If, for example, a toy project needs two identical silhouettes, you can tack-nail or tape together two pieces of wood and cut them as if they were a solid piece. With a cutting depth of 2 inches, you can make a pad of eight pieces of $\frac{1}{4}$-inch plywood and have eight pieces exactly alike after a single cutting.

There are many types of blades available for jigsaws. **Figure 20** lists the most common ones and makes suggestions for their use.

Another type of jigsaw is the "Moto-Saw" shown in **Figure 21**. The tool weighs only 9 pounds, but has a 12-inch throat and can cut soft woods up to $1\frac{1}{2}$ inches thick. It's a comparatively quiet tool, so it's not impossible to think of using it in the house. Four rubber feet will keep the tool steady on most surfaces—it doesn't need a permanent mounting.

A *hacksaw* is needed to cut metal; for example, to shorten a bolt or to cut steel rod for an axle. The one shown in **Figure 22** can handle 10- or 12-inch blades. There are a variety of blades, but a $\frac{1}{2}$-inch-wide blade with 32 teeth per inch will be most useful.

**Fig. 21.** The "Moto-Saw" is a self-contained unit that weighs only 9 lbs. but can cut soft woods up to $1\frac{1}{2}$ inches thick. It can even be used on the kitchen table.

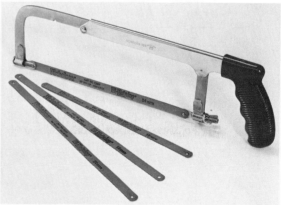

**Fig. 22.** The hacksaw is a metal cutting tool. It's handy for such jobs as cutting steel rods for axles or shortening bolts.

**Hammers and Nails.** A 16-ounce, curved *claw hammer* **(Figure 23)** is a good choice for general woodworking. It is not so light that it can't do a good job driving large nails, or so heavy that it becomes tiring and unwieldy. The one shown is a relatively modern version, having a steel handle and a vinyl grip. Some workers, especially those who work outdoors where steel feels colder than wood, prefer a wooden handle. The grip really doesn't matter as long as the tool is a good one. Hammers displayed in bargain bins are usually poor investments.

A small hammer, usually called a *tack hammer* **(Figure 24),** is a wise addition since it can be used to drive brads (small nails) as well as tacks. Some have heads that are magnetized—useful when what you are driving is too small to finger-hold.

A way to avoid damaging fingers when driving small nails is shown in **Figure 25.** The holder is just a strip of wood with a slot that is slim enough to grip the nail until you have it started.

The sizes and gauges of *common* and *box* nails are shown in **Figure 26.** Box nails are slimmer and are better to use when there is a chance that common nails might split the wood. In any case, if splitting becomes a nuisance on a particular piece of wood, it's a good idea to drill small pilot holes before driving the nails.

Don't drive nails so deep that the hammer head mars the wood. Just tap the heads flush.

**Fig. 23.** A 16 oz. curved claw hammer, for general woodworking. Good ones are also available with wood handles.

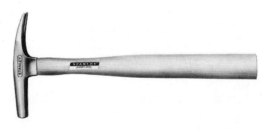

**Fig. 24.** A tack hammer is also good for driving brads. Some have striking areas that are magnetic to help you pick up and position tacks.

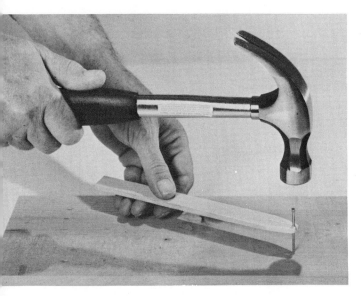

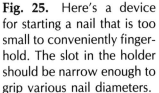

**Fig. 25.** Here's a device for starting a nail that is too small to conveniently finger-hold. The slot in the holder should be narrow enough to grip various nail diameters.

It's okay to use common or box nails when exposed nail heads don't matter; but if you wish to conceal the heads, switch to finishing nails **(Figure 27)**. The chart also lists "casing" nails. These are slightly heavier in gauge than finishing nails, and can be handy when you want a little more strength in a joint. They are frequently used by builders for cabinetwork and on interior trim.

Whether you use finishing or casing nails, the nail heads should be "set" below the surface of the wood, and the small hole that remains is filled with a wood putty, preferably one that is colored to match the wood.

*Nail sets* come in different sizes (the tips range from $\frac{1}{32}$ to $\frac{1}{8}$ inch in diameter). It's wise to have a set equal to the size of the nail, so that you won't have to make and fill holes larger than necessary.

The tool shown in **Figure 28** is a *self-centering* nail set. It's a handy gadget that makes nail-setting easier without marring adjacent surfaces. After the nail is driven to the point where you would use a conventional nail set (it should project about $\frac{1}{8}$ inch), place the tool over the nail and set it by striking the plunger.

## COMMON AND BOX NAIL SIZES

| Size d (penny) | 2 | 3 | 4 | 5 | 6 | 7 | 8 | 9 | 10 | 12 | 16 | 20 | 30 | 40 | 50 | 60 |
|---|---|---|---|---|---|---|---|---|---|---|---|---|---|---|---|---|
| Length in inches | 1 | $1\frac{1}{4}$ | $1\frac{1}{2}$ | $1\frac{3}{4}$ | 2 | $2\frac{1}{4}$ | $2\frac{1}{2}$ | $2\frac{3}{4}$ | 3 | $3\frac{1}{4}$ | $3\frac{1}{2}$ | 4 | $4\frac{1}{2}$ | 5 | $5\frac{1}{2}$ | 6 |
| *Common Nails* | | | | | | | | | | | | | | | | |
| Gauge | 15 | 14 | $12\frac{1}{2}$ | $12\frac{1}{2}$ | $11\frac{1}{2}$ | $11\frac{1}{2}$ | $10\frac{1}{4}$ | $10\frac{1}{4}$ | 9 | 9 | 8 | 6 | 5 | 4 | 3 | 2 |
| Approximate number/lb. | 845 | 540 | 290 | 250 | 165 | 150 | 100 | 90 | 65 | 60 | 45 | 30 | 20 | 17 | 13 | 10 |
| *Box Nails* | | | | | | | | | | | | | | | | |
| Gauge | $15\frac{1}{2}$ | $14\frac{1}{2}$ | 14 | 14 | $12\frac{1}{2}$ | $12\frac{1}{2}$ | $11\frac{1}{2}$ | $11\frac{1}{2}$ | $10\frac{1}{2}$ | $10\frac{1}{2}$ | 10 | 9 | 9 | 8 | — | — |
| Approximate number/lb | 1010 | 635 | 473 | 406 | 236 | 210 | 145 | 132 | 94 | 88 | 71 | 52 | 46 | 35 | — | — |

2  3  4  5  6  7

**Fig. 26.** This chart indicates actual lengths of *common* and *box* nails, though only common nails are shown. Box nails are slimmer but come in the same d (penny) lengths.

**Fig. 27.** Facts and dimensions on finishing and casing nails and brads.

### FINISHING-HEAD NAILS

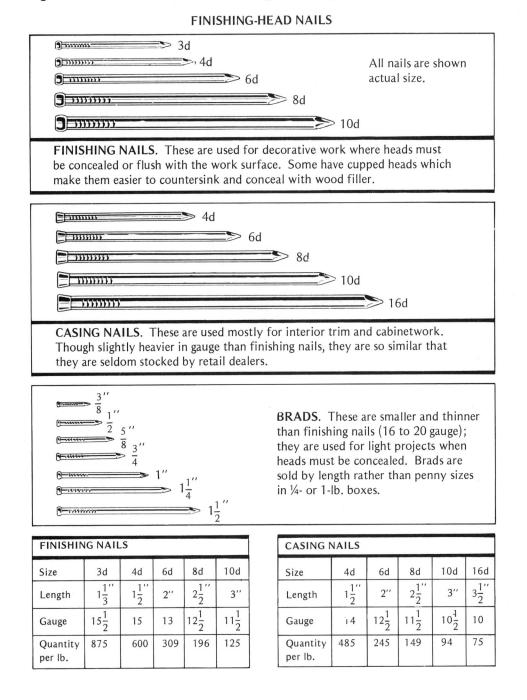

**FINISHING NAILS.** These are used for decorative work where heads must be concealed or flush with the work surface. Some have cupped heads which make them easier to countersink and conceal with wood filler.

**CASING NAILS.** These are used mostly for interior trim and cabinetwork. Though slightly heavier in gauge than finishing nails, they are so similar that they are seldom stocked by retail dealers.

**BRADS.** These are smaller and thinner than finishing nails (16 to 20 gauge); they are used for light projects when heads must be concealed. Brads are sold by length rather than penny sizes in ¼- or 1-lb. boxes.

| FINISHING NAILS | | | | | |
|---|---|---|---|---|---|
| Size | 3d | 4d | 6d | 8d | 10d |
| Length | $1\frac{1}{3}''$ | $1\frac{1}{2}''$ | $2''$ | $2\frac{1}{2}''$ | $3''$ |
| Gauge | $15\frac{1}{2}$ | 15 | 13 | $12\frac{1}{2}$ | $11\frac{1}{2}$ |
| Quantity per lb. | 875 | 600 | 309 | 196 | 125 |

| CASING NAILS | | | | | |
|---|---|---|---|---|---|
| Size | 4d | 6d | 8d | 10d | 16d |
| Length | $1\frac{1}{2}''$ | $2''$ | $2\frac{1}{2}''$ | $3''$ | $3\frac{1}{2}''$ |
| Gauge | 14 | $12\frac{1}{2}$ | $11\frac{1}{2}$ | $10\frac{1}{2}$ | 10 |
| Quantity per lb. | 485 | 245 | 149 | 94 | 75 |

**Fig. 28.** A self-centering punch makes it easy to set finishing nails.

**Fig. 29.** This type of hand drill can be used for holes up to about $\frac{1}{4}$ inch. The hollow handle stores bits.

Don't drive nails as if you were trying for a prize in a carnival. Nails driven home with reasonable force will actually hold better, because they will cause the least amount of distortion in the wood fibers. Remove any nail that starts to bend. Even if you can save it, the bend may cause the point of the nail to travel crooked in the wood. It's better to use a new nail.

**Drills.** Small old-fashioned *hand drills,* those that work something like an egg beater **(Figure 29),** are still good for holes up to about $\frac{1}{4}$ inch. You can use them with small twist drills or special drill points such as those shown in **Figure 30.** Actually, heavy-duty versions with chuck jaws that can handle $\frac{3}{8}$-inch drills are available. Some have a "high" and "low" adjustment that allows you to choose extra torque or greater speed.

A *bit brace* **(Figure 31)** is the tool to use for hand-drilling holes $\frac{1}{4}$ inch and larger. They are available in light- and heavy-duty versions. The major difference between them is the diameter of the swing of the handle, called the "sweep." The greater the sweep, the more torque you can apply.

The chucks on most braces are specially designed to hold bits with tapered shanks, but some have universal jaws and can be used with straight shank bits up to $\frac{1}{2}$ inch as well. A good brace will have a rachet action that allows you to take full or partial swings either clockwise or counterclockwise. With a screwdriver bit, the reversing action allows you to remove screws as well as drive them.

**Fig. 30.** Special sets of drill points for use in hand drills are available, but you can also work with small twist drills.

**Fig. 31.** With correct cutting tools, the hand brace can be used to form holes as large as 3 inches. The gadget attached to the bit is an adjustable stop that lets you drill holes to a specific depth.

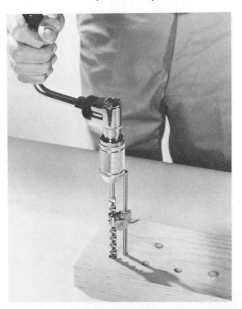

**Fig. 32.** Most hand braces are used with auger bits that have a tapered tang. Some have universal chucks so that they can also grip round-shank bits.

In **Figure 32** you see a typical *auger bit* that is used in a brace. The lead point is threaded to pull the bit into the work. Sizes of augers start at $\frac{1}{4}$ inch and increase by sixteenths to 1 inch. Numbers are often used to indicate bit size. For example, a number 9 bit will form a $\frac{9}{16}$-inch diameter hole.

The difference between brace auger bits and those that can be used in a drill press, for example, is shown in **Figure 33.** Never use a screw-tip bit for power drilling.

**Fig. 33.** Hand brace bits have a feed-screw point that pulls the bit into the work. They should not be used with power drills. Bits with brad points are safe to use with power tools.

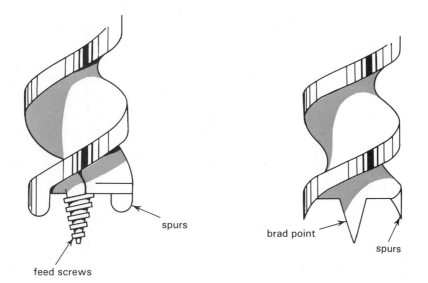

**Fig. 34.** Expansion, or expansive, bits are designed for cutting large holes. Cutters are adjustable to allow you to bore odd-size holes.

*Expansive,* or *expansion bits* as they are sometimes called, are used to form holes larger than 1 inch. Most come with two cutters **(Figure 34),** and it's wise to work with the smallest one that serves the job at hand. Commonly, two sizes are available: one for holes from $\frac{5}{8}$ to $1\frac{3}{4}$ inches, the other for holes from $\frac{7}{8}$ to 3 inches. An advantage of this type of tool is that the cutters are infinitely adjustable, so you can form odd-diameter holes. It's feasible, for example, to bore a hole that falls between $\frac{3}{4}$ and $\frac{13}{16}$ inch.

Both types of bits are rather long; you can form deeper holes than possible with, say, a regular twist drill. Bit extensions that run from 12 to 18 inches long can do such jobs as boring cord holes through tall wooden lamp bases.

The portable *electric drill* is one of the tools that practically revolutionized homeshop woodworking. Few tool chests today lack one. It can do all the jobs of hand drills faster and easier, and, just as important, it can be equipped with accessories for jobs that range from sawing to sanding. Features on today's electric drills include double-insulation, variable speeds, and forward or reverse chuck actions.

Common electric-drill sizes are $\frac{1}{4}$, $\frac{3}{8}$, and $\frac{1}{2}$ inch. The fraction indicates the maximum chuck opening—but not necessarily the largest hole you can drill. Some drilling tools, like spade bits which can form holes up to $1\frac{1}{2}$ inches, have shank sizes that can be gripped in small drills. Spade bits are good tools for electric drills because they operate best at high speeds. Thus they can be used even in a "small" $\frac{1}{4}$-inch drill.

Generally, drill size indicates power and speed. A $\frac{1}{2}$-inch drill will have more torque but less speed than either a $\frac{3}{8}$- or $\frac{1}{4}$-inch drill. This makes sense, because the larger tool must stand up under heavy-duty functions such as drilling in steel or concrete. A $\frac{3}{8}$-inch drill is an acceptable compromise since its top speed is adequate for small-hole drilling and it has power for some big jobs. In truth, it's good to have both a $\frac{3}{8}$-inch drill and a $\frac{1}{4}$-inch version for general woodworking.

The portable drills are designed for hand use, but you can set them up like a drill press by acquiring a stand like the ones shown in **Figure 35.** These can be a great convenience on many jobs. Most important, they eliminate the chance of human error when it's critical for a hole to be perpendicular in the wood.

For accuracy when drilling, mark lines that intersect where the hole must be. Then use a punch or an awl to make a small indentation at the intersec-

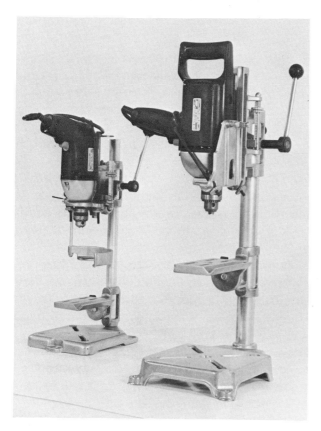

**Fig. 35.** Special stands are available for most of the electric drills on the market. A portable drill on a drill press allows accurate work.

**Fig. 36.** For accurate drilling, draw lines that intersect where the hole will be. Then punch a point at the center to help guide the drill at the start.

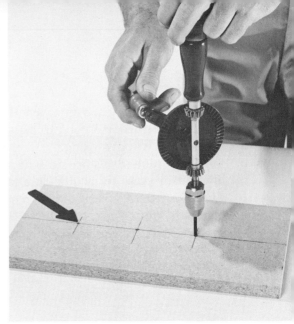

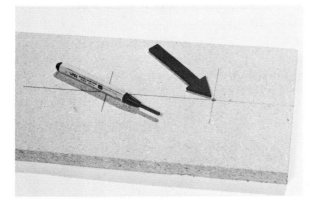

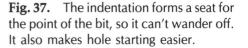

**Fig. 37.** The indentation forms a seat for the point of the bit, so it can't wander off. It also makes hole starting easier.

tion **(Figure 36)**. This makes it easy to seat the bit accurately and start the hole **(Figure 37)**.

Often it's a good idea to drill a pilot hole first. A pilot hole is a smaller hole than the final one you need. This makes drilling easier, increases accuracy, and results in cleaner holes. Always use a backup block when the hole must go through the work. This will minimize, if not eliminate, feathering and splintering where the bit comes through.

A small guide block such as the one shown in **Figure 38** can help you to drill squarely. When it is correctly sized, the guide block can also serve as a stop gauge when you are drilling to a specific depth. Another way to judge hole depth is simply to wrap a piece of masking tape around the bit **(Figure 39)**. You stop drilling when the tape touches the work.

When a hole is required at a critical angle, use a guide block as shown in **Figure 40**. First drill the correct-size hole (or a pilot hole) through a square block of wood. Then saw off the base of the block so it will provide the correct angle, and use the block as a guide for the bit.

**Figure 41** shows a secure jig you can make from a handscrew clamp for holding small parts while drilling. The matching V-cuts that are made in the jaws of the clamp will securely grip square or round pieces. The holder can be secured to a bench, held in a vise, or clamped to a drill-press table.

**Figure 42** shows a similar way to do the same job. Here a conventional drill vise is used with a V-block to grip a small, round piece that requires a concentric hole. It's an accurate and safe way to work.

**Fig. 38.**   A small guide block can help you to drill holes square to the surface. The block can also be sized to gauge holes of specific depth.

**Fig. 39.**   Another way to drill to a predetermined depth is simply to wrap a piece of masking tape around the bit.

**Fig. 40.**  Angular holes are difficult to "eyeball." It's better to work with a guide block like this one.

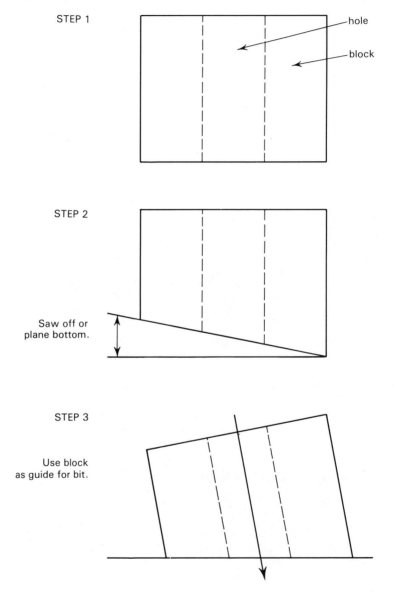

STEP 1

hole

block

STEP 2

Saw off or
plane bottom.

STEP 3

Use block
as guide for bit.

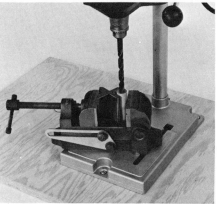

**Fig. 41.** Make matching V-cuts in the jaws of a handscrew and you have a tool that will securely grip small, square, or round pieces.

**Fig. 42.** A drill vise used with a V-block is one means for drilling straight, concentric holes through dowels and similarly shaped parts.

**Screwdrivers and Screws.** Conventional screwdrivers have a wing-type driving tip and are used to turn most of the common type of slotted-head screws used in woodworking: roundheads, ovalheads, and flatheads. Flatheads are often called "countersunk" screws because they are always driven flush with the work surface.

The efficient way to drive a screw is with a blade that closely fits the slot in the screw. Since there are many sizes of screws, it is good to buy the drivers in sets **(Figure 43).** Using a small screwdriver to seat a 14 or 16 gauge screw is difficult, and will probably damage the tool.

The tool shown in **Figure 44** is a *spiral ratchet screwdriver*—a real time and labor saver. It automatically turns the screw when you push down on the handle. Most of these screwdrivers can drive or retract a screw or be locked in a fixed position for use as a conventional driver. They can be fitted with different-size blades for various screws. Incidentally, the tool's chuck will also grip drill bits—you can drill small holes quickly with it.

The tool shown in **Figure 45** is the kind of screwdriver bit that is used in a bit brace. Similar types, without the tapered shank, can be used in a

**Fig. 43.** The blade of a screwdriver should fit snugly in the screw-head slot. It's a good idea to buy these tools in large sets.

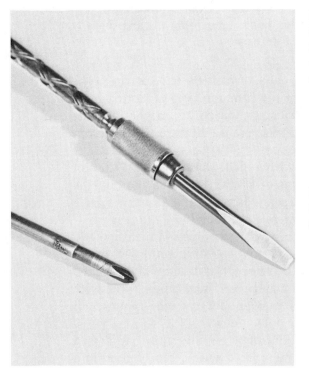

**Fig. 44.** You can drive or loosen screws faster and easier by working with a spiral-ratchet screwdriver. This tool can be used with various types and sizes of blades, as well as with small drill bits.

**Fig. 45.** Screwdriver blades like this big one, made in different styles and sizes, are also used in a hand brace.

portable electric drill. With a set of these blades and an electric drill with variable forward and reverse speeds, you would be well-equipped for most screwdriving chores.

Unless you are working with tiny screws and soft wood, you can drive screws easily and obtain maximum holding strength by drilling both a pilot and a shank hole **(Figure 46).** The depth of the shank hole can equal the full thickness of the top piece of wood being attached. The depth of the pilot hole should be about one-half the length of the threaded portion of the screw. Recommendations for sizes of pilot and shank holes are shown in **Figure 47.**

**Fig. 46.** Cross sections of two holes drilled for screws. The wood plugs that are inserted in holes for counterbored screws (below) are sanded smooth; the buttons leave a decorative touch.

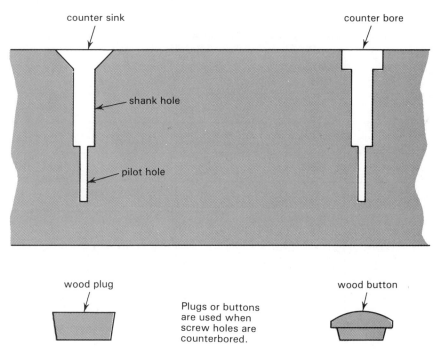

**Fig. 47.** If you follow these suggestions, wood screws will be easier to drive and will hold with maximum power.

| Screw Number | Pilot Holes | | | | Shank Holes | | Counterbore |
| --- | --- | --- | --- | --- | --- | --- | --- |
| | Hardwood | | Softwood | | Twist Drill* | Drill Gauge** | Auger Bit Number |
| | Twist Drill* | Drill Gauge** | Twist Drill* | Drill Gauge** | | | |
| 0 | $\frac{1}{32}$ | 66 | $\frac{1}{64}$ | 75 | $\frac{1}{16}$ | 52 | — |
| 1 | — | 57 | $\frac{1}{32}$ | 71 | $\frac{5}{64}$ | 47 | — |
| 2 | — | 54 | $\frac{1}{32}$ | 65 | $\frac{3}{32}$ | 42 | 3 |
| 3 | $\frac{1}{16}$ | 53 | $\frac{3}{64}$ | 58 | $\frac{7}{64}$ | 37 | 4 |
| 4 | $\frac{1}{16}$ | 51 | $\frac{3}{64}$ | 55 | $\frac{7}{64}$ | 32 | 4 |
| 5 | $\frac{5}{64}$ | 47 | $\frac{1}{16}$ | 53 | $\frac{1}{8}$ | 30 | 4 |
| 6 | — | 44 | $\frac{1}{16}$ | 52 | $\frac{9}{64}$ | 27 | 5 |
| 7 | — | 39 | $\frac{1}{16}$ | 51 | $\frac{5}{32}$ | 22 | 5 |
| 8 | $\frac{7}{64}$ | 35 | $\frac{5}{64}$ | 48 | $\frac{11}{64}$ | 18 | 6 |
| 9 | $\frac{7}{64}$ | 33 | $\frac{5}{64}$ | 45 | $\frac{3}{16}$ | 14 | 6 |
| 10 | $\frac{1}{8}$ | 31 | $\frac{3}{32}$ | 43 | $\frac{3}{16}$ | 10 | 6 |
| 11 | — | 29 | $\frac{3}{32}$ | 40 | $\frac{13}{64}$ | 4 | 7 |
| 12 | — | 25 | $\frac{7}{64}$ | 38 | $\frac{7}{32}$ | 2 | 7 |
| 14 | $\frac{3}{16}$ | 14 | $\frac{7}{64}$ | 32 | $\frac{1}{4}$ | D | 8 |
| 16 | — | 10 | $\frac{9}{64}$ | 29 | $\frac{17}{64}$ | I | 9 |
| 18 | $\frac{13}{64}$ | 6 | $\frac{9}{64}$ | 26 | $\frac{19}{64}$ | N | 10 |
| 20 | $\frac{7}{32}$ | 3 | $\frac{11}{64}$ | 19 | $\frac{21}{64}$ | P | 11 |
| 24 | $\frac{1}{4}$ | D | $\frac{3}{16}$ | 15 | $\frac{3}{8}$ | V | 12 |

HOLE SIZE RECOMMENDED FOR WOOD SCREWS

*nearest size in fractions of an inch
**this will provide maximum holding power

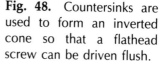

**Fig. 48.** Countersinks are used to form an inverted cone so that a flathead screw can be driven flush.

Countersinking, done with a spiral ratchet screwdriver in **Figure 48,** can be done after shank and pilot holes are drilled. Don't countersink to full depth if the wood is soft. Tightening the screw will bring it flush. Countersink to full depth if the wood is hard.

Usually, counterboring is done to conceal a screw. There are two ways to prepare the hole. Start with the pilot hole, then counterbore, and finally drill the shank hole or first do the counterbore, then the pilot hole, and finish with the shank hole.

Counterbored holes can be filled with short pieces of dowel or special wood plugs, both of which are sanded flush, or with decorative wood buttons. Both of these counterbore fillers are shown in **Figure 46.**

Whether you countersink or counterbore or do neither depends on the job you are doing and the design of the screw head **(Figure 49).** Flathead and ovalhead screws are always countersunk; the ovalhead requiring a shallower indentation than the flathead. The roundhead screw is often left exposed. Any of the screws can be concealed with either a plug or a button if you counterbore.

phillips head

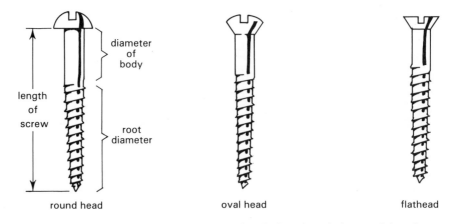

round head       oval head       flathead

**Fig. 49.** Common screw-head designs. The flathead and the oval head require countersinking.

Screw gauges and the lengths that are available in each category are shown in **Figure 50.**

**Wood Plugs and Short Dowels.** The cutter shown in **Figure 51** is used to make plugs for filling counterbored holes. The chamfered end that the cutter forms makes it easy to insert the plugs and also provides some room for excess glue. The cutter can pierce thin stock (up to about $\frac{1}{2}$ inch) and can be used to produce small, disc-type wooden parts. On thick stock you can cut to the full depth of the tool and then free the individual pieces by snapping them off with a screwdriver, as shown in **Figure 52.**

**Fig. 50.** This shows gauges and lengths of wood screws. When you buy screws, specify the following: (1) length; (2) gauge number; (3) flat, round, or oval head; material such as brass, steel, bronze; (5) finish such as bright, steel blued, cadmium, nickel, or chromium.

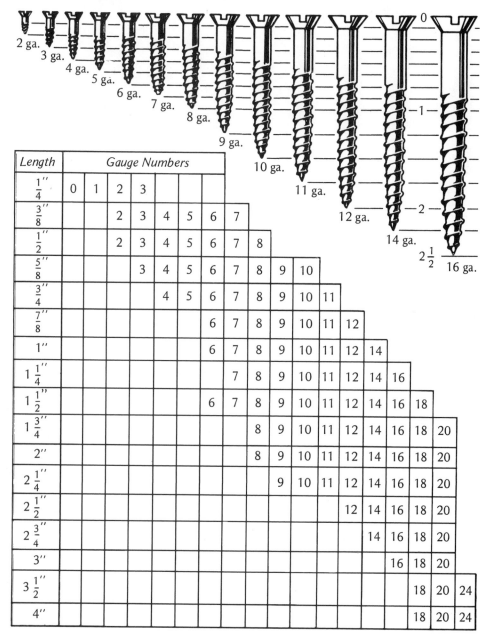

| Length | Gauge Numbers | | | | | | | | | | | | | | | | | |
|---|---|---|---|---|---|---|---|---|---|---|---|---|---|---|---|---|---|---|
| $\frac{1}{4}''$ | 0 | 1 | 2 | 3 | | | | | | | | | | | | | | |
| $\frac{3}{8}''$ | | | 2 | 3 | 4 | 5 | 6 | 7 | | | | | | | | | | |
| $\frac{1}{2}''$ | | | 2 | 3 | 4 | 5 | 6 | 7 | 8 | | | | | | | | | |
| $\frac{5}{8}''$ | | | | 3 | 4 | 5 | 6 | 7 | 8 | 9 | 10 | | | | | | | |
| $\frac{3}{4}''$ | | | | | 4 | 5 | 6 | 7 | 8 | 9 | 10 | 11 | | | | | | |
| $\frac{7}{8}''$ | | | | | | | 6 | 7 | 8 | 9 | 10 | 11 | 12 | | | | | |
| $1''$ | | | | | | | 6 | 7 | 8 | 9 | 10 | 11 | 12 | 14 | | | | |
| $1\frac{1}{4}''$ | | | | | | | | 7 | 8 | 9 | 10 | 11 | 12 | 14 | 16 | | | |
| $1\frac{1}{2}''$ | | | | | | | 6 | 7 | 8 | 9 | 10 | 11 | 12 | 14 | 16 | 18 | | |
| $1\frac{3}{4}''$ | | | | | | | | | 8 | 9 | 10 | 11 | 12 | 14 | 16 | 18 | 20 | |
| $2''$ | | | | | | | | | 8 | 9 | 10 | 11 | 12 | 14 | 16 | 18 | 20 | |
| $2\frac{1}{4}''$ | | | | | | | | | | 9 | 10 | 11 | 12 | 14 | 16 | 18 | 20 | |
| $2\frac{1}{2}''$ | | | | | | | | | | | | | 12 | 14 | 16 | 18 | 20 | |
| $2\frac{3}{4}''$ | | | | | | | | | | | | | | 14 | 16 | 18 | 20 | |
| $3''$ | | | | | | | | | | | | | | | 16 | 18 | 20 | |
| $3\frac{1}{2}''$ | | | | | | | | | | | | | | | | 18 | 20 | 24 |
| $4''$ | | | | | | | | | | | | | | | | 18 | 20 | 24 |

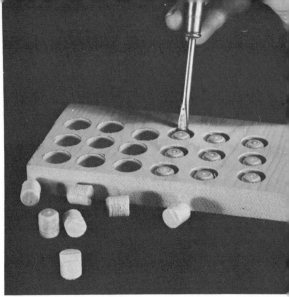

**Fig. 51.** This cutter forms the short plugs that are used in counterbored holes to conceal screws. The tool chamfers one end, and the plugs can be used like buttons.

**Fig. 52.** After drilling, snap the plugs off with a screwdriver. The boring tool (Fig. 51) can also be used to cut through material, but the stock can't be much more than $\frac{1}{2}$ inch thick.

If you use the plug to conceal a screw, insert it with the broken end out and then sand it flush with adjacent surfaces **(Figure 53)**. If the project calls for the plug to project (a decorative detail), insert it in the counterbored hole with the chamfered end up.

**Fig. 53.** When used to conceal, the plugs are inserted with the chamfered side down. Trim off excess with a knife or chisel, and then sand smooth.

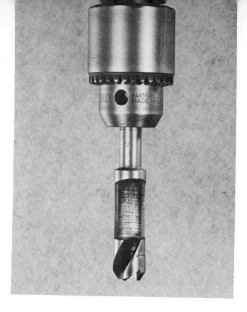

**Fig. 54.** This type of cutter can be used to form plugs, but it cuts deeper and can produce short dowels as well.

The tool shown in **Figure 54** is also called a plug cutter, but it can form dowels up to 2 inches long. An advantage of both tools is that you can form plugs and short dowels from material that matches wood you have used for the project; for example, pine plugs for a pine project. If you work very carefully you can match the plug's grain direction, even the grain pattern, to surrounding areas.

Don't use cutters like this with hand drills. You *might* be successful if you work with a portable electric drill, but the cutter will be most efficient when used with a portable drill in a drill stand or when chucked in a regular drill press.

**Smoothing, Shaping, Finishing.** No matter how carefully you saw wood, you'll find that the edge can use additional attention before the part is acceptable for assembly. Sometimes, just sanding will do the job, but more often a pass or two with a hand plane should be the preliminary step **(Figure 55)**. A plane can be used simply to remove material—for example, to reduce a board's width to the required size. But it best serves its purpose when it does a finishing chore. The cutter is set to produce a shaving thin enough almost to see through.

There are *jack* planes, *fore* planes, *jointer* planes, and others, but the one that is most suitable for general woodworking—or, at least, the one that makes sense to start with—is the *smooth* plane **(Figure 56)**. This is the

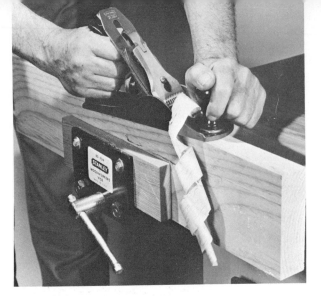

**Fig. 55.** The hand plane can be used to remove a lot of material but it's essentially a finishing tool—set to remove ultrathin shavings.

smallest member of the *bench plane* family, usually running about 10 inches long and with a cutting blade about 2 inches wide. The plane's size and weight make it convenient to handle, without reducing its efficiency. Chances are that no matter how many hand planes you add to a collection, you'll never consider the smooth plane obsolete.

The *block plane* (**Figure 57**) is a slightly larger than palm-size tool that is especially good for smoothing end grain and plywood edges. Its blade is set at a more acute angle than that of a bench plane, and the bevel on the blade

**Fig. 56.** A *smoothing* plane about 10 inches long and with a 2-inch-wide blade is useful as a general-purpose tool.

**Fig. 57.** The *block* plane is slightly larger than palm-size. It does a good job on end grain and plywood.

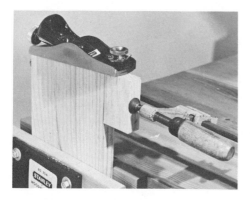

**Fig. 58.** Back up the work with a scrap block when planing end grain. The scrap, instead of the work, will take the feathering and splintering that will occur at the end of the pass.

**Fig. 59.** The block plane is handy for jobs like this—reducing a dowel for a precise fit.

faces up instead of down. On some jobs, waste made by the tool will resemble sawdust more than shavings.

Any plane, when used across the edge of stock, will cause some splintering at the end of the pass. To prevent this, work as shown in **Figure 58.** The clamped-in-place scrap block splinters instead of the work.

The block plane is useful for chamfering or beveling whether you are working with or across the grain, and can be used delicately enough for jobs such as the one shown in **Figure 59**—reducing a dowel, or any cylinder, just enough to size it for a particular hole.

There are *files* and there are *rasps,* the latter **(Figure 60)** suitable for shaping wood. The basic difference between files and rasps is in the tooth arrangement. Files have continuous, comparatively small teeth that can easily be clogged by wood. When a file is used for woodworking, it should have what is called a "bastard cut," and it should be at least 10 inches long. (Note: File cuts indicate spacing of teeth and are classified as *course, bastard, second,* and *smooth.*)

**Fig. 60.** Some conventional files can be used to shape wood, but *rasps* like these are much better. Tooth design lets them cut fast and with minimum clogging.

The teeth on a rasp are large, individually cut, and spaced so they can be used on soft material with minimum clogging. Of all the file and rasp shapes—*flat, round, three-square,* and so on—the one called *half-round* will be most functional. In cross-section, the file is shaped like the segment of a circle: one side flat, the other convex. The flat side can be used on flat edges and surfaces and on convex shapes; the half-round side does a good job shaping concave forms **(Figure 61).**

The tangs on files and rasps are sharp enough to injure you; they must never be used without a suitable handle. Grasp the free end of the file carefully. You can scrape fingers if the file moves and your hand doesn't. Wear a glove if you wish, but not a floppy one. Wearing any kind of loose apparel that can snag is poor shop practice. Consider files and rasps as shapers, not finishers. They leave a texture that requires further attention.

**Fig. 61.** A half-round cross section is handy on a rasp— the flat side can be used on contours and the half-round side on concave forms.

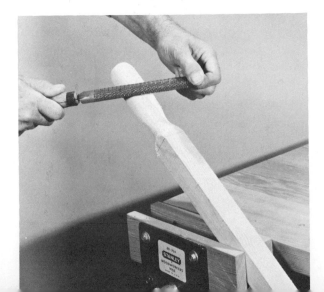

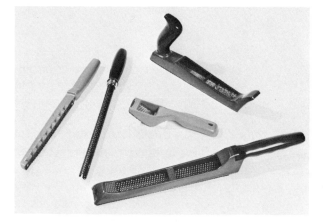

**Fig. 62.** Formers like these Surform tools are handy. They cut fast, don't clog, and come in sizes and shapes to fit most kinds of work.

Formers, like the Surform tools shown in **Figure 62,** are fine wood shapers. If you've ever used a cheese grater, you'll know how these tools work —the tooth designs and cutting actions are very similar.

The blades of the formers are tool steel. The hundreds of teeth are razor-sharp, and each has a generous "waste route" so clogging is practically nonexistant. As you work, the shavings accumulate inside the tool **(Figure 63)** or fall away from the work area. To clear a tool, simply invert it and tap it gently on a bench-top. The tools can be used cross-grain, but, as with hand planes, results are smoothest when you stroke with the grain of the wood.

The item shown in **Figure 64** is of the Surform family but is designed for use in a portable electric drill or drill press. It does a fast job of preliminary smoothing of regular or irregular curves and of circular, inside cutouts.

**Fig. 63.** The Surform tools cut on the forward stroke. Shavings will be light or heavy depending on the pressure you apply.

**Fig. 64.** This type of Surform tool is designed for power drills on inside or outside curves.

*Sandpaper* is the ultimate finishing tool. Neglect this phase of woodworking and you downgrade all previous effort. This applies to all projects, not just for the sake of appearance but also, in the case of toys, for safe use. Being fastidious with sanding, especially on edges and corners, is the way to avoid splinters. To make a point—any toy in use should be frequently checked to be sure that no damage has occurred that can result in splinters. Such areas should be sanded back smooth.

A good deal of sanding can be done simply by wrapping sandpaper around a block of wood that you can easily grip. This tool can be used to smooth surfaces, edges, round corners, and so on. For *soft* sanding you can cement a piece of indoor-outdoor carpeting, or something similar, to the block of wood **(Figure 65).** This makes the tool more suitable for smoothing contours, dowels, cylinders **(Figure 66),** etc. It can even be used on those dowels and cylinders to take them down a smidgen for a more precise fit.

**Fig. 65.** To make a *soft* sanding block, cement a piece of indoor-outdoor carpeting (or something similar) to a block of wood.

**Fig. 66.** Soft sanding is good for many jobs but especially useful for smoothing contours and round parts. The sandpaper can be held in place with tape, or you can use thumb tacks.

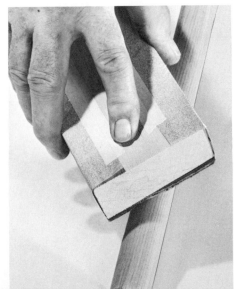

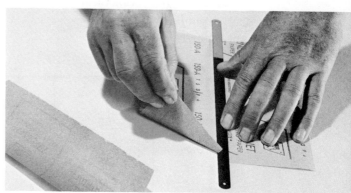

**Fig. 67.** Strips of sandpaper used like shoe-polishing rags help smooth edges like this. You can buy the abrasive in strips or make your own from standard sheets.

**Fig. 68.** This is a good way to cut sandpaper. Hold a hacksaw blade firmly down on the paper, and then pull up the paper against the blade's serrated edge.

An efficient way to smooth contours, rounded edges, and the like is shown in **Figure 67**: A strip of sandpaper is gripped and run back and forth like a shoe-polishing rag. You can buy sandpaper in strips, or you can make your own abrasive ribbons from standard sheets. The sheets can be cut with shears, or you can size pieces as shown in **Figure 68**. Hold a hacksaw blade firmly down on the paper; then pull up against the blade's serrated edge.

If you work with power sanders, remember that the *belt sander* is generally used to remove a lot of material quickly. The fine finishing is best done with a *pad sander.*

There are many types and grades of sandpaper, generally classified as *fine, medium,* and *coarse.* The general rule is to work through progressively finer grits of sandpaper until you are satisfied with the smoothness of the wood. But you should judge what grit to start with by the original condition of the wood. It's wrong to automatically reach for coarse paper when the wood is smooth enough to work with only a fine-grit paper.

You can often extend the life of sandpaper if you take this point of view: A worn *coarse* paper might serve for a while longer as *medium* grade; used *medium* paper can often do further duty as a *fine* grade.

| Identification of Abrasive Grits | | Choose from the categories in relation to the condition of the wood. Some jobs can be done by working with the "fine" category only. | |
|---|---|---|---|
| *By Name* | *By Grit No.* | *By Grade No.* | *General Use* |
| Very fine | 400<br>360<br>320<br>280<br>240<br>220 | 10/0<br><br>9/0<br>8/0<br>7/0<br>6/0 | For polishing and smoothing between finishing coats and for smoothing the final coat; use after applications of stain, shellac, sealers; also for super-fine finish on raw wood. |
| Fine | 180<br>150<br>120 | 5/0<br>4/0<br>3/0 | For final smoothing before the application of stains or sealers. |
| Medium | 100<br>80<br>60 | 2/0<br>1/0<br>1/2 | Intermediate smoothing; to prepare wood for fine sanding; remove any remaining roughness. |
| Coarse | 50<br>40<br><br>36 | 1<br><br>$1\frac{1}{2}$<br><br>2 | For initial sanding when necessary; to prepare wood for medium and fine work. |
| Very coarse | 30<br>24<br>20<br>16 | $2\frac{1}{2}$<br>3<br>$3\frac{1}{2}$<br>4 | For very rough work only; may be used on unplaned wood; often used in place of a file to round edges. |

**Fig. 69.** A guide to abrasives.

The charts in **Figures 69** and **70** provide information on abrasive types and grits and make suggestions for correct use.

## Basic Facts about Various Abrasives

| Type | Grits | | | | | | | Generally Available in | Use on | | Suggested Applications |
|------|-------|--|--|--|--|--|--|------------------------|--------|--|------------------------|
| | Super fine | Extra fine | Very fine | Fine | Medium | Coarse | Very coarse | | Wood | Metal | |
| Flint paper | | | X | X | X | X | X | 9 x 10" sheets 4½ x 5" packets | X | | Rough work and finishing chores; lacks toughness and durability. |
| Garnet paper | | | 220 A | 120 C | 80 D | 50 D | 30 D | 9 x 11" sheets | X | | Excellent general abrasive for all woodworking projects. |
| Aluminum oxide paper | | | 220 A | 120 C | 80 D | 50 D | 30 D | 9 x 11" sheets | X | X | Good for hardwoods, metals, plastics and other materials; long lasting. |
| Aluminum oxide cloth | | | 120 | 80 | 50 | 30 | | in belt form for electric sanders | X | X | Cloth-backed belts are very strong and are a first choice for power-tool sanding. |
| Silicon carbide waterproof paper | 400 A | 320 A | 220 A | | | | | 9 x 11" sheets | X | X | Very good for wet sanding after primer coats and between finish coats; can be used with oil and similar lubricants or water. |

**Note:** Letter designation following the grit number indicates the degree of flexibility of the backing: A indicates a thin, soft backing; C and D indicate progressively stiffer and tougher backing.

**Fig. 70.** The different types of abrasive grits.

**Clamps and Glue.** It is often said that a woodworking shop can't have too many clamps. It's ideal to have a vast assortment; but the scope of your projects should influence what you invest in. For example, you may never make a project that requires the use of a six-foot bar clamp. More-ordinary clamps make better sense, at least to start with.

*C-clamps* are so useful for general shop work that several sizes are often included in lists of basic tools. Maximum openings of C-clamps—which indicate the thickness of parts they can grip—range from as little as $\frac{5}{8}$ inch to as much as 18 inches. The smallest ones on up to about 4 or 5 inches are very useful. Another consideration is the depth of the throat. On small standard C-clamps, the throat depth relates to the opening. For example, a $\frac{5}{8}$-inch clamp has a $\frac{7}{8}$-inch throat; a $1\frac{1}{2}$-inch clamp has a 2- or a 3-inch throat. There are also deep-throat C-clamps; for example, a $2\frac{1}{2}$-inch clamp with a 6-inch throat. Deep throats allow you to apply pressure farther in from the edges of stock.

Always use a piece of scrap between the clamp's bearing points and the work **(Figure 71).** This prevents the clamp from marring the work, and it also spreads the clamp pressure over a wider area.

*Spring clamps* **(Figure 72)**, which provide you with powerful, tireless fingers, open up to 4 inches. The overall size of the tool and its gripping

**Fig. 71.** Use protective pads under the jaws of clamps to prevent mars like the one indicated by the arrow.

**Fig. 72.** Spring clamps are available in many sizes. Some have protective covers over jaws and handles so they're easier to grip and won't mar the work.

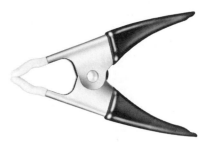

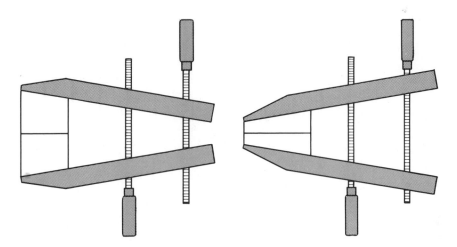

**Fig. 73.** These are *standard handscrews*—the jaws can be adjusted at an angle. Jaws on nonadjustable types will always remain parallel.

power increase with the maximum opening. The spring on larger ones is so strong, you need two hands to spread the jaws. The pressure applied by the clamp is always at the end of the jaws, so you can pinpoint the grip at any place within the tool's reach.

Spring clamps can be used to hold glued assemblies (as long as the spring pressure is adequate for the job on hand) and for grasping and holding parts you are working on. For example, it can hold several pieces together while you drill through the lot. Some spring clamps have jaws specially designed to grip round objects like dowels or tubing.

*Handscrews* **(Figure 73)** rate high among woodworkers because they easily adjust to apply parallel pressure over broad areas of the work without marring surfaces. Also, *standard* handscrews have jaws that can be adjusted at an angle; they can be used to hold assemblies of parts that have an angular configuration.

Like most clamps, handscrews come in different sizes. There are three factors to consider: the maximum opening between the jaws, the overall length of the jaws, and the *reach,* which means the grip area. Sizes range

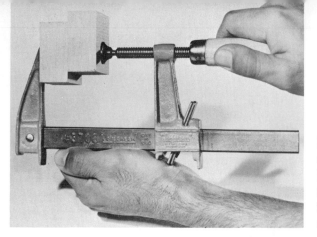

**Fig. 74.** This is an example of a sliding head bar clamp. Because the head is movable, the clamp can be used to grip any length up to its maximum opening.

from a 2-inch jaw opening with an overall jaw length of 4 inches and a reach of 2 inches, all the way up to a 17-inch jaw opening with a 24-inch jaw length and a reach of 12 inches.

**Figure 74** shows an example of a *sliding head bar clamp.* These are available with maximum openings from 6 to more than 72 inches. Generally, you should consider the maximum opening, not the minimum. Because the head slides on the bar, the clamp with the longest opening can be used to grip the thinnest assemblies.

If the scope of your work calls for extra-long clamps, you can use *clamp fixtures* **(Figure 75).** The advantage with these is that with a few sets of fixtures you can make any number of different-length bar clamps merely

**Fig. 75.** A pipe clamp fixture mounted on black pipe. With a few sets of fixtures and an assortment of pipe, you'll have clamps of whatever length you need.

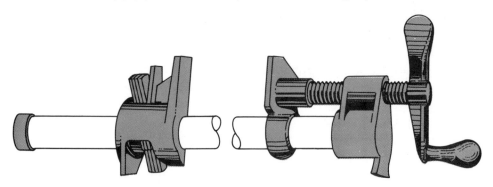

**Fig. 76.** The traditional woodworker's vise is an integral part of the workbench. The top edges of the vise's jaws are flush with the surface of the bench.

by mounting the fixtures onto various lengths of black pipe. The fixtures are available for mounting on $\frac{1}{2}$- and $\frac{3}{4}$-inch pipe so you can have light-duty or heavy-duty "bar" clamps of any length you wish.

A vise is used primarily to steady stock while you work. The traditional *woodworker's vise* (**Figure 76**) is built into the edge of a workbench with its jaws flush with the bench-top. It has replaceable jaws, usually of wood to avoid marring the work. There are different vise sizes and some variables in design. For example, some vises have a retractable stop, called a dog, in the top edge of the front jaw. When the dog is raised, the vise can be used to apply pressure to work that is backed up by a stop on the top of the bench. It's a way to grip pieces that are wider or longer than the vise's maximum opening.

The example in **Figure 77** is also a woodworker's vise, but is designed for attachment to any surface not more than $2\frac{1}{4}$ inches thick. Thus it can be used on a workbench, a table—even outdoors on a piece of thick plywood that spans a couple of sawhorses. The jaws of this unit are faced with tempered hardboard. They can be replaced, when necessary, with similar material or with wood.

There are many types of glues available for woodworking. When wisely selected and correctly used, the adhesive will form a bond that will hold

**Fig. 77.** This is also a woodworker's vise, but it can be secured anywhere. The jaw faces, which can be hardboard or wood, are replaceable.

even when surrounding areas fail. Some types of wood are more porous than others, but all are more absorbent at end grain than along edges or on surfaces. It's a good idea, on end grain, first to apply a thinned coat of glue as a sealer. After this soaks in and dries, apply the full-strength bonding coat. You can tell just by looking whether the surface has a uniform coat.

Much of the glue we use today is squeezed out of plastic bottles. This is convenient but often tempts workers to lay the glue in a wavy bead. It's better, after the bead is down, to spread the glue uniformly with a small, stiff brush.

Using too much glue is unnecessary and wasteful, but don't be miserly. The amount of glue that oozes out when parts are put together should be minimal. Remove the excess immediately with a knife or similar tool. Then wipe the area with a damp, lint-free cloth. Glue can act as a sealer to prevent stain or other finishes from penetrating.

The characteristics and uses of most common wood glues are given in **Figure 78.** You should also carefully read the manufacturer's instructions that are printed on the container's label. The label will be specific only for that product and will also tell you of any safety precautions you should follow.

**Nuts and Bolts and Washers.**   These are usually considered heavy-duty fasteners, yet the types that are shown in **Figure 79** do come in sizes that are usable on small projects. Unlike screws, bolts do not thread into wood

**Fig. 78.** Glues for the woodworker and their uses.

| Type | Preparation | Clamping Time | | Best Temperature °Fahrenheit | Moisture Resistance | Waterproof | Remarks |
|---|---|---|---|---|---|---|---|
| | | Softwood | Hardwood | | | | |
| Animal liquid hide | Ready to use | 3-4 hours | 2 hours | 70 degrees or over; warm the glue if the room is cold. | Good | No | Good choice for general furniture work but not for outdoor projects. Provides some strength even when joints are poorly fitted. Will resist heat and mold, and is easy to use. |
| Powdered casein | Mix with water. | 3-4 hours | 2 hours | Must be above freezing; works best at warmer temperature | Good | No | Especially good for oily woods like yew, teak, lemon, but it will stain woods like redwood. Works fairly well as a joint filler. Okay for general woodworking but do not use on outdoor projects. |
| Polyvinyl white glue | Ready to use | 1½-2 hours | 1 hour | 60 degree minimum | Good | No | This is a very good all-around glue. It's quick-setting, easy to use, and does not require maximum clamping. Do not use on outdoor projects. |
| Plastic powdered resin | Mix with water. | 16 hours | 16 hours | 70 degree minimum | High | No | Best for wood projects that will be exposed to considerable moisture and joints that are close fitting and clamped tightly. Not good for oily woods. |
| Resorcinal | 2-part mix; follow directions on container. | 16 hours | 16 hours | 70 degree minimum | High | Yes | This is the glue to use for outdoor projects, boats, wooden water containers. It is also excellent for joints that are poorly fitted, but do not use when temperature is below 70°F. |
| Urea resin | 2-part mix; follow directions on container. | Requires only seconds with high frequency heat | | 70 degree minimum | High | No | This is not a typical home workshop adhesive. It works best when moisture content of wood is minimal. |
| Contact cement | Ready to use | Bonds on contact; no clamping required | | 70 degree minimum | High | No | Not used for general woodworking. Use for bonding thin materials such as veneers, laminates, plastics and so forth. But remember that parts can't be shifted after contact is made. Read directions carefully. |
| Epoxy cement | 2-part mix | Amount of clamping depends on product but will set faster with heat. Some require none; read directions on the package. | | | | Yes | This is not a general woodworking adhesive, but it is good for bonding dissimilar materials. Some types can be used to fill holes. Use carefully. Read directions on the package. |

Most Common Wood Glues

**Fig. 79.**   Specifications for bolts, types of nuts, washers, and carriage bolts.

## MACHINE BOLTS

| Diameter in inches | Length in inches |
|---|---|
| $\frac{1}{4}$ | $\frac{1}{2}$ to 8 |
| $\frac{5}{16}$ | $\frac{1}{2}$ to 10 |
| $\frac{3}{8}$ | $\frac{3}{4}$ to 12 |
| $\frac{7}{16}$ | 1 to 12 |
| $\frac{1}{2}$ | 1 to 25 |

hex head

countersunk head

oval or button head

## STOVE BOLTS

| Diameter in inches | Length in inches |
|---|---|
| $\frac{1}{8} - \frac{5}{32}$ | $\frac{3}{8}$ to 2 |
| $\frac{3}{16}$ | $\frac{3}{8}$ to 6 |
| $\frac{1}{4}$ | $\frac{1}{2}$ to 6 |
| $\frac{5}{16} - \frac{3}{8}$ | $\frac{3}{4}$ to 6 |
| $\frac{1}{2}$ | 1 to 4 |

button head   countersunk head   truss head

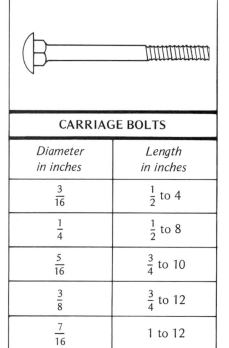

## CARRIAGE BOLTS

| Diameter in inches | Length in inches |
|---|---|
| $\frac{3}{16}$ | $\frac{1}{2}$ to 4 |
| $\frac{1}{4}$ | $\frac{1}{2}$ to 8 |
| $\frac{5}{16}$ | $\frac{3}{4}$ to 10 |
| $\frac{3}{8}$ | $\frac{3}{4}$ to 12 |
| $\frac{7}{16}$ | 1 to 12 |
| $\frac{1}{2}$ | 1 to 20 |

## NUTS

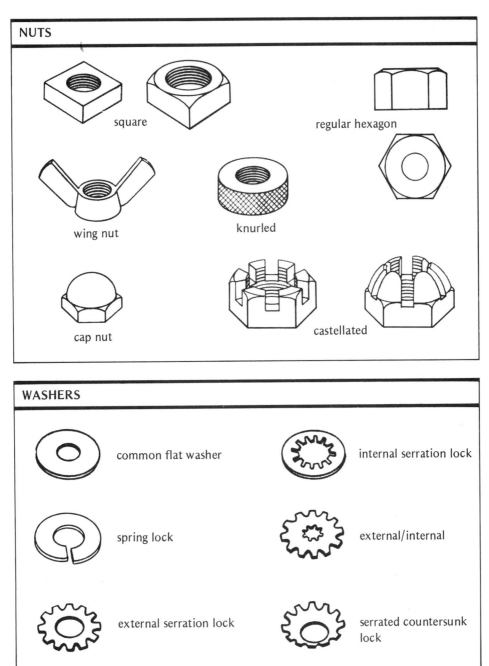

square

regular hexagon

wing nut

knurled

cap nut

castellated

## WASHERS

common flat washer

internal serration lock

spring lock

external/internal

external serration lock

serrated countersunk lock

but pass through full-size holes. Because they are easy to remove, bolts are often chosen for projects, like outdoor furniture, that you might want to break down for storage.

A useful, not unattractive, fastener for woodworking is the *carriage bolt,* which is available with either a round or an oval head. This bolt has a square shoulder directly under the head that bites into the wood, preventing the bolt from turning when you tighten the nut. The carriage bolt takes a washer only under the nut. Other types, unless they have countersunk heads, can be used with washers under both head and nut.

**Using Throw-Aways.** **Figures 80** and **81** show typical items we usually throw away but which can serve, sometimes with modification, as project components. For example, some caps from fancy bottles of perfume or cologne are nicely shaped for use as a stack on a toy locomotive. Others seem to have been specially designed to serve as a horn button on a car or as ready-to-glue-on headlights. Items like the reels of adding-machine

**Fig. 80.** Caps from fancy perfume and cologne bottles and similar containers can be ready-made components of toys, such as stacks for locomotives and horn buttons for cars.

**Fig. 81.** Other recyclable items are shown here. Some can be used as is; others can be altered to serve as bushings, spacers, etc.

tapes can serve as short dowels, bushings, or spacers. Some wood caps after being plugged are attractive ready-made wheels.

Other items that can be recycled include mailing tubes, jar covers, the handles of discarded brooms, coat hangers (when you need a piece of wire), the round containers that salt and some cereals are packed in, and so on. It's a question of seeing the items as usable material. Some containers can serve as major components. In the project section are some attractive lamps with bases made from oil cans and cookie tins.

**Copying Patterns.**    Many of the patterns in the book, especially the silhouette forms in the toys section, can be reproduced by using the enlarging-by-squares method **(Figure 82).** The system is this: Assume the drawing in the book is done on graph paper. You draw a graph with squares sized as the drawing suggests and then mark points where the pattern crosses lines. Then it's a matter of connecting the points.

Once the pattern is drawn, you can transfer it to the wood by using carbon paper. As an alternative you can cement the pattern directly to the wood. Or, if you wish to keep the design for future use, use the pattern to make a permanent template of thin plywood or hardboard. Of course, you can also draw the enlarging graph (with very light lines) directly onto the wood. You can also take a photograph of the book drawing and then enlarge it in the darkroom.

The enlarging-by-squares method can also be used in reverse. For example, if you happen onto an illustration in a magazine that you'd like to reproduce but that is too large for your purposes, put a graph over the illustration and transfer the pattern to a sheet of paper with squares of smaller size.

**Finishing.**    As we said earlier, children don't object to the natural look of wood **(Figure 83).** A very careful sanding job followed by a coat or two of nontoxic sealer or clear finish makes a presentable finale. For decorative touches, you can work with materials like self-adhesive stars, felt, tapes, letters, and numbers—all of which are available in a stationery store. Of course, work with colors if you prefer. It's important to choose nontoxic

**Fig. 82.**   This illustrates how to enlarge or reduce a drawing when transferring it from a pattern to the work. The procedure is known as enlarging by squares.

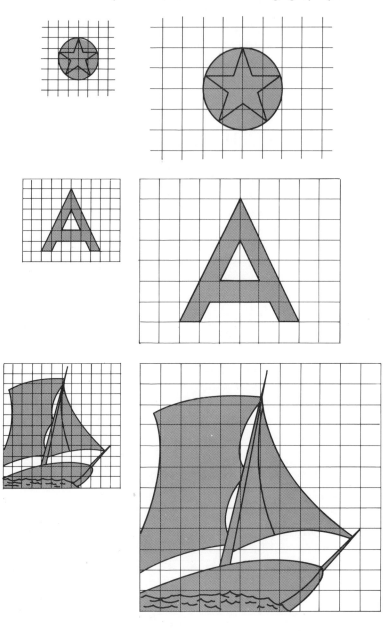

**Fig. 83.** Children don't seem to mind that the toy projects have a natural wood finish. You can add decorative details by working with some of the self-adhesive materials suggested in the text.

paints, which isn't difficult to do these days since lead and other poison bases have been outlawed.

Finishes for other types of projects are also available in nontoxic form. These include polyurethanes that can serve as primers, sealers, or finishes in themselves **(Figure 84).** Some require brush applications; others can simply be wiped on with a cloth. Instructions on the container will list the correct methods of application.

Polyurethanes are not recommended for use on projects such as cutting boards. Polyurethane flakes may present a health hazard, and marks from knife blades will mar the finish.

There is a special finish called "Salad Bowl Finish" that is a good choice for final touches on cutting boards, salad bowls, and the like. Because of its nontoxic formulation, it's also a good finish for toys and other projects used by children.

**Fig. 84.** Modern polyurethane materials that are non-toxic can be used on toys and other projects. Some are applied with a brush, others with a cloth. Follow the instructions on the container.

Another way to finish projects that come into contact with food is to use mineral oil. Apply a generous amount and allow it to soak in for 30 minutes or so. Then wipe off the excess. You can renew the finish when necessary simply by applying more of the oil. Don't use cooking oils for this purpose —they can turn rancid.

# II.
# MAINLY
# FOR
# KIDS:

# TOYS

# WHEELS
# AND AXLES

The easiest way to make small wheels is to slice them from dowels. Typically, dowels are made of maple or birch, come in 3- or 4-foot lengths, and range in diameters from $\frac{1}{8}$ inch up to more than 1 inch. Larger diameters and longer lengths are available as "rounds." The term includes a variety of molding products such as *half rounds* and *quarter rounds, closet rods* or "poles," and *hand rails* which are shown in **Figure 1.** Closet-rod diameters are usually about $1\frac{5}{8}$ or $1\frac{3}{4}$ inches. The hand rail is shown because the flat it has makes it easy to attach the cylinder to a flat surface; for, say, the boiler on a toy locomotive.

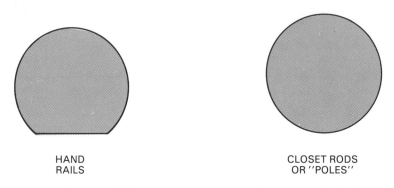

HAND
RAILS

CLOSET RODS
OR "POLES"

**Fig. 1.** "Rounds" are available as closet rods or poles, or as hand rails. Rails have a "flat" which makes the part suitable for attachment to a flat surface.

**Figure 2** shows how dowels can be sliced on a table saw. It is never a good or safe practice to use the rip fence as a stop to gauge the thickness of the cutoff. The cutoff piece might be captured between the fence and saw blade and could be thrown back or up at the operator, or the wood may bind the blade. The fence is used only as a holder for the jig, which serves as a stop. The distance from the front edge of the jig—which is clamped to the rip fence well forward of the saw blade—to the saw blade determines the

**Fig. 2.** Always use a stop—not the rip fence—to determine the thickness of cutoffs. Hold the work firmly against the stop and stand clear of the cutting path.

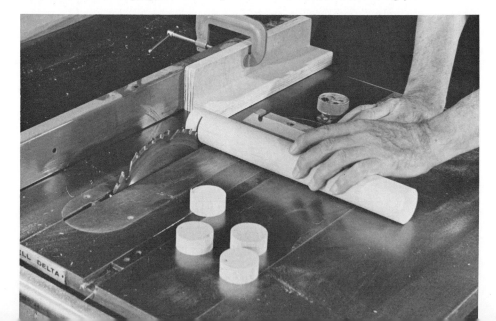

thickness of the cutoff. The setup provides a lot of room between rip fence and blade, so the cutoff can't be trapped.

Because the dowel pieces are round, after they are cut off they can still roll back toward you, but not with any force. Still, it's always a good idea to stand out of line of the saw blade. Scrap pieces of wood are often used as stops in this application, but you will find it more convenient to make the special jig **(Figure 3)** which you can keep on hand as an accessory.

**Fig. 3.** Here is a cut-off gauge, shown in the previous photo, that you can make and keep as an accessory. Glue and nail the parts together. Sand the wood smooth, round off corners, and apply a coat of sealer.

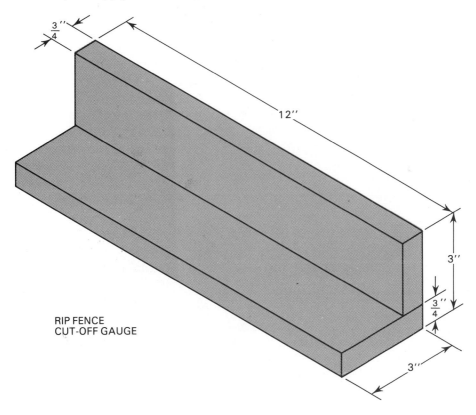

Dowels and rounds can be cut freehand with a hand saw, but an accurate job will demand great care. A better way is to make the cutoff box shown in **Figure 4.** This is a smaller version of the miter box we have already talked about, but it has a single guide kerf and its size is more suitable for the materials you will be cutting. A more sophisticated version of the cutoff box is shown in **Figure 5.** Here the base of the project has a V-channel so that rounds can be seated more securely. Either unit can be used with a conventional hand saw, but the cut edges will be easier to smooth if you work with a backsaw.

To locate the center of the cut-off dowel—so you can drill them for axles

**Fig. 4.** The cut-off box resembles a miter box, but has a single guide-kerf and is sized to be more suitable for dowels and other cylinders.

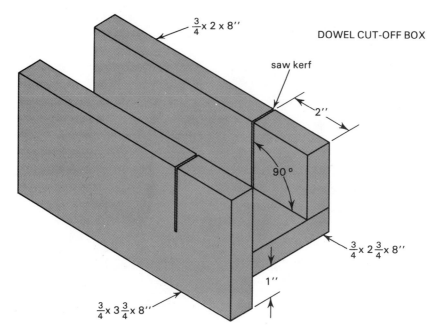

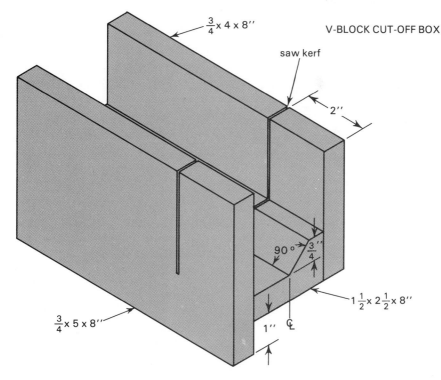

**Fig. 5.** This version of cut-off box has a V-shape channel in the base to hold round forms more securely.

—you can use a commercial center finder, or make one of the two styles shown in **Figure 6.** You may find the alternative design easier to build since it only calls for straight cuts. Either project serves the purpose and is used as follows: Place the round in the V and mark a diameter along the centered edge of the guide. Turn the part about 90 degrees and mark a second diameter. The center of the round will be where the lines intersect.

The center finder isn't limited to marking wheel centers. It can also be used for other jobs, such as marking mounting points on the ends of stock that will be turned in a lathe.

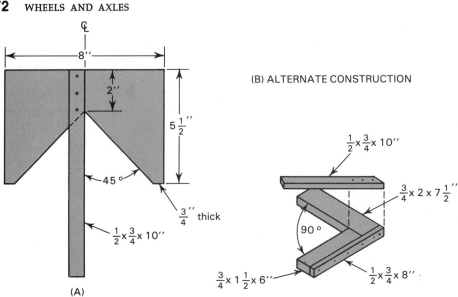

**Fig. 6.** Two ways to make a center finder for sawing. Each can be used to mark the center of round or square stock.

## DRILLING AXLE HOLES

Wheels can be individually marked and drilled, but this practice poses the possibility of error. That can be a nuisance if you are producing in quantity. A better strategy is to make the center-drilling jig shown in **Figure 7.** It can be used on a drill press or on a portable drill stand.

The jig works as follows: Use the center finder to mark the center location of one piece. Place the piece in the V of the jig, and then clamp the jig in place so that the center mark of the workpiece will be exactly under the drill bit. Then you can drill through as many parts as you wish without further layout. It's a good idea to use this jig to drill pilot holes. Later, the holes can be enlarged to whatever size is needed.

Construction details of the jig are shown in **Figure 8.** To make the T-slot, first form the $\frac{3}{16} \times \frac{5}{8}$-inch dado clear across the base of the jig. Then cut the $\frac{1}{4}$-inch-wide slot. The guides form a V whose point should be exactly

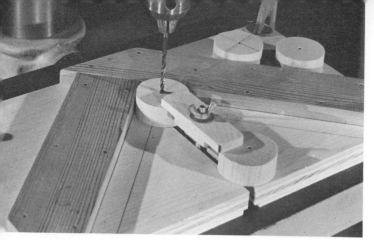

**Fig. 7.** The center-drilling jig makes it easy to accurately drill center holes in one or more pieces. Layout is done only on first piece, the one that is used to position the jig on the drill table.

**Fig. 8.** Construction details of the center-drilling jig. The text explains how the T-slot is formed.

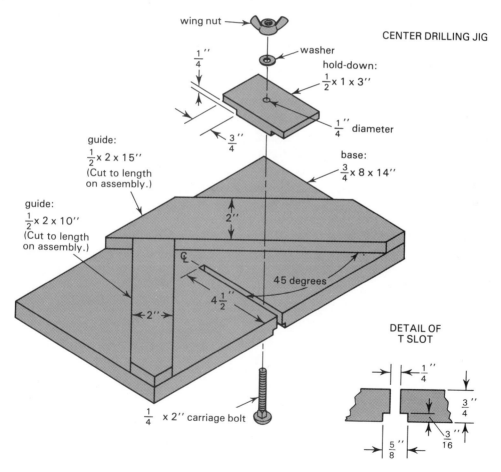

CENTER DRILLING JIG

wing nut

$\frac{1}{4}$"

washer

hold-down:
$\frac{1}{2}$ x 1 x 3"

$\frac{1}{4}$" diameter

$\frac{3}{4}$

guide:
$\frac{1}{2}$ x 2 x 15"
(Cut to length
on assembly.)

base:
$\frac{3}{4}$ x 8 x 14"

guide:
$\frac{1}{2}$ x 2 x 10"
(Cut to length
on assembly.)

2"

₵

45 degrees

$4\frac{1}{2}$"

2"

$\frac{1}{4}$ x 2" carriage bolt

DETAIL OF
T SLOT

$\frac{1}{4}$"

$\frac{3}{4}$"

$\frac{3}{16}$"

$\frac{5}{8}$"

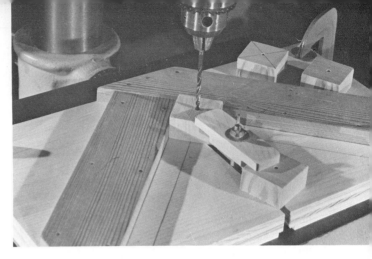

**Fig. 9.** The center-drilling jig can also be used to drill center holes in square pieces. The procedure does not change.

on the centerline of the T-slot. The hold-down makes sense since it's often inconvenient, sometimes unsafe, to hand-hold small parts. As shown in **Figure 9,** the jig can also be used to drill center holes in square pieces.

## LARGE WHEELS

Several types of tools can be used to form wheels with larger diameters than you can get from the largest ready-made rounds or dowels. *Hole saws* are available as individual units that mount on a universal mandrel. Each saw cuts a particular size disc, sizes can exceed 4 inches.

Another type of hole saw is shown in **Figure 10.** Because it comes with various blades, the one tool can be used to form discs that range in size from

**Fig. 10.** This type of hole saw comes with various blades—so the tool is usable for different size discs. All the blades mount on the single hub.

**Fig. 11.** Both the work and the back-up block should be securely clamped. The tool has a drill-pilot that bores a center or axle hole as it cuts the disc.

$1$–$2\frac{1}{2}$ inches. The saw is available with blade lengths that can penetrate $\frac{3}{4}$-inch stock, or with extra-long blades that can cut 2 inches deep.

Tools like this can be used in a portable drill or in a drill press **(Figure 11)**. With either tool, back up the work with scrap so the hole will be clean where the saw breaks through. Also, be sure that the work and the back-up block are securely clamped. One advantage of these saws is that they have a center drill. Thus, an exactly centered axle hole is formed as you cut the disc.

The tools shown in **Figure 12** are called *fly cutters* or *circle cutters.* They come in several sizes. "Small" ones can typically cut circles from about $1\frac{1}{8}$ inches up to better than 5 inches; "large" ones range from $1\frac{3}{4}$ inches to better than 8 inches. Tools like these require that you first drill a center hole for the pilot, and the cutters *must* be used in a drill press **(Figure 13)** at very slow speeds. Both the work and a back-up block should be securely clamped, and the feed pressure (the amount you pull on the drill press handle) should be light. Keep hands well away from the cutting area, since even at a slow speed the cutter will be a blur.

The fly cutter can be used to shape decorative, concentric grooves **(Figure 14)**. Simply cut smaller, limited-depth circles before you cut through for the disc. If you wish, you can grind a special point on a cutter for this kind of work. For example, a half-round shape that will produce cove-shaped grooves. You can also form decorative grooves with the hole saws. Just make shallow grooves with a number of smaller hole saws before you use the one that cuts through the material.

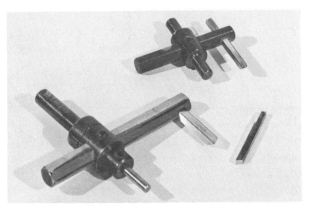

**Fig. 12.** Two sizes of fly cutters: like the hole saws, they are meant to cut holes, but they also cut out discs which make great wheels.

**Fig. 13.** The fly cutters are used in a drill press, *never* with a portable drill. Keep work and back-up block securely clamped. Use a slow speed and very light feed pressure.

**Fig. 14.** Forming decorative grooves by making smaller-than-wheel-size, limited-depth cuts. The same thing can be done with hole saws.

## OTHER WHEEL-FORMING TECHNIQUES

**Figure 15** shows a drill-press pivot-cutting method that can be used to cut circles or grooves of almost any size. Drive a nail through a back-up block, and then clamp the block to the drill table so that the distance from the nail to the cutter (a router bit) equals the radius of the circle. The work is drilled to fit the pivot nail, and then placed in position for cutting. Use a high drill-press speed, and if necessary, make repeat passes to achieve full depth of cut; lower the router bit a little for each rotation of the work. The depth of each cut will depend on the hardness of the wood. In general, a few shallow cuts will produce smoother results than a single, deep one.

The pivot-cutting method can also be used with a portable router. Drill a hole for a small nail at one end of a length of dowel or steel rod. Lock the other end of the rod in one of the holes normally used for the router's edge guide. The distance from the nail to the router bit will be the radius

**Fig. 15.** This drill-press, pivot technique lets you cut wheel discs of almost any size. Hold the work firmly and rotate it slowly against the router bit's direction of rotation.

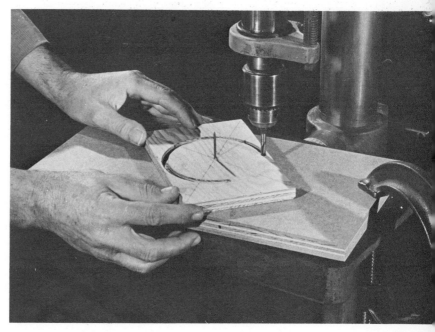

**Fig. 16.** The pivot-cutting method can also be used with a portable router. The size of the disc is limited only by the size of the material. Thus you can cut table tops as well as wheels for toys.

of the circle. The router is then pivoted about the nail to form a perfect circle **(Figure 16).** Here too, results will be better if you make several passes, deepening the cut each time. Techniques like this are not limited to wheel-making. They can be used to form circular pieces for table tops and the like.

## SMOOTHING WHEEL RIMS

Wheel rims can be sanded by hand, but there are methods that will make this chore easier and more accurate. One way is to mount a pair of wheels, or more, on a bolt, and secure them with a nut. Lock the free end of the bolt in the chuck of a portable drill, and secure the drill in a vise. Wrap a piece of sandpaper around a block of wood, and then apply the sandpaper to the turning wheels.

If you want to chamfer the wheel rims or round them off, mount the wheels individually on the bolt. This method can also be used on a drill press.

The jig shown in **Figure 17** allows fast sanding of circular edges with great accuracy. The jig is shown clamped to a disc-sander table, but it is just as usable on a belt sander or even a drill press that is turning a drum sander.

The jig is clamped to the tool's table so that its forward edge clears the abrasive surface. The work is mounted on the dowel/pivot, and the guide bar moved forward until the disc touches the abrasive. Then the guide bar

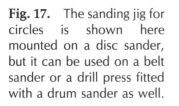

**Fig. 17.** The sanding jig for circles is shown here mounted on a disc sander, but it can be used on a belt sander or a drill press fitted with a drum sander as well.

is clamped into place and the work rotated. Make alignment marks on the guide bar and the jig (arrow in **Figure 17**) so duplicate pieces can be accurately reproduced **(Figure 18).** The dowel/pivot is long enough so that you can mount pairs of $\frac{3}{4}$-inch-thick wheels. If the wheels are thicker, and the capacity of the sanding tool permits it, you can substitute a longer dowel. Of course, you can also simultaneously sand a set of four wheels if wheel thickness, dowel/pivot length, and tool capacity are compatible. It is possible to pivot-sand four $\frac{1}{2}$- or $\frac{3}{4}$-inch-thick wheels. Four wheels that

**Fig. 18.** The work is mounted on the dowel/post and rotated. Pairs of wheels can be mounted and sanded simultaneously for a perfect match.

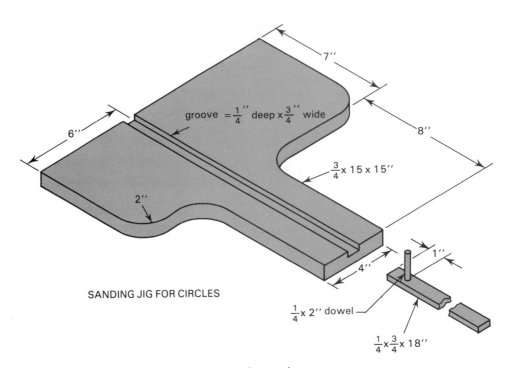

groove $=\frac{1}{4}''$ deep x $\frac{3}{4}''$ wide

7''

6''

8''

$\frac{3}{4}$ x 15 x 15''

2''

SANDING JIG FOR CIRCLES

4''

1''

$\frac{1}{4}$ x 2'' dowel

$\frac{1}{4}$ x $\frac{3}{4}$ x 18''

**Fig. 19.** How to make the sanding jig for circles.

are $1\frac{1}{2}$ inches thick would present problems. Better do them individually or, at most, in pairs. Construction details of the circular sanding jig are shown in **Figure 19.**

## WHEELS FROM READY-MADES

Wheels can be made from items like the curtain rings shown in **Figure 20.** These come in different sizes and are available in wood, metal, and plastic. The wooden ones in the photograph have an outside diameter of

$2\frac{3}{4}$ inches; the metal ones have an outside diameter of $1\frac{1}{2}$ inches. The rings have hangers, but they're not difficult to remove. Hangers on the wooden rings are just screw eyes that you simply unwind; on others the hangers can be removed by filing.

To turn the rings into wheels, cut snug-fitting wood or hardboard discs and press them into place—the rings become "tires" **(Figures 21 and 22).** You can size the discs for a nice fit with a fly cutter. It should require a *little* force to seat the discs, but be careful when working with wooden rings. If the discs are too large the rings will split. Coat the perimeter of the discs with glue before you install them.

**Figure 23** is an example of novelty wheels. These were made from tops of fancy bottles of cologne. The tops will usually have threaded inserts of metal or plastic. To remove the metal inserts, bend the top edge with a small screwdriver and use pliers to break the bond that holds the insert. The plastic inserts can simply be broken away, but protect your eyes from flying chips. The final step is to glue a center-drilled wooden plug into the hole.

**Fig. 20.** Curtain rings provide ready-made materials for wheels. They come in different sizes and are made of wood, plastic, and metal.

**Fig. 21.** The rings become good-looking wheels when they are filled with discs of wood or hardboard. Size discs for wooden rings carefully so that when you press them into place they won't split the ring.

**Fig. 22.** Plastic or metal rings also make handsome wheels. Such curtain rings have hangers (usually a loop) that must be filed off.

**Fig. 23.** Novelty wheels were made from the wooden tops from fancy bottles of cologne. The threaded inserts are removed, and the hole is filled with a predrilled wooden plug.

## WHEEL RIMS OR "TIRES"

Rims can be added to wooden wheels for a decorative touch, to protect floors or furniture, or to make the wheels more durable. **Figure 24** shows small wheels rimmed with plastic obtained from the canisters that 35mm film is packed in. The idea is to size a dowel or a turned cylinder to make a very tight fit in the canister. Then simply cut the canister into wheel thicknesses. Note that the rim and the outside surface of the wheel can be covered if you utilize the bottom of the canister. Many similar containers can be adapted for wheels of various diameters.

A "soft" rim is shown in **Figure 25.** This is simply a strip of cork that is attached with contact cement or white glue. If you use white glue, coat both the cork and the wheel rim. Use a heavy rubber band to hold the cork until the glue dries.

To make a wooden wheel more durable you can rim it with metal **(Figure 26).** Metals that work easily include aluminum or various types of flashing —the material used on roofs. Either material can be attached with contact cement or very small nails. If using nails, put two on each side of the joints and two or three more about the wheel's perimeter. Use a file to chamfer the edges of the metal, and then sand the edges smooth with emery paper.

**Fig. 24.** The plastic rims on these wheels came from 35-mm film canisters. Similar throwaways can serve as rims for wheels of various sizes.

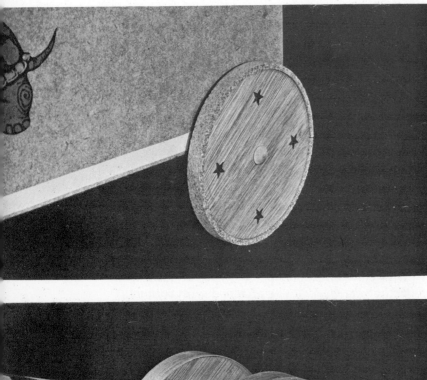

**Fig. 25.** This wheel is rimmed with cork to prevent marring of floors or furniture. A cork rim will also be quieter than a wooden one. Note the wood button used as a hub and the self-adhesive decorative stars.

**Fig. 26.** Metal rims make wooden wheels more durable. The metal can be easy-to-form aluminum or flashing, and can be secured with contact cement. These are the wheels on the Hobby Horse which will be shown later.

## MAKING RIMS AND WOODEN TUBES

Parts like those shown in **Figure 27** are not difficult to make from large rounds or turned cylinders if you work very carefully and use a drilling procedure like the one demonstrated in **Figure 28.**

**Fig. 27.** Wooden rings and tubes can be made from rounds or lathe-turned cylinders. Don't make the wall thickness of the pieces too thin, or they won't hold up.

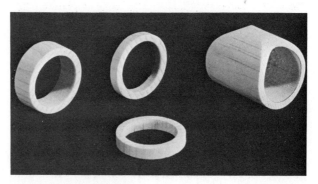

**Fig. 28.** Here's a way to make a wooden tube, which can be used as is or sliced into rings. This is a fly cutter, but one that removes material much as a conventional hole former does. Caution: Use care to avoid wood breakage here.

The drilling tool being used is a type of fly cutter, but instead of cutting circular grooves, it removes material just like a conventional drill bit. It's very important that the work be held securely and that the drilling pressure be very light. The advantage of the fly cutter is that you can form tubes of various inside diameters. Of course, for small tubes, you can work with conventional drills or spade bits. For rims and short tubes, the job can be done with a hole saw.

You can do some of this work with an electric hand drill, or even with a hand brace, but generally it's recommended that the operation be performed on a drill press.

## WHEEL AND AXLE ASSEMBLIES

The four most common wheel assemblies for push or pull toys are shown in **Figure 29.** Sometimes the choice is arbitrary; other times you can opt for a design that provides necessary stability. For example, design A of **Figure 29** will do for a small animal silhouette on wheels. But if the figure is tall, it will be less likely to topple if the wheels are spread by spacers or if it has a base, designs B or C.

Wheels can rotate on the axles, or axles and wheels can turn together **(Figure 30).** One advantage of using dowels as axles is that dowels are generally available a bit oversize. This means that if you want a $\frac{1}{4}$-inch dowel to fit tightly in a wheel or body of a toy, you just drill a $\frac{1}{4}$-inch hole. If the dowels you buy are more precise than usual, you can still work with the dowel-size hole if you use some glue to bond the connection.

If the wheel must turn on the axle or the axle must turn in the body of the toy, drill holes that are just oversize enough to permit the action—$\frac{5}{16}$-inch holes for $\frac{1}{4}$-inch dowels, $\frac{7}{16}$-inch holes for $\frac{3}{8}$-inch dowels, $\frac{9}{16}$-inch holes for $\frac{1}{2}$-inch dowels, and so on.

Wheels that turn on wooden axles are often secured with a short dowel **(Figure 31).** The dowel must fit the hole through the axle tightly and be located so the wheel can't bind. When you drive home a dowel retainer, do

**Fig. 29.** Here are basic wheel assemblies for pull or push toys. Wider-spread wheels give toys more stability.

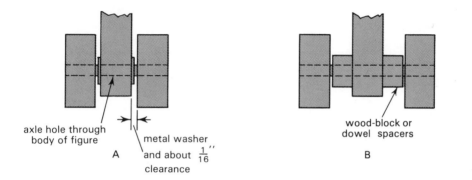

axle hole through
body of figure

A

metal washer
and about $\frac{1}{16}$″
clearance

wood-block or
dowel spacers

B

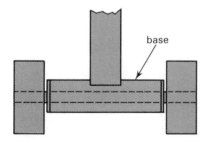

base

C

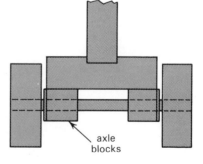

axle
blocks

D

**Fig. 30.** This drawing tells what conditions must be met for the wheels to turn independently or to rotate with the axles. It's always a good idea to use a washer (metal or hardboard) between the body and wheels.

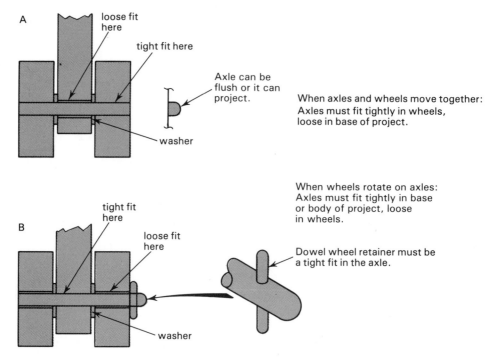

A

loose fit here

tight fit here

Axle can be flush or it can project.

washer

When axles and wheels move together: Axles must fit tightly in wheels, loose in base of project.

When wheels rotate on axles: Axles must fit tightly in base or body of project, loose in wheels.

tight fit here

loose fit here

B

Dowel wheel retainer must be a tight fit in the axle.

washer

**Fig. 31.** Wheels that rotate independently of the axle can be secured with a dowel that passes through the axle. Place the dowel so that the wheel can turn without binding.

it gently to avoid splitting the axle. Chamfering the ends of the retainer will make it easier to insert and will also add to appearance.

## WHEEL/AXLE ASSEMBLIES FOR ACTION

One way to make the head, ears, or tail of an animal pull toy nod or waggle is to use an axle that is bent into a U-shape at its center **(Figure 32)**. One end of the connecting rod loops around the base of the U, and the other end links to the part that moves. Make the axles from wire that is at least

**Fig. 32.** This is a popular method for producing action in a toy. The free end of the connecting rod, or drive wire, connects to the part that nods or waggles.

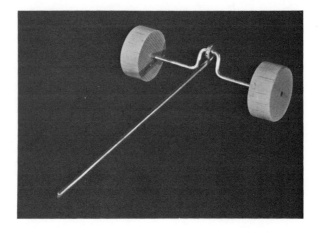

**Fig. 33.** Don't overdo the depth of the U-shape (dimension B) in the axle. A $\frac{1}{2}$-inch U-depth will result in a 1-inch stroke, and that will produce quite visible action.

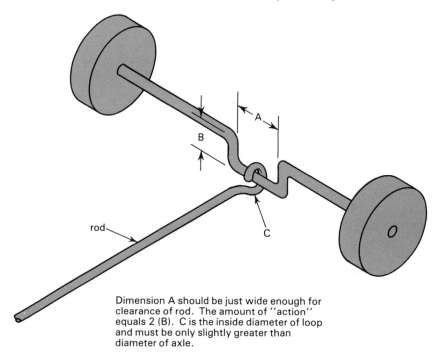

rod

Dimension A should be just wide enough for clearance of rod. The amount of "action" equals 2 (B). C is the inside diameter of loop and must be only slightly greater than diameter of axle.

No. 10 gauge ($\frac{1}{8}$-inch diameter). The connecting rod or drive wire can be of similar material or thinner wire, say No. 16 gauge ($\frac{1}{16}$-inch diameter).

The U-shape can be made with a pair of flat-nose pliers. Grip the length of wire close to its center, and bend the ends so you will have the base of the U. Then use the pliers to grip at the sides of the U and bend the free ends of the wire 90 degrees. Some gentle tapping with a hammer with the wire resting on a piece of hardwood or a metal block will straighten imperfections. It's best to work with a piece of wire that is longer than you need. Then you can be sure that the U will be centered by trimming the ends of the wire.

Form loops on the connecting rod by bending the wire around a piece of steel. Start the loop by gripping the wire against the rod with pliers. Move the pliers as you continue to form the loop. **Figure 33** illustrates some facts that apply to this type of action-axle.

Animal pull toys such as bunnies can be made to hop if you use an off-center axle at either the front or the rear of the toy **(Figure 34).** Don't

**Fig. 34.** Axles placed off-center will cause animal pull toys to hop. There is a limit to the amount of offset you can use. Too much, and the wheels won't turn.

off center

true center

**Fig. 35.** An eccentric cam placed on the axle will move the part placed on it up and down.

overdo the offset or the wheels won't turn as the toy is pulled. An offset of about $\frac{1}{4}$ inch will cause an easily noticeable hopping action.

Another way to make a toy hop or have an up-and-down action is to mount a cam on the axle **(Figure 35).** The animal, or whatever, that must move is pivot-mounted at one end. The other end rests on the cam and hops because of the eccentric cam rotation. **Figure 36** shows an important factor

**Fig. 36.** Situate the eccentric cam so that it won't bind against the surface the wheels are rolling on.

Distance A must be less than distance B.
Axle must fit tight into wheels *and* cam.

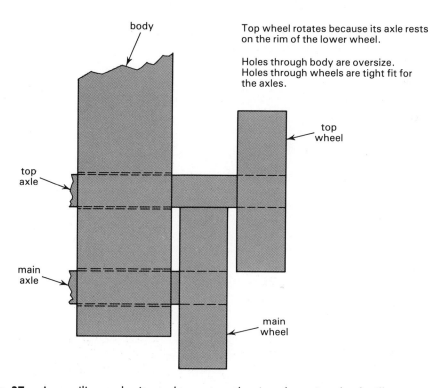

body

Top wheel rotates because its axle rests on the rim of the lower wheel.

Holes through body are oversize. Holes through wheels are tight fit for the axles.

top
wheel

top
axle

main
axle

main
wheel

**Fig. 37.** An auxiliary axle situated to rest on the rim of a main wheel will cause other parts to turn. This is the action that is used on the Pinwheel Toy shown later.

about cam action. You don't want the cam so big that it touches the same plane (or ground) that the wheels roll on.

Wheels can be organized to turn accessory axles and to rotate other parts of the project **(Figure 37).** The idea is to locate the extra axle to rest on the perimeter of the main wheel. All of these action designs are used on some of the projects that will follow.

## AT THE END OF THE AXLE

Three ways to finish the ends of wooden axles are shown in **Figure 38.** Most times, the choice is optional. These ideas apply when wheels and axles

**Fig. 38.** Three ways to end an axle. These ideas apply mostly to wooden axles.

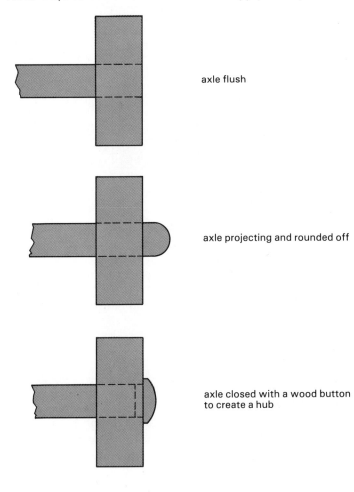

axle flush

axle projecting and rounded off

axle closed with a wood button
to create a hub

**Fig. 39.** These axle hubs were made by cutting off the ends of pens that were no longer usable. Similarly, many other throwaways can be recycled.

turn together. When the wheel turns on the axle, the axle must project and a retainer of some sort is used to keep the wheel in place. When the axle is wood, the dowel retainer we talked about can be used. If the axle is metal, you can tap on metal *caps,* which are generally available. Or use *shaft collars,* which lock in place with a set screw. Both items come in various sizes.

**Figure 39** shows examples of hubs made from throwaways. These were cut from the ends of used pens, but there are many other items that will serve the same purpose. Choose something that is a reasonably good fit for the axle. Use glue or cement to bond the hub in place.

# BASIC PULL TOYS

**Puppy Pull Toy.
Hippo Pull Toy.
Whale of a Pull.
Spotty Dog.
Drag a Dragon.**

The Puppy Pull Toy was painted in a tan tone. Details were done with a black felt-tip pen. Wheels and axles are natural. The spacers are a contrasting color. Scale drawings for similar toys are shown on upcoming pages.

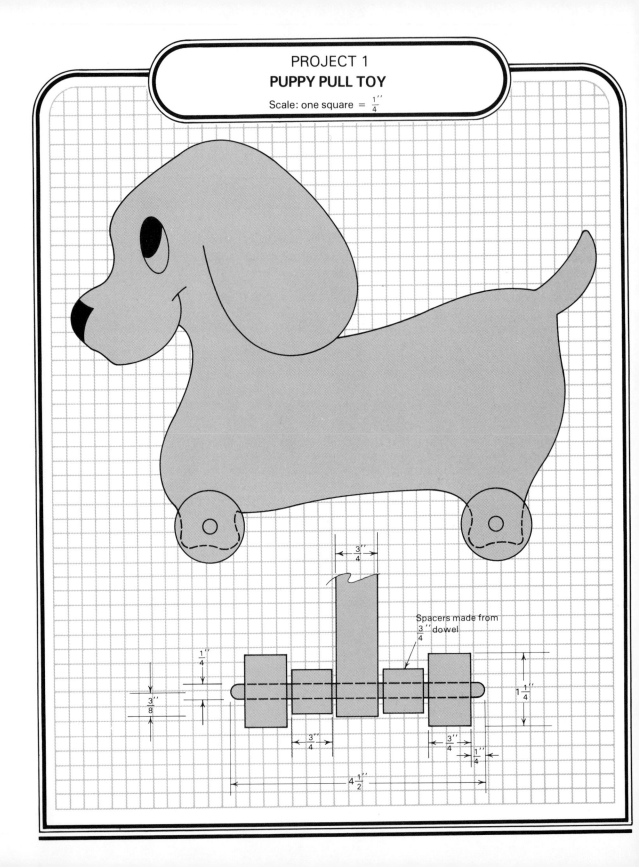

# PROJECT 1
## PUPPY PULL TOY

Scale: one square = $\frac{1}{4}$''

These projects are typical of pull toys that merely involve cutting silhouettes and then mounting them on wheels. Duplicate the figure by following one of the methods that were suggested on page 61, such as the enlarging-by-squares method. You can cut with a coping saw or saber saw, or on a jigsaw. If you wish, you can use a saber saw or a jigsaw to produce two silhouettes with a single cutting by making a layer or stack of two pieces of $\frac{3}{4}$-inch stock. Of course, the cutting can also be done on a band saw equipped with a narrow blade. Common band saws have a 6-inch depth of cut, which allows the pads to be considerably thicker—a good idea for producing in quantity.

You can work with either lumber or plywood. In either case, be sure that cut edges are sanded smooth and that edges are slightly rounded. Plywood edges will require more attention than lumber. Be sure to fill any voids with wood dough. For a natural finish, apply more sealer to edges than to surfaces. Allow it to soak in, and when dry, repeat the application if necessary.

A good way to prepare plywood edges for paint is as follows: Choose a putty, like Duratite's, which comes as a white powder. You mix the powder with water for use, to control the consistency. Thus you can produce a thin or a thick coating and brush it on the plywood edges. Allow the coating to dry, sand it smooth, and you have a respectable base for paint.

The drawing of Project 1 details the wheel/axle arrangement, and tells what the hole sizes should be. In this case, wheels and axles turn together. The spacers are made from dowel, but you can substitute if you wish.

**project 1**

**Puppy Pull Toy**

## MATERIALS LIST

Axles $= \frac{1}{4}''$ dowel $\times 4\frac{1}{2}''$
Holes through body *and* spacers $= \frac{5}{16}''$
Holes through wheels $= \frac{1}{4}''$
Body lumber or plywood $= \frac{3}{4} \times 8 \times 10''$

Sections cut from plastic or cardboard tubes that have thick walls will serve as well.

Use a length of strong string as the pull, tying it at one end to a small screweye placed in the figure. The free end of the string can simply be knotted, or you can use a wooden bead as a "handle." Wood beads of various sizes are available in craft supply stores, or you can make your own by drilling a hole through a short length of dowel. Place the screweye down low on the figure. The toy will more likely tip over if the pull is high.

## PROJECTS 2, 3, 4, and 5

These projects are made by following the same procedures outlined for the Puppy Pull Toy. Each silhouette pattern (see drawings) shows the location of axle holes and suggests wheel sizes. The wheel/axle arrangement can be like the one used on the puppy, or you can substitute one of the ideas that were shown in wheel-and-axle section earlier.

Some of the patterns are whimsical; children seem to enjoy this. Don't feel that artistic realism is a must when you design original forms. Often, you can "draw" with a compass and French curve and similar drafting instruments.

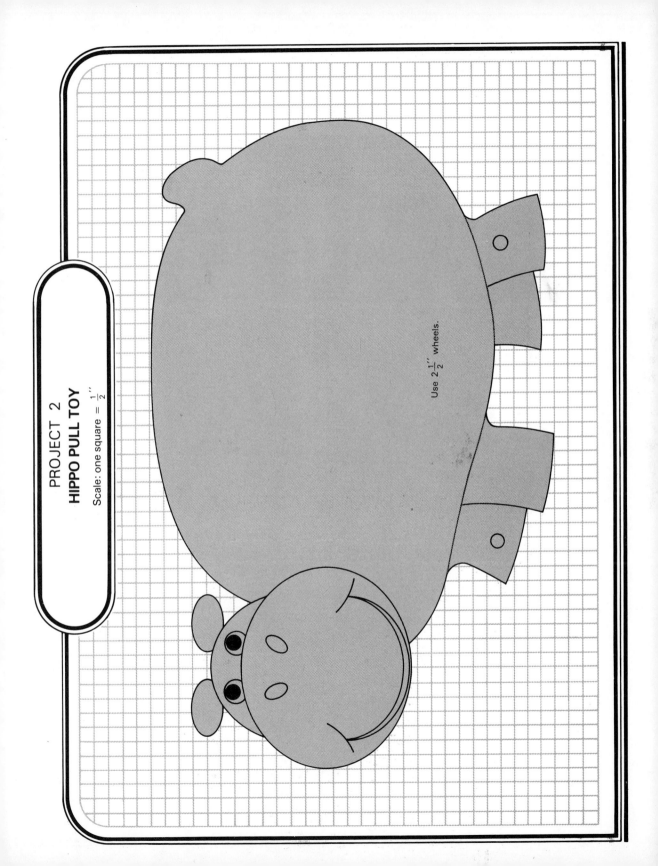

PROJECT 2
**HIPPO PULL TOY**

Scale: one square = $\frac{1}{2}$"

Use 2 $1\frac{1}{2}$" wheels.

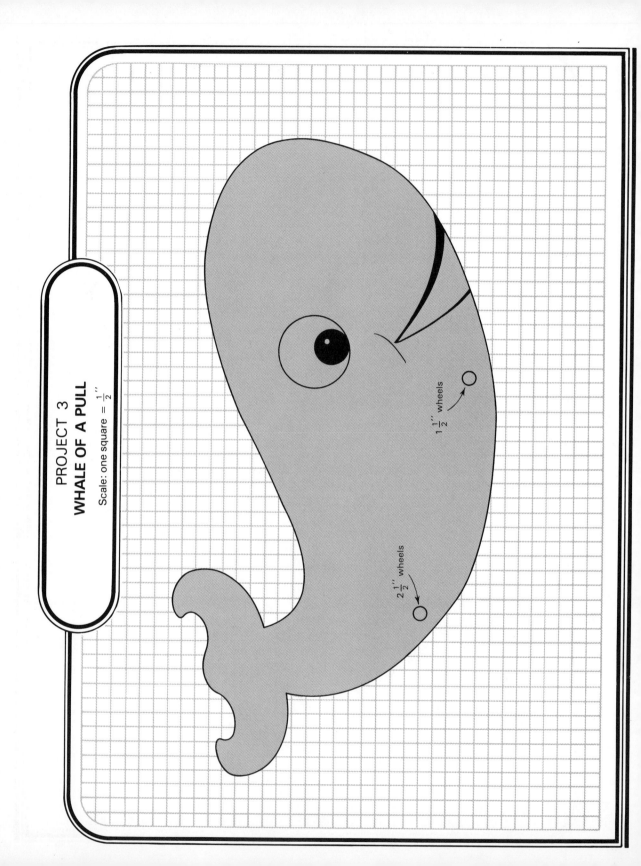

PROJECT 3
WHALE OF A PULL

Scale: one square = $\frac{1}{2}$

$2\frac{1}{2}''$ wheels

$1\frac{1}{2}''$ wheels

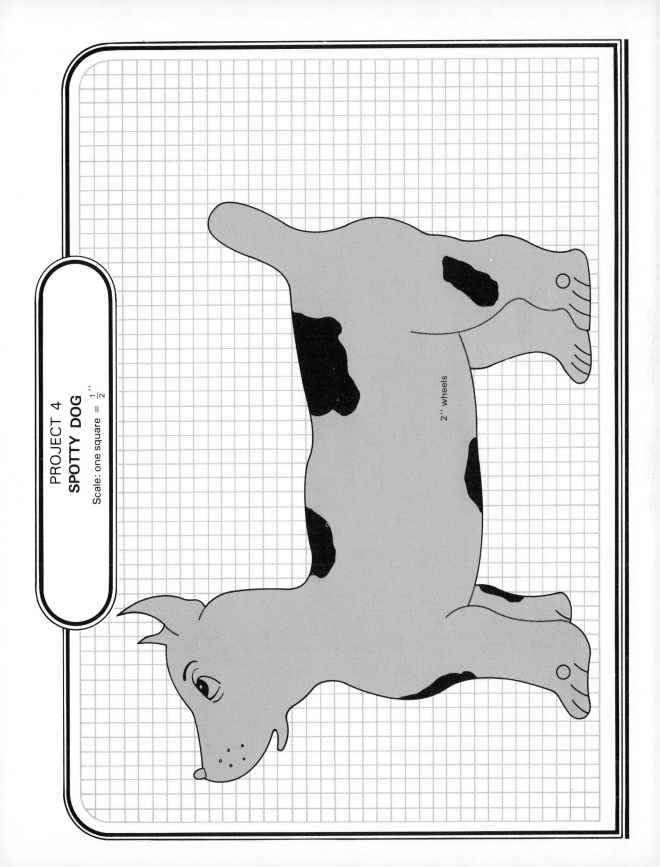

PROJECT 4
**SPOTTY DOG**

Scale: one square = $\frac{1}{2}$"

2" wheels

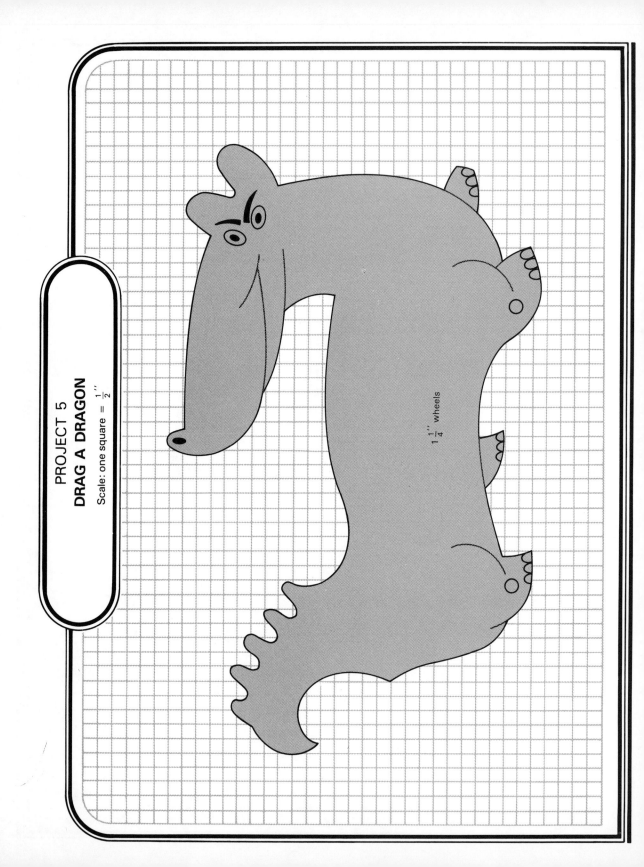

PROJECT 5
**DRAG A DRAGON**

Scale: one square = $\frac{1}{2}''$

$1\frac{1}{4}''$ wheels

# Toting Dachshund

This pull toy is a departure, because it is made so that it can be used to carry small objects. Start by making a pad of two pieces of $\frac{1}{2} \times 8 \times 18$-inch plywood. Draw the figure, but before cutting it to shape, locate and drill the holes for the axles.

Next, for the tote assembly, cut two pieces of plywood $\frac{1}{2} \times 2\frac{1}{2} \times 3$ inches and one piece $\frac{1}{2} \times 3 \times 9\frac{1}{2}$ inches and assemble them, as shown in the drawing, with glue and 4d nails.

Attach the sides of the project to the tote assembly by using glue and 4d finishing nails. Set the nail heads and conceal with wood dough. It's a good

The Toting Dachshund has a $\frac{1}{2}$-inch plywood body. The ears and wheels were cut from pine. The axles are hardwood dowels. Finishing was done with a nontoxic sealer.

idea, when doing this part of the job, to have the axles on hand. Put them in place before attaching the sides and they will serve as guides for correct alignment of the two pieces.

To make the ears, draw the pattern on a piece of $\frac{3}{4}$-inch stock. Drill the axle hole, cut the part to shape, and then saw it in half to get two identical parts each about $\frac{3}{8}$ inch thick.

Check the drawing for wheel sizes and for wheel/axle, ear/axle arrangements.

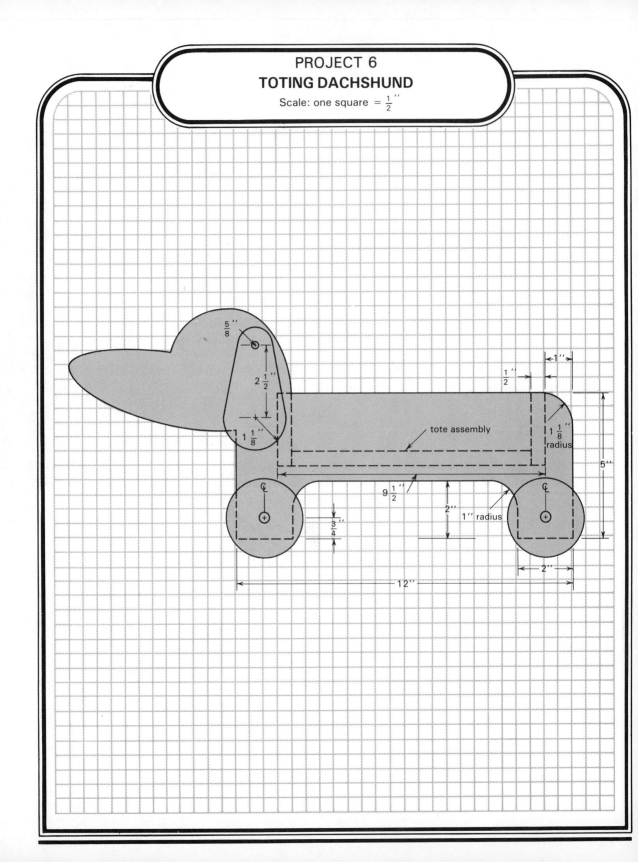

# PROJECT 6
# TOTING DACHSHUND
Scale: one square = $\frac{1}{2}''$

$\frac{5}{8}''$

$2\frac{1}{2}''$

$1\,1\frac{1}{8}''$

tote assembly

$\frac{1}{2}''$

$1''$

$1\frac{1}{8}''$ radius

$5''$

$9\frac{1}{2}''$

1'' radius

$2''$

$\frac{3}{4}''$

$2''$

$12''$

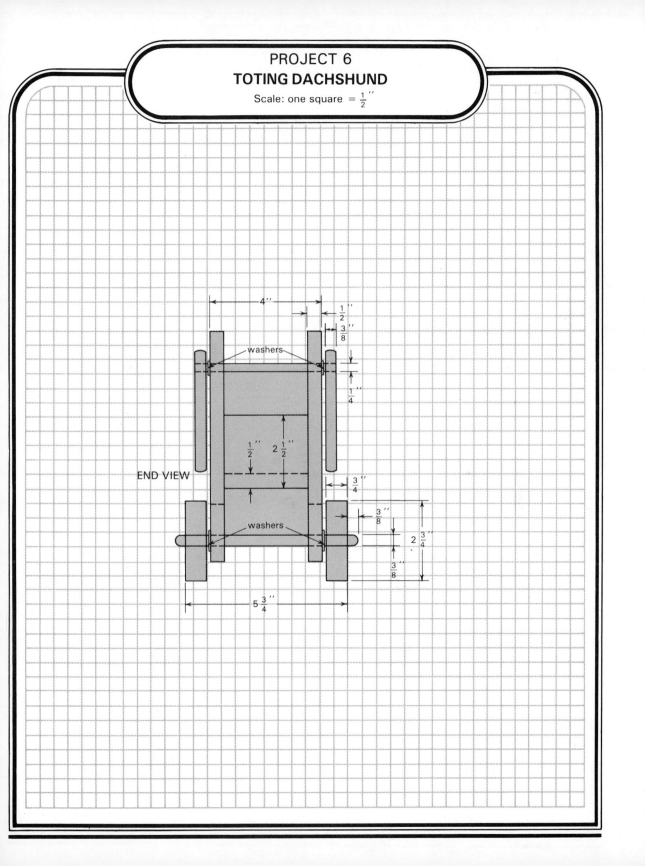

# PROJECT 6
## TOTING DACHSHUND
Scale: one square = $\frac{1}{2}$"

4"

$\frac{1}{2}$"

$\frac{3}{8}$"

washers

$\frac{1}{4}$"

$\frac{1}{2}$"    $2\frac{1}{2}$"

END VIEW

$\frac{3}{4}$"

$\frac{3}{8}$"

washers

$2\frac{3}{4}$"

$\frac{3}{8}$"

$5\frac{3}{4}$"

# PULL TOYS WITH ACTION

# Hopping Bunny Pull Toy

The bunny seems to hop as it is pulled because the axle holes in the front wheels are offset.

Draw and cut out the animal silhouette in the usual fashion. Make the base from a piece of $\frac{3}{4} \times 3 \times 7\frac{1}{2}$-inch lumber. The centered groove is easy to cut on a table saw, and it can be done with hand tools. But if it's a chore for you, skip it. Just butt-joint the figure to the base. Drill the axle holes

The Hopping Bunny Pull Toy was painted white and detailed with a black, felt-tip pen. The wheels have a natural finish. For a decorative touch on the wheels, apply perfect or erratically cut circles of self-adhesive felt.

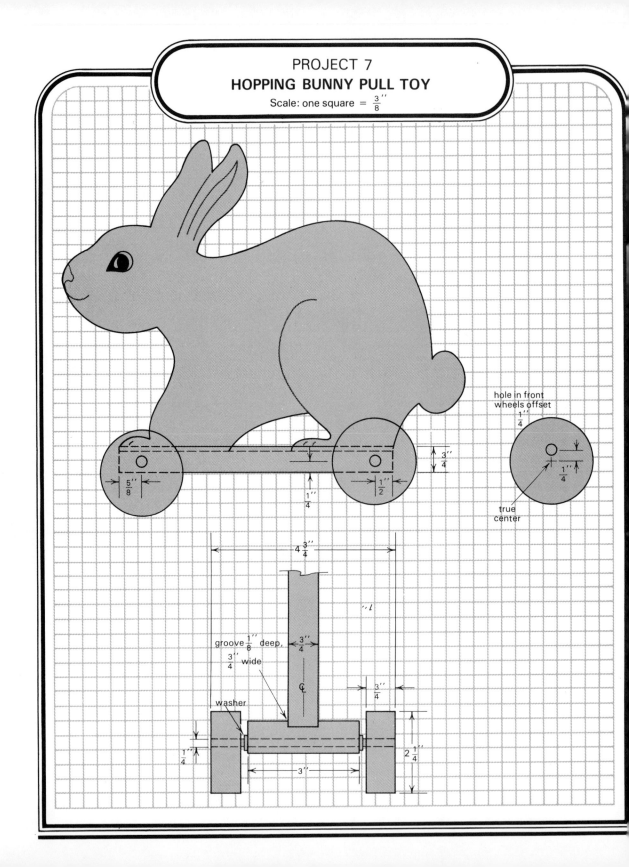

# PROJECT 7
## HOPPING BUNNY PULL TOY
Scale: one square = $\frac{3}{8}''$

through the base very carefully. If you are working with hand tools, it may be wise to mark the hole location on each edge of the stock so you can form half-way holes from each edge. Attach the figure to the base with glue and 7d nails.

The axle holes in the rear wheels are center-drilled, but those in the front wheels are offset in the amount shown in the drawing. This will cause an obvious hopping action while still allowing the wheels to turn freely.

The wheel/axle arrangements are detailed in the drawing.

# Walking Ducks Pull Toy

This toy employs the cam action that was described on page 92. The bar to which the ducks are attached pivots at one end and has an up-and-down movement, because the free end rests on the eccentric cam rotated by the axle of the front wheels.

Start the project by making the sides and ends of the base and assembling them with glue and small finishing nails. Next, cut the dadoes in the base

The Walking Ducks Pull Toy has a natural finish. All of the round parts were cut from hardwood dowels. The wheels and cam are plywood; other parts are pine. If you have a hole punch you can make small discs of black paper and paste them on as eyes; otherwise, draw the eyes with black ink.

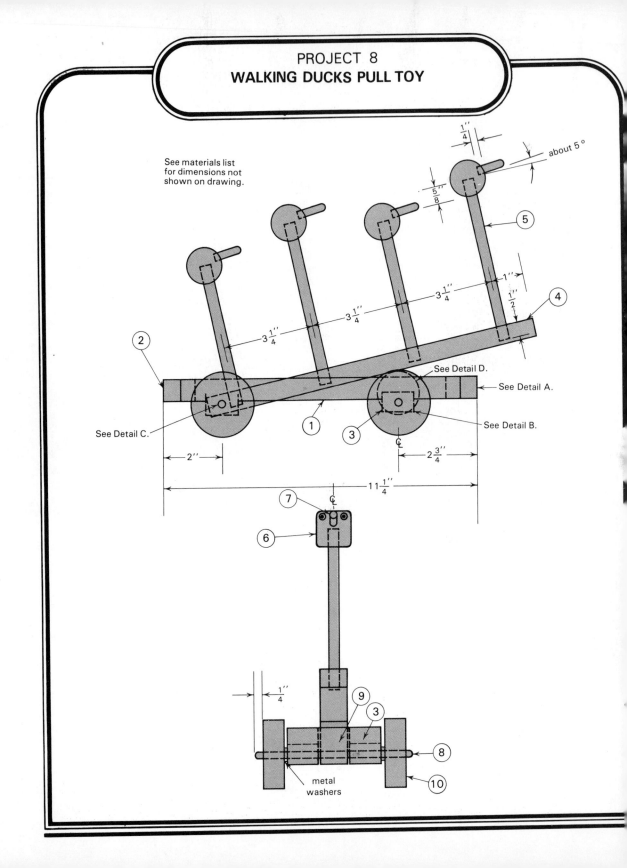

See materials list
for dimensions not
shown on drawing.

about 5°

See Detail D.

See Detail A.

See Detail C.

See Detail B.

metal
washers

## project 8
### Walking Ducks Pull Toy

# MATERIALS LIST

| Part No. | Name | Pieces | Size | Material |
|---|---|---|---|---|
| 1 | base sides | 2 | $\frac{3}{4} \times 1\frac{1}{8} \times 10''$ | lumber |
| 2 | base ends | 2 | $\frac{3}{4} \times 1\frac{1}{8} \times 3\frac{3}{8}''$ | " |
| 3 | axle blocks | 4 | $\frac{3}{4} \times 1\frac{1}{8} \times 1\frac{1}{8}''$ | " |
| 4 | bar | 1 | $\frac{3}{4} \times 1 \times 12''$ | " |
| 5 | necks | 2 | $\frac{3}{8} \times 5\frac{3}{4}''$ | dowel |
| | | 2 | $\frac{3}{8} \times 5''$ | " |
| 6 | heads | 4 | $1\frac{1}{4} \times 1\frac{1}{4}''$ | dowel |
| 7 | noses | 4 | $\frac{1}{4} \times 1''$ | " |
| 8 | axles | 2 | $\frac{1}{4} \times 5\frac{3}{4}''$ | " |
| 9 | cam | 1 | $\frac{3}{4} \times 1\frac{1}{2}''$ dia. | lumber |
| 10 | wheels | 4 | $\frac{3}{4} \times 2\frac{3}{8}''$ dia. | " |

Holes through wheels $= \frac{1}{4}''$
Holes through axle blocks $= \frac{5}{16}''$
Hole through cam $= \frac{1}{4}''$
Pivot hole through bar $= \frac{5}{16}''$
Hole in bar and heads for necks $= \frac{3}{8}''$
Holes for noses $= \frac{1}{4}''$

for the axle blocks. Make the axle blocks and use glue to install them in the base.

Cut the bar (part 4 in the drawing) to size. Drill the pivot hole, as show in Detail C, and the holes for the dowels which serve as necks for the d Make the heads and noses by slicing off sections of dowel, and th the head-piece holes. Be sure the pieces are firmly held, r whether you form the holes on a power tool or by hand. Ac angles are not really critical; they can even differ from the neck pieces to length and then assemble necks, finally, put the assemblies in place on the bar. If t

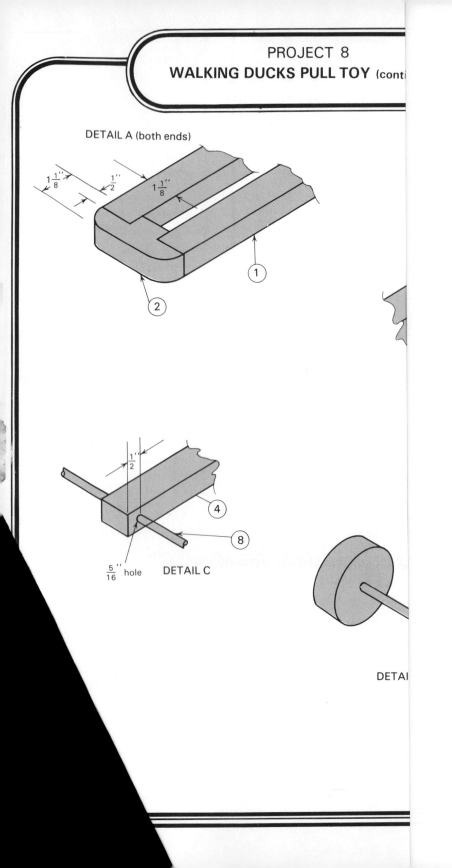

DETAIL A (both ends)

$1\frac{1}{8}''$

$\frac{1}{2}''$

$1\frac{1}{8}''$

①

②

$\frac{1}{2}''$

④

⑧

$\frac{5}{16}''$ hole    DETAIL C

DETAI

in the holes you've drilled for them, apply some glue before making the connections.

The next step is to make the axles, wheels, and cam. When you assemble the rear axle and wheels, put the bar in place so the axle will pass through the pivot hole. Detail D in the drawing shows how the cam mounts on the front axle. This too should be placed in the center opening of the base so the front axle can be forced through it. The cam must be a tight fit if it is to turn as the axle turns.

# Dog with Waggly Ears

The dog's ears flap happily when the toy is pulled because of the drive wire that runs from the rear wheels to the cam mounted on the ear-axle.

Start the project by drawing the silhouette on one of three pieces of $\frac{3}{4} \times 9\frac{1}{2} \times 13\frac{1}{2}$-inch lumber. Because the total thickness of the parts will be $2\frac{1}{4}$ inches, it will be difficult to saw them as a pad by hand or even with a saber saw or jigsaw. Best bet is to saw a pad of two pieces, and then use one of them as a pattern for the third piece. The center piece of the body is cut as shown by the dotted lines in the drawing. This provides the open area that is needed for the cam and the drive wire.

All of the wooden parts for the Dog with the Waggly Ears are pine lumber. Finishing was done with several coats of sealer. Details were added with a felt-tip pen.

Next, cut all the remaining parts—cam, axles, wheels, and ears. To do the ears, draw the pattern on a piece of $\frac{3}{4}$-inch lumber. After drilling the ear-axle hole and cutting the part to shape, slice it in half so you will have two identical pieces. Before going farther, study Section A-A and Details A and B in the drawing. These show how the cam is mounted and how the rear axle should be shaped.

Put one side of the body and the center pieces together temporarily by using small clamps. You can then mount the cam and rear axle and test to see exactly how long the drive wire must be and whether it has sufficient

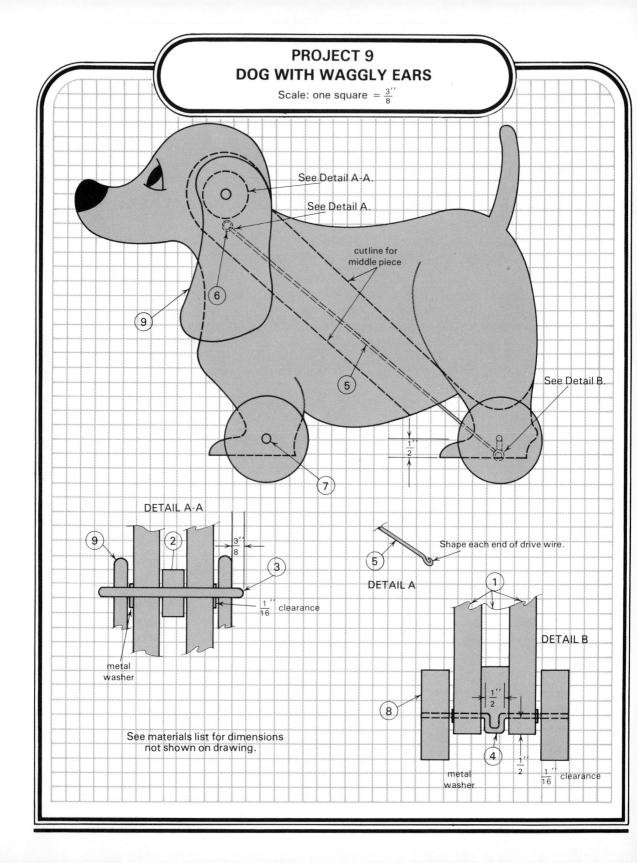

# PROJECT 9
# DOG WITH WAGGLY EARS

Scale: one square = $\frac{3''}{8}$

See Detail A-A.

See Detail A.

cutline for middle piece

See Detail B.

$\frac{1''}{2}$

DETAIL A-A

$\frac{3''}{8}$

$\frac{1}{16}''$ clearance

metal washer

Shape each end of drive wire.

DETAIL A

DETAIL B

$\frac{1''}{2}$

$\frac{1''}{2}$

$\frac{1}{16}''$ clearance

metal washer

See materials list for dimensions not shown on drawing.

**project 9**
**Dog with Waggly Ears**

# MATERIALS LIST

| Part No. | Name | Pieces | Size | Material |
|---|---|---|---|---|
| 1 | body parts | 3 | $\frac{3}{4} \times 9\frac{1}{2} \times 13\frac{1}{2}''$ | lumber |
| 2 | ear cam | 1 | $\frac{3}{4} \times 1\frac{1}{4}''$ dia. | " |
| 3 | ear axle | 1 | $\frac{1}{4} \times 4''$ | dowel |
| 4 | rear axle* | 1 | 10 ga. (or $\frac{1}{8}''$) $\times$ 6″ | wire |
| 5 | drive wire* | 1 | 16 ga. (or $\frac{1}{16}''$) $\times$ 12″ | " |
| 6 | connector | 1 | $\frac{1}{4}''$ | screweye |
| 7 | front axle | 1 | $\frac{1}{4} \times 4''$ | dowel |
| 8 | wheels | 4 | $\frac{3}{4} \times 2\frac{3}{8}''$ dia. | lumber |
| 9 | ears | 2 | $\frac{3}{8} \times 3\frac{1}{2} \times 5\frac{1}{2}''$ | " |

*Lengths are oversize so parts may be checked on assembly.
Hole through body for front axle $= \frac{5}{16}''$
Hole through front wheels $= \frac{1}{4}''$
Hole through ear cam $= \frac{1}{4}''$
Holes through body for ear axle $= \frac{5}{16}''$
Holes through ears $= \frac{1}{4}''$
Hole in wheels for rear axle $= \frac{3}{32}''$
Hole through body for rear axle $= \frac{5}{32}''$

clearance. When you are satisfied that the action is smooth, you can do the permanent assembly.

The body parts—with the axle-mounted cam, drive wire, and rear axle in place—can be bonded together with glue and clamps, or you can skip the clamping by driving a half dozen or so 6d finishing nails at strategic points around the perimeter from both sides. Set the nail heads and fill the holes with wood dough.

Now add the wheels and ears. Be sure the rear wheels fit very tightly on the axle. We call for a $\frac{3}{32}$-inch hole, which worked fine for the 10 gauge axle-wire used. It might pay to do a test! Drill a hole in some scrap wood and see how the wire you use will fit.

# Elephant with Nodding Head

The elephant will keep nodding as long as he is moved along. The action is caused by the same type of mechanism used on Project 9, except that the drive wire connects to the front axle.

The body consists of four separate pieces—two similar outside pieces, the center piece (or divider), and the head and trunk. You can cut the two similar pieces as one by stacking them. The other two are cut individually

**124**

The Elephant with the Nodding Head has a natural finish and black details. The decorative touches are self-adhesive stars that you can buy in a stationery store.

as shown by the dotted lines on the drawing. The lines noted as "marked lines" are details that you can add with a felt-tip pen after the project is assembled. They are not cut-lines.

Because there is access to the mechanism at the front of the toy, there is no need to do a temporary assembly for testing. Mount the head on its axle, and then with the head-axle and the front axle in place, bond the three

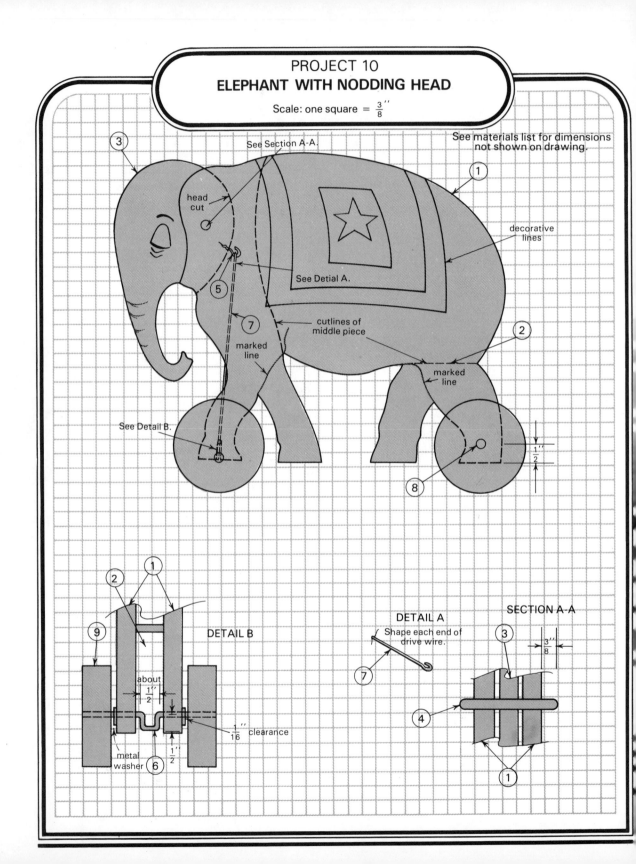

## project 10
### Elephant with Waggly Trunk

# MATERIALS LIST

| Part No. | Name | Pieces | Size | Material |
|---|---|---|---|---|
| 1 | body piece (outside) | 2 | $\frac{1}{2} \times 9 \times 10''$ | lumber or plywood |
| 2 | body piece (middle) | 1 | $\frac{3}{4} \times 6\frac{1}{2} \times 7\frac{1}{2}''$ | " |
| 3 | head | 1 | $\frac{1}{2} \times 3\frac{3}{4} \times 6''$ | " |
| 4 | head axle | 1 | $\frac{1}{4} \times 2\frac{5}{8}''$ | dowel |
| 5 | connector | 1 | $\frac{1}{4}''$ | screweye |
| 6 | front axle* | 1 | 10 ga. (or $\frac{1}{8}''$) $\times$ 6'' | wire |
| 7 | drive wire* | 1 | 16 ga. (or $\frac{1}{16}''$) $\times$ 7$\frac{1}{2}''$ | " |
| 8 | rear axle | 1 | $\frac{1}{4} \times 3\frac{5}{8}''$ | dowel |
| 9 | wheels | 4 | $\frac{3}{4} \times 2\frac{1}{2}''$ dia. | lumber |

*Lengths are oversize so parts may be checked on assembly.
Hole through body for front axle $= \frac{5}{32}''$
Holes in wheels for front axle $= \frac{3}{32}''$
Hole through body for rear axle $= \frac{5}{16}''$
Hole through rear wheels $= \frac{1}{4}''$
Hole through head $= \frac{5}{16}''$
Hole through body for head axle $= \frac{1}{4}''$

body parts together with glue and clamps, or with glue and 3d or 4d finishing nails.

It's a good idea first to form a loop only at one end of the drive wire. Connect it to the screweye in the elephant's head and then manually cause the head to nod so you can judge how long the wire should be. Be sure to place the screweye so that the trunk will not hit the drive wire at the end of the head's down stroke.

Section A-A and Details A and B show the way the head is mounted and the front wheel/axle arrangement.

# Rolling Drum Push or Pull Toy

This project intrigues children because the figures (or whatever design you care to use on the drum) rotate as the toy is moved. How you decorate the drum is optional. The figure we used on our project was cut from self-adhesive wallpaper that has designs especially appropriate for a youngster's room. The figure was applied after the drum was painted white.

Start the project by cutting the parts for the base. The axle holes in the sides of the base can be drilled before or after the pieces are assembled. Detail A shows how the base end-pieces are shaped. If you choose to avoid

The figure on the drum was cut from self-adhesive wall paper. There are other ways to decorate. Use a variety of small figures, paint an original design, or draw a spiral. The perimeter of the drum is covered with $\frac{3}{4}$-inch-wide red tape.

The flanges on the rotators might be considered optional, but they make the drum less likely to tip over. The wheels here were cut from hardboard-veneered plywood, but only because there happened to be a scrap piece available. The wheels can be either lumber or plywood.

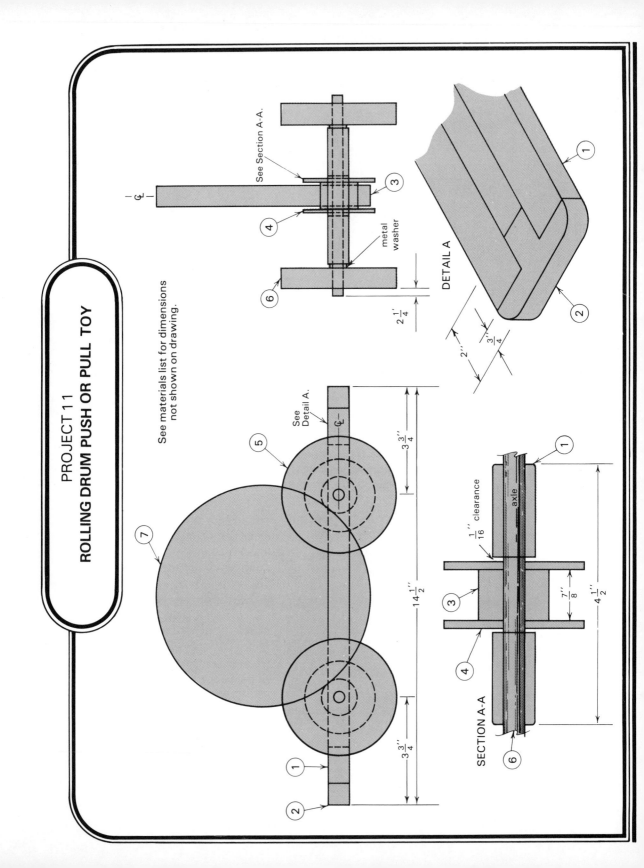

PROJECT 11
ROLLING DRUM PUSH OR PULL TOY

See materials list for dimensions not shown on drawing.

DETAIL A

See Section A-A.

metal washer

$2\frac{1}{4}$

See Detail A.

$3\frac{3}{4}''$

$14\frac{1}{2}''$

$3\frac{3}{4}''$

$2''$

$\frac{3}{4}''$

$\frac{1}{16}''$ clearance

axle

$\frac{7}{8}''$

$4\frac{1}{2}''$

SECTION A-A

### project 11
### Rolling Drum Push or Pull Toy

## MATERIALS LIST

| Part No. | Name | Pieces | Size | Material |
|---|---|---|---|---|
| 1 | base sides | 2 | $\frac{3}{4} \times 1\frac{5}{8} \times 13''$ | lumber |
| 2 | base ends | 2 | $\frac{3}{4} \times 2 \times 4\frac{1}{2}''$ | " |
| 3 | rotators | 2 | $1\frac{1}{4} \times \frac{7}{8}''$ | dowel |
| 4 | flanges | 4 | $\frac{1}{8} \times 2\frac{1}{2}''$ dia. | plywood |
| 5 | wheels | 4 | $\frac{3}{4} \times 4''$ dia. | lumber |
| 6 | axles* | 2 | $\frac{3}{8} \times 7''$ | dowel |
| 7 | drum | 1 | $\frac{3}{4} \times 7\frac{1}{2}''$ dia. | lumber or plywood |

*Length is oversize; trim on assembly.
Holes through base $= \frac{7}{16}''$
Holes through rotators, flanges, and wheels $= \frac{3}{8}''$

the notching that is shown, just use a $\frac{3}{4}$-inch-thick piece and butt-joint it to the ends of the side pieces. In either case, use glue and 6d finishing nails to bond the parts together.

Make the rotators from dowel and the flanges from $\frac{1}{8}$-inch-thick plywood or hardboard. The axle holes can be predrilled in individual pieces, or you can form them after the flanges are glued to the rotators. Remember that the rotator/flange assemblies must be a tight fit on the axles. Put them in place by setting them in the opening in the base and then passing the axle through. The axles will pass easily through the holes in the base, but will have to be tapped with a hammer to pass through the rotator/flange assemblies.

The final construction step is to cut the disc for the drum—which you can do by following one of the methods described beginning on page 74.

# Push or Pull Ferris Wheel

This toy takes a bit of time to make, but the results are satisfying. It proved to be one of the favorite action toys among the children who tested these toy projects.

Start the project by doing a careful layout on one of two pieces of $\frac{1}{2} \times 7 \times 7$-inch plywood or lumber. Pad, or stack, the pieces and cut them as one to get two identical parts. Be sure to drill the holes for the seat axles and the main axle before separating the pieces.

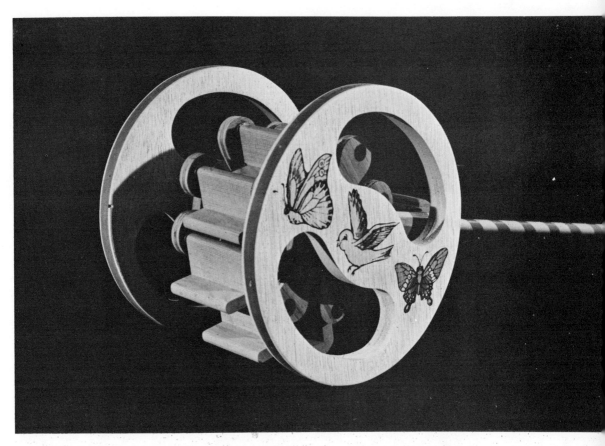

Little David and many other children loved the Ferris Wheel. The handle of the toy was spiral-wound with a colorful tape.

The outside of the main wheels were painted white and then decorated with small figures cut from self-adhesive, children's-room wall paper. The perimeters of the wheels were covered with tape.

The best way to make the seats is to cut a 25- or 26-inch length of $2 \times 4$ (actual size is $1\frac{1}{2} \times 3\frac{1}{2}$ inches) so that it measures $1\frac{1}{2} \times 1\frac{3}{4}$ inches. Then reduce the piece by making a rabbet cut so you will end up with an L-shaped part with leg thicknesses of $\frac{1}{2}$ inch. Then the part can be cut into 3-inch-long sections. If this procedure is a chore for you, make the seats by gluing and nailing together suitably sized pieces of $\frac{1}{2}$-inch stock.

The seat axle holes won't be difficult to form on a drill press. If you work by hand, you will be more accurate if you drill half-way holes from each end. Cut the seat axles to length and then make an assembly of the seats, axles, and ferris wheels. The axles must be a loose fit in the seat holes, but a tight fit in the wheels.

Next, draw the outline of the yoke on a piece of $1\frac{1}{2} \times 5\frac{5}{8} \times 9\frac{1}{4}$-inch lumber and mark the locations of the holes required for the main axle and for the handle. It is best to drill these holes. Drill about $1\frac{3}{4}$ inches deep for the handle hole and about $\frac{3}{4}$ inches deep for the axle holes before cutting the yoke to shape.

Cut the handle to length and insert it into the yoke after coating the end with glue. You can add a couple of 3d finishing nails as reinforcement; just drive them through the yoke so that they penetrate the handle. The handle grip is a ready-made wooden draw pull. It will already have a center for drilling since it is marked for screw attachment. Hold the ball securely with a clamp or in a vise when you form the hole for the handle. Attach the ball with glue.

The main wheels are discs 10 inches in diameter cut from $\frac{3}{4}$-inch-thick plywood or lumber. Make the layout shown in the drawing on one of two pieces that you pad for simultaneous cutting. Be sure to drill the hole for the main axle before separating the pieces.

All you have to do now is the final assembly. Remember that only the main wheels and the ferris wheels must be a tight fit on the main axle. The axle holes through the yoke are large enough so the yoke can pivot freely.

## project 12
### Push or Pull Ferris Wheel

# MATERIALS LIST

| Part No. | Name | Pieces | Size | Material |
|---|---|---|---|---|
| 1 | ferris wheel | 2 | $\frac{1}{2} \times 7 \times 7''$ | plywood or lumber |
| 2 | seats | 8 | $1\frac{1}{2} \times 1\frac{3}{4} \times 3''$ | lumber |
| 3 | seat axles | 8 | $\frac{1}{4} \times 4\frac{1}{2}''$ | dowel |
| 4 | main axle | 1 | $\frac{1}{2} \times 8\frac{1}{2}''$ | " |
| 5 | yoke | 1 | $1\frac{1}{2} \times 5\frac{5}{8} \times 9\frac{1}{4}''$ | lumber |
| 6 | handle | 1 | $\frac{1}{2} \times 21''$ | dowel |
| 7 | handle grip | 1 | 2'' ball | ready-made draw pull |
| 8 | main wheels | 2 | $\frac{3}{4} \times 10 \times 10''$ | plywood or lumber |

Holes for seat axles (in ferris wheel) $= \frac{1}{4}''$
Axle hole in seats $= \frac{5}{16}''$
Center hole in ferris wheel $= \frac{1}{2}''$
Hole through yoke (for main axle) $= \frac{9}{16}''$
Hole through main wheels $= \frac{1}{2}''$
Holes for handle in yoke and handle grip $= \frac{1}{2}''$

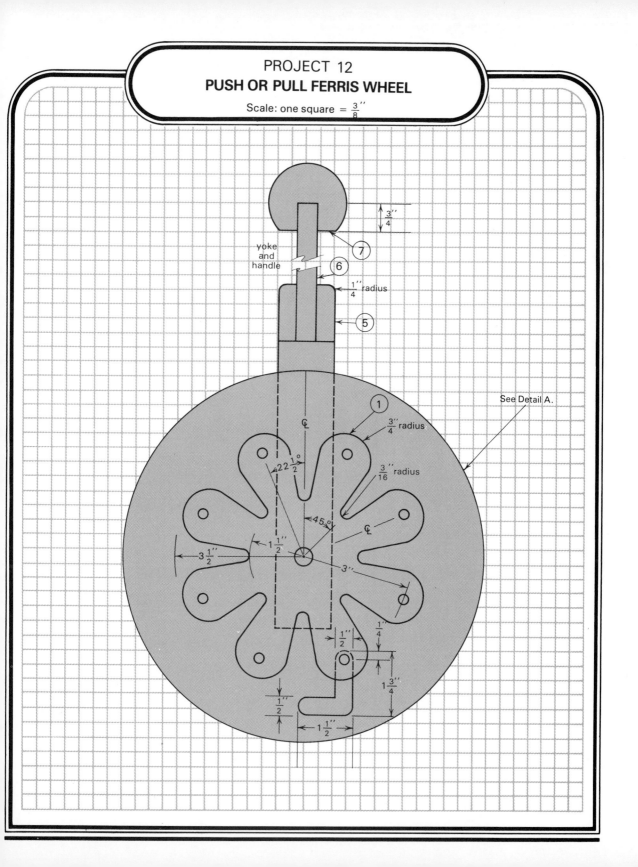

# PROJECT 12
## PUSH OR PULL FERRIS WHEEL
Scale: one square = $\frac{3}{8}''$

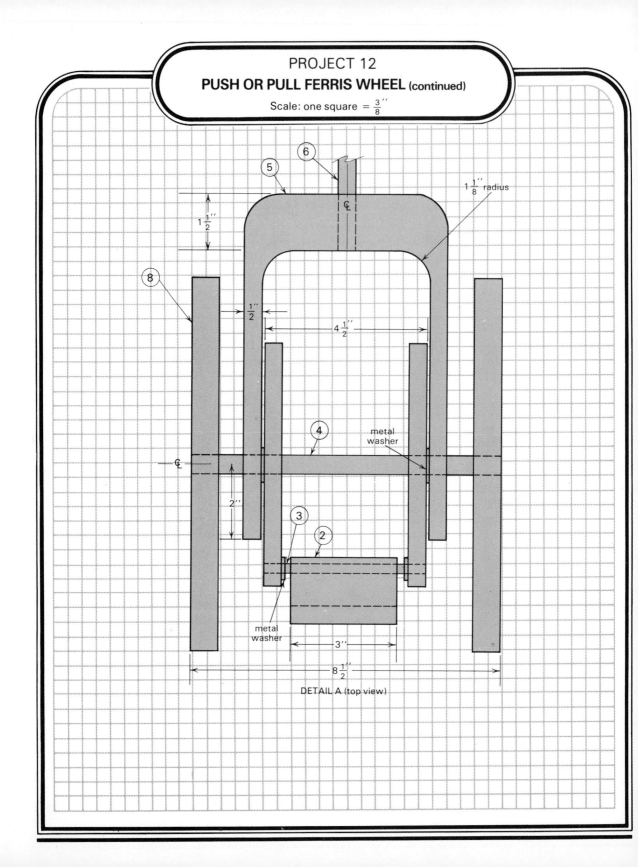

# PROJECT 12
## PUSH OR PULL FERRIS WHEEL (continued)

Scale: one square = $\frac{3}{8}''$

DETAIL A (top view)

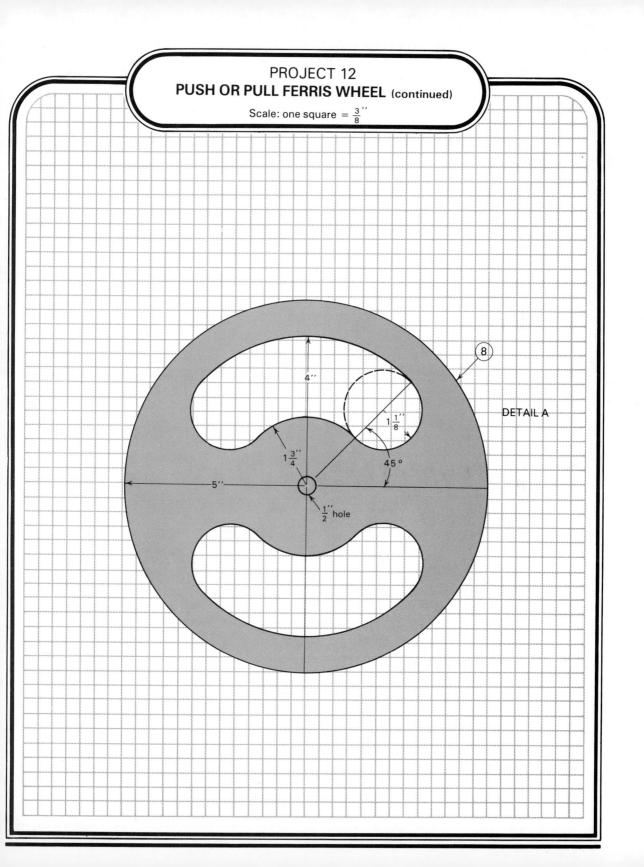

# PROJECT 12
## PUSH OR PULL FERRIS WHEEL (continued)
Scale: one square = $\frac{3}{8}''$

4''

$1\frac{1}{8}''$

$1\frac{3}{4}''$

45°

5''

$\frac{1}{2}''$ hole

8

DETAIL A

# Pinwheel Pull Toy

The "pinwheels" of this toy rotate because their axles rest on the perimeter of the wheels that the toy rolls on.

Start the project by forming the body from a piece of $1\frac{1}{2} \times 5\frac{1}{2} \times 11$-inch lumber. It's a good idea to mark the locations for all the axles before you make the angular cuts on the body. Use care when marking hole locations and when drilling. If you're not near perfect, the top wheels may not turn or they may bind.

Cut the discs that are needed for the main wheels, pinwheels, and washers, and after cutting the axles to length, do the final assembly. All the

The body of the toy has a natural finish but its edges are trimmed with colorful tape. The pinwheels are painted, then rimmed with tape, and decorated with black circles, semicircles, and self-adhesive stars. Or you might decide on spirals, figures, or more stars.

wheels must fit tightly on the axles. The axle holes through the body of the toy and the washers are a bit oversize so that axle/wheel assemblies can turn freely.

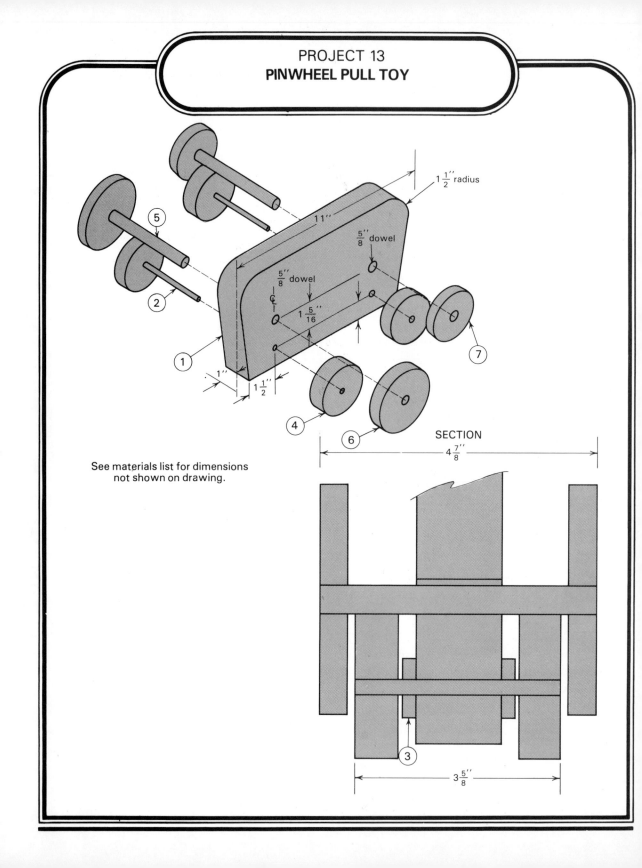

$1\frac{1}{2}''$ radius

11''

$\frac{5}{8}''$ dowel

$\frac{5}{8}''$ dowel

$1\frac{5}{16}''$

1''

$1\frac{1}{2}''$

See materials list for dimensions
not shown on drawing.

SECTION

$4\frac{7}{8}''$

$3\frac{5}{8}''$

**project 13**
**Pinwheel Pull Toy**

# MATERIALS LIST

| Part No. | Name | Pieces | Size | Material |
|---|---|---|---|---|
| 1 | body | 1 | $1\frac{1}{2} \times 5\frac{1}{2} \times 11''$ | lumber |
| 2 | wheel axles | 2 | $\frac{1}{4} \times 3\frac{5}{8}''$ | dowel |
| 3 | washers | 4 | $\frac{1}{4} \times 1''$ dia. | dowel |
| 4 | wheels | 4 | $\frac{3}{4} \times 2\frac{1}{2}''$ dia. | lumber |
| 5 | pinwheel axles | 2 | $\frac{1}{2} \times 4\frac{7}{8}''$ | dowel |
| 6 | large pinwheel | 2 | $\frac{1}{2} \times 4''$ dia. | plywood |
| 7 | small pinwheel | 2 | $\frac{1}{2} \times 2\frac{1}{2}''$ dia. | " |

Holes through body for wheels $= \frac{5}{16}''$
Holes through wheels $= \frac{1}{4}''$
Holes through washers $= \frac{5}{16}''$
Holes through body for pinwheel axles $= \frac{5}{8}''$
Holes through pinwheels $= \frac{1}{2}''$

# Swiveling Crocodile

Start this project with a 21-inch length of 2×4 (the actual cross-section dimensions will be $1\frac{1}{2}$ × $3\frac{1}{2}$ inches). The location of the axle holes, which are pivot points for the body sections, are shown in the lower part of the drawing. Drill these holes and then draw the profile of the crocodile on one surface of the stock. Add the cut-lines that separate the body sections. Saw the figure to profile shape, and then cut the five body pieces.

The inside ends of the head and the tail and both ends of the intermediate pieces are shaped as shown in the top view of the construction drawing.

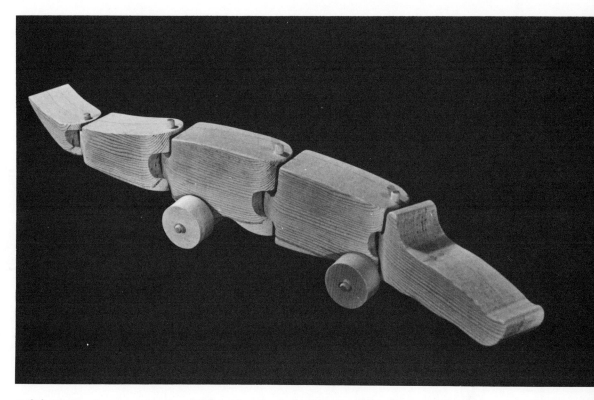

It didn't seem important to the children that the Swiveling Crocodile have a pull cord. They seemed happy just to sit and move the toy about with their hands. All of the parts are pine, except for axles which are hardwood dowels.

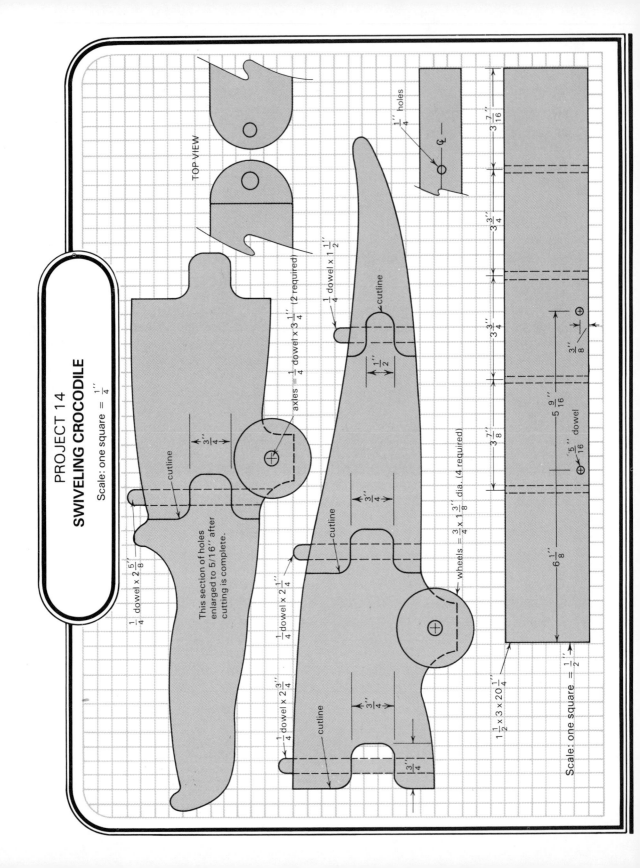

# PROJECT 14
## SWIVELING CROCODILE

Scale: one square = $\frac{1}{4}$''

TOP VIEW

$\frac{1}{4}$'' holes

$\frac{1}{4}$ dowel x $2\frac{5}{8}$''

cutline

This section of holes enlarged to 5/16'' after cutting is complete.

$\frac{3}{4}$''

axles = $\frac{1}{4}$ dowel x $3\frac{1}{4}$'' (2 required)

$\frac{1}{4}$ dowel x $1\frac{1}{2}$''

cutline

$\frac{1}{2}$''

$\frac{1}{4}$ dowel x $2\frac{1}{4}$''

cutline

$\frac{3}{4}$''

wheels = $\frac{3}{4}$ x $1\frac{3}{8}$'' dia. (4 required)

$\frac{1}{4}$ dowel x $2\frac{3}{4}$''

cutline

$\frac{3}{4}$''

$3\frac{7}{16}$''

$3\frac{3}{4}$''

$3\frac{3}{4}$''

$\frac{3}{8}$''

$3\frac{7}{8}$''

$5\frac{9}{16}$''

$\frac{5}{16}$'' dowel

$6\frac{1}{8}$''

$1\frac{1}{2}$ x 3 x $20\frac{1}{4}$''

Scale: one square = $\frac{1}{2}$''

Actually, the suggested shape can be modified depending on how much swivel action you feel the joints should have. It's possible to provide enough relief for the body parts to turn at right angles to each other.

The hole in the projecting part of the first four sections is enlarged to $\frac{5}{16}$ inch, so that the pivot dowel is loose in this hole but tight in the holes of the mating section.

After the crocodile's body has been assembled and swivels to your satisfaction, make the wheels and axles and put them in place.

# TRUCKS AND CARS

## projects 15, 16

# Cab.
# Log Carrier.

### THE TRUCKING SYSTEM

The Trucking System consists of four projects: a cab and three trailers, each of which is designed for a different function. This was a change from the original design which was just a one-piece sand carrier. The child who tested the vehicle used it in ways that suggested that interchangeable trailers would be more enjoyable.

The Cab and Log Carrier. Both projects were painted green except for staves, wheels, and headlights which were left natural. The headlights are faced with discs cut from self-adhesive aluminum tape. The wheel hubs are discs of felt, also self-adhesive, which you can buy ready-made. The wheels are cut from maple.

Start by cutting the bed, or bottom, to size and then drilling the hole for the coupling post. Pad, or stack, two pieces of $\frac{1}{2} \times 5 \times 7$-inch plywood or lumber and then cut them both at once to form the cab sides. Attach these to the base with glue and 4d nails. Cut the back and front, beveling the top edge of the front piece so that it conforms to the angle on the sides. These parts are also attached with glue and 4d nails.

Make and attach the hood and roof. In each case use glue and nails—$\frac{5}{8}$-inch brads for the hood, and 2d or 3d nails for the roof. Attach the axle

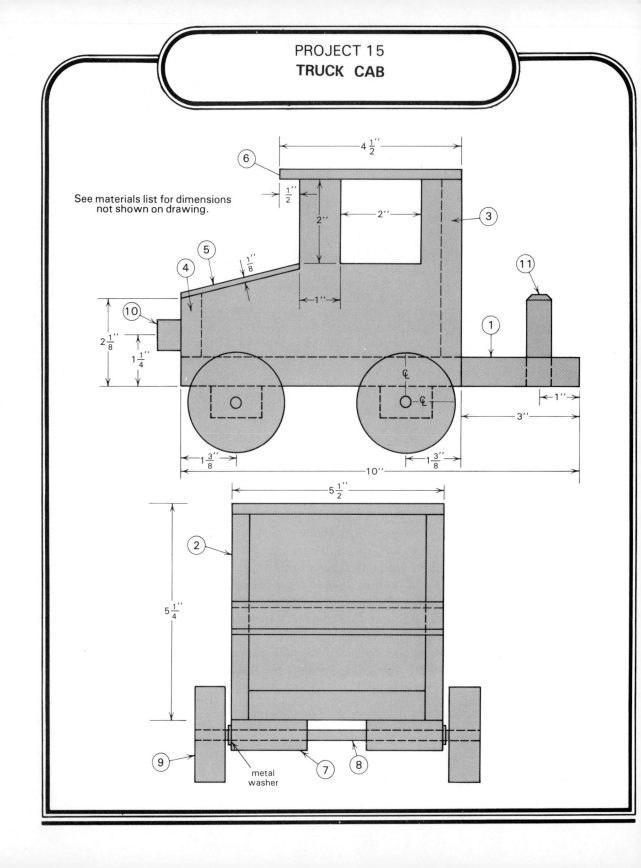

# PROJECT 15
## TRUCK CAB

See materials list for dimensions
not shown on drawing.

metal
washer

**project 15**
**Cab**

# MATERIALS LIST

| Part No. | Name | Pieces | Size | Material |
|---|---|---|---|---|
| 1 | bed | 1 | $\frac{3}{4} \times 4\frac{1}{2} \times 10''$ | plywood or lumber |
| 2 | sides | 2 | $\frac{1}{2} \times 5 \times 7''$ | " |
| 3 | back | 1 | $\frac{1}{2} \times 4\frac{1}{4} \times 4\frac{1}{2}''$ | " |
| 4 | front | 1 | $\frac{1}{2} \times 1\frac{1}{2} \times 4\frac{1}{2}''$ | " |
| 5 | hood | 1 | $\frac{1}{8} \times 3\frac{1}{2} \times 5\frac{1}{2}''$ | plywood |
| 6 | roof | 1 | $\frac{1}{4} \times 4\frac{1}{2} \times 5\frac{1}{2}''$ | " |
| 7 | axle blocks | 4 | $\frac{3}{4} \times 1\frac{1}{4} \times 2''$ | lumber |
| 8 | axles | 2 | $\frac{1}{4} \times 7\frac{5}{16}''$ | dowel |
| 9 | wheels | 4 | $\frac{3}{4} \times 2\frac{3}{8}''$ dia. | lumber |
| 10 | headlights | 2 | $\frac{3}{4} \times \frac{5}{8}''$ | dowel |
| 11 | coupling post | 1 | $\frac{5}{8} \times 2\frac{1}{4}''$ | " |

Hole through wheels $= \frac{1}{4}''$
Hole through axle blocks $= \frac{5}{16}''$
Hole in bed for coupling post $= \frac{5}{8}''$

blocks with glue and 4d nails. Have the axles on hand so you can insert them in the blocks for correct alignment during assembly.

The headlights are sections of dowel. Drill a small center hole through them so you can easily drive the 3d nail that, with glue, holds them in place. The last step is to make and install the wheels and the coupling pin.

# PROJECT 16
## LOG CARRIER

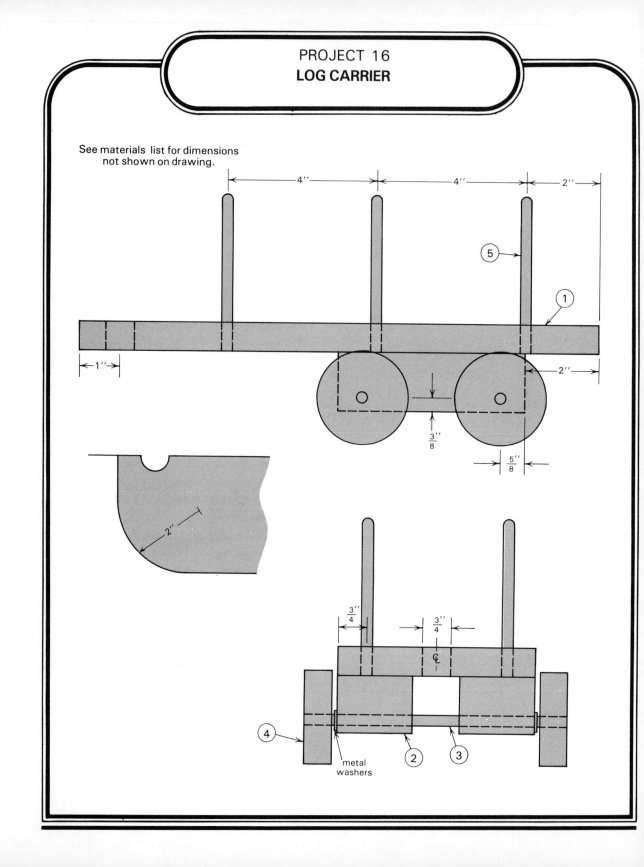

See materials list for dimensions not shown on drawing.

metal washers

**project 16**

**Log Carrier**

## MATERIALS LIST

| Part No. | Name | Pieces | Size | Material |
|---|---|---|---|---|
| 1 | bed | 1 | $\frac{3}{4} \times 6 \times 14''$ | plywood or lumber |
| 2 | axle blocks | 2 | $1\frac{1}{2} \times 2 \times 5''$ | lumber |
| 3 | axles | 2 | $\frac{1}{4} \times 7\frac{3}{4}''$ | dowel |
| 4 | wheels | 4 | $\frac{3}{4} \times 2\frac{3}{8}''$ dia. | lumber |
| 5 | staves | 6 | $\frac{1}{4} \times 4''$ | dowel |

Holes through wheels $= \frac{1}{4}''$
Holes through axle blocks $= \frac{5}{16}''$
Holes in bed for staves $= \frac{1}{4}''$

Cut the bed piece to size, and then drill the $\frac{3}{4}$-inch hole at the front and the $\frac{1}{4}$-inch holes for the staves. Form the axle blocks and put them in place with glue. Nail the blocks down from the top of the bed with 5d or 6d nails. Use the axles as a gauge to be sure the blocks will have correct alignment. Make the staves, taking care to round off the top edges, and put them in place with glue. Then make and attach the wheels.

A parent suggested that the design be changed so that the top ends of the staves would not be exposed. If you feel the point is valid, you can take this extra step. Cut two 9- or 10-inch-long pieces of $\frac{3}{4} \times \frac{3}{4}$-inch stock and in each of them drill three blind holes that are located to suit the spacing of the staves. Sand the pieces to eliminate all sharp edges, and then glue them into place as rails.

# Moving Van

Cut the bed to size, shape the front end, and drill the $\frac{3}{4}$-inch hole for the coupling post attachment. You'll note in the drawing that the design calls for rabbet cuts in the sides, front, and roof. These will be easy to form on a table saw, or they can be cut by hand; but if it's too big a chore, you can substitute butt joints. Just be sure that you make necessary dimensional changes.

In either case, the procedure is to attach the sides to the bed; then attach the front, and then the roof. Use glue and nails in all joints. Correct nail lengths will differ depending on whether you have made rabbet or butt joints. A reasonable guide is to choose a nail that is two to three times as long as the thickness of the part being secured.

**154**

The Moving Van trailer was finished with several coats of nontoxic sealer. Decorative touches are supplied by strips of $\frac{3}{4}$-inch-wide, white tape.

Make and attach the axle blocks by following the procedure outlined for the Log Carrier. Then cut the back door to size. This should be dressed—that is, reduced in size—just enough so that it will be a loose fit in the opening. Round off the top and bottom edges of the door, and then install its handle.

Use the following procedure to mount the door: Mark the location of the door pivots on the sides of the van and drill a small pilot hole. Hold the

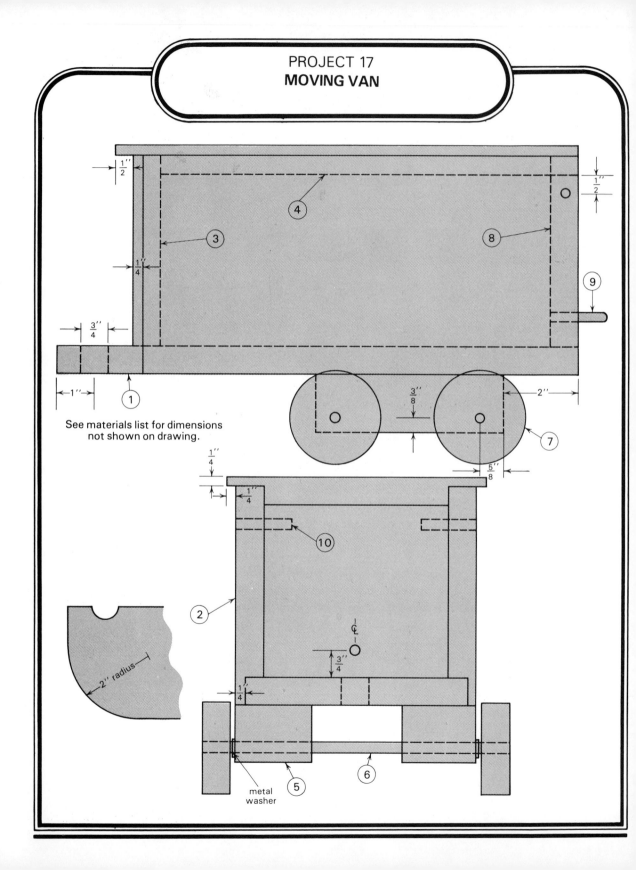

# PROJECT 17
## MOVING VAN

$\frac{1}{2}$''

$\frac{1}{2}$''

4

3

8

$\frac{1}{4}$''

9

$\frac{3}{4}$''

$\frac{3}{8}$''

2''

1

7

See materials list for dimensions
not shown on drawing.

$\frac{1}{4}$''

$\frac{1}{4}$''

1''

$\frac{5}{8}$''

10

2

2'' radius

C
L

$\frac{3}{4}$

$\frac{1}{4}$''

5

6

metal
washer

**project 17**

**Moving Van**

## MATERIALS LIST

| Part No. | Name | Pieces | Size | Material |
|---|---|---|---|---|
| 1 | bed | 1 | $\frac{3}{4} \times 6 \times 14''$ | plywood or lumber |
| 2 | sides | 2 | $\frac{3}{4} \times 5\frac{3}{4} \times 11\frac{3}{4}''$ | " |
| 3 | front | 1 | $\frac{3}{4} \times 5 \times 6\frac{1}{2}''$ | " |
| 4 | roof | 1 | $\frac{3}{4} \times 7 \times 12\frac{1}{2}''$ | " |
| 5 | axle blocks | 2 | $1\frac{1}{2} \times 2 \times 5''$ | lumber |
| 6 | axles | 2 | $\frac{1}{4} \times 8\frac{1}{4}''$ | dowel |
| 7 | wheels | 4 | $\frac{3}{4} \times 2\frac{3}{8}''$ dia. | lumber |
| 8 | back door | 1 | $\frac{3}{4} \times 4\frac{1}{2} \times 5''$ | plywood or lumber |
| 9 | door handle | 1 | $\frac{1}{4} \times 1\frac{1}{2}''$ | dowel |
| 10 | door pivots | 2 | $\frac{1}{4} \times 1\frac{1}{2}''$ | dowel |

Hole through wheels $= \frac{1}{4}''$
Hole through axle blocks $= \frac{5}{16}''$
Pivot hole through sides $= \frac{1}{4}''$
Pivot holes in door $= \frac{5}{16}''$
Hole for door handle $= \frac{1}{4}''$

door in position and drill through the pilot holes into the edges of the door. Enlarge the door holes to $\frac{5}{16}$ inch (about 1 inch deep) and the holes in the sides to $\frac{1}{4}$ inch. Put the door in place and tap the door pivots into position. It might be wise to cut the door pivots longer than necessary to begin with. Then you can easily remove them should some adjustment be necessary to prevent the door from binding.

# Sand Carrier

The construction procedure is pretty much the same as that outlined for the preceding projects. Make the bed, then form and install the remaining parts in this order: sides, axle blocks, front, gate, axles, and wheels. The gate is installed in exactly the same manner as the door on the van.

The Sand Carrier trailer has a plywood bed. All body parts are pine. Wheels are maple.

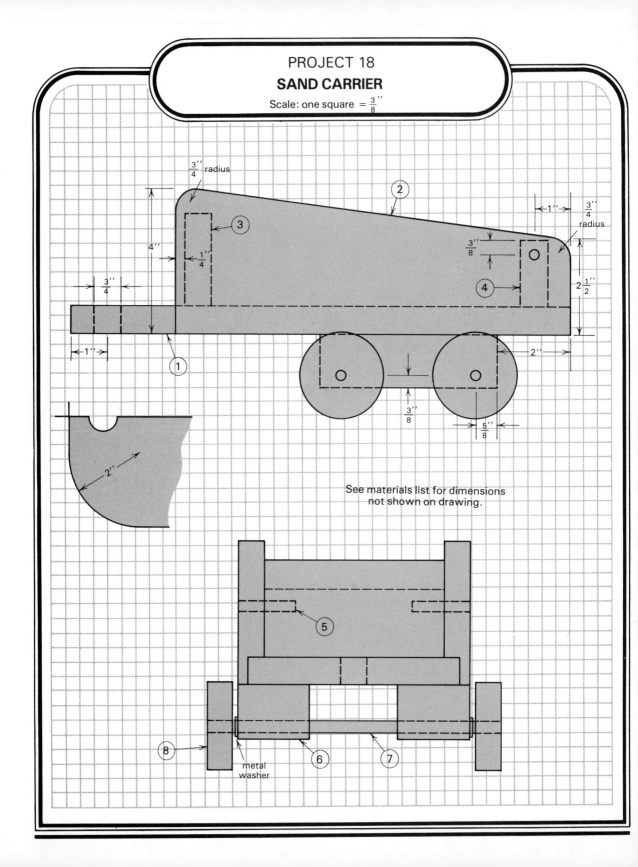

# PROJECT 18
## SAND CARRIER

Scale: one square = $\frac{3}{8}''$

See materials list for dimensions
not shown on drawing.

metal
washer

**project 18**
**Sand Carrier**

## MATERIALS LIST

| Part No. | Name | Pieces | Size | Material |
|---|---|---|---|---|
| 1 | bed | 1 | $\frac{3}{4} \times 6 \times 14''$ | plywood or lumber |
| 2 | sides | 2 | $\frac{3}{4} \times 4 \times 11''$ | " |
| 3 | front | 1 | $\frac{3}{4} \times 2\frac{1}{2} \times 5''$ | " |
| 4 | gate | 1 | $\frac{3}{4} \times 1\frac{3}{4} \times 5''$ | " |
| 5 | gate pivots | 2 | $\frac{1}{4} \times 1\frac{1}{2}''$ | dowel |
| 6 | axle blocks | 2 | $1\frac{1}{2} \times 2 \times 5''$ | lumber |
| 7 | axles | 2 | $\frac{1}{4} \times 8\frac{1}{4}''$ | dowel |
| 8 | wheels | 4 | $\frac{3}{4} \times 2\frac{3}{8}''$ dia. | lumber |

Holes through wheels $= \frac{1}{4}''$
Holes through axle blocks $= \frac{5}{16}''$
Pivot hole through sides $= \frac{1}{4}''$
Pivot hole in gate $= \frac{5}{16}''$

# Bug.
# Sports Car.
# Bus.

All three of the projects are made by following a similar procedure. Cut the piece of wood required for the body of the car and then draw the pattern of the car's outline. Mark the location of holes required for windows and axles and drill them as specified on the drawings. Cut the parts to shape of the outline, and then nicely round all edges with sandpaper. The perime-

The Bug's body was made from a piece of kiln-dried fir. The wheels are birch. All parts have a natural finish.

ter of the window in the Sports Car is chamfered. This can be done with a file or with sandpaper, and you can also chamfer the windows in the other car projects.

After the bodies are formed, complete the projects by making and adding the wheels and axles. Projects of this nature can be pull toys, but children also seem to enjoy just sitting with them and rolling them about.

You have many options for toy size. There is no reason you can't make any of the cars twice or even three times as large as the drawing suggests.

Materials can be fir, pine, maple, or birch. Often the choice is based on what suitabe-size pieces of scrap wood are available.

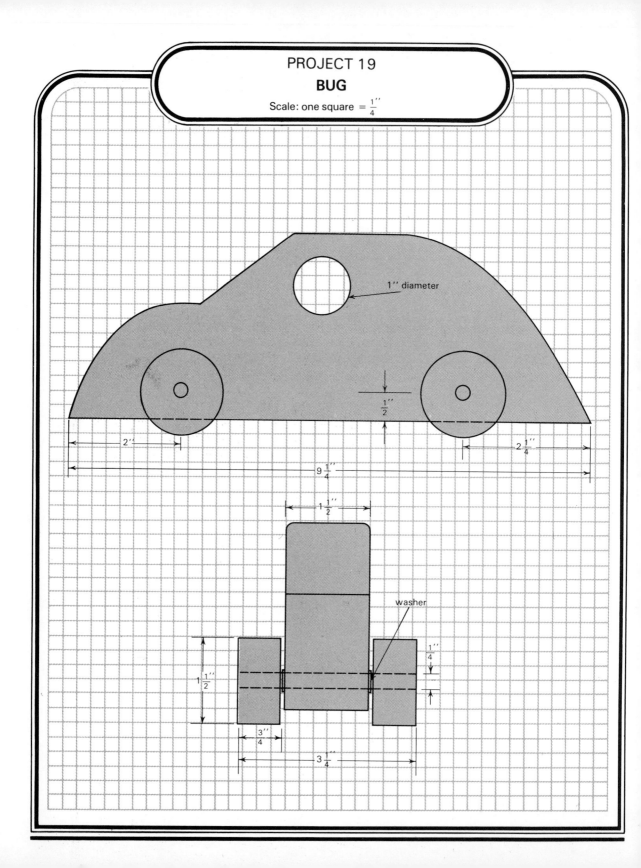

# PROJECT 19
## BUG

Scale: one square $= \frac{1''}{4}$

1'' diameter

$\frac{1''}{2}$

2''

$2\frac{1''}{4}$

$9\frac{1''}{4}$

$1\frac{1''}{2}$

washer

$\frac{1''}{4}$

$1\frac{1''}{2}$

$\frac{3''}{4}$

$3\frac{1''}{4}$

## project 19
### Bug

# MATERIALS LIST

Axles $= \frac{1}{4}''$ dowel $\times$ $3\frac{1}{4}''$
Holes through wheels $= \frac{1}{4}''$
Body piece $= 1\frac{1}{2} \times 9\frac{1}{4} \times \frac{1}{2}''$
Holes through body $= \frac{5}{16}''$

The Sports Car's body is pine, tinted with diluted, brown mahogany stain. The wheels are teak, but only because I had some small leftovers.

## project 20
### Sports Car

## MATERIALS LIST

Axles = $\frac{1}{4}$" dowel $\times$ $2\frac{3}{4}$"
Holes through wheels = $\frac{1}{4}$"
Body piece = $1\frac{1}{2} \times 12 \times \frac{3}{8}$"
Holes through body = $\frac{5}{16}$"

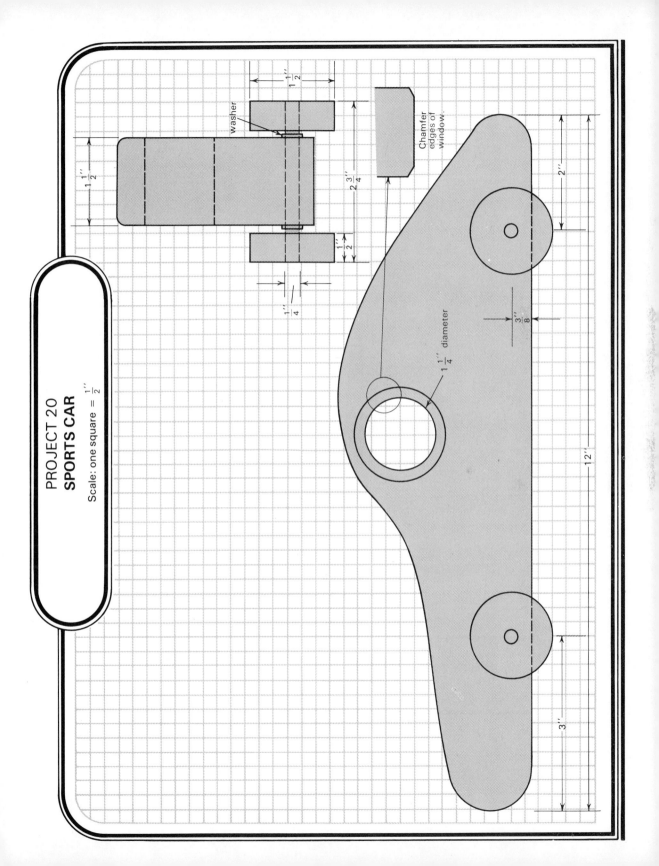

PROJECT 20
**SPORTS CAR**

Scale: one square = $\frac{1}{2}''$

washer

$1\frac{1}{2}''$

$2\frac{3}{4}''$

$\frac{1}{2}''$

$\frac{1}{4}''$

Chamfer edges of window.

$1\frac{1}{4}''$ diameter

$2''$

$\frac{3}{8}''$

$12''$

$3''$

The Bus is kiln-dried fir. The wheels were cut from scrap pieces of cabinet-grade oak plywood.

## project 21
### Bus

# MATERIALS LIST

Axles $= \frac{1}{4}''$ dowel $\times 3\frac{1}{4}''$
Holes through wheels $= \frac{1}{4}''$
Body piece $= 1\frac{1}{2} \times 4\frac{1}{2} \times 13''$
Holes through body $= \frac{5}{16}''$

# PROJECT 21
## BUS

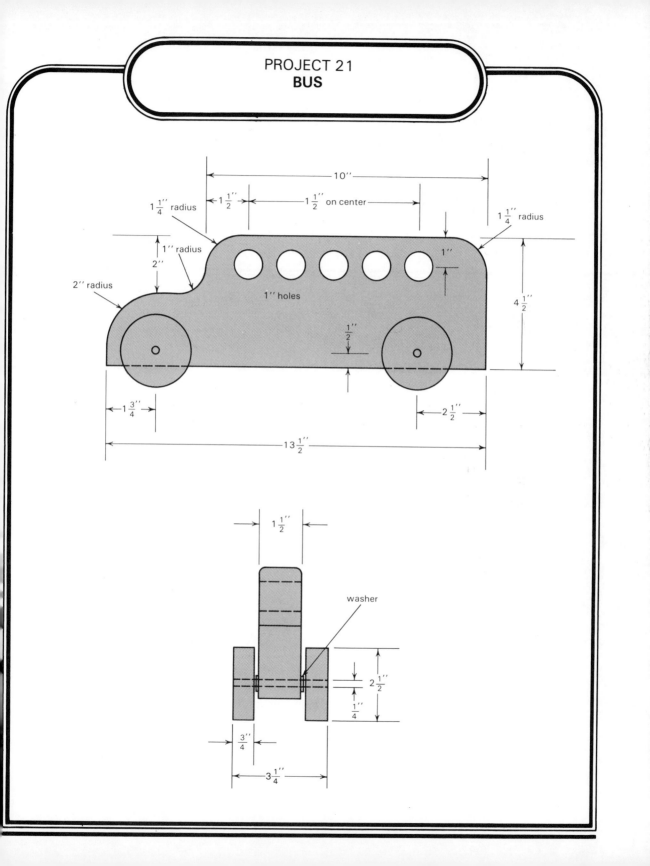

# ON-TRACK TRAIN

# Locomotive. Passenger Cars. Track.

**ON-TRACK TRAIN**

The projects consist of a locomotive and a passenger-car design. You can build the locomotive and a single car, but you'll be surprised at how much more enjoyable a child will find the projects when there are more cars—and

All of the parts of the Long Train have a natural finish. The larger pieces are pine; wheels and axles are hardwood. The boiler is a section of fancy hand rail that was on hand.

the coupling system is easy to use. Pull one car, pull six cars, drop some off to be picked up later—it's all part of the fun of being the engineer.

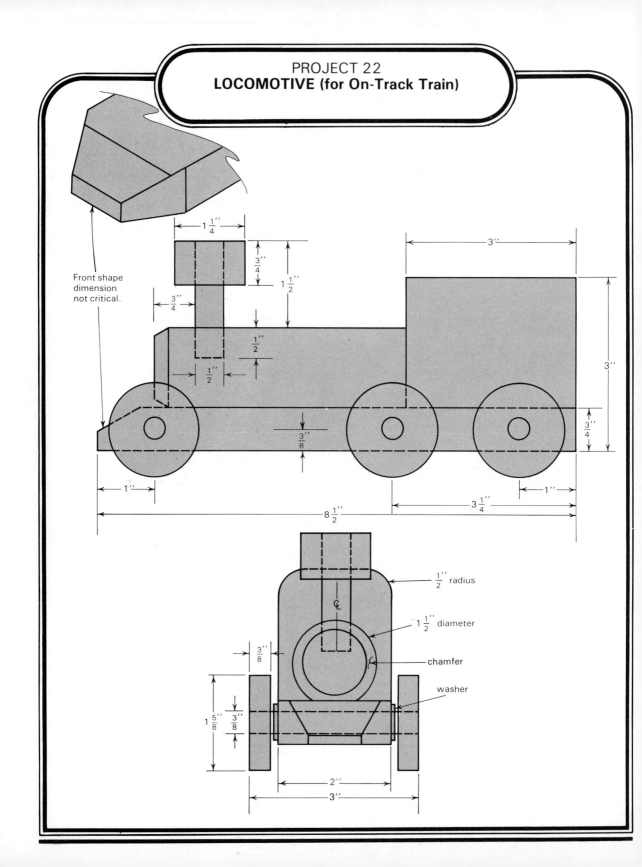

Front shape dimension not critical.

$1\frac{1}{4}''$

$\frac{3}{4}''$

$1\frac{1}{2}''$

$\frac{3}{4}''$

$3''$

$\frac{1}{2}''$

$\frac{1}{2}''$

$3''$

$\frac{3}{8}''$

$\frac{3}{4}''$

$1''$

$8\frac{1}{2}''$

$3\frac{1}{4}''$

$1''$

$\frac{1}{2}''$ radius

$1\frac{1}{2}''$ diameter

chamfer

washer

$\frac{3}{8}''$

$1\frac{5}{8}''$ $\frac{3}{8}''$

$2''$

$3''$

**project 22**

**Locomotive**

## MATERIALS LIST

Axles = $\frac{3}{8}$" dowel $\times$ 3"
Holes through wheels = $\frac{3}{8}$"
Holes through body = $\frac{7}{16}$"

The bed, or bottom, is a piece of 2 $\times$ 8$\frac{1}{2}$ $\times$ $\frac{3}{4}$-inch stock. Shape the front end as shown in the drawing, paying more attention to the form than to any particular dimension. Locate and drill the holes for the axles. The cab measures 2 $\times$ 2$\frac{1}{4}$ $\times$ 3 inches. You can cut it from a piece of 4$\times$4 or make it by gluing together pieces cut from a 2$\times$4. Round off its top edges, and then attach the cab to the bed with glue and 6d nails driven up through the bottom of the bed.

The boiler can be made from a round or lathe-turned cylinder, or it can be a length of hand rail. The flat on a round can be formed with a plane or by using a rasp and then sanding. Drill the hole for the stack and then attach the boiler to the bed as you did for the cab. Make the stack assembly, glue it into place, and then add axles and wheels.

# PROJECTS 23 & 24
## PASSENGER CARS (for On-Track Train)

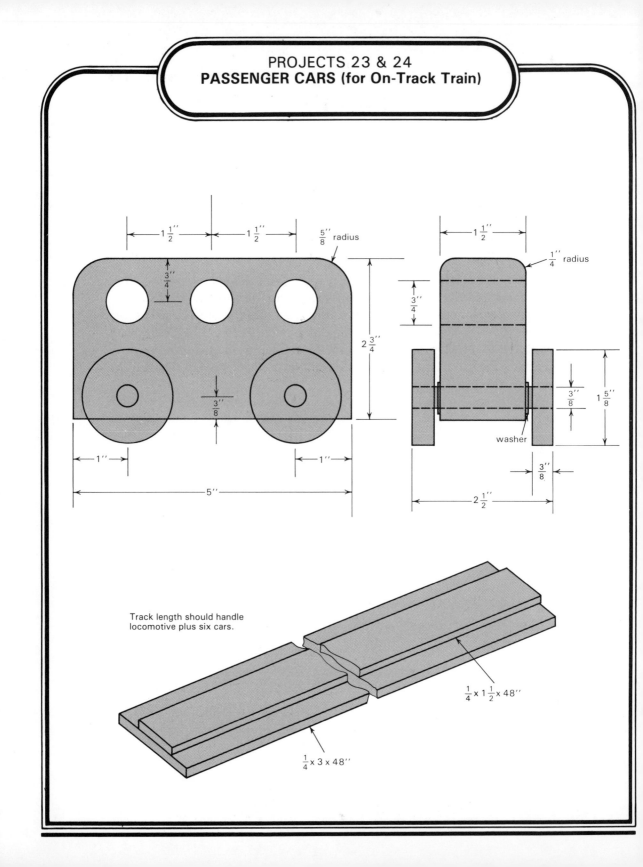

$\frac{5}{8}''$ radius

$1\frac{1}{2}''$    $1\frac{1}{2}''$

$\frac{3}{4}''$

$2\frac{3}{4}''$

$\frac{3}{8}''$

$1''$    $1''$

$5''$

$1\frac{1}{2}''$

$\frac{1}{4}''$ radius

$\frac{3}{4}''$

$\frac{3}{8}''$

$1\frac{5}{8}''$

washer

$\frac{3}{8}''$

$2\frac{1}{2}''$

Track length should handle
locomotive plus six cars.

$\frac{1}{4}$ x $1\frac{1}{2}$ x 48''

$\frac{1}{4}$ x 3 x 48''

**project 23**

**Passenger Cars**

# MATERIALS LIST

Axles = $\frac{3}{8}''$ dowel $\times$ $2\frac{1}{2}''$
Holes through wheels = $\frac{3}{8}''$
Holes through body = $\frac{7}{16}''$

Cut a number of pieces (I made six) of $1\frac{1}{2}$-inch-thick stock to measure $2\frac{3}{4} \times 5$ inches. Form the two top ends on each piece to about a $\frac{5}{8}$-inch radius, and then work with sandpaper to round off all edges. Mark the locations of the window and axle holes on one piece. Drill pilot holes and then use the piece as a template to mark hole locations on the other parts. This is easy to do if you hold the template piece against another and pass the drill bit through the pilot holes.

Open the holes to full size, and then make and install the axles and wheels.

The track goes where the Long Train goes. The coupling system consists of a small screweye in one car, a small screw hook in the following one. If the screw hooks you buy have sharp points, blunt them with a file.

**project 24**

**Track**

# MATERIALS LIST

Track length suitable for locomotive plus six cars
Material $= \frac{1}{4}''$ plywood

---

The track is made by assembling two pieces of $\frac{1}{4}$-inch plywood. The plywood can be glued and then held with clamps, or you can substitute $\frac{1}{2}$-inch staples for the clamps.

My original thought was that the child could use the track to display the On-Track Train when he wasn't playing with it, but it became as important in his play activities as the train itself. In fact, we're being harassed to build more track, even curved ones!

# THE TRAIN

# Locomotive.
# Tender.

This locomotive has a lot more detail than the one designed for the On-Track Train; so it will take more time and care to make.

Start by forming the bed from a piece of $\frac{3}{4} \times 3\frac{3}{4} \times 16$-inch stock. Shape the back and front ends, and then drill the hole for the coupling pin. Make and attach the cab's sides with glue and 3d or 4d nails. The front and the roof are rabbeted as the drawing shows, but an alternative method is to use butt joints. If you use butt joints, make any necessary dimensional changes. The front can still be $\frac{1}{2}$-inch stock, but it will be better to use $\frac{1}{4}$-inch material for the roof.

**178**

The drive rod adds interest to the Train project. All parts have a natural finish.

The boiler's diameter is $2\frac{1}{2}$ inches, and it's not likely that you'll find that size in a ready-made round. It can be made on a lathe, or it can even be made by hand if you start with square stock, cutting off corners with a saw and finishing with a plane and sandpaper. That will take some time, but it can be done. Another solution is to check the ready-made spindles available in do-it-yourself centers to see if you can cull a suitable piece. When the part is on hand, drill it for the stacks, and then attach it to the bed with glue and 5d or 6d nails driven up through the bottom of the bed.

Make and attach the axle blocks with glue and 5d nails. If you have the axles on hand, they can be used to help you make sure the blocks are correctly aligned. Shape a piece of wood to the cow-catcher form shown on the drawing. The angles don't have to be perfect. Attach the part with glue and 5d nails driven up through the bottom of the bed.

Now you can make and install the stacks and headlight. The headlight will be easier to attach if you first drill a small center hole for a 5d or 6d nail.

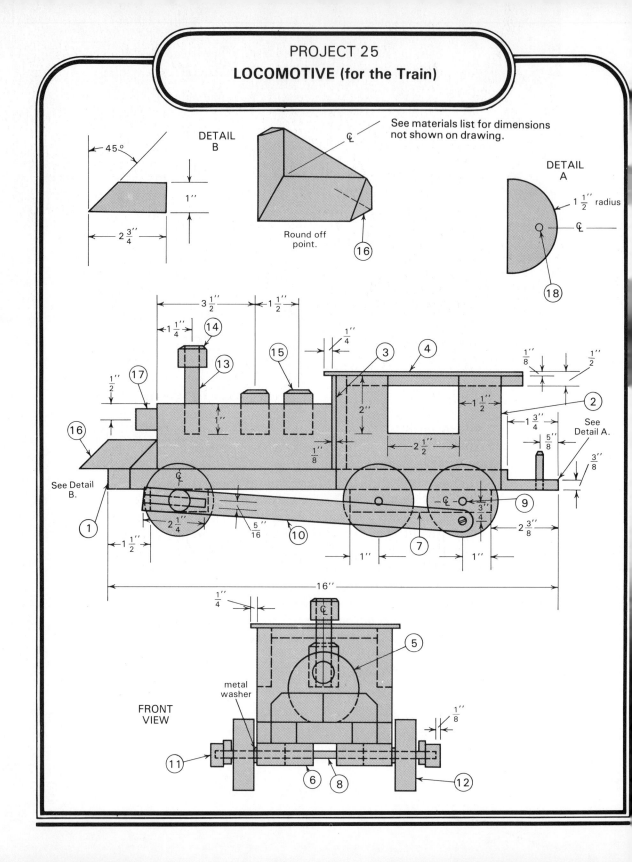

# PROJECT 25
# LOCOMOTIVE (for the Train)

DETAIL B

45°

1″

2 3/4″

See materials list for dimensions not shown on drawing.

℄

16

Round off point.

DETAIL A

1 1/2″ radius

℄

18

3 1/2″   1 1/2″

1 1/4″   14

15   1/4″

17   13   3   4

1/2″   2″

1/8″   1/2″

1″   1 1/2″   2

1 3/4″   See Detail A.

5/8″   3/8″

16   1/8″

℄

2 1/4″

See Detail B.   1

5/16″   10   7   9

3/4″

2 3/8″

1 1/2″   1″   1″

16″

1/4″

℄

5

metal washer

FRONT VIEW

1/8″

11   6   8   12

# project 25

## Locomotive

## MATERIALS LIST

| Part No. | Name | Pieces | Size | Material |
|---|---|---|---|---|
| 1 | bed | 1 | $\frac{3}{4} \times 3\frac{3}{4} \times 16''$ | lumber |
| 2 | cab sides | 2 | $\frac{1}{2} \times 4 \times 6''$ | lumber or plywood |
| 3 | cab front | 1 | $\frac{1}{2} \times 3\frac{1}{4} \times 4\frac{3}{4}''$ | " |
| 4 | cab roof | 1 | $\frac{1}{2} \times 5\frac{1}{4} \times 7''$ | " |
| 5 | boiler | 1 | $2\frac{1}{2}''$ dia. $\times 6\frac{1}{4}''$ | lumber (turned) |
| 6 | front axle blocks | 2 | $\frac{3}{4} \times 2 \times 2''$ | lumber |
| 7 | rear axle blocks | 2 | $\frac{3}{4} \times 1 \times 5''$ | " |
| 8 | front axle | 1 | $\frac{1}{4} \times 8''$ | dowel |
| 9 | rear axles | 2 | $\frac{1}{4} \times 6\frac{5}{8}''$ | " |
| 10 | drive rod | 2 | $\frac{1}{4} \times \frac{3}{4} \times 12''$ | lumber |
| 11 | front axle caps | 2 | $\frac{3}{4} \times \frac{1}{2}''$ | dowel |
| 12 | wheels | 6 | $\frac{3}{4} \times 2\frac{3}{8}''$ dia. | lumber |
| 13 | tall stack | 1 | $\frac{1}{2} \times 3''$ | dowel |
| 14 | tall stack cap | 1 | $1''$ dia. $\times \frac{3}{4}''$ | dowel |
| 15 | short stacks | 2 | $1''$ dia. $\times 1\frac{1}{2}''$ | " |
| 16 | cow catcher | 1 | $1 \times 2\frac{3}{4} \times 3\frac{3}{4}''$ | lumber |
| 17 | headlight | 1 | $\frac{3}{4} \times \frac{3}{4}''$ | dowel |
| 18 | coupling pin | 1 | $\frac{1}{4} \times 1\frac{1}{4}''$ | dowel |

Holes through wheels = $\frac{1}{4}''$
Holes through axle blocks = $\frac{5}{16}''$
Hole for coupling pin = $\frac{1}{4}''$

Make the drive rods, cutting the slots at the front end just wide enough to avoid binding the axle. Make and install the axles and wheels, and then add the drive rod. Use a $\frac{5}{8}$- or $\frac{3}{4}$-inch round- or pan-head screw to attach the rod to the rear wheel. The screw, of course, merely acts as a pivot; don't

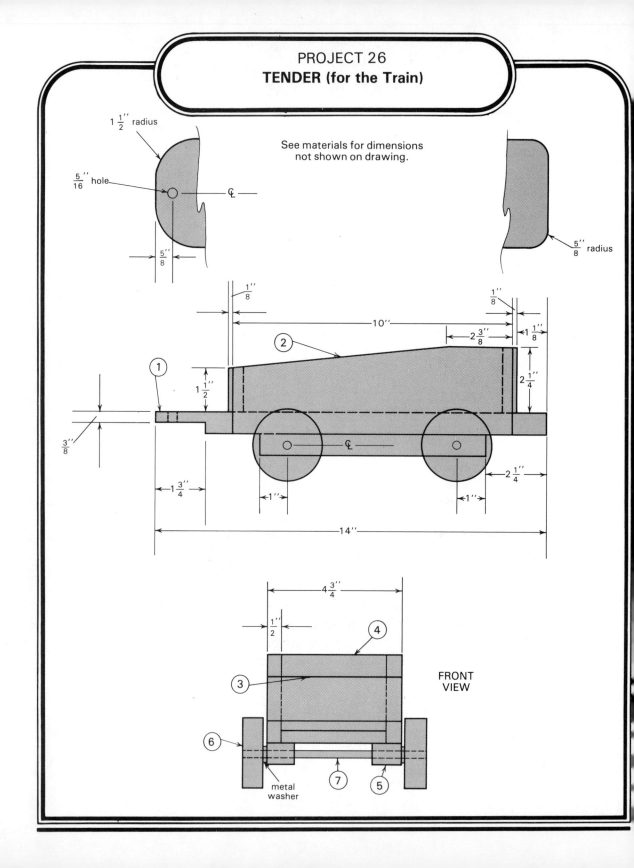

# PROJECT 26
## TENDER (for the Train)

$1\frac{1}{2}''$ radius

See materials for dimensions
not shown on drawing.

$\frac{5}{16}''$ hole

CL

$\frac{5}{8}''$

$\frac{5}{8}''$ radius

$\frac{1}{8}''$

$\frac{1}{8}''$

10''

$2\frac{3}{8}''$

$1\frac{1}{8}''$

2

1

$1\frac{1}{2}''$

$2\frac{1}{4}''$

$\frac{3}{8}''$

CL

$1\frac{3}{4}''$

1''

1''

$2\frac{1}{4}''$

14''

$4\frac{3}{4}''$

$\frac{1}{2}''$

4

3

FRONT
VIEW

6

7

5

metal
washer

tighten it. Drill the hole through the drive rod just large enough for the rod to move freely.

Make the front axle caps by drilling a $\frac{1}{4}$-inch-deep center hole in pieces of $\frac{3}{4}$-inch dowel that are $\frac{1}{2}$ inch thick. Glue them in place at the ends of the front axle. There must be enough clearance between the wheel and the cap so that the drive rod will move without binding.

**project 26**

**Tender**

## MATERIALS LIST

| Part No. | Name | Pieces | Size | Material |
|----------|------|--------|------|----------|
| 1 | bed | 1 | $\frac{3}{4} \times 3\frac{3}{4} \times 14''$ | lumber |
| 2 | sides | 2 | $\frac{1}{2} \times 3 \times 10''$ | lumber or plywood |
| 3 | front | 1 | $\frac{1}{2} \times 1\frac{1}{2} \times 4\frac{3}{4}''$ | " |
| 4 | back | 1 | $\frac{1}{2} \times 2\frac{1}{4} \times 4\frac{3}{4}''$ | " |
| 5 | axle blocks | 2 | $\frac{3}{4} \times 1 \times 8''$ | lumber |
| 6 | wheels | 4 | $\frac{3}{4} \times 2\frac{3}{8}''$ dia. | " |
| 7 | axles | 2 | $\frac{1}{4} \times 6\frac{5}{8}''$ | dowel |

Holes through axle blocks $= \frac{5}{16}''$
Holes through wheels $= \frac{1}{4}''$

Cut the bed to size, then shape the front and rear ends and drill the hole that will couple the tender to the locomotive. Make and attach the sides to the bed with glue and 4d nails. Add the front and the back. These pieces are rabbeted, but butt joints may be substituted if you change dimensions to suit. Form and drill the axle blocks, and attach them with glue and 4d nails driven from the bottom of the blocks. Then make and install the axles and wheels.

# GAMES

# Tick-Tack-Toe Board and Men

## TICK-TACK-TOE PLUS GAME

Tick-Tack-Toe will be more fun to play on a special board with posts and "game-men" of various shapes than on paper with pencils. The version here includes two extra, small projects that extend the fun and can also be used as teaching aids.

**184**

The Tick-Tack-Toe Plus Game consists of a main board for the basic game, plus two extra projects that add to the fun and can be used as teaching aids.

# PROJECT 27
## TICK-TACK TOE BOARD AND MEN

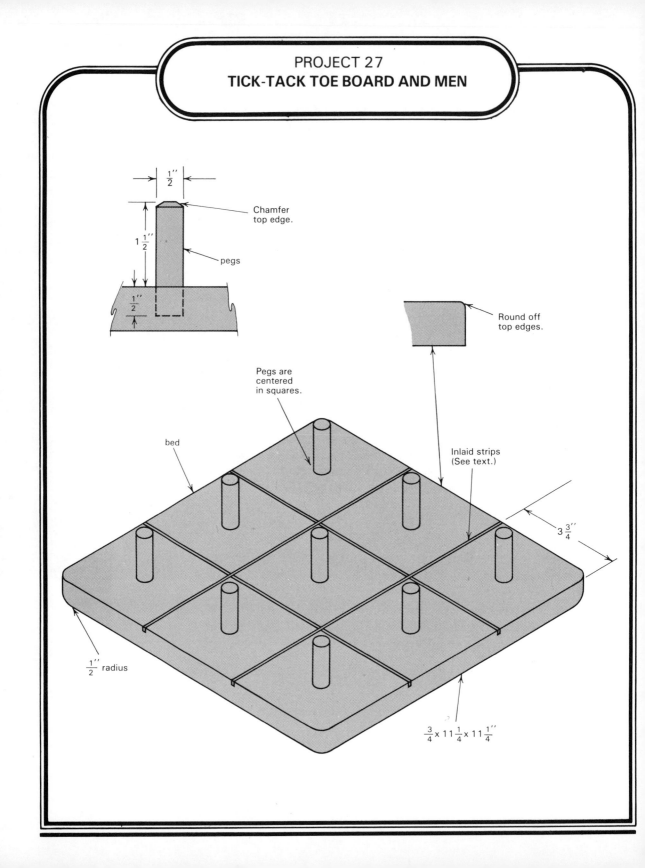

$\frac{1}{2}''$

Chamfer
top edge.

$1\frac{1}{2}''$

pegs

$\frac{1}{2}''$

Round off
top edges.

Pegs are
centered
in squares.

bed

Inlaid strips
(See text.)

$3\frac{3}{4}''$

$\frac{1}{2}''$ radius

$\frac{3}{4} \times 11\frac{1}{4} \times 11\frac{1}{4}''$

Start by cutting a piece of $\frac{3}{4}$-inch-thick lumber to measure $11\frac{1}{4}$ inches square. I inlaid strips to divide the board into squares by following this procedure on a table saw: Set the blade's height to project about $\frac{1}{8}$ inch. Lock the rip fence so that the distance to the blade (which will actually be the center of the kerf the blade cuts) is $3\frac{3}{4}$ inches. Cut one groove, then turn the stock so the opposite edge is against the fence, and cut a second groove. Cut strips from a contrasting material to fit the grooves and glue them into place. The thickness of the strips will depend on how wide a kerf the blade cuts. A good procedure is to cut strips as wide as the kerf from a piece of, say, $\frac{1}{2}$-inch-thick stock. The strips can then be sliced lengthwise with a sharp knife. After the strips are in place, the excess projecting above the board can be sanded flush.

With the first two strips in place, repeat the kerf cutting procedure for the two grooves that cross the first ones. Then install the second set of strips. When you work this way, the joints where the strips cross will be perfect. The grooves can also be formed with a hand saw, or you can avoid them entirely by marking the board into squares with paint or ink or by applying narrow strips of self-adhesive tape.

Draw diagonals connecting opposite corners of each square to locate centers and then drill the "blind" holes for the posts. Cut the posts to length, round off or chamfer their top ends, and glue them into place.

*(Continued)*

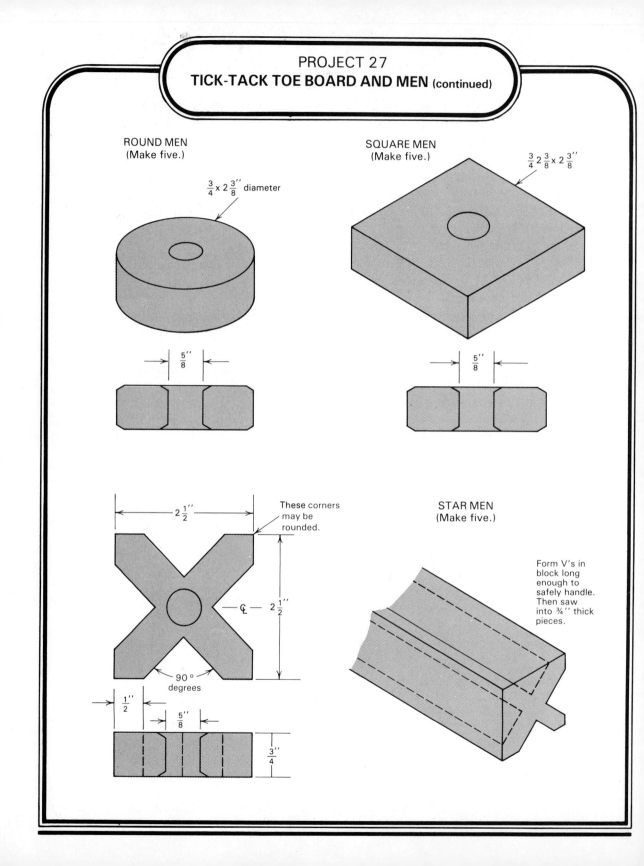

ROUND MEN
(Make five.)

$\frac{3}{4} \times 2\frac{3}{8}''$ diameter

$\frac{5}{8}''$

SQUARE MEN
(Make five.)

$\frac{3}{4} \ 2\frac{3}{8} \times 2\frac{3}{8}''$

$\frac{5}{8}''$

$2\frac{1}{2}''$

These corners may be rounded.

$\frac{C}{L} - 2\frac{1}{2}$

$90°$ degrees

$\frac{1}{2}''$

$\frac{5}{8}''$

$\frac{3}{4}''$

STAR MEN
(Make five.)

Form V's in block long enough to safely handle. Then saw into ¾'' thick pieces.

## THE MEN

The round and the square men are fairly easy to make; the star men take a little more doing. If you work on a table saw, you can start with a $2\frac{1}{2}$-inch square block of wood that is long enough to handle safely. Cut V-grooves down the center of each side, and then slice off as many $\frac{3}{4}$-inch-thick pieces as you want. If you work with hand saws, it will be better to make individual $\frac{3}{4}$-inch-thick by $2\frac{1}{2}$-inch-square pieces and then cut the V-shapes in each. With a band saw you can cut V-grooves in stock that is long enough to be sliced into the number of parts that are needed.

# Single Post

The single post can be used to stack the men haphazardly or in some alternating pattern of shapes or colors. It can also be used to teach counting and the meaning of numbers. Put on three stars and one round and one square, and how many pieces do you have?

The project is simply a base with a centered $\frac{1}{2}$-inch dowel $12\frac{1}{2}$ inches long.

All parts of the Single Post, except for the hardwood-dowel post, were made from pine lumber. The star men are white, the round ones are stained, and the square ones have a natural finish. You can use brighter colors if you wish.

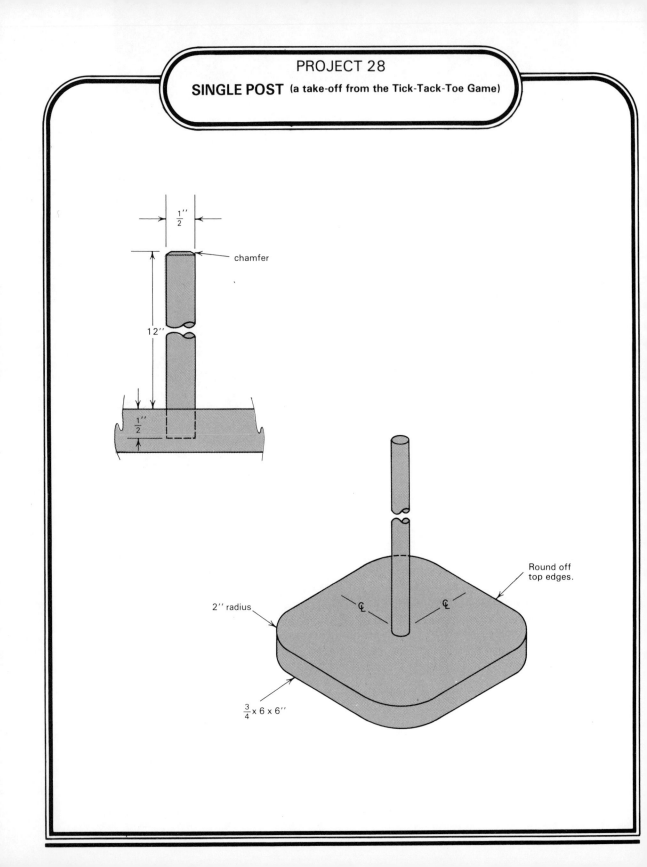

$\frac{1}{2}''$

chamfer

12''

$\frac{1}{2}''$

Round off
top edges.

2'' radius

$\frac{3}{4}$ x 6 x 6''

# Triple Post

This too is used with the Tick-Tack-Toe men for play or used like the Single Post as a teaching aid. Cut the base to shape, and draw a 5-inch-diameter circle around its center. The center of the holes for the posts are 120 degrees apart on the circumference of the circle.

The base of the Triple Post project is plywood, but lumber will do just as well. It can be used as a teaching aid for distinguishing shapes and colors.

# PROJECT 29

## TRIPLE POST (a take-off from the Tick-Tack-Toe Game)

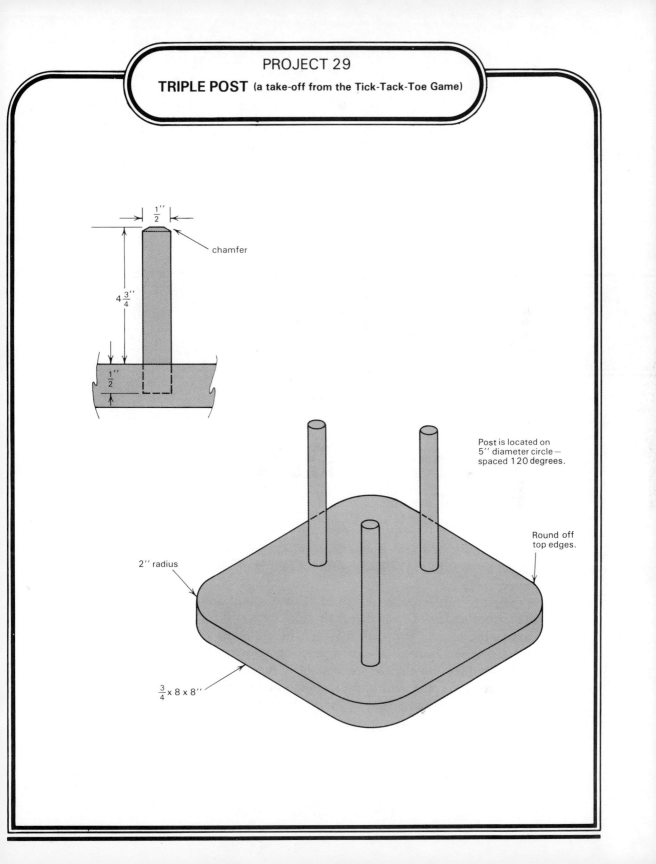

$\frac{1}{2}''$

chamfer

$4\frac{3}{4}''$

$\frac{1}{2}''$

Post is located on
5'' diameter circle —
spaced 120 degrees.

Round off
top edges.

2'' radius

$\frac{3}{4} \times 8 \times 8''$

# Spiral Game

The object of spiral games is to tilt the wooden base to make the ball travel the length of the spiral without falling off. Skilled players may want to compete for time.

Start the project with a piece of cabinet-grade plywood $\frac{3}{4}$ inch thick and 12 inches square. Draw diagonals from opposite corners of the square to locate the center, and drill a $\frac{1}{4}$-inch hole at that point. Make the spiral marker shown in the drawing. The string, which can be stapled to both the pencil holder and the dowel, should be just long enough so the starting radius of the spiral will be $5\frac{5}{8}$ inches. The pencil should have a slip fit so that the holder can rest flat on the work. The string wraps around the dowel

**196**

The waste that results when you cut the spiral groove in the square piece can be used to make a second project. The spiral-cut pieces are mounted on plywood or hardboard bases. A natural finish is suitable.

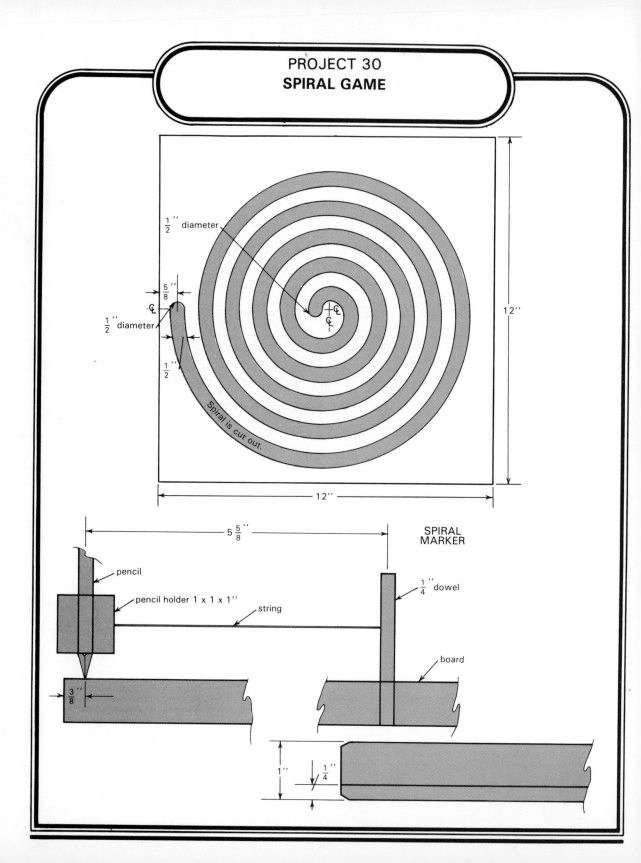

as you rotate the holder to produce the spiral pattern. Be sure to keep the string taut.

The next step is to drill the $\frac{1}{2}$-inch hole at the start of the spiral. Be sure to locate its center at the center of the spiral track. Use the hole to insert the blade of whatever tool you will saw with—saber saw, jigsaw, deep-throat coping saw. Don't try to be overly precise in making the cut. Some slight irregularities will add to the difficulty of playing the game.

When the cut is complete, place the work on a bench and use a compass to draw a second parallel spiral. Set the compass to a $\frac{1}{2}$-inch width and keep the point of the compass in the saw-cut as a guide.

The second cut you make results in a $\frac{1}{2}$-inch-wide spiral groove in the square piece and a spiral-shaped waste piece that can be used for a second game. The spiral-cut piece is mounted on a base of $\frac{1}{4}$-inch plywood or hardboard. Coat mating surfaces with glue and then hold them together with a weight of some sort until the glue is dry. The result is another spiral-pattern groove and a second game to play with.

# Zig-Zag Traveler

The toy in the photos has one traveling piece, but there are others you can add to increase interest. For example, substitute small jig-sawed figures for the block or use a steel rod instead of a dowel. The extra weight of the steel will often cause a hesitation at the top of a slope which reverses the pinwheel's direction of rotation.

Start by making a pad of two pieces of $6 \times 14 \times \frac{1}{2}$-inch-thick plywood or lumber. Drill the hole in the upper right-hand corner for the $\frac{3}{8}$-inch-diameter dowel tie, and then make the layout for the zig-zag route. Do the cutting very carefully—you want a smooth path for the traveler. The waste

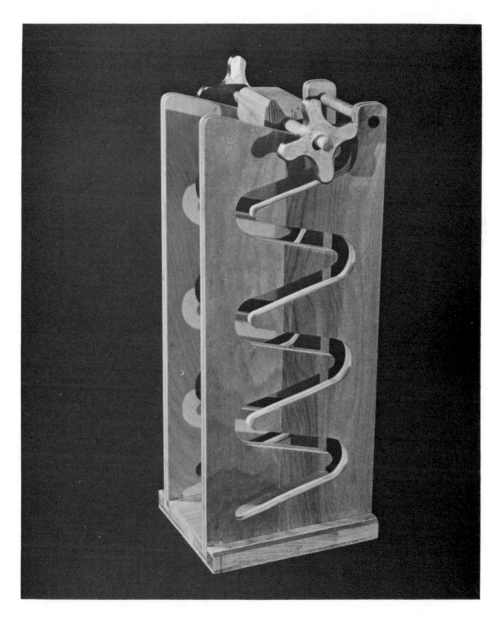

The traveler follows a zig-zag path down the sides of the toy.

# PROJECT 31
## ZIG - ZAG TRAVELER

Scale: one square $= \frac{1}{2}''$

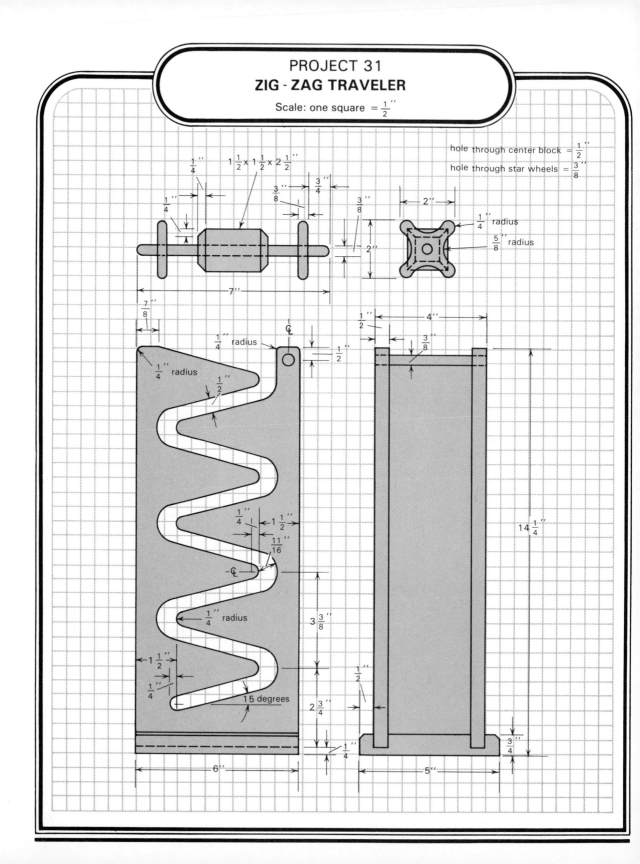

hole through center block $= \frac{1}{2}''$

hole through star wheels $= \frac{3}{8}''$

$1\frac{1}{2} \times 1\frac{1}{2} \times 2\frac{1}{2}''$

$\frac{1}{4}''$

$\frac{3}{8}''$

$\frac{3}{4}''$

$\frac{1}{4}''$

$\frac{3}{8}''$

$2''$

$2''$

$\frac{1}{4}''$ radius

$\frac{5}{8}''$ radius

$7''$

$\frac{7}{8}''$

$\frac{1}{4}''$ radius

$\frac{1}{4}''$ radius

$\frac{1}{2}''$

$\frac{1}{2}''$

$\frac{1}{2}''$

$4''$

$\frac{3}{8}''$

$14\frac{1}{4}''$

$\frac{1}{4}''$

$1\frac{1}{2}''$

$\frac{11}{16}''$

$\frac{1}{4}''$ radius

$3\frac{3}{8}''$

$1\frac{1}{2}''$

$\frac{1}{4}''$

$\frac{1}{2}''$

$2\frac{3}{4}''$

15 degrees

$\frac{1}{4}''$

$6''$

$5''$

$\frac{3}{4}''$

You can make travelers in addition to the one shown here. A little experimenting should prompt you toward a few original designs.

material has an interesting pattern, and should be stored for possible use on a future project.

The base—plywood or lumber—measures $\frac{3}{4} \times 5 \times 6$ inches and is grooved to receive the sides. Install the sides by using glue and driving a few 3d nails up through the bottom of the base. Add the dowel tie, meanwhile checking to be sure the sides of the project are parallel.

Construction details of the traveler are shown in the drawing. It will be easy to make duplicate star wheels if you draw the pattern on a piece of $\frac{3}{4}$-inch stock and then slice the piece into two parts after the star's outline has been formed. The star wheels fit tightly on the axle; the center block does not.

# Marble Ride

Teddy, age 12, was so impressed with this project and the Marble Roller Coaster **(Project 33)** which comes next, he found it difficult to wait until he could take complete possession. Interestingly, he tried to keep marbles constantly moving while his brother David, age 4, was content to let a marble run the entire course before starting another.

The best way to begin construction is to make the *returns* that are shown in Detail A in the drawing. Cut 6 pieces of stock (a few back-ups won't hurt) so they measure $1\frac{1}{2}$ inch square and 3 inches long. Bore a $\frac{3}{4}$-inch-diameter center hole in each piece $2\frac{1}{2}$ inches deep. Next, as shown in Step 3, bore a $\frac{3}{4}$-inch hole through one wall of the return. Then, working with a file or something similar, form the semicircular opening at the bottom of

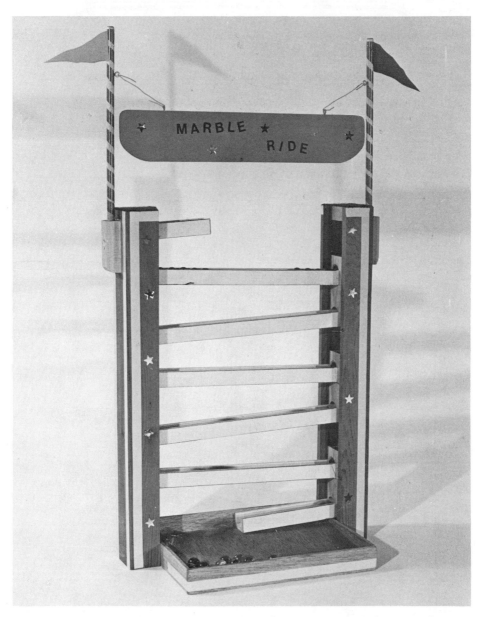

All main parts of the Marble Ride have a natural finish. Decorative touches were added with self-adhesive tapes and stars. The banner was painted and then titled with the self-adhesive letters sold in stationery stores. The flag poles, which are removable, have a spiral-winding of colorful tape.

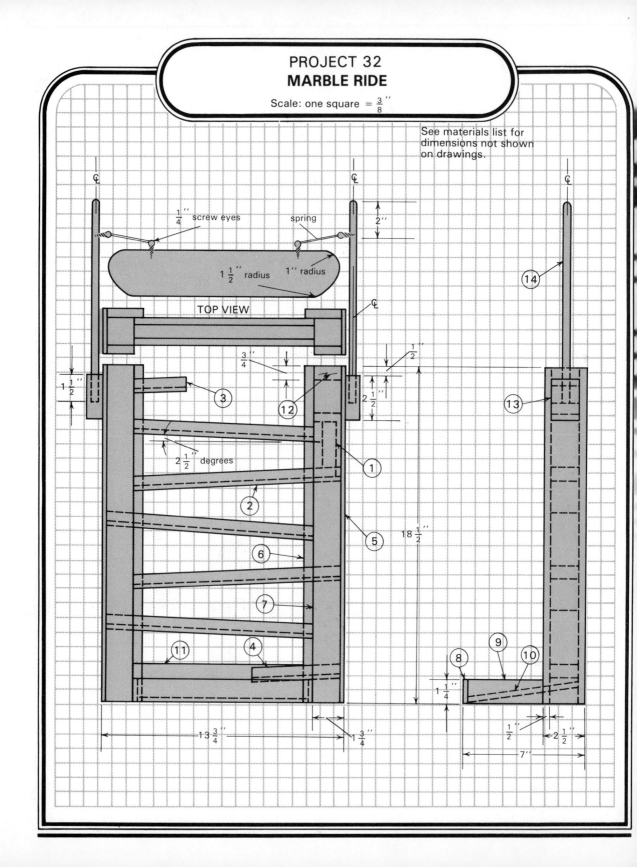

# PROJECT 32
# MARBLE RIDE

Scale: one square = $\frac{3}{8}$ "

See materials list for dimensions not shown on drawings.

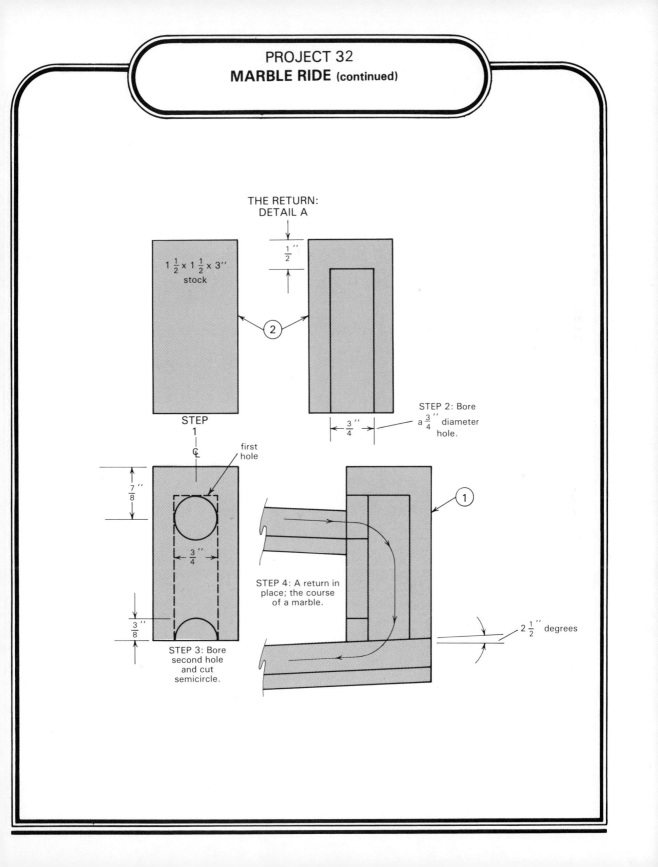

THE RETURN:
DETAIL A

$\frac{1}{2}''$

$1\frac{1}{2} \times 1\frac{1}{2} \times 3''$ stock

STEP 1

STEP 2: Bore a $\frac{3}{4}''$ diameter hole.

$\frac{3}{4}''$

first hole

$\frac{7}{8}''$

$\frac{3}{4}''$

$\frac{3}{8}''$

STEP 3: Bore second hole and cut semicircle.

STEP 4: A return in place; the course of a marble.

$2\frac{1}{2}''$ degrees

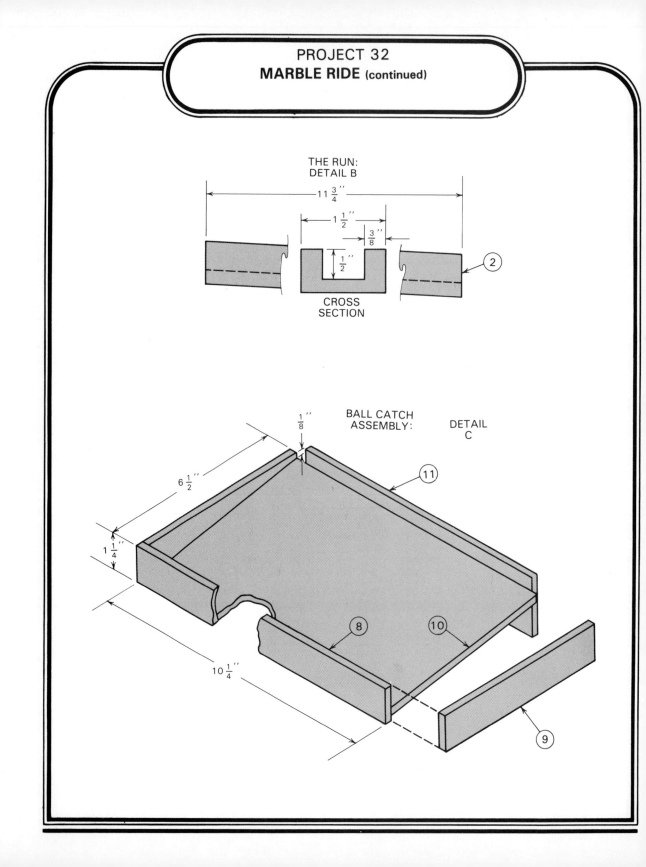

THE RUN:
DETAIL B

$11\frac{3}{4}''$

$1\frac{1}{2}''$

$\frac{3}{8}''$

$\frac{1}{2}''$

CROSS
SECTION

②

BALL CATCH
ASSEMBLY:

DETAIL
C

$\frac{1}{8}''$

$6\frac{1}{2}''$

$1\frac{1}{4}''$

$10\frac{1}{4}''$

⑪

⑧

⑩

⑨

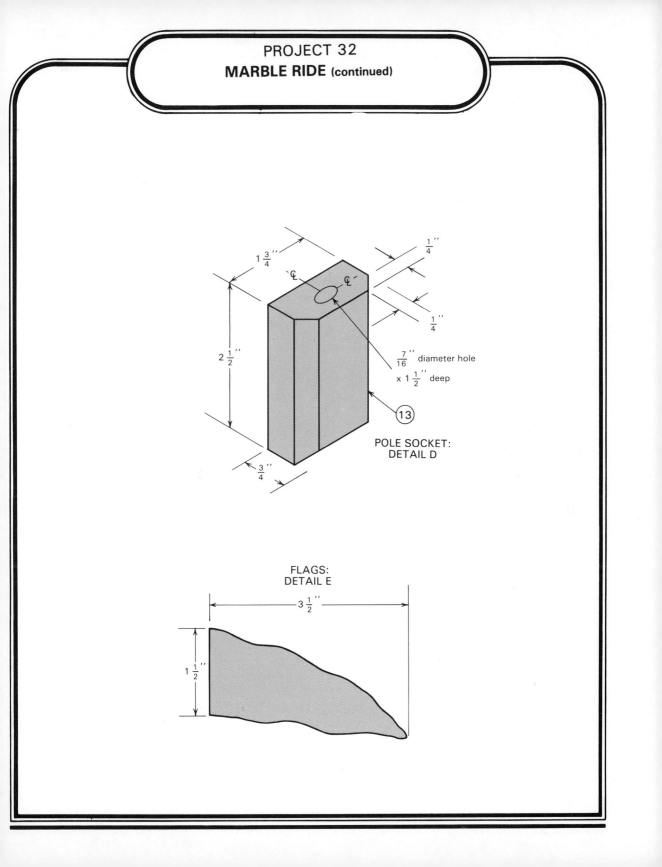

$1\frac{3}{4}''$

$\frac{1}{4}''$

$\frac{1}{4}''$

$2\frac{1}{2}''$

$\frac{7}{16}''$ diameter hole

x $1\frac{1}{2}''$ deep

(13)

POLE SOCKET:
DETAIL D

$\frac{3}{4}''$

FLAGS:
DETAIL E

$3\frac{1}{2}''$

$1\frac{1}{2}''$

the part. Step 4 (of Detail A) shows how the marbles travel through the returns after the *runs* have been installed.

Make the *runs* to the shape and size shown in Detail B. Here it may be more convenient to form the $\frac{1}{2} \times \frac{3}{4}$-inch-wide groove in a piece of stock that is long enough to be cut up into the number of runs that are required. The runs can also be made by gluing and nailing $\frac{3}{8} \times \frac{1}{2}$-inch-wide side pieces to a $\frac{1}{4} \times 1\frac{1}{2}$-inch-wide base.

The ends of the runs and the bottom of the returns are angled $2\frac{1}{2}$ degrees. This is easy to do on a disc or belt sander and can be done by hand if you work with coarse sandpaper or files. In either case, form the angle on one part and then use the piece as a pattern to mark the others.

Start assembly by using glue and 1-inch brads to join the ends (part no. 5) to the backs (part 6). Make a U-shaped jig by tack-nailing three strips of wood to a bench-top. The legs of the U must be parallel, 90 degrees to the base, with inside surfaces $13\frac{3}{4}$ inches apart. Place the L-shaped assemblies you have (parts 5 and 6), open end up, against the legs of the U and with one end snug against the base. You can use small C-clamps or spring clamps to keep the two assemblies in place.

Add the returns and the runs in this fashion, applying glue to mating surfaces before installing each piece. First install the top left return, then the first run, then the top right return and the second run, and so on. The idea is to eliminate the need for clamping by making the runs just long enough so they must be forced into position. The bottom of the entry hole in the returns must align with the bottom of the groove in the runs. The procedure is not complicated if you take it step-by-step. If you wish, you can do a dry run: Before doing the final assembly, put parts together without glue in order to check positions.

The short *entry* and *exit* runs are attached with glue and reinforced with $\frac{5}{8}$-inch brads that are driven at a slant (toe-nailed) through the top edges of the runs into the returns.

The final step, while the parts are still in the jig, is to add the two *fronts* (part 7) with glue and a few 1-inch brads located to avoid the holes in the returns or the grooves in the runs.

The *ball-catch* assembly is shown in Detail C. This can be assembled as

## project 32
### Marble Ride

# MATERIALS LIST

| Part No. | Name | Pieces | Size | Material |
|---|---|---|---|---|
| 1 | returns | 6 | $1\frac{1}{2} \times 1\frac{1}{2} \times 3''$ | lumber |
| 2 | runs* | 5 | $\frac{3}{4} \times 1\frac{1}{2} \times 12\frac{1}{2}''$ | " |
| 3 | entry run | 1 | $\frac{3}{4} \times 1\frac{1}{2} \times 3\frac{1}{2}''$ | " |
| 4 | exit run | 1 | $\frac{3}{4} \times 1\frac{1}{2} \times 6''$ | " |
| 5 | ends | 2 | $\frac{1}{4} \times 2\frac{1}{2} \times 18\frac{1}{2}''$ | plywood |
| 6 | backs | 2 | $\frac{1}{2} \times 2 \times 18\frac{1}{2}''$ | plywood or lumber |
| 7 | front | 2 | $\frac{1}{2} \times 1\frac{1}{2} \times 18\frac{1}{2}''$ | " |
| | **Ball Catch Parts** | | | |
| 8 | front | 1 | $\frac{1}{4} \times 1\frac{1}{4} \times 10\frac{1}{4}''$ | plywood |
| 9 | sides | 2 | $\frac{1}{4} \times 1\frac{1}{4} \times 6\frac{1}{4}''$ | " |
| 10 | bottom* | 1 | $\frac{1}{4} \times 7 \times 9\frac{3}{4}''$ | " |
| 11 | back | 1 | $\frac{1}{4} \times 2 \times 9\frac{1}{4}''$ | " |
| 12 | filler block | 1 | $\frac{3}{4} \times 1\frac{1}{2} \times 1\frac{1}{2}''$ | lumber |
| 13 | pole socket | 2 | $\frac{3}{4} \times 1\frac{3}{4} \times 2\frac{1}{2}''$ | " |
| 14 | flag poles | 2 | $\frac{3}{8} \times 11''$ | dowel |
| 15 | banner | 1 | $\frac{1}{4} \times 2\frac{1}{2} \times 13''$ | plywood |

*Length of runs and the width of ball catch bottom are listed oversize so they may be fitted on assembly.

a unit, but be sure the total width will match the distance between the inside edges of the front pieces (part 7).

The *pole sockets,* which are glued to the unit, are shaped as shown in Detail D. Make the *flag poles* from $\frac{3}{8}$-inch dowel and the *banner,* shaped as shown in the main drawing, from $\frac{1}{4}$-inch plywood. The *flags* (Detail E) are cut from heavy construction paper and attached to the poles with cement or glue.

# Marble Roller Coaster

The action of the Marble Roller Coaster is different from that of the Marble Ride. Here, the balls make quick U-turns at the end of each run, and they are always visible. At the end of travel, the balls fall through an opening in the bottom basin and are collected in a "barrel."

Start construction by making the *runs* and the *returns*. The runs are made from strips of $\frac{3}{4} \times 1\frac{1}{2}$-inch stock that are V-cut to the dimensions shown in Detail C in the drawing. This V shape can be either cut in a long piece that you then cut off into individual parts, or in pieces that are precut to

**212**

The Marble Roller Coaster was finished in natural tones and decorated with strips of self-adhesive aluminum tape. The titles were done on a label maker, but you can substitute self-adhesive letters from stationery stores.

## project 33
### Marble Roller Coaster

# MATERIALS LIST

| Part No. | Name | Pieces | Size | Material |
|---|---|---|---|---|
| 1 | returns* | 8 | $\frac{3}{4} \times 2 \times 3\frac{1}{2}''$ | lumber |
| 2 | runs** | 8 | $\frac{3}{4} \times 1\frac{1}{2} \times 12\frac{1}{2}''$ | " |
| 3 | ends | 2 | $\frac{5}{8} \times 3\frac{1}{2} \times 18\frac{3}{4}''$ | lumber or plywood |
| 4 | sides | 4 | $\frac{1}{4} \times 2\frac{5}{8} \times 15\frac{1}{2}''$ | " |
| 5 | bottom | 1 | $\frac{3}{4} \times 3\frac{1}{2} \times 15\frac{3}{4}''$ | lumber |
| 6 | height block | 1 | $\frac{3}{4} \times 1\frac{1}{2} \times 3\frac{1}{2}''$ | " |
| 7 | ball return | 1 | made from mailing tube (see text) | |
| 8 | ball guides | 2 | $\frac{1}{2} \times \frac{3}{4} \times 14\frac{1}{4}''$ | lumber |
| 9 | closure | 2 | $\frac{3}{4} \times 1\frac{1}{2} \times 12''$ | " |
| 10 | backstops | 7 | $\frac{3}{4} \times 2 \times 3\frac{1}{2}''$ | " |
| | **Parts for Marble Barrel** | | | |
| 11 | barrel | 1 | 3" dia. $\times$ 3" | mailing tube |
| 12 | barrel bottom | 1 | cut to suit | plywood or lumber |

*See text for actual size.
**Length is oversize so parts may be fitted on assembly.

length. In either case, cut the pieces longer than necessary so they can be trimmed to exact length on assembly.

The returns, shown in Detail A, require semicircular V-grooves that will mate with the V-grooves in the runs. The best way to make them is to use the pivot-cutting technique that is shown in Detail B and in the photograph. The pivot block is a scrap piece of wood with a nail through it. The block is clamped to the tool's table so the distance from the nail to the point of the router bit equals $\frac{7}{8}$ inch. Then the stock is mounted as shown in the photo and rotated against the cutter's direction of rotation. Use a high speed

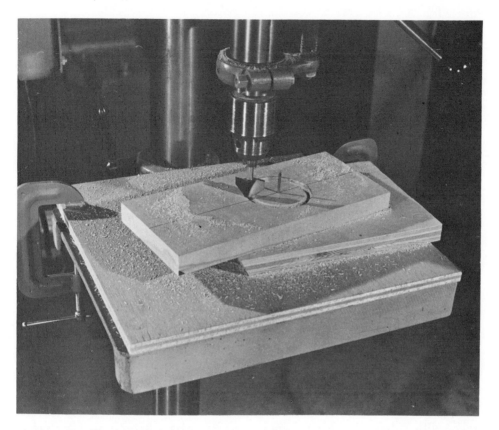

The setup used to form the circular V-grooves for the returns. The cutter is a 45-degree V-groove router bit. The grooves will be smoothest if you get to the full depth of cut by making repeat passes.

and achieve full depth-of-cut by making repeat passes, cutting about $\frac{1}{8}$ inch deep for each.

Start with a piece of wood that is well oversize so that you can work without getting your fingers close to the cutter. After the V-groove is formed, cut the entire piece $3\frac{1}{2}$ inches wide and 4 inches long. Be sure the circular groove and the work have a common centerline. Slice the part in half and you have two returns. This will make the piece a bit smaller than the 2-inch dimension called for, but the change will not be critical.

Next, make a U-shaped jig by tack-nailing strips of wood to a bench-top. The legs of the U must be parallel, with inside edges 17 inches apart. Make the *ends* (part 3) and the *sides* (part 4) and assemble one side—the back one —to each end with glue and 1-inch brads. Put these subassemblies in the jig, back surface down, and with top edges butting against the base of the U.

Put the top left and the top right returns in approximate position, and then use the top run to determine the exact position of the returns. Repeat this procedure with a second run and a second return, and this will reveal the distance the returns should be spaced. Now, after carefully marking their positions, you can install all the returns by using glue and short brads driven through the sides that have been installed. Add the remaining two sides, again using glue and short brads, and then return the parts to the jig.

Now it's time to install the runs. Cut them overlong—just enough so they must be forced into position between the returns. Coat mating surfaces with glue, put the runs in place, and then allow the assembly to sit until the glue is dry. The free end of the bottom run can be held against the side piece with a small clamp after the mating areas have been coated with glue.

Make the ball-catch as a subassembly as shown in Detail E. First shape the bottom (part 5), and check it on assembly to be sure it will fit correctly. Add the remaining parts and install the unit with glue and 1-inch brads that you drive through the side pieces. The ball return (part 7) is cut from a 3-inch mailing tube and is connected to the height block with glue and small nails. Use glue and 4d finishing nails to attach the closure pieces (part 9).

The final step is to make the backstops that are shown in Detail D. A quick procedure is to use a hole saw or fly cutter to form a $2\frac{1}{2}$-inch-diameter

The marble barrel was painted white and then decorated with colorful, self-adhesive tapes and stars.

hole in a piece of suitable-size stock, and then saw the piece in half to get two parts. Round off the front corners as the drawing shows, then coat the edges and the bottom of the pieces with glue and slip them into place. Press them by hand to make good contact, and then let them sit until the glue is dry.

Detail F shows how the Marble Barrel is made. Use the section of mailing tube as a template to mark the size of the disc used as a base. Install the disc with glue and with four 2d nails spaced 90 degrees apart.

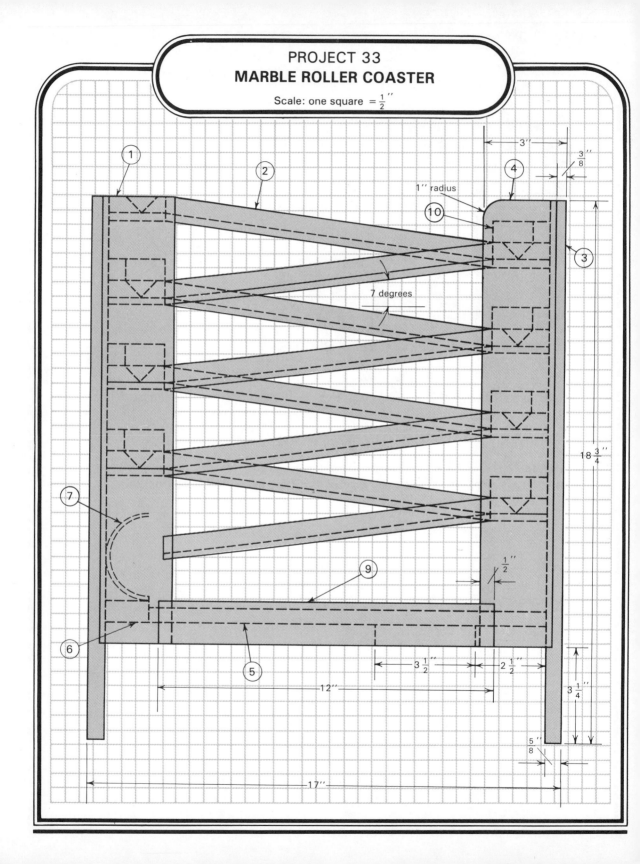

PROJECT 33
MARBLE ROLLER COASTER
Scale: one square = $\frac{1}{2}$″

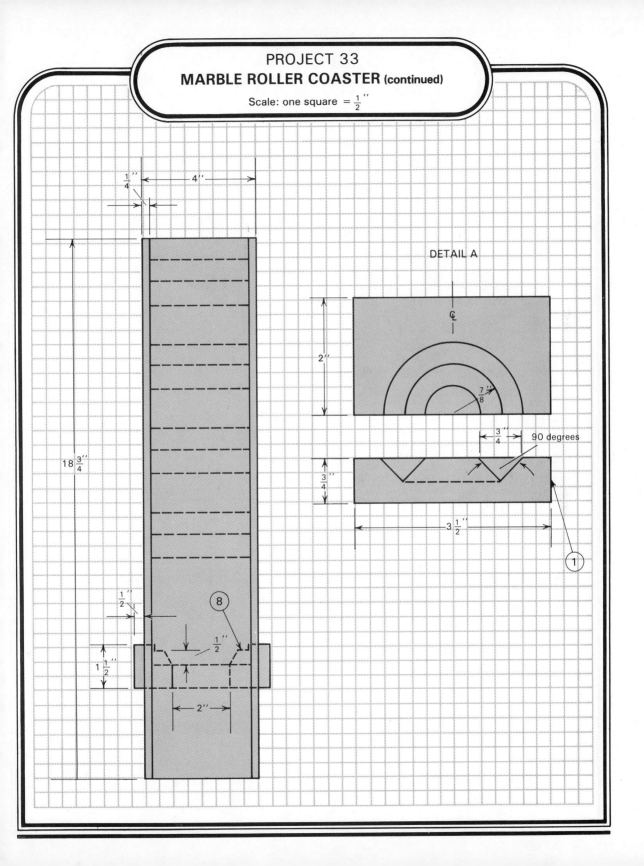

DETAIL A

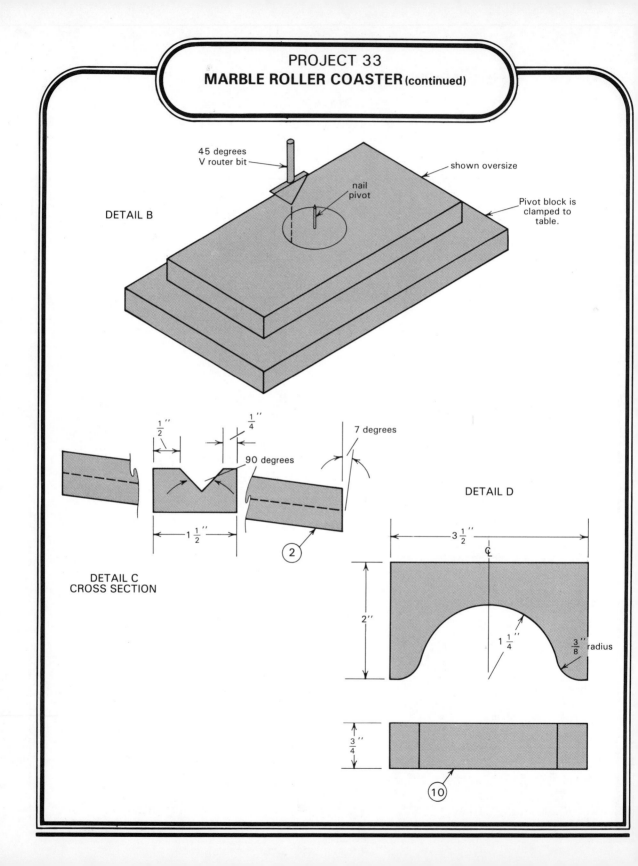

DETAIL B

45 degrees
V router bit

nail
pivot

shown oversize

Pivot block is
clamped to
table.

DETAIL C
CROSS SECTION

$\frac{1}{2}$''

$\frac{1}{4}$''

90 degrees

$1\frac{1}{2}$''

7 degrees

②

DETAIL D

$3\frac{1}{2}$''

2''

$1\frac{1}{4}$''

$\frac{3}{8}$'' radius

$\frac{3}{4}$''

⑩

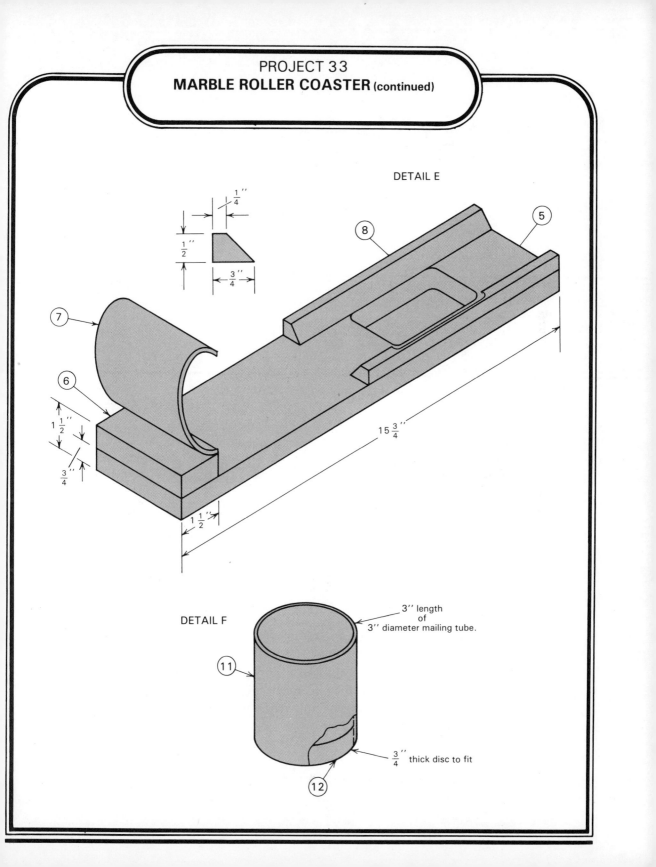

DETAIL E

$\frac{1}{4}''$

$\frac{1}{2}''$

$\frac{3}{4}''$

8

5

7

6

$1\frac{1}{2}''$

$\frac{3}{4}''$

$1\frac{1}{2}''$

$15\frac{3}{4}''$

DETAIL F

3'' length
of
3'' diameter mailing tube.

11

$\frac{3}{4}''$ thick disc to fit

12

# WAGONS

# Toy-Tote Wagon

Kids like to be transported, but they also enjoy being the transporter. The Toy-Tote Wagon is maneuverable and sized especially to suit the stuffed toys and animals a child is likely to have. Maybe it's a way for youngsters to emulate the parent who pulls them about in a large wagon.

Make the bed first, and then add the front and rear pieces, securing them with glue and 6d box nails. Form the sides using $\frac{1}{4}$-inch hardboard or plywood, and put them in place with glue and 4d box nails. If you use hardboard, drill small pilot holes for the nails so that they will be less likely to bend when you hammer them.

Make and attach the axle blocks, using a length of $\frac{1}{2}$-inch dowel as a gauge so the two pieces will be correctly aligned. The piece for the yoke, sized $\frac{3}{4} \times 3\frac{1}{2} \times 11$ inches to begin with, is shaped at the front as shown

All parts have a natural finish. The stripes and stars are self-adhesive products. The turtle was cut from children's-room wallpaper.

Proud owner of new transport system. The Toy-Tote Wagon proved to be a big deal for David. It was his to load and pull indoors and outdoors.

in the detail drawing. Attach it to the underside of the bed with glue and the screws called for in the drawing.

Next, make the rear axle and wheels. The length of the axle should be just enough to leave about an $\frac{1}{8}$-inch recess in the wheel holes so that the wood button, which serves as a hub, can be glued into place. Coat the ends of the axle with glue before pressing the wheels into place. If it is easier for you to eliminate the wood button, let the axle ends come flush with the outside surfaces of the wheels and then glue on a 1-inch-diameter disc of $\frac{1}{8}$- or $\frac{1}{4}$-inch-thick hardboard or plywood. The wheel "tires" (part 8) are strips cut from sheet cork which are put in place with contact cement or glue. If you use glue, hold the tires in place with a heavy rubber band until the glue dries.

The front wheel is a swivel-type plate caster with a 2-inch-diameter plastic wheel. Attach the caster to the underside of the yoke with the screws that are supplied with the unit.

Cut the handle to size and drill a hole at the bottom end for the axle and one at the top end for the grip. The hole at the top must provide a tight fit for the grip. At the bottom, the axle must fit tightly in the yoke, but be loose in the handle.

**project 34**
**Toy-Tote Wagon**

# MATERIALS LIST

| Part No. | Name | Pieces | Size | Material |
|---|---|---|---|---|
| 1 | bed | 1 | $\frac{3}{4} \times 12 \times 16\frac{1}{2}''$ | plywood |
| 2 | front | 1 | $\frac{3}{4} \times 5 \times 12''$ | " |
| 3 | rear | 1 | $\frac{3}{4} \times 4 \times 12''$ | " |
| 4 | sides | 2 | $\frac{1}{4} \times 7\frac{1}{2} \times 18''$ | hardboard |
| 5 | axle blocks | 2 | $1\frac{1}{8} \times 1\frac{1}{2} \times 3\frac{1}{2}''$ | lumber |
| 6 | yoke | 1 | $\frac{3}{4} \times 3\frac{1}{2} \times 11''$ | " |
| 7 | rear wheels | 2 | $\frac{1}{2} \times 5\frac{1}{4}''$ diameter | plywood (or lumber) |
| 8 | wheel "tires" | 2 | $\frac{1}{8} \times \frac{1}{2} \times 18''$ | cut from sheet cork |
| 9 | axle | 1 | $\frac{1}{2} \times 13\frac{1}{2}''$ | dowel |
| 10 | hubs | 2 | $\frac{1}{2}''$ | wood buttons |
| 11 | handle | 1 | $\frac{3}{4} \times 1\frac{1}{4} \times 22''$ | lumber |
| 12 | handle grip | 1 | $\frac{3}{8} \times 4''$ | dowel |
| 13 | handle axle | 1 | $\frac{3}{8} \times 4''$ | " |
| 14 | front wheel | 1 | $2''$ | swivel type plate caster with plastic wheel |

Hole through axle blocks $= \frac{9}{16}''$
Hole through rear wheels $= \frac{1}{2}''$
Hole through yoke $= \frac{3}{8}''$
Hole through handle $= \frac{7}{16}''$
Hole for handle grip $= \frac{3}{8}''$

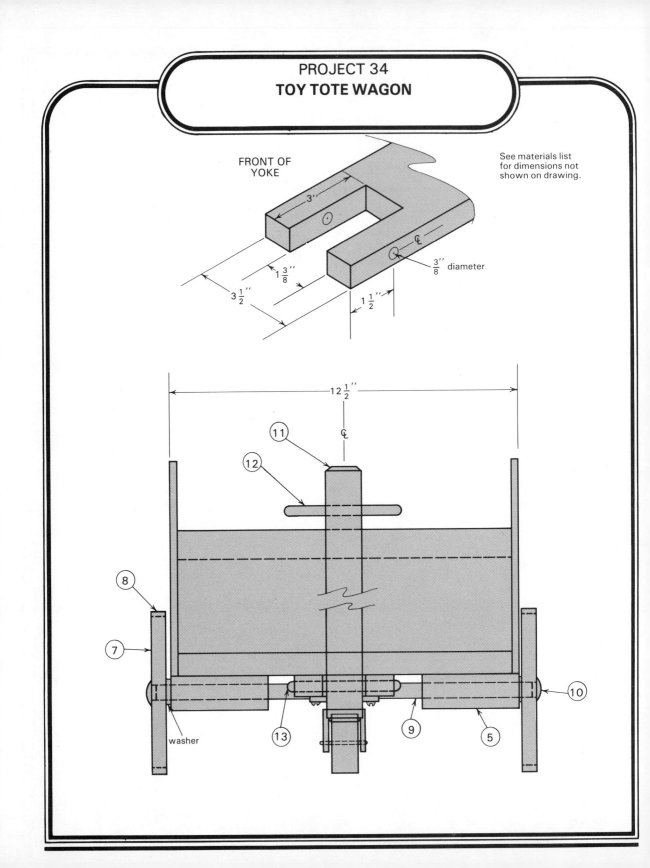

# PROJECT 34
## TOY TOTE WAGON

FRONT OF
YOKE

3''

See materials list
for dimensions not
shown on drawing.

$1\frac{3}{8}''$

$3\frac{1}{2}''$

$1\frac{1}{2}''$

$\frac{3}{8}''$ diameter

$12\frac{1}{2}''$

11

12

8

7

washer

13

9

5

10

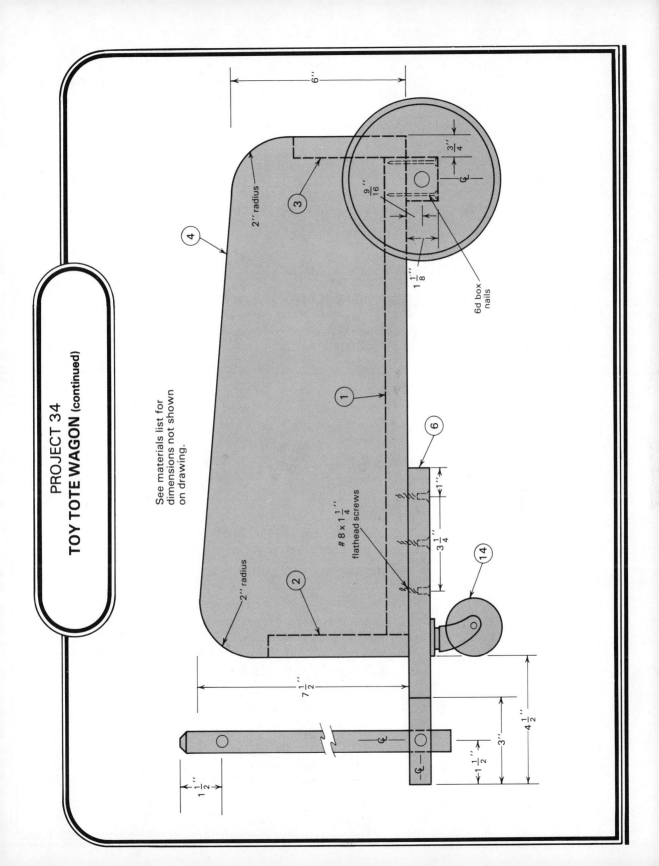

PROJECT 34
TOY TOTE WAGON (continued)

See materials list for
dimensions not shown
on drawing.

2" radius

2" radius

6"

3"
4

9"
16

1 1"
8

6d box
nails

#8 x 1 1"
4
flathead screws

1"

3 1"
4

7 1"
2

1 1"
2

1 1"
2

3"

4 1"
2

# Express Wagon

Start the project by making the bed—a piece of $\frac{3}{4}$-inch-thick, cabinet-grade plywood that will measure 16 inches wide by $24\frac{1}{4}$ inches long. Mark the locations of the screws that will be driven through the bed to secure the rear axle block and the front cleat. For now, drill small pilot holes at these points. They will be used to locate matching holes required in the axle block and cleat.

Cut the front and the back pieces to size, and after forming the rabbet in the bottom edges, attach them to the bed with glue and 4d box nails.

Cut the material that is required for the front and rear side pieces (parts 4 and 5). Mark these so you can identify which surface of each piece must face the inside of the wagon. This is important, because the direction of the rabbet cuts and dadoes must face the proper way when the parts are

The removable sides, bed, front, and rear pieces are plywood. All other parts are lumber. Finishing was done with coats of sealer. The wheel washers were rimmed with red tape.

installed. The rabbet cuts along the bottom edge of each piece should be $\frac{3}{4}$ inch deep by 1 inch wide. The grooves that are needed for the removable sides are $\frac{3}{4}$ inch deep and $\frac{5}{8}$ inch wide. If you are working on a table saw,

The steering post and yoke arrangement. A lock nut on the handle bolt provides security while still allowing the handle to pivot.

be aware, because the pieces are relatively small. The safest way to form the grooves is with a tenoning jig. If you lack such an accessory, do the cutting on pieces that are large enough to be safely handled. Then saw the pieces to final size.

Shape the front pieces as shown in the drawing, round off the inside corner of the rear pieces, and then attach the parts to the bed with glue and 5d or 6d nails. Make and install the front and rear posts using glue and 5d finishing nails.

Next, cut two 14-inch lengths of $1\frac{1}{2} \times 3\frac{1}{2}$-inch stock, and in each of them form the V-groove shown in Detail A. Saw one of them so it will produce both the front cleat (part 10) and the front axle block (part 12). The remaining piece, shaped as shown in Detail B, will be the rear axle block (part 9). Bore the $\frac{3}{4}$-inch-diameter hole that will be used for the steering post (Detail

**project 35**

**Express Wagon**

# MATERIALS LIST

| Part No. | Name | Pieces | Size | Material |
|---|---|---|---|---|
| 1 | bed | 1 | $\frac{3}{4} \times 16 \times 24\frac{1}{4}''$ | plywood |
| 2 | front | 1 | $\frac{3}{4} \times 5\frac{1}{2} \times 16''$ | plywood or lumber |
| 3 | back | 1 | $\frac{3}{4} \times 4\frac{1}{4} \times 16''$ | " |
| 4 | sides (front) | 2 | $1\frac{1}{2} \times 5\frac{1}{2} \times 7''$ | lumber |
| 5 | sides (rear) | 2 | $1\frac{1}{2} \times 4\frac{1}{4} \times 5''$ | " |
| 6 | front posts | 2 | $\frac{5}{8} \times \frac{7}{8} \times 7''$ | " |
| 7 | rear posts | 2 | $\frac{5}{8} \times \frac{7}{8} \times 5''$ | " |
| 8 | removable sides | 2 | $\frac{1}{2} \times 4\frac{1}{2} \times 12\frac{1}{2}''$ | plywood |
| 9 | rear axle block | 1 | $1\frac{1}{2} \times 3\frac{1}{2} \times 14''$ | lumber |
| 10 | front cleat | 1 | $1\frac{1}{2} \times 1\frac{1}{2} \times 14''$ | " |
| 11 | washer | 1 | $\frac{1}{4} \times 3''$ dia. | temp. hardboard |
| 12 | front axle block | 1 | $1\frac{1}{2} \times 1\frac{3}{4} \times 14''$ | lumber |
| 13 | rear axle | 1 | $\frac{3}{4} \times 20''$ | dowel |
| 14 | front axles | 2 | $\frac{3}{4} \times 8\frac{1}{2}''$ | " |
| 15 | washers | 8 | $\frac{1}{4} \times 2''$ dia. | temp. hardboard |
| 16 | wheels | 4 | $1\frac{1}{2} \times 5\frac{1}{4}''$ dia. | lumber |
| 17 | wheel locks | 4 | $\frac{1}{4} \times 2''$ | dowel |
| 18 | steering post | 1 | $\frac{3}{4} \times 5\frac{1}{2}''$ | " |
| 19 | steering post retainer | 1 | $1\frac{1}{4} \times 1\frac{1}{4} \times 1\frac{1}{2}''$ | lumber |
| 20 | yoke | 1 | $1\frac{1}{2} \times 7 \times 7''$ | " |
| 21 | handle | 1 | $\frac{3}{4} \times 22''$ | aluminum tube |
| 22 | handle grip | 1 | $1 \times 2 \times 7''$ | lumber |
| 23 | handle bolt | 1 | $\frac{3}{8} \times 2\frac{1}{2}''$ | bolt w/two washers and a *lock* nut |

C) in the front cleat, and then proceed to attach cleat and rear axle to the bed. Put them temporarily into position and bore screw-starting holes by drilling through the pilot holes you already have in the bed. Enlarge the pilot holes to $\frac{3}{16}$ or $\frac{7}{32}$ inch, coat mating surfaces with glue, and then drive home the 2-inch flathead screws.

Bore the $\frac{3}{4}$-inch-diameter hole required for the steering post through the front axle block, then cut to length and attach the two front axles and the single rear one (Detail A). Do not, at this point, drill the wheel-lock holes through the axles.

The steering-post arrangement is shown in Detail C. Make the antifriction washer (part 11) and the retainer (part 19) and assemble the unit as illustrated. Attach the steering post (in the hole in the front cleat) with glue and two #6 1-inch screws. Add the washer and the axle block, then the metal washer, and finally the retainer—which you only attach with screws.

The yoke is shaped as shown in Detail D. The easiest way to form the notch is to first bore a 1-inch hole with its center $3\frac{1}{2}$ inches from the yoke's end. Then saw out the waste piece. Attach the yoke to the front axle block with glue and four #10 $1\frac{3}{4}$-inch screws.

Cut the wheel washers (part 15) by working as if you were making small wheels. Make the four wheels and then add washers and wheels to the axles. Drill holes through the axles for the $\frac{1}{4}$-inch dowels used as wheel locks. Locate the locks so that they allow just enough clearance for the wheels to turn. Detail E shows an optional wheel arrangement. The bushing can be aluminum tubing that has a $\frac{3}{4}$-inch inside diameter. Size the hole through the wheel so that the bushing can be a press fit. If the wheel doesn't turn freely on the axle, work with fine sandpaper and dress the axle to suit.

Final steps are to make the removable sides and the handle assembly. Bore the hole in the handle grip before you cut the part to outline shape. Attach it to the handle with two #6 1-inch screws. The bolt that passes through the yoke and the handle is secured with a *lock nut.* Lock nuts are sold in auto-supply stores if not available at your hardware store. Lock nuts will stay put at any point on the bolt.

One more point: The handle length in the drawing is okay for youngsters, but too short when adults are pulling the wagon. An extra, longer handle will prevent back cricks.

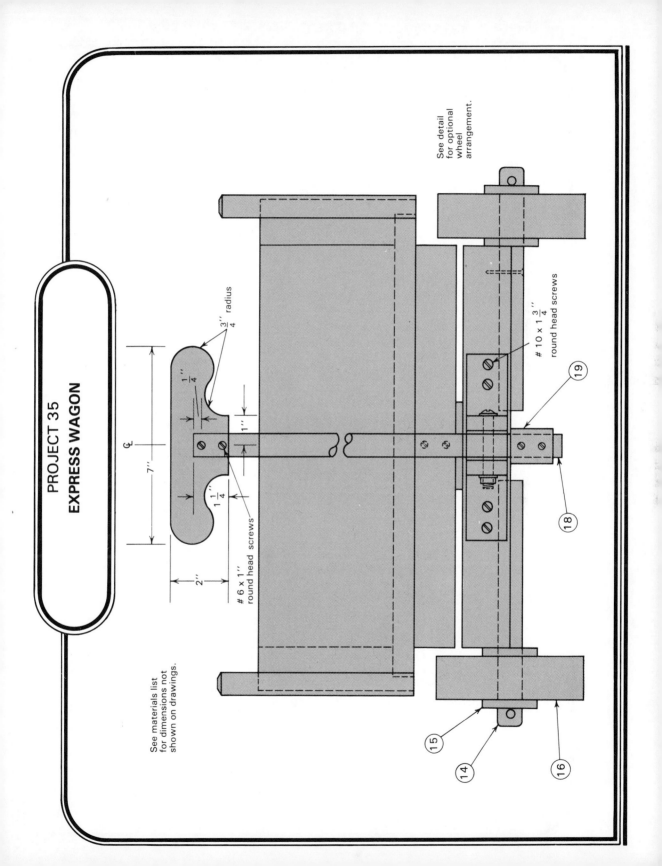

# PROJECT 35
# EXPRESS WAGON

See materials list for dimensions not shown on drawings.

See detail for optional wheel arrangement.

$\frac{3}{4}$'' radius

$\frac{1}{4}$''

$1$''

$1\frac{1}{4}$''

$7$''

$2$''

# 6 x 1'' round head screws

# 10 x 1$\frac{3}{4}$'' round head screws

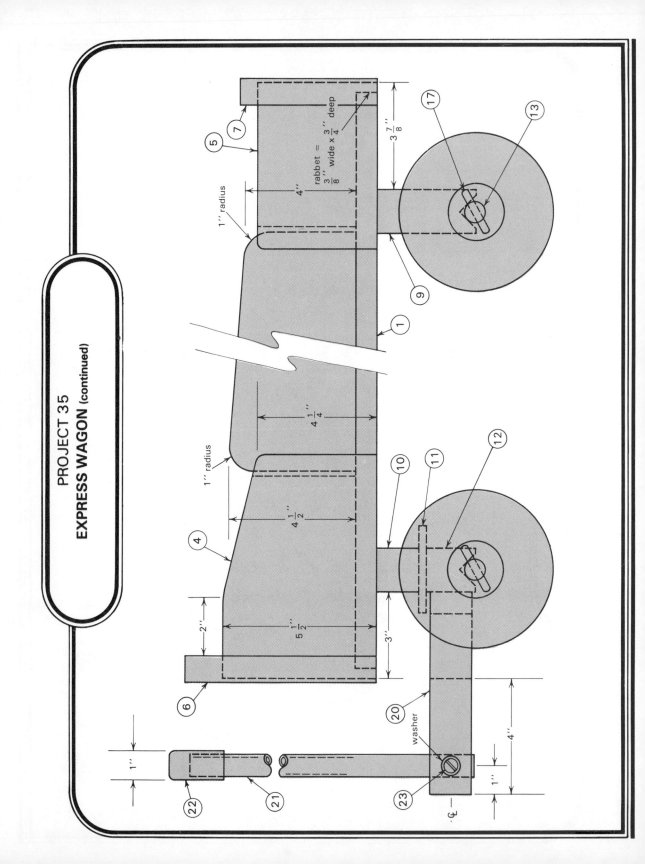

PROJECT 35
EXPRESS WAGON (continued)

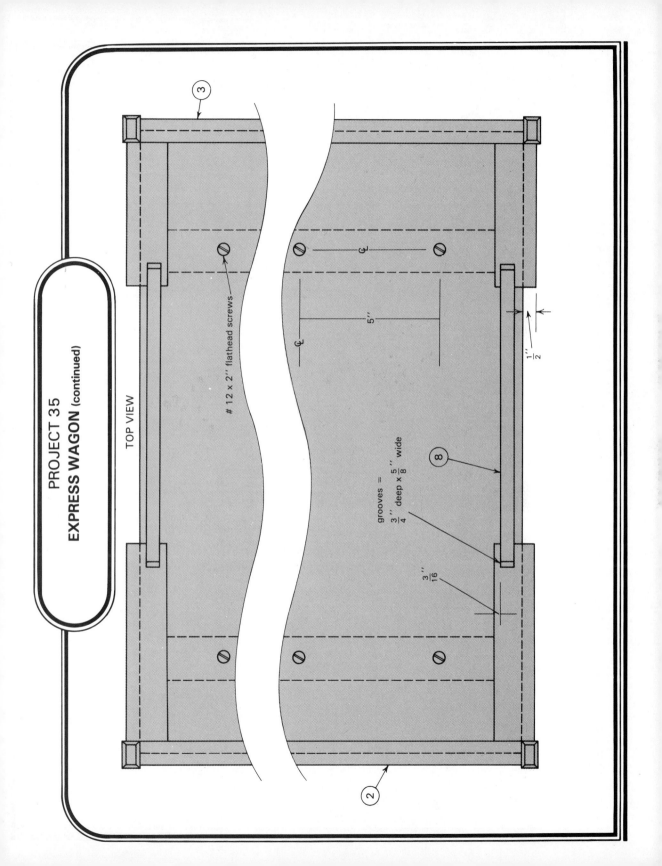

# PROJECT 35
## EXPRESS WAGON (continued)

TOP VIEW

# 12 x 2" flathead screws

grooves =
$\frac{3}{4}$" deep x $\frac{5}{8}$" wide

$\frac{3}{16}$"

5"

$\frac{1}{2}$"

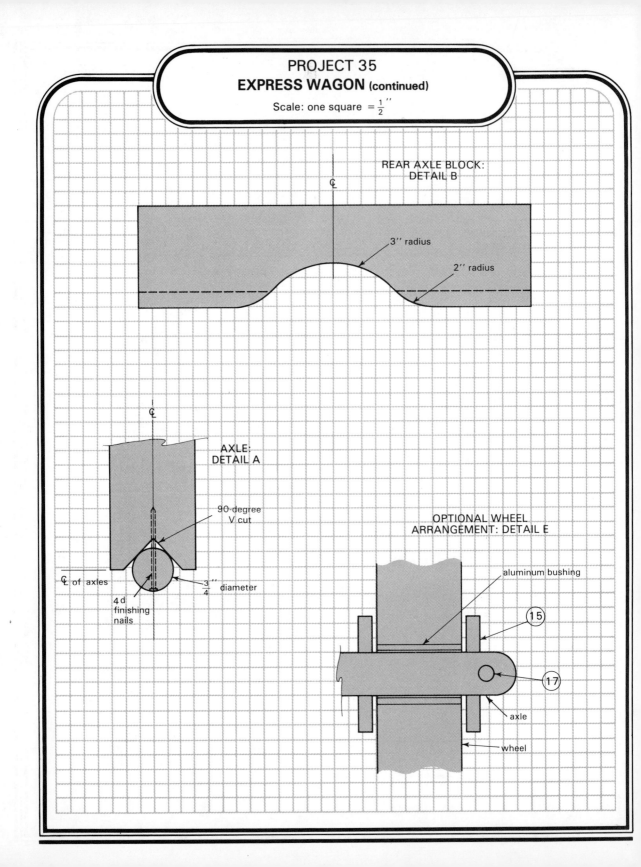

# PROJECT 35
## EXPRESS WAGON (continued)
Scale: one square $= \frac{1}{2}''$

REAR AXLE BLOCK:
DETAIL B

3'' radius

2'' radius

AXLE:
DETAIL A

90-degree
V cut

OPTIONAL WHEEL
ARRANGEMENT: DETAIL E

aluminum bushing

$\frac{3}{4}''$ diameter

15

17

$\mathcal{C}$ of axles

4 d
finishing
nails

axle

wheel

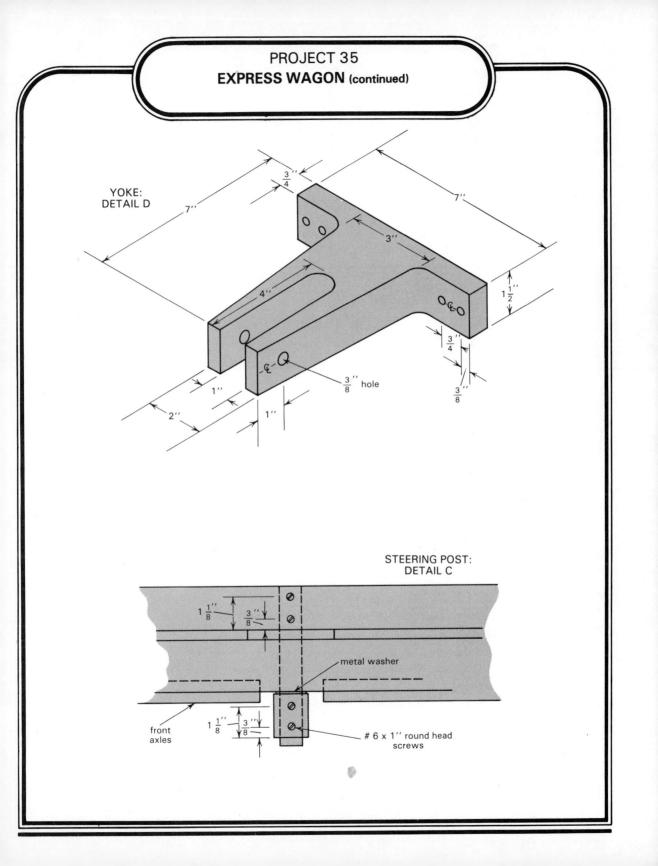

YOKE:
DETAIL D

STEERING POST:
DETAIL C

metal washer

front axles

# 6 x 1'' round head screws

# RIDING TOYS

# Kiddie
# Car

Kids like to be mobile—whether they're on wheels, straddling a project and pretending to ride, or just rocking. These are major reasons why the projects in this section will always be popular. The first three are traditional. The fourth, the No-Gas Car, is the "ultimate driving machine" for the youngster who hasn't yet cast his eyes on a full-size bike and is far from thoughts of a motorcycle or automobile.

**238**

The Kiddie Car was finished by first applying a coat of sealer and then a coat of yellow paint. The pad on the seat is a piece of indoor-outdoor carpeting. It can be attached with glue, contact cement, or even with strips of heavy double-face tape.

## project 36
### Kiddie Car

# MATERIALS LIST

| Part No. | Name | Pieces | Size | Material |
|---|---|---|---|---|
| 1 | seat | 1 | $1 \times 10 \times 20''$ | plywood or lumber |
| 2 | wheel posts (rear) | 2 | $1\frac{1}{2} \times 2\frac{1}{2} \times 8''$ | lumber |
| 3 | rear support | 1 | $1\frac{1}{2} \times 2\frac{3}{8} \times 7\frac{1}{2}''$ | " |
| 4 | wheel posts (front) | 2 | $1\frac{1}{2} \times 2\frac{1}{2} \times 7\frac{3}{4}''$ | " |
| 5 | front support | 1 | $1\frac{1}{2} \times 2\frac{1}{4} \times 5''$ | " |
| 6 | brace | 1 | $1\frac{1}{2} \times 2\frac{3}{8} \times 8\frac{1}{4}''$ | " |
| 7 | steering column | 1 | $1\frac{1}{2} \times 1\frac{1}{2} \times 4''$ | " |
| 8 | steering post | 1 | $\frac{3}{4} \times 9\frac{1}{4}''$ | aluminum tube |
| 9 | washers | 2 | $\frac{1}{4} \times 3''$ dia. | temp. hardboard |
| 10 | wheels | 3 | $1\frac{1}{2} \times 5\frac{1}{2}''$ dia. | lumber |
| 11 | washers | 2 | $\frac{1}{4} \times 2''$ dia. | temp. hardboard |
| 12 | washers | 2 | $\frac{1}{4} \times 1\frac{1}{2}''$ dia. | " |
| 13 | rear axle | 1 | $\frac{3}{4} \times 12\frac{1}{2}''$ | dowel |
| 14 | front axle | 1 | $\frac{3}{4} \times 6\frac{1}{2}''$ | " |
| 15 | handlebars | 1 | $1\frac{1}{2} \times 2\frac{1}{4} \times 12''$ | lumber |
| 16 | plug | 1 | $\frac{3}{4} \times 1''$ | dowel |
| 17 | cap | 1 | to suit | salvage |

Hole through front wheel and washers $= \frac{7}{8}''$
Hole through front wheel supports $= \frac{3}{4}''$
Hole through rear wheels $= \frac{3}{4}''$
Hole through rear wheel supports and washers $= \frac{7}{8}''$

# PROJECT 36
## KIDDIE KAR

Scale: one square = $\frac{1}{2}$''

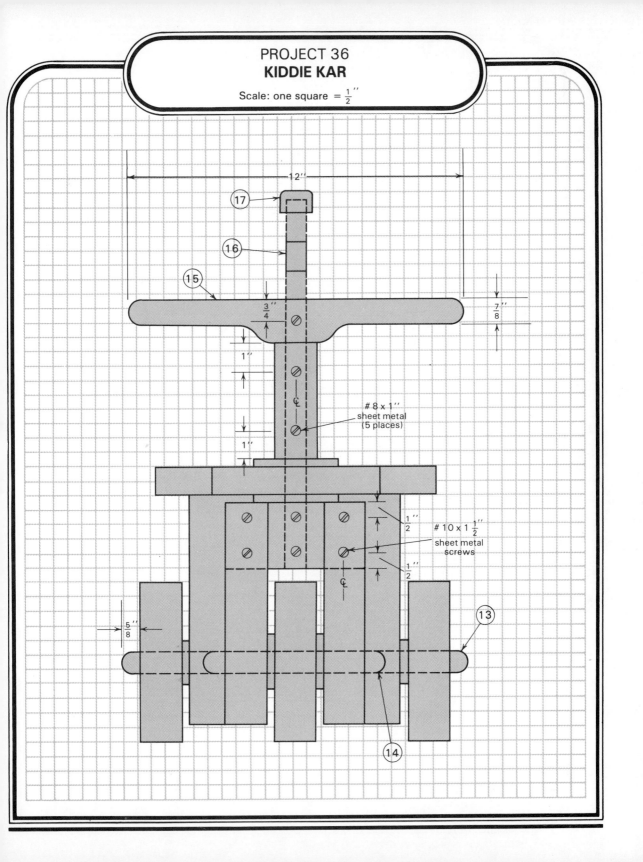

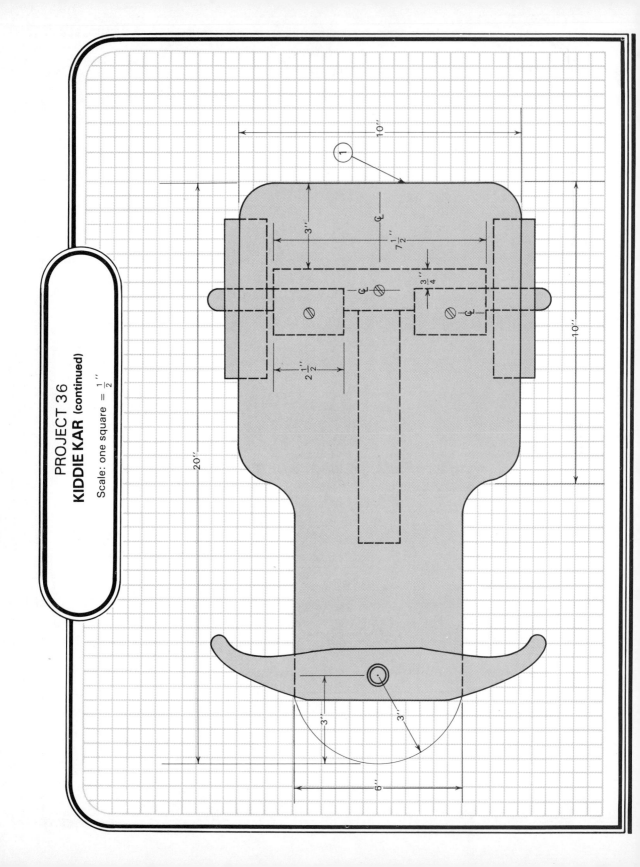

10"

10"

20"

① 1

3"

$7\frac{1}{2}$"

$\frac{3}{4}$"

$2\frac{1}{2}$"

6"

3"

3"

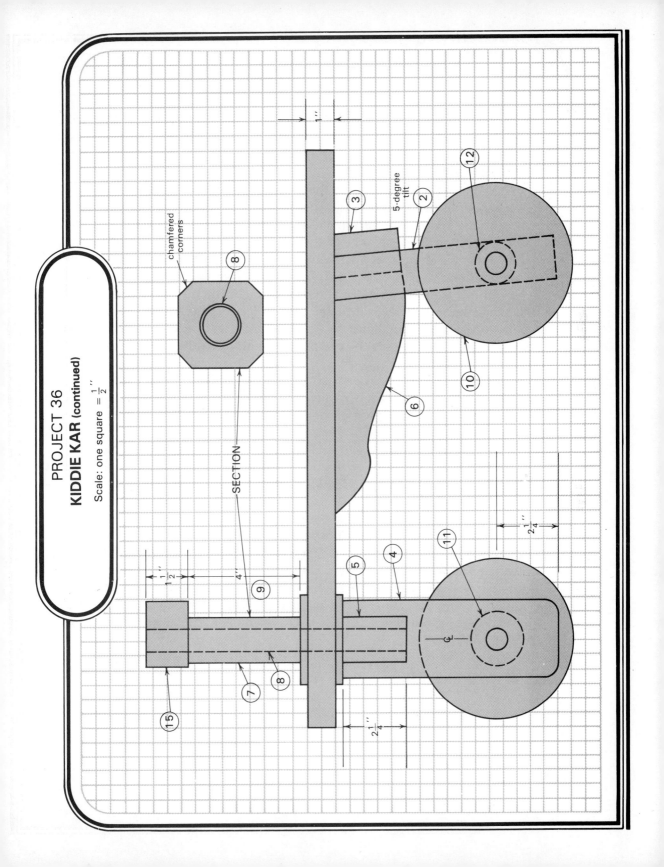

PROJECT 36
KIDDIE KAR (continued)

Scale: one square = $\frac{1}{2}$''

Start the project by shaping the seat and boring the $\frac{3}{4}$-inch steering-post hole at the front, and three pilot holes at the rear for the screws that will be used to attach the rear-wheel support assembly. Chamfer or round off the top and bottom edges of the seat and do a thorough sanding job, especially if you use plywood.

Next, make the rear posts and the support (parts 2 and 3). Bore the $\frac{7}{8}$-inch axle holes through the posts and form the rabbet cuts in the support to the dimensions shown in the top view of the drawing. Shape the top end of the posts and the top edge of the support to an angle of 5 degrees, and then assemble the pieces with glue and 6d box nails driven through the support.

Hold the assembly in place and drill through the pilot holes in the seat so you'll know where to drill the lead holes for the attachment screws. Enlarge the seat pilot holes to $\frac{3}{16}$ or $\frac{7}{32}$ inch, and after coating mating surfaces with glue, attach the parts permanently by driving home the three #12 $2\frac{1}{4}$-inch screws.

Make the assembly that consists of parts 4 and 5. Drill the $\frac{3}{4}$-inch steering-post hole through the support and the $\frac{3}{4}$-inch axle holes through the posts before assembling the pieces with glue and the #10 $1\frac{1}{2}$-inch sheet-metal screws.

Make the brace (part 6) and attach it with glue and by toenailing at the front and rear. The shape of the brace really isn't critical, so you can skip the layout that is shown and just draw something similar by working with a French curve.

Next, make the parts that compose the steering assembly—the steering post, which is a length of aluminum tubing; two washers; the steering column; and the handlebars. Assemble the parts in this order: Place the steering post in the hole that is in the front support. Add a washer and then pass the post through the hole in the seat. Add the second washer, then the steering column, and finally, the handlebars. Drill $\frac{1}{16}$-inch holes through the parts as you place them, for the #8 1-inch sheet-metal screws that are called for.

The cap, which is a recycled bottle top, adds a decorative touch, but is there primarily to seal the hole at the top of the steering post in which little fingers can sometimes get caught. Size the plug so that it will have to be forced into the post, and then glue on the cap.

Make and install the axles, wheel washers, and wheels. The rear wheels turn *with* the axle; the front wheel rotates independently.

# Hobby Horse

Make a pad of the three pieces required for the horse's head. Draw the silhouette, and then drill the $\frac{1}{2}$-inch-diameter hole that is needed for the handle and two pilot holes for the screws that will secure the head to the post. Saw the pad to outline shape, and after separating the parts, do the additional sawing required on the $\frac{3}{4}$-inch-thick center piece (dotted lines on the drawing).

Assemble the three pieces using glue and clamps, or glue and 4d finishing nails that you drive at strategic points from both sides of the assembly.

The post is a solid piece that you can cut from a 2×3 or a 2×4. Cut the part to length and then chamfer all four corners. With a saw, reduce the post's thickness at the top end so it will fit the slot in the head. The curved

**246**

A young rider reins in his trusty steed.

portion of the post which will abut the head at the bottom of the slot can be shaped with a rasp.

Drill the $\frac{11}{16}$-inch axle hole through the post. After coating the insertion area with glue, put the post in place and drive home the two #10 $1\frac{1}{2}$-inch panhead sheet-metal screws.

Make the wheels, and rim them with strips of sheet aluminum or flashing material. The metal can be attached with contact cement or with 1-inch nails. If you work with nails, use two on each side of the joint and three others spaced 90 degrees apart. Make and install the axle and the washers, and mount the wheels. The wheels and axles turn as a unit.

The handle grips can be made from dowel, or you can drill center holes through ready-made, ball-shape draw pulls. The handle grips should fit tightly on the handle, and the handle should be a tight fit in the head.

The Hobby Horse is yellow; the features are black. The mane was made by stapling short pieces of macrame cord and then unraveling them. The post was spiral-wound with $\frac{3}{4}$-inch-wide, green self-adhesive tape.

# PROJECT 37
# HOBBY HORSE

Scale: one square $= \frac{1}{2}''$

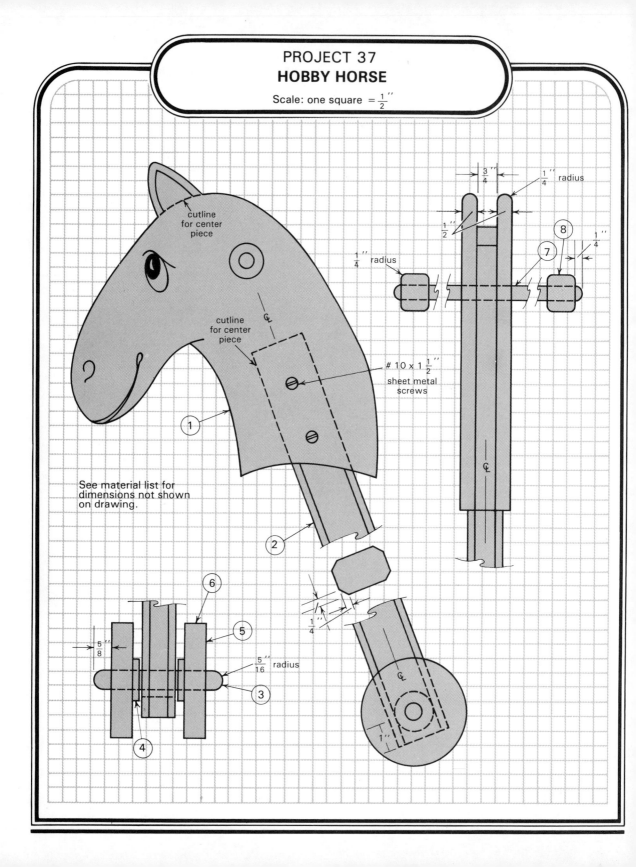

cutline for center piece

cutline for center piece

See material list for dimensions not shown on drawing.

# 10 x 1 $\frac{1}{2}''$ sheet metal screws

$\frac{3}{4}''$

$\frac{1}{4}''$ radius

$\frac{1}{2}''$

$\frac{1}{4}''$ radius

$\frac{1}{4}''$

$\frac{5}{8}''$

$\frac{5}{16}''$ radius

$\frac{1}{4}''$

$1''$

## project 37
### Hobby Horse

# MATERIALS LIST

| Part No. | Name | Pieces | Size | Material |
|---|---|---|---|---|
| 1 | head | 2 | $\frac{1}{2} \times 12 \times 12''$ | lumber or plywood |
|  |  | 1 | $\frac{3}{4} \times 12 \times 12''$ | " |
| 2 | post | 1 | $1\frac{1}{4} \times 2 \times 28\frac{1}{2}''$ | lumber |
| 3 | axle | 1 | $\frac{5}{8} \times 4\frac{3}{4}''$ | dowel |
| 4 | washers | 2 | $\frac{1}{4} \times 1\frac{1}{2}''$ dia. | temp. hardboard |
| 5 | wheels | 2 | $\frac{3}{4} \times 4''$ dia. | lumber |
| 6 | rims* | 2 | $\frac{3}{4} \times 13''$ | sheet aluminum or flashing material |
| 7 | handle | 1 | $\frac{1}{2} \times 12''$ | dowel |
| 8 | handle grips | 2 | $1\frac{1}{4} \times 1''$ | " |

*Length is oversize—to be trimmed on assembly.

Hole for handle through head and grips $= \frac{1}{2}''$. Hole through post for axle and through washers $= \frac{11}{16}''$. Hole through wheels $= \frac{5}{8}''$.

# Rocking Horse

The drawings show an easy method for tracing the arc required for the rockers. Select a piece of plywood or lumber of any width that is at least 50 inches long. Mark a centerline down the length of the material. Cut a 32-inch length of $1\frac{1}{2}$-inch-thick by 6-inch-wide lumber and clamp or tack-nail it to the first piece so that it is centered and at right angles to the centerline. Drive a nail on the centerline, 48 inches from the outside edge of the stock. Make a "compass" by tying one end of a piece of string to the nail and the other end to a pencil; the distance between pencil point and nail should be 48 inches. Keep the string taut as you move the pencil to

The Rocking Horse has a natural finish. Head details are black; short pieces of macrame material do for the mane. Use $\frac{1}{4}$- or $\frac{3}{8}$-inch-diameter smooth rope for the reins which pass through the horse's head and the upper part of the front leg.

form the arc. Reduce the length of the string by $2\frac{1}{4}$ inches and mark a second, parallel arc. While the stock is still in square form, mark the location of the holes needed for the stretchers.

If you have a band saw you can pad, or stack, the stock together so a single cutting will produce two rockers. Otherwise, saw and sand one rocker and then use it as a template to mark its twin. Drill the $\frac{5}{8}$-inch-diameter holes required for the stretchers, and then chamfer and sand outside edges so that a cross section of the pieces will look like that in Section A-A in the drawing. Cut and install the stretchers, making sure that the rockers are parallel and that the distance between outside surfaces equals 12 inches. Use glue and one 6d finishing nail to secure the stretchers.

Make the back leg, shaping the center cutout and the base notches to the dimensions that are shown in the front view of the drawing. Next, cut the piece required for the front leg, and form as the drawing shows. You can use the back leg as a template to mark the cut lines of the lower portion of the front leg.

To make the seat, first cut the material to overall size. Then form the dado in which the back leg fits and the 5-degree bevel at the front, and saw the part to shape. It's a good idea, while the seat is still free and easy to handle, to make and attach the backrest (part 7) by following the instructions shown in Detail C. At this point, you can also attach the seat to the back leg and install the brace. At first, cut the brace longer than necessary. After it is attached, cut the front end to conform to the bevel on the front edge of the seat.

Now put this assembly and the front leg temporarily in position so that you can judge exact locations. Mark the leg positions on the inside of the rockers, and make and install the glue blocks shown in Detail B. Secure them with glue and 6d finishing nails and then permanently attach the legs. Use glue and one #8 $1\frac{3}{4}$-inch screw through the legs into each glue block. Use glue and 6d finishing nails to make the bond between the front leg and the seat.

Shape the head by following the pattern shown in Detail A. Here you can do some carving if you wish—depressions for the nostrils, lips, raised eyebrows, and so on. The least you should do is round off all edges, paying particular attention to the area between mane and nose.

**project 38**

**Rocking Horse**

# MATERIALS LIST

| Part No. | Name | Pieces | Size | Material |
|---|---|---|---|---|
| 1 | rockers | 2 | $1\frac{1}{2} \times 6 \times 32''$ | lumber |
| 2 | stretchers | 3 | $\frac{5}{8} \times 13''$ | dowel |
| 3 | back leg | 1 | $\frac{3}{4} \times 10 \times 13''$ | lumber or plywood |
| 4 | front leg | 1 | $\frac{3}{4} \times 10 \times 23\frac{1}{2}''$ | " |
| 5 | seat | 1 | $1 \times 10 \times 18''$ | plywood or lumber |
| 6 | brace | 1 | $\frac{3}{4} \times 2\frac{1}{4} \times 18''$ | lumber |
| 7 | backrest | 1 | $1\frac{1}{2} \times 4 \times 8''$ | " |
| 8 | glue blocks | 4 | $1 \times 1\frac{1}{2} \times 3''$ | " |
| 9 | head | 1 | $1\frac{1}{2} \times 7 \times 9''$ | " |
| 10 | screw covers | 2 | $\frac{1}{2}''$ | wood buttons |
| **Parts for Stirrups (Optional)** | | | | |
| 11 | sides | 4 | $\frac{3}{4} \times 1\frac{1}{4} \times 4''$ | lumber |
| 12 | bottom rung | 2 | $\frac{1}{2} \times 4''$ | dowel |
| 13 | top rung | 2 | $\frac{1}{2} \times 3\frac{1}{4}''$ | " |
| 14 | strap | 1 | $1\frac{1}{4}''$ wide $\times$ app. 30″ | leather (or similar) |

Also needed:  about 36″ of $\frac{3}{8}''$-diameter nylon rope
(for reins)
macrame material for mane and tail
Stretcher holes through rockers $= \frac{5}{8}''$

Hayley gets the Rocking Horse. She thought the stirrups were a good idea.

If you wish to add the stirrups, they can be made as shown in the detail drawing. The strap can be made from an old belt. It can be cut to a specific length or made adjustable by installing button snaps—which, if you don't have equipment for that kind of thing, can be done for you at a shoe repair shop.

Secure the strap to the seat with a couple of $\frac{3}{4}$-inch, panhead sheet-metal screws. Use washers under the heads.

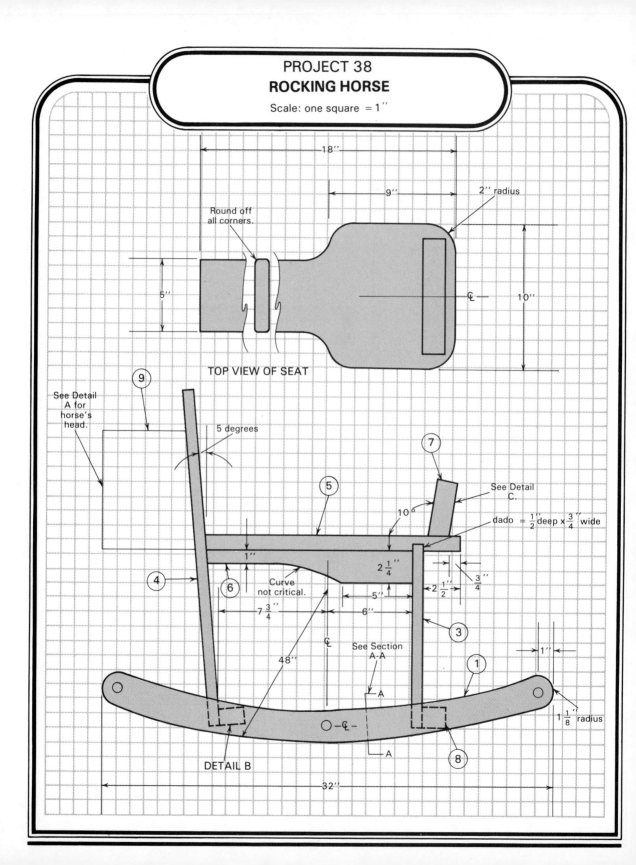

# PROJECT 38
## ROCKING HORSE

Scale: one square = 1″

18″

9″

2″ radius

Round off all corners.

5″

10″

℄

**TOP VIEW OF SEAT**

See Detail A for horse's head.

5 degrees

⑨

⑤

⑦

See Detail C.

10°

dado = $\frac{1}{2}$″ deep x $\frac{3}{4}$″ wide

1″

$2\frac{1}{4}$″

$\frac{3}{4}$″

④

⑥

Curve not critical.

$2\frac{1}{2}$″

$7\frac{3}{4}$″

6″

5″

③

℄

48″

See Section A-A

A

①

1″

$1\frac{1}{8}$″ radius

℄

A

⑧

**DETAIL B**

32″

# PROJECT 38
## ROCKING HORSE (continued)

Scale: one square = 1"

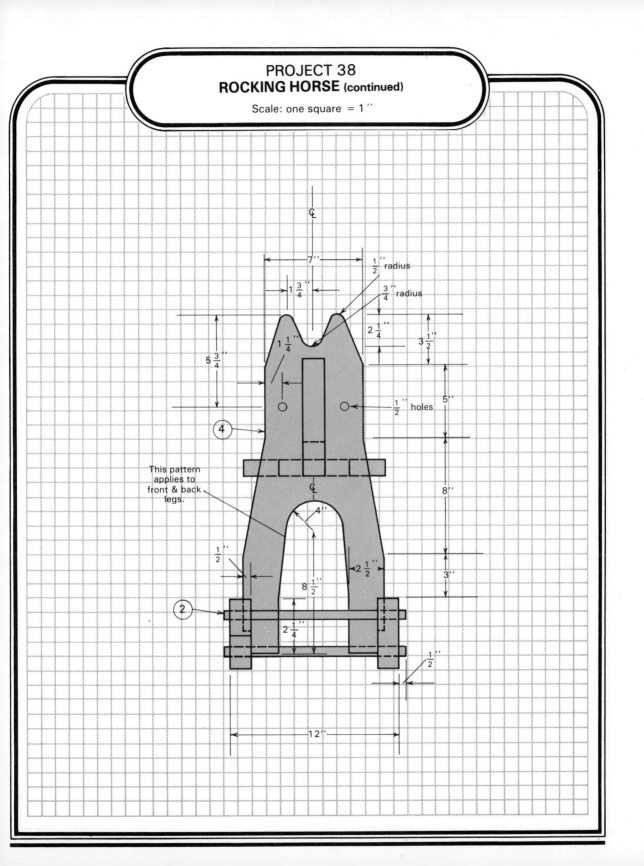

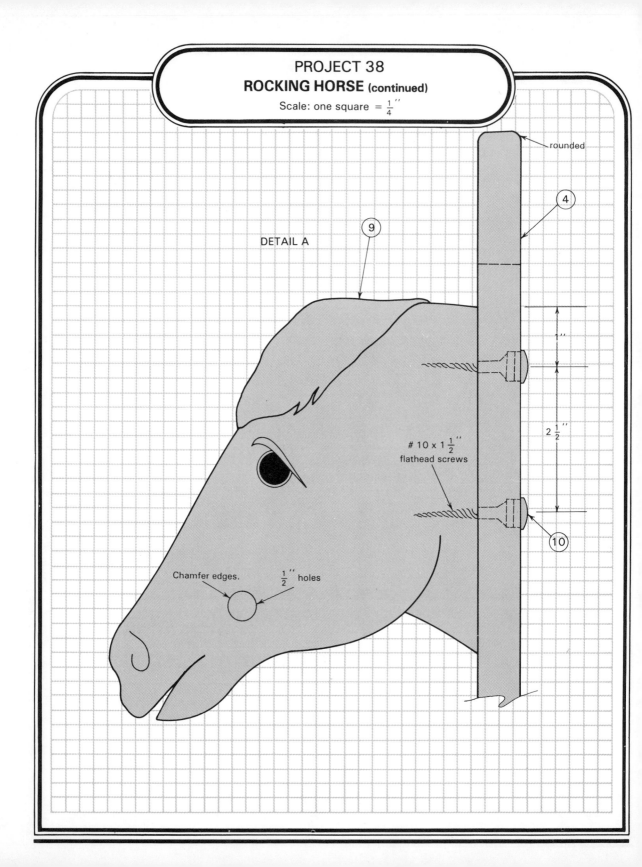

# PROJECT 38
## ROCKING HORSE (continued)
Scale: one square = $\frac{1}{4}$"

rounded

DETAIL A

④

⑨

1"

2 $\frac{1}{2}$"

# 10 x 1 $\frac{1}{2}$"
flathead screws

⑩

Chamfer edges.   $\frac{1}{2}$" holes

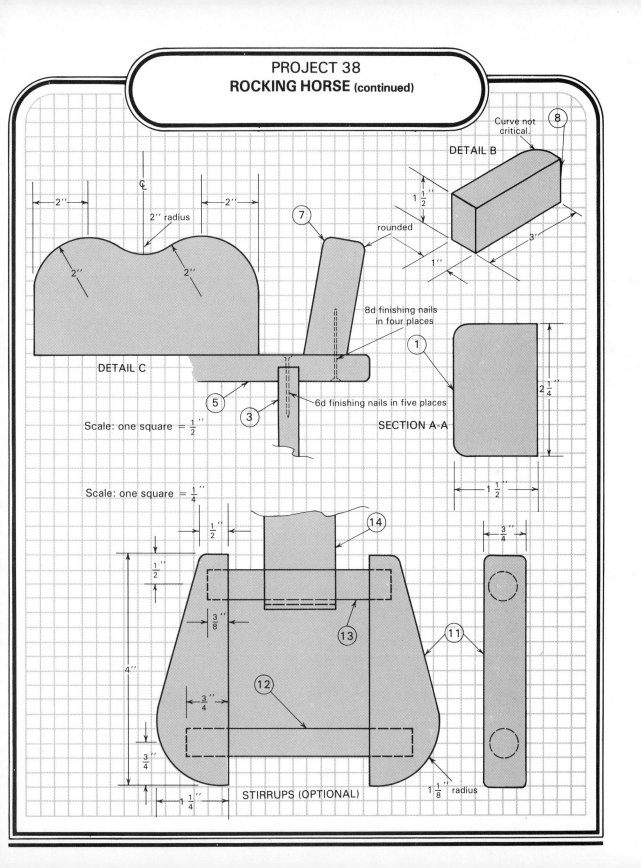

# PROJECT 38
## ROCKING HORSE (continued)

DETAIL B

Curve not critical.

⑧

$1\frac{1}{2}''$

$3''$

$1''$

2'' radius

2''

2''

2''

2''

C̶

DETAIL C

rounded

⑦

8d finishing nails
in four places

6d finishing nails in five places

⑤

③

Scale: one square = $\frac{1}{2}''$

①

SECTION A-A

$2\frac{1}{4}''$

$1\frac{1}{2}''$

Scale: one square = $\frac{1}{4}''$

$\frac{1}{2}''$

$\frac{1}{2}''$

⑭

$\frac{3}{4}''$

$\frac{3}{8}''$

⑬

⑪

4''

$\frac{3}{4}''$

⑫

$\frac{3}{4}''$

$1\frac{1}{8}''$ radius

STIRRUPS (OPTIONAL)

$1\frac{1}{4}''$

# No-Gas Car

It's not surprising that this project was one of the most popular with the test crew. It steers like the real thing, has a brake system, and because the store-bought wheels are good ones with permanently lubricated bearings, the car rolls well even on slight slopes. It will take a little time to make, but the rewards are great. Your only problem will be keeping the recipient calm until delivery time. The answer is to keep him or her busy helping with the construction.

Start the project with the bed, a piece of $\frac{3}{4} \times 16 \times 39\frac{3}{4}$-inch cabinet-grade plywood. Work from the top view of the main drawing and mark the location of all the holes and the brake-handle slot. Drill pilot holes for the screws that will secure the rear axle block and the front cleat. The two holes

The back "motor" area and steering wheel assembly of the No-Gas Car are yellow. All other parts of the car have a natural finish. The material for the steering cable was purchased in a boat supply store. Choose substantial wheels—too many have balloon-thin tires and plastic hubs.

at the front for the steering cable and the two at the rear for the brake-shoe bar can be drilled full size. To form the slot, bore two 1-inch holes with centers 3 inches apart and cut out the waste. Form the bed to its outline shape.

Next, cut two pieces of $1\frac{1}{2} \times 3\frac{1}{2}$-inch stock 18 inches long. Make the V-cut shown in Detail C in one edge of each piece and then saw one of them to produce both the front cleat (part 3) and the front axle block (part 5). Bore the $\frac{3}{4}$-inch hole (see Detail A) required for the steering post through the cleat and the front axle block, and then attach the cleat and the *rear* axle block to the bed with glue and the screws called for. You can easily locate the lead holes in the cleat and axle block by holding the parts in place and drilling through the pilot holes that are already in the bed.

The next step involves putting together the steering post assembly—shown in Detail A. The post, a $4\frac{1}{8}$-inch length of $\frac{3}{4}$-inch (outside diameter) aluminum tubing, is secured in the front cleat with two sheet-metal screws. Drill $\frac{1}{16}$-inch holes through the cleat and tube before driving the screws. Make and add the antifriction washer (part 4), then the front axle block and the metal washer, and finally the shaft collar, which is a ready-made part with its own locking set screw.

Now hacksaw $\frac{1}{2}$-inch-diameter steel rods to the lengths needed for the rear axle and the two front axles. The axles are drilled for and attached with $1\frac{1}{4}$-inch, #8 sheet-metal screws as shown in Detail C. The wheels you buy may have a different hub width than those we used; so be sure the axles extend beyond the ends of the blocks a distance that equals the sum of the thickness of the metal washer, plus the wheel width, plus the shaft collar, and an additional $\frac{1}{8}$ inch.

Shape the front and the rear walls (parts 9 and 10). The rear wall is shorter by $\frac{3}{4}$ inch and has a $2\frac{1}{4}$-inch-diameter hole through which the steering column passes. Both parts are attached with glue and 7d box nails—the front wall is butt-jointed at the end of the bed, and the rear wall has nails driven up from the bottom of the bed.

## THE STEERING MECHANISM

The parts that are required for steering and their relationships are shown in Detail B. Start by cutting to length the 1-inch outside diameter aluminum tube that will be the steering column. Next, cut to length the $1\frac{1}{2} \times 3\frac{1}{2}$-inch

The steering wheel and the brake handle are wrapped with black tape. The "horn" is a cap salvaged from a one-gallon bottle. Decorative touches were added with $\frac{1}{2}$-inch-wide red tape.

pieces of stock that will be the steering column supports. It's best to cut these pieces longer than necessary, so you can trim them to exact size after checking on assembly.

Don't try to drill the 1-inch-diameter holes for the steering column at a 30 degree angle. Instead, bore the holes square through the stock and then bevel the bottom end of the parts. This will "tilt" the holes to the angle needed. First make the front support (part 11), putting it in the position shown in Detail B, and secure it with glue and by toenailing with 2d box nails. Temporarily position the steering column as a guide to help you install the rear steering-column support (part 12). This part is secured with glue and toenailed at the bottom end, and a brace (part 16) is added at the top end.

Next install the steering column. Drill a $\frac{1}{8}$-inch hole through the column about $\frac{1}{2}$ inch from one end. Pass this end through the holes in the column supports, and slip on the washer and insert the cotter pin needed at the lower end. Drill the hole for the other cotter pin on assembly after slipping on the second washer.

At a point midway between the inside surfaces of the column supports, drill a $\frac{1}{16}$-inch hole through one wall of the steering column for the sheet-metal screw that will lock the steering cable.

Use the following procedure to install the cable: Use a couple of clamps to hold the front axle block in line with the front cleat. Secure an end of the cable to the left end of the axle block as shown in Detail B-2. Using very small screweyes, secure the cable by hammering the eyes so they clinch the cable. Pass the free end of the cable through its hole in the bed, and tightly wrap it clockwise about eight turns around the steering column. Pass the free end through the second hole in the bed, and while holding the cable taut, secure it to the right end of the axle block. Now drive home the sheet-metal screw so there is an equal number of cable coils on each side of it.

The next step is to make the keepers (part 14). When they are installed, the keepers hold the cable tightly and keep it from unwinding as the steering column is turned. Detail B-3 shows how to make two keepers from one block of wood. First drill the $1\frac{1}{4}$-inch hole $\frac{1}{2}$ inch deep, and then make the 1-inch hole through the stock. Cut the piece on the centerline, and install the keepers as shown in Detail B, with the ties (part 15) which are held in place with sheet-metal screws. Before you set the keepers, place a glob of paste wax or grease on the area that bears against the cable.

Shape two pieces of $\frac{3}{4} \times$ 3-inch pieces of stock to resemble the part shown in Detail B-1. These are glued and nailed to the underside of the bed so the steering cable rides over the rounded edge. They act as guides and also serve to tighten the cable.

The hood is made from a piece of thin plastic laminate (the kind used to cover counter tops), and is secured with sheet-metal screws spaced about 2 inches apart. The laminate is easy to bend and strong enough for the job.

## THE BACK ASSEMBLY

Make the two sides and the center piece (parts 19 and 20) and put them into place with glue and 6d box nails. Add the reinforcement pieces (part 21), bonding them with glue and toenailing along the top and bottom edges with 1-inch brads.

We used the kerfing method to make the back parts pliable enough to conform to the arc at the back of the bed. This is just a matter of cutting saw-blade-wide grooves across the short dimension of the pieces. Make the grooves' depth a little more than half the material's thickness and space them about $\frac{1}{2}$ inch apart. It will pay here to do the kerfing on a test piece. The closer the kerf spacing the easier it will be to make the bend. When you are satisfied with results, make the parts and put them into place with glue and 3d box nails driven between the kerfs. If you wish, you can cover the kerfs with a thin veneer that you bond with contact cement.

The top trim is made from a length of $\frac{1}{2}$-inch-diameter hose (or something similar) that you slit and then press into place. Secure the hose with 2d nails where it makes contact with the sides and the center piece.

Now make the brake handle support and the foot rests (parts 24 and 25).

These are shaped as shown in Details D and E and are attached with glue and screws in the positions shown on the main drawing. Be sure the notch in the brake handle support lines up with the slot that is through the bed.

Before going further, mount the wheels on the axles. First put on a metal washer, then the wheel, and then the wheel lock, which is a ready-made, $\frac{1}{2}$-inch-bore shaft collar.

## THE BRAKE SYSTEM

Make the assembly consisting of the shoe bar and shoe shown in Detail F. A good way to make the shoes is to mark an 8-inch-diameter circle on a suitable-size piece of stock, and form the notches needed for the bar before you saw the piece to produce two shoes. Attach the bar with glue and with a single screw.

Clamp the assembly to the bed so that the shoe lines up with the wheel and the bar is centered under the $\frac{5}{16}$-inch carriage bolt hole. Drill through the hole in the bed to form the matching hole in the bar.

Next make the brake handle, shaping the top end with rasp and sandpaper to a reasonably round form. Drill the pivot hole ($\frac{5}{16}$ inch), and then mount the handle by tapping in the $\frac{1}{4}$-inch dowel pivot. The pivot should fit tightly in the holes that are in the brake handle support.

Now you can make the ties (part 30). Connect them at the handle end with a $\frac{1}{4}$-inch bolt and lock nut, and at the shoe bar end with a sheet-metal screw. We used aluminum U-channel for the ties, but you can substitute strips of $\frac{1}{4}$-inch-thick maple or birch.

The positions of the stops (part 33) and springs (part 32) are shown on the top view of the main drawing. Attach the stops with glue and a small nail or screw. Attach the springs to small screweyes that you place in the rear axle block and the shoe bar. We made the springs by cutting lengths from a screen door spring and then working with pliers to form hooks at the ends. The length of the springs should provide enough tension to keep the shoe bar snug against the stop.

The shape of the brake shoe conforms to the circumference of the wheel. The neutral-position clearance is maintained because of the springs that connect between the shoe bar and the rear axle block. Stops, which are attached to the underside of the bed, keep the springs from pulling the shoes too far forward.

The bumper was metalized with self-adhesive aluminum tape. The headlights have fronts of the same material. The letters are self-adhesive, from a stationery store. The hood louvers are strips of black tape.

## THE STEERING ASSEMBLY

All the parts required for the steering assembly are shown in Detail G. Make the hub, and after drilling through it to pierce the steering column, secure it with four *panhead* sheet-metal screws set 90 degrees apart.

Shape the steering wheel and its hub, and clamp them in the correct position to a flat surface so that you can mark perpendicular diameters across both pieces. Using the marks as a guide, drill through the wheel and into the hub. Drill pilot holes first, and then enlarge them to $\frac{1}{4}$ inch. Of course, you can do the job on a drill press by holding the parts with a vise or clamp and using the blade from a square, or something similar, to align the drill with the diameter marks on the work.

Put the pieces together by adding the four $\frac{1}{4}$-inch dowel spokes and then attaching the assembly to the steering column hub with four screws. Finally, make an assembly of the plug and the horn. The plug should be sized to fit tightly in the steering column hole.

## HEADLIGHTS AND BUMPER

Fashion the bumper from a piece of $1\frac{1}{2} \times 3\frac{1}{2}$-inch stock, attaching it by drilling a pilot hole and enlarging it to a depth of about $2\frac{3}{4}$ inches with a $\frac{1}{2}$-inch bit. Coat mating surfaces with glue, and then drive home the two screws. Seal the holes by gluing on two $\frac{1}{2}$-inch wood buttons.

The headlights can be cut from lumber, or you can slice them from a round or large dowel. It is not critical that the diameter be the listed size. Attach the pieces, after drilling a centered pilot hole, with glue and 5d box nails.

## project 39
### No-Gas Car

# MATERIALS LIST

| Part No. | Name | Pieces | Size | Material |
|---|---|---|---|---|
| 1 | bed | 1 | $\frac{3}{4} \times 16 \times 39\frac{3}{4}''$ | plywood |
| 2 | rear axle block | 1 | $1\frac{1}{2} \times 3\frac{1}{2} \times 18''$ | lumber |
| 3 | front cleat | 1 | $1\frac{1}{2} \times 1\frac{3}{4} \times 18''$ | " |
| 4 | washer | 1 | $\frac{1}{4} \times 4''$ dia. | temp. harboard |
| 5 | front axle block | 1 | $1\frac{1}{2} \times 1\frac{1}{2} \times 18''$ | lumber |
| 6 | steering post | 1 | $\frac{3}{4}''$ O.D. $\times 4\frac{1}{8}''$ | aluminum tubing |
| 7 | washer | 1 | $\frac{3}{4}''$ | metal |
| 8 | lock | 1 | $\frac{3}{4}''$ bore | shaft collar |
| 9 | front wall | 1 | $\frac{3}{4} \times 10 \times 10''$ | plywood or lumber |
| 10 | rear wall | 1 | $\frac{3}{4} \times 9\frac{1}{4} \times 10''$ | " |
| 11 | front steering column support | 1 | $1\frac{1}{2} \times 3\frac{1}{2} \times 7''$ | lumber |
| 12 | rear steering column support | 1 | $1\frac{1}{2} \times 3\frac{1}{2} \times 9\frac{1}{2}''$ | " |
| 13 | steering cable | 1 | $\frac{1}{8} \times 36''$ | wire cable |
| 14 | keepers | 2 | $1\frac{1}{4} \times 3\frac{1}{2} \times 4''$ | lumber |
| 15 | ties | 4 | $\frac{1}{4} \times 2 \times 2\frac{1}{4}''$ | plywood |
| 16 | brace | 1 | $\frac{3}{4} \times 3\frac{1}{2} \times 5''$ | lumber |
| 17 | steering column | 1 | $1''$ O.D. $\times 18''$ | aluminum tubing |
| 18 | hood | 1 | $10 \times 26''$ | plastic laminate |
| **Back Assembly** | | | | |
| 19 | sides | 2 | $\frac{3}{4} \times 4 \times 6''$ | lumber |
| 20 | center | 1 | $\frac{3}{4} \times 6 \times 6''$ | " |
| 21 | glue blocks | 3 | $1\frac{1}{2} \times 2 \times 2''$ | " |
| 22 | backs | 2 | $\frac{1}{4} \times 6 \times 15''$ | hardboard |
| 23 | trim | 1 | $\frac{1}{2} \times 32''$ | hose (or similar) |
| 24 | brake handle support | 1 | $1\frac{1}{2} \times 3\frac{1}{2} \times 7''$ | lumber |

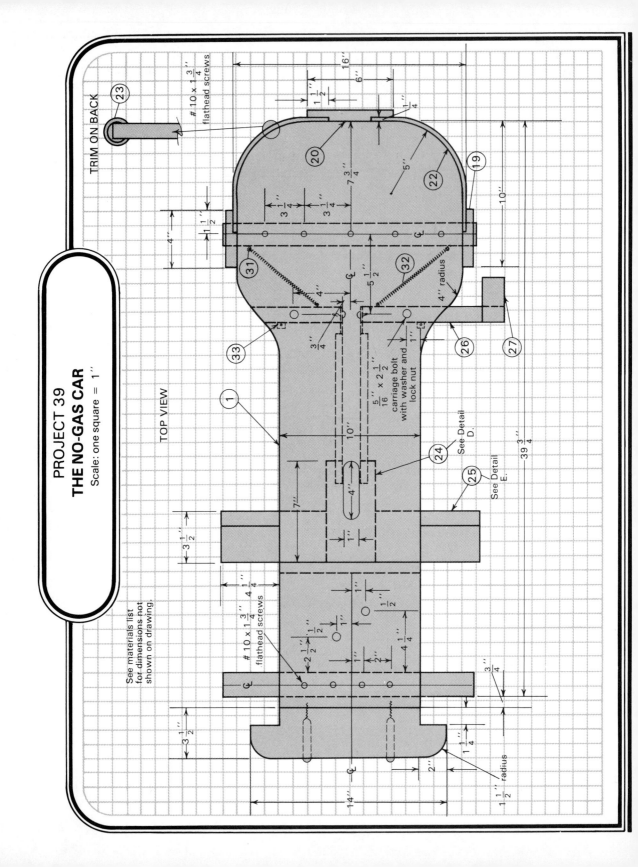

# PROJECT 39
## THE NO-GAS CAR

Scale: one square = 1''

TOP VIEW

TRIM ON BACK

See materials list for dimensions not shown on drawing.

#10 x 1 3/4'' flathead screws

carriage bolt with washer and lock nut

5/16'' x 2 1/2''

See Detail D.

See Detail E.

4'' radius

1 1/2'' radius

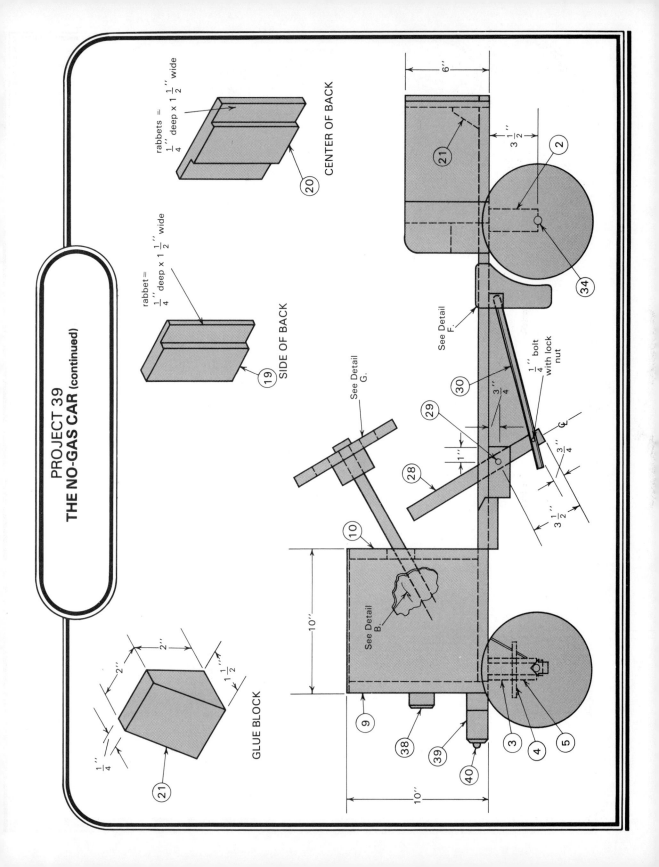

# PROJECT 39
# THE NO-GAS CAR (continued)

CENTER OF BACK

rabbets = $\frac{1}{4}$'' deep x 1$\frac{1}{2}$'' wide

SIDE OF BACK

rabbet = $\frac{1}{4}$'' deep x 1$\frac{1}{2}$'' wide

GLUE BLOCK

2''

2''

1$\frac{1}{2}$''

$\frac{1}{4}$''

See Detail B.

See Detail G.

See Detail F.

$\frac{1}{4}$'' bolt with lock nut

6''

3$\frac{1}{2}$''

3''

$\frac{3}{4}$''

$\frac{3}{4}$''

1''

3$\frac{1}{2}$''

10''

10''

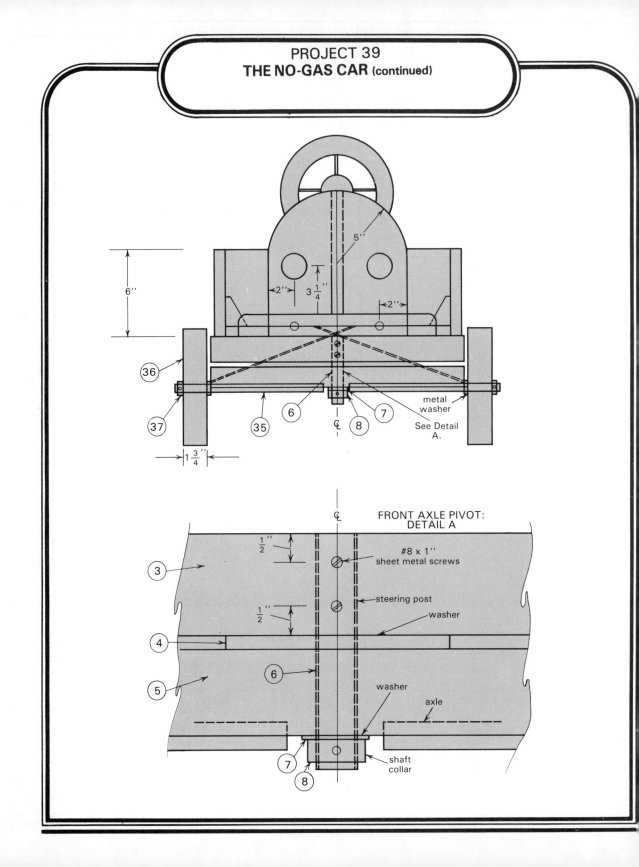

FRONT AXLE PIVOT:
DETAIL A

#8 x 1''
sheet metal screws

steering post

washer

washer

axle

shaft
collar

metal
washer

See Detail
A.

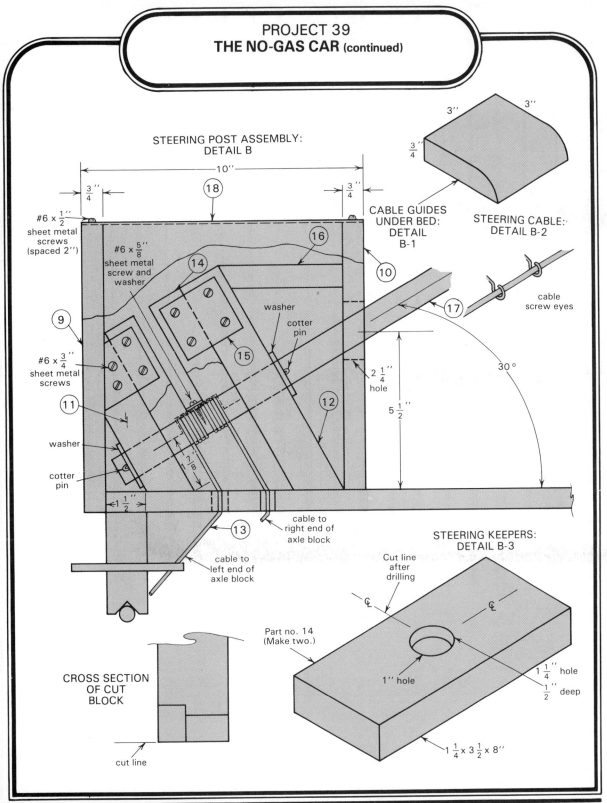

STEERING POST ASSEMBLY:
DETAIL B

10''

3/4

18

3/4

#6 x 1/2''
sheet metal
screws
(spaced 2'')

#6 x 5/8''
sheet metal
screw and
washer

16

CABLE GUIDES
UNDER BED:
DETAIL
B-1

3''      3''

3/4

STEERING CABLE:
DETAIL B-2

14

10

cable
screw eyes

9

15

washer

cotter
pin

17

#6 x 3/4''
sheet metal
screws

2 1/4''
hole

30°

11

5 1/2''

washer

7/8

cotter
pin

1 1/2''

cable to
right end of
axle block

13

cable to
left end of
axle block

STEERING KEEPERS:
DETAIL B-3

Cut line
after
drilling

12

CROSS SECTION
OF CUT
BLOCK

cut line

Part no. 14
(Make two.)

1'' hole

1 1/4'' hole
1/2'' deep

1 1/4 x 3 1/2 x 8''

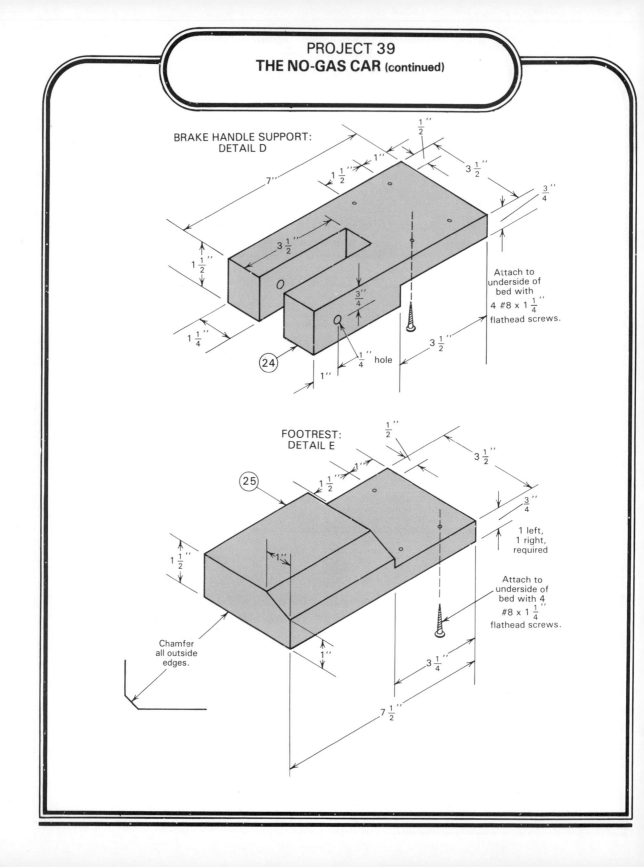

BRAKE HANDLE SUPPORT:
DETAIL D

7''

1 1/2''

1''

1/2''

3 1/2''

3/4''

3 1/2''

1 1/2''

1 1/2''

1 1/4''

3/4''

Attach to underside of bed with 4 #8 x 1 1/4'' flathead screws.

3 1/2''

(24)

1/4'' hole

1''

FOOTREST:
DETAIL E

1/2''

1''

3 1/2''

1 1/2''

(25)

3/4''

1 left, 1 right, required

1 1/2''

1''

Attach to underside of bed with 4 #8 x 1 1/4'' flathead screws.

Chamfer all outside edges.

1''

3 1/4''

7 1/2''

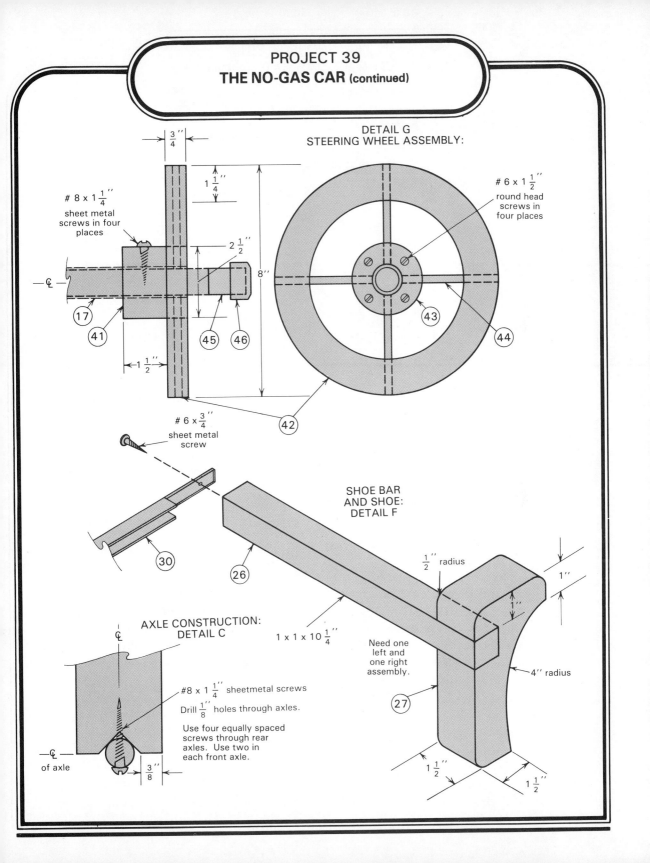

DETAIL G
STEERING WHEEL ASSEMBLY:

$\frac{3}{4}''$

$1\frac{1}{4}''$

# 8 x $1\frac{1}{4}''$ sheet metal screws in four places

# 6 x $1\frac{1}{2}''$ round head screws in four places

$2\frac{1}{2}''$

8''

17

41

45

46

43

44

$1\frac{1}{2}''$

# 6 x $\frac{3}{4}''$ sheet metal screw

42

SHOE BAR AND SHOE:
DETAIL F

30

26

$\frac{1}{2}''$ radius

1''

1''

AXLE CONSTRUCTION:
DETAIL C

1 x 1 x $10\frac{1}{4}''$

Need one left and one right assembly.

4'' radius

#8 x $1\frac{1}{4}''$ sheetmetal screws

Drill $\frac{1}{8}''$ holes through axles.

Use four equally spaced screws through rear axles. Use two in each front axle.

of axle

$\frac{3}{8}$

27

$1\frac{1}{2}''$

$1\frac{1}{2}''$

# ODDS AND ENDS

# Building Blocks

This project was placed at this point in the book because the "parts" are bits and pieces, cutoffs, and extras which accumulated as other projects were constructed. The idea here is a departure from commercial products which usually consist of square or rectangular pieces. Our test group of kids affirmed my thought that an assortment of shapes and sizes can be more fun and challenging to play with—and can be more imaginatively used to assemble buildings, ramps, cars, and so on.

The blocks also lend themselves well to a game too. Each player gets to

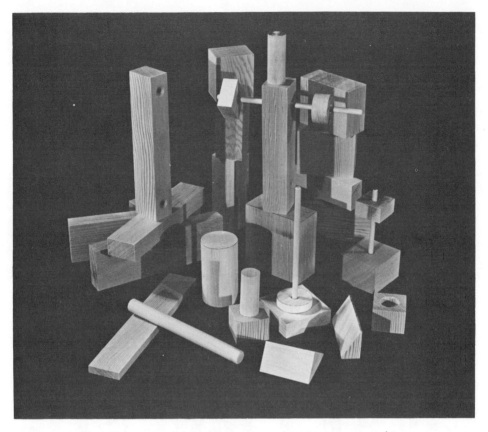

Elements for fanciful constructions may accumulate in your scrap bin.

place a block of his choice on the piece already in place. The idea is to see how high the construction can be built before it topples. Placement of one piece can make it very rough for the person who follows. This is a good game for parents to play with children—even for adults to play with one another. One rule of the game: You can't place a dowel, or any cylinder, horizontally unless it is through a hole in the preceding piece.

Whatever pieces you use should be thoroughly sanded and finished with sealer.

# Clown Plaque I.
# Clown Plaque II.
# Clown Plaque III.
# Cheshire Cat.

All plaques are made using the same procedure. Draw the full-size silhouette on $\frac{3}{4}$-inch-thick plywood or lumber. (These are saleable items. If you are interested in spare-time cash, you might want to make a permanent pattern of $\frac{1}{8}$-inch-thick hardboard.) Cutting can be done with most any sawing tool—deep-throat coping saw, saber saw, or jigsaw. How many pieces you can pad for simultaneous cutting depends on the tool you use. If you work on a band saw, you can easily cut four or five at a time.

Drill a hole at the back, so the plaques can hang on a small nail. A $\frac{1}{4}$-inch hole about $\frac{1}{2}$ inch deep will do. A hole *through* the plaque will detract from the project's appearance.

Do a careful sanding job on edges. Check plywood edges for voids and fill any with wood dough. A small drum sander—they're available down to $\frac{1}{2}$-inch diameter—used in a portable drill or a drill press will help speed the smoothing job.

To finish, first apply a coat of sealer. Let the sealer penetrate for fifteen minutes or so, and then wipe off excess with a lint-free cloth. When the sealer is dry, brush on a coat of white latex paint. This will be dry to the touch in about an hour, but it's best to wait much longer before proceeding.

Outline the details with a black, felt-tip pen, and then fill in with bright poster paints—yellows, greens, reds. Of course, you can do your own finishing composition with materials of your choice.

PROJECT 41
CLOWN PLAQUE I

Scale: one square = $\frac{1}{4}$″

$\frac{3}{4}$ x 10 x 14″

Clown Plaque I. Base material is $\frac{3}{4} \times 10 \times 14$ inches.

# PROJECT 42
## CLOWN PLAQUE II
Scale: one square = $\frac{3}{8}$''

$\frac{3}{4}$ x 8 x 21''

Clown Plaque II. Base material is $\frac{3}{4} \times 8 \times 21$ inches.

# PROJECT 43
## CLOWN PLAQUE III
Scale: one square = $\frac{1}{2}''$

$\frac{3}{4} \times 11\frac{1}{4} \times 23''$

Clown Plaque III. Base material is $\frac{3}{4} \times 11\frac{1}{4} \times 23$ inches.

# PROJECT 44
## CHESHIRE CAT PLAQUE
Scale: one square = $\frac{1}{4}$''

$\frac{3}{4}$ x 8 x 11''

Cheshire Cat Plaque. Base material is $\frac{3}{4} \times 8 \times 11$ inches.

# III.
# MAINLY FOR ADULTS:

# GIFTS AND FURNITURE

These projects are mainly for the home, patio, or garden. Some are practical. Some are decorative. Some are both. A short course on lathe work precedes the wood-turning projects.

# LATHE PROJECTS

## A SHORT COURSE IN LATHE WORK

The lathe is a fascinating tool—the project immediately starts taking shape as soon as the cutting tools are applied. It's also true that small lathe projects make saleable items and fine gifts. At a local store that sells only handcrafted products, we were told that the fastest-moving turnings were things like candle sticks, bud vases, and small bowls. These projects are covered later.

Many people shy away from lathe work because they feel it requires special expertise to do acceptable work. It's true that the more involved you get, the more adept you must be at handling the chisels. But, in essence, that is the major difference between the professional and the amateur. The

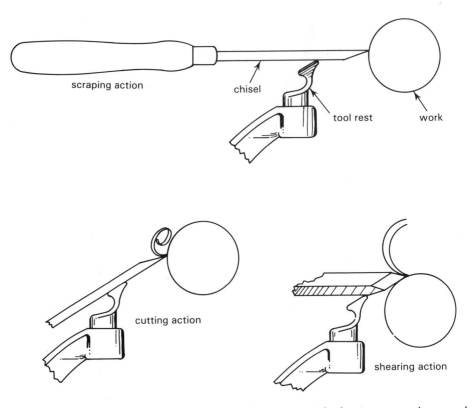

**Fig. 1.** The three chisel actions used to do lathe turnings. The beginner can do a good job using the scraping action almost exclusively while occasionally taking a stab at the other techniques. The illustrations show the tool rest much farther away from the work than it should be, so that the chisel-contact area can be seen more clearly.

techniques are there for all to learn, and the amateur can avoid, at least in the beginning, the *shearing* and *cutting* actions of the expert and arrive at similar results by using the *scraping* action which is easily mastered. Scraping leaves a rougher surface than shearing and cutting; so more sanding is required. But who will know when viewing the finished project what techniques were used to obtain smooth results?

If you are a lathe beginner, study the illustrations that follow before starting on the projects. A good idea is to mount stock in the lathe and experiment to get the feel of the tools. Take very light cuts; there's no point in rushing. The results won't matter too much, but even so you're likely to produce something usable.

## UPCOMING LATHE PROJECTS

The drawings for the lathe projects are done so you can choose one of two methods to duplicate the pieces. With the enlarging-by-squares draw-

**Fig. 2.**  A typical set of lathe chisels. Probably the least important of these are the *squarenose* and the *spear point.* An ordinary butt chisel can do the job of the squarenose, and the skew, held flat and used to scrape, can substitute for the spear point. It's important to keep the chisels clean and sharp.

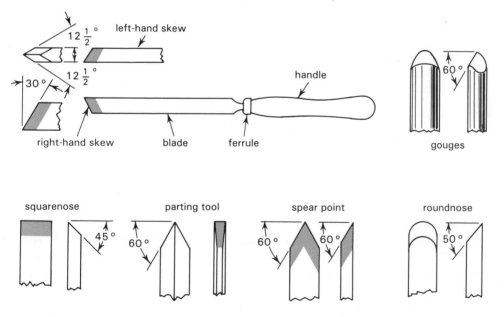

**Fig. 3.** This chart suggests reasonable speeds for the type of cut and the size of the work. Stay as close as possible to these speeds. The general rule is to decrease speed as work size increases. Use the *finishing-cut* speed when sanding.

| Material and Diameter | Roughing cut revolutions per minute | Shaping cut revolutions per minute | Finishing cut revolutions per minute |
|---|---|---|---|
| wood up to 2" | 910 | 2,590 | 4,250 |
| wood to 2" to 4" | 810 | 2,375 | 3,380 |
| wood 4" to 6" | 650 | 1,825 | 2,375 |
| wood 6" to 8" | 650 | 1,200 | 1,825 |
| wood 8" to 10" | 650 | 910 | 1,025 |
| wood over 10" | 650 | 650 | 650 |
| plastics up to 3" | 2,200 | 3,125 | 3,875 |
| plastics over 3" | 1,025 | 1,200 | 1,680 |
| nonferrous metals up to 3" (with carbide-tipped tools) | 650 | 1,300 | 3,125 |

ing you can make a profile template, or you can simply work from the major dimensions that are listed. The latter method requires that you decide the form of what we call *transitional* areas; that is, the line that flows between points where specific diameter and "thickness" dimensions are given. This is not a heavy burden; you can easily judge from the drawing how the area should be shaped. A slight variation will not affect appearance.

Some of the projects—for example, the bud vases—require center holes. These can be drilled with the stock in the lathe by substituting a chuck and drill bit for the center in the tailstock. You can also drill the hole into the stock before it is mounted. This poses no problem if the project is small enough to be mounted on a screwcenter or if the work is on a faceplate. A cone-shape piece (like the one shown in the drawing can also be used to hold pre-drilled stock by placing it between the work and the tailstock center. The cone can be shaped on a screwcenter and should be retained as a permanent accessory—it will be usable on other projects regardless of the center hole's size.

**Fig. 4.** This is theoretically the correct position for the tool rest. There will be times when you can't work this way, but you should stay as close to it as you can. The idea is to provide maximum support for the chisel as close to the work as possible.

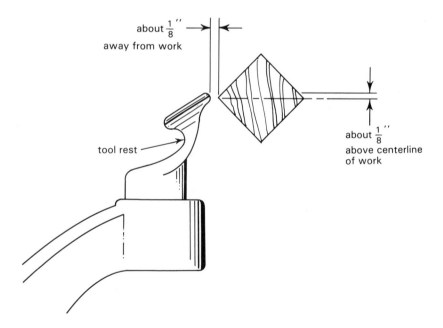

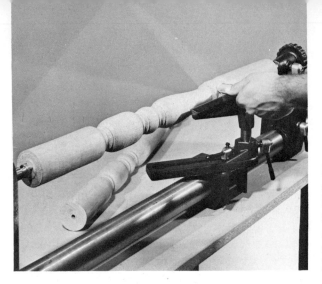

**Fig. 5.** This is *spindle turning.* The work is mounted between the *spur center* in the headstock and the *cup center* in the tailstock. The tool rest is moved to the area being shaped.

**Fig. 6.** Use the center finder shown in chapter on wheel making to mark the center at each end of a spindle turning. Use an awl to form an indentation at the mark. When the wood is hard, use a small saw to cut shallow grooves for the wings on the spur center. Note that the marker can be used to find the center of round or square stock.

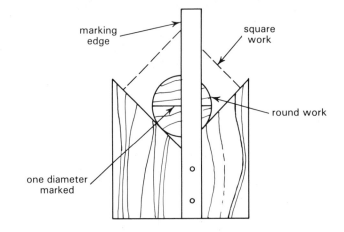

marking edge

square work

round work

one diameter marked

It's a good idea on all lathe projects to remove as much waste as possible before mounting the stock. If the project is round (a bowl or base), saw the raw stock to a slightly oversize diameter. If the stock is square, saw off its corners so that what you mount will have an octagonal cross section. Preparing stock this way minimizes tedious waste removal chores.

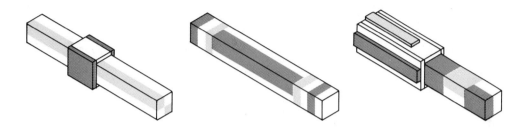

**Fig. 7.** Stock for lathe turnings can be made by assembling pieces of contrasting wood. Very interesting inlay effects result when the part is shaped. These examples are for spindle turning, but the same idea can apply to *faceplate* work. A good glue job is critical.

**Fig. 8.** Bowls, bases, and dish-type projects are turned on a *faceplate*. The faceplate is centered and then attached to the work with screws. The screws should be heavy enough to secure the work, but not so long that you will cut into them when shaping the project.

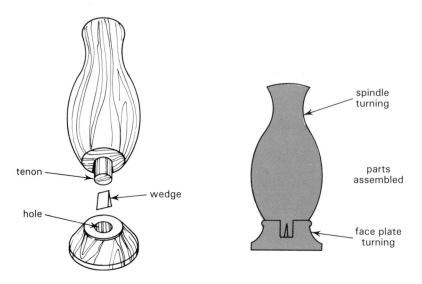

tenon

wedge

hole

spindle
turning

parts
assembled

face plate
turning

**Fig. 9.** There are times when it is necessary or more convenient to make a project by assembling a spindle and a faceplate turning. The tenon on this piece is an integral part of the spindle turning. The wedge-shape piece, which penetrates a slot cut into the tenon, is not essential, but does make a stronger bond between the two pieces.

**Fig. 10.** Work too small to turn as a spindle or mount on a faceplate can be secured on a *screwcenter*. The holder mounts on the headstock in place of the spur center. This is a good means for making fancy-looking wheels for toys.

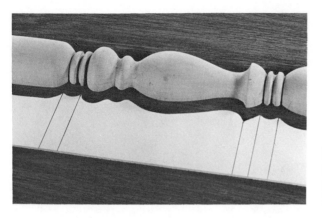

**Fig. 11.** It's a good idea to make an outline template when you have to turn similar pieces.

**Fig. 12.** When using the scraping action, hold the chisel firmly and move it very slowly forward into the work. Retract it frequently to clear chips. Here, a roundnose chisel is forming a cove. The chisel can be used to do basic forming of other shapes as well.

**Fig. 13.** A job ordinarily done with a squarenose chisel is here being done with a butt chisel. The chisel can be used to shape cylinders, form grooves, or even to do ball shapes. Use a light touch—and keep the tool sharp.

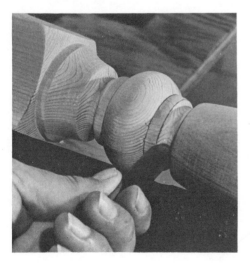

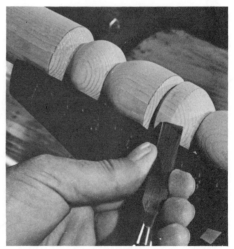

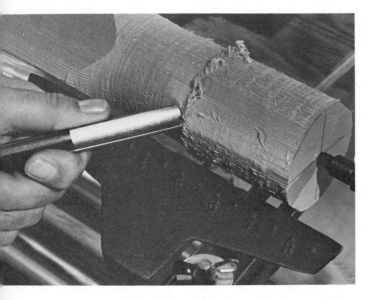

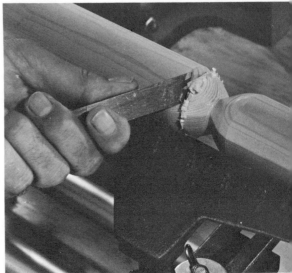

**Fig. 14.** Here, a gouge is used in a shearing cut. The tool is placed almost on edge and moved parallel to the work. The gouge is the tool most often used to remove waste material quickly, for such jobs as turning square stock into a cylindrical shape.

**Fig. 15.** Experts use the skew chisel this way. The action can shear away large amounts of material while leaving a surface that requires little sanding. It takes practice to master this technique.

**Fig. 16.** Here a skew is used in a scraping action to form a sharp corner.

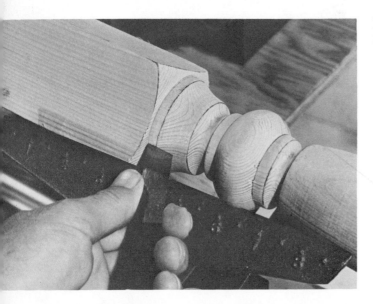

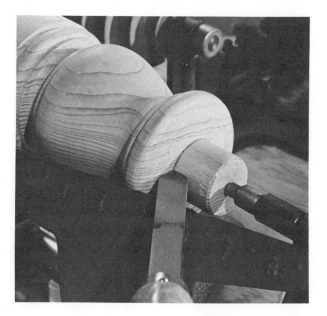

**Fig. 17.** A spear point is also a good tool to use for cleaning out corners. Even the experts will usually use this tool with a scraping action. The shape of the point makes the chisel ideal for forming V-grooves.

**Fig. 18.** Tools not made for lathes can often be used to speed up or make some jobs easier to accomplish. The Surform plane is easier to handle than a conventional chisel for doing the final shaping on a cylinder. The rough surface it leaves can be quickly smoothed with sandpaper. This is a good way to form cylinders before slicing them up into wheels.

**Fig. 19.** A round file can be used to touch up or to form coves. Of course, the work is turning as the file is applied. Move the file to and fro and frequently remove waste that begins clogging the teeth.

**Fig. 20.** Most of the shaping on faceplate work is done with a roundnose chisel and a scraping action. It isn't always possible to set the tool rest as close to the cutting area as you might like, so hold the chisel firmly and cut lightly and carefully.

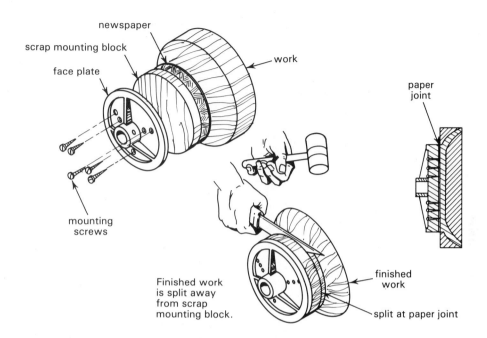

newspaper

scrap mounting block

face plate

work

paper joint

mounting screws

Finished work is split away from scrap mounting block.

finished work

split at paper joint

**Fig. 21.** This is a way to set up when doing faceplate turning and when the work —or the work's base—is too thin to take screws. The work is glued to a scrap block, but with a sheet of newspaper in the joint. You'll find the pieces are not difficult to split apart when the forming is complete.

**Fig. 22.** Another face-plate-turning technique— one you can use to make spoked wheels, or a fancier version of the steering wheel we used on the No-Gas Car. The parts, roughly precut to circular shape, are mounted with rear-driven screws to a piece of scrap that can be attached to the faceplate. Spoke locations can be marked, and even the drilling can be done, while the pieces remain mounted on the lathe.

**Fig. 23.** Turnings can be sanded to perfection while they are still in the lathe. It's best to cut sandpaper strips that are especially suitable for the form you are smoothing. Of course, the sanding is done while the work is turning. This removes a lot of material quickly, so use a light touch, especially on details.

**Fig. 24.** Finishing can also be done before removing the work from the lathe. Work with a lint-free cloth, but don't pick up too much finishing material. Otherwise, overspray may greet you.

# Bud Vase (for wet display)

This project uses an inner liner—such as a laboratory test tube—to keep the plant water away from the wood. Have the glass test tube on hand before starting the project so you'll know exactly what size hole to drill. Test tubes are often available in hobby supply stores or you might buy one from a pharmacist. Actually, it isn't essential that the inner container be a test tube. There are many products that come in usable, vial-type glass or plastic bottles. Whatever you use, drill the hole so that the container will be easy to slip in or out of place.

**Proj. 45.**   The material used was maple, but it was stained a red mahogany. The finishing coat was just paste wax.


**Fig. 1.**   A cone-shaped piece, that you form on a screwcenter, will let you mount predrilled stock between headstock and tailstock centers.

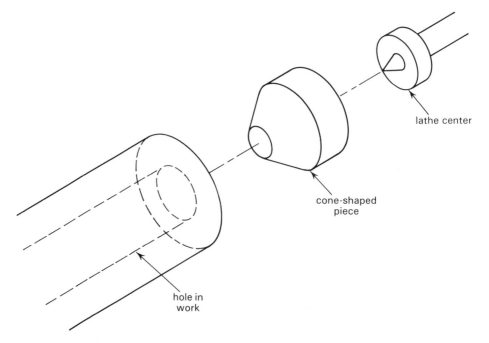

lathe center

cone-shaped
piece

hole in
work

# PROJECT 45
## BUD VASE (for wet display)
Scale: one square = $\frac{1}{4}''$

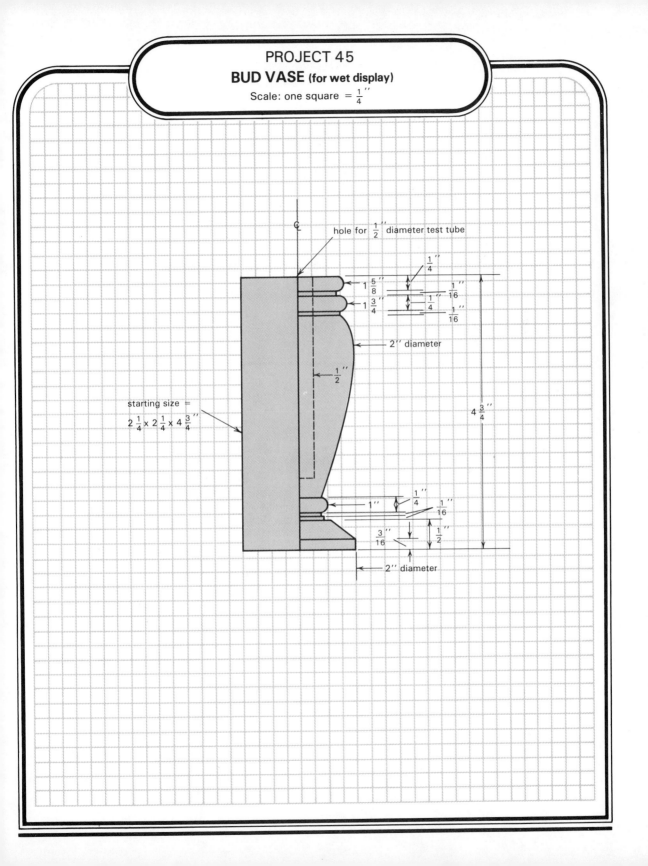

hole for $\frac{1}{2}''$ diameter test tube

$1\frac{5}{8}''$

$1\frac{3}{4}''$

$\frac{1}{4}''$

$\frac{1}{16}''$

$\frac{1}{4}''$

$\frac{1}{16}''$

2'' diameter

$\frac{1}{2}''$

$4\frac{3}{4}''$

starting size =
$2\frac{1}{4} \times 2\frac{1}{4} \times 4\frac{3}{4}''$

1''

$\frac{1}{4}''$

$\frac{1}{16}''$

$\frac{3}{16}''$

$\frac{1}{2}''$

2'' diameter

# project 46

# Bud Vase
# (for dry display)

This project is small enough so that you can predrill it and then mount it on a screwcenter for turning. Despite its slight appearance, the project proved very popular for gifts and for selling. We made mine by cutting a section from the fallen limb of a walnut tree. The imperfection was deliberately ignored and became an asset, probably because the blemish said "handcrafted" and was a welcome departure from sleek, production turnings.

**Proj. 46.** The project began as a section from a fallen walnut limb. Finishing steps included sanding and application of a single coat of sealer. The knot blemish adds a pleasing accent.

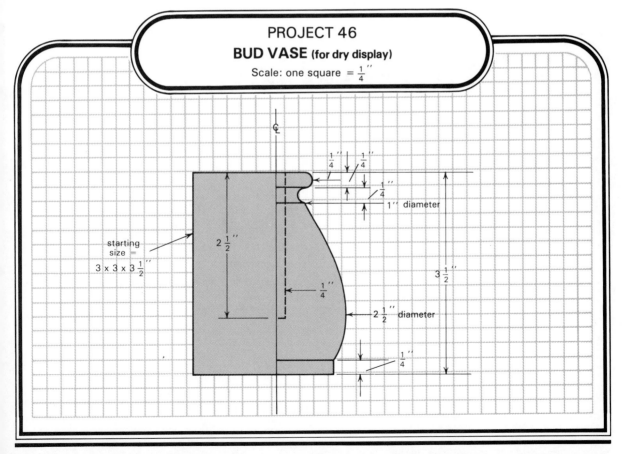

# PROJECT 46
## BUD VASE (for dry display)
Scale: one square = $\frac{1}{4}''$

$\frac{1}{4}''$  $\frac{1}{4}''$

$\frac{1}{4}''$

1'' diameter

starting size = $3 \times 3 \times 3\frac{1}{2}''$

$2\frac{1}{2}''$

$\frac{1}{4}''$

$3\frac{1}{2}$

$2\frac{1}{2}''$ diameter

$\frac{1}{4}''$

# Candlestick I

This project is typical of those that are best done by shaping the base on a faceplate and the spindle, with an integral tenon, between centers. The two parts are then joined with glue. Size the tenon carefully for a slip-fit in the base. For reinforcement, you can use the wedge technique mentioned before, or you can drive a flathead screw up through the bottom of the base into the tenon. Apply a piece of self-adhesive felt to the base (a good idea on all projects of this type) to hide the screw.

**Proj. 47.**   The wood is maple; the tone was achieved with diluted walnut stain. Varnish or something similar would have been suitable too. You can achieve a good sheen by applying several coats of paste wax, while the parts are still in the lathe.

# PROJECT 47
## CANDLESTICK I
Scale: one square = $\frac{1}{4}''$

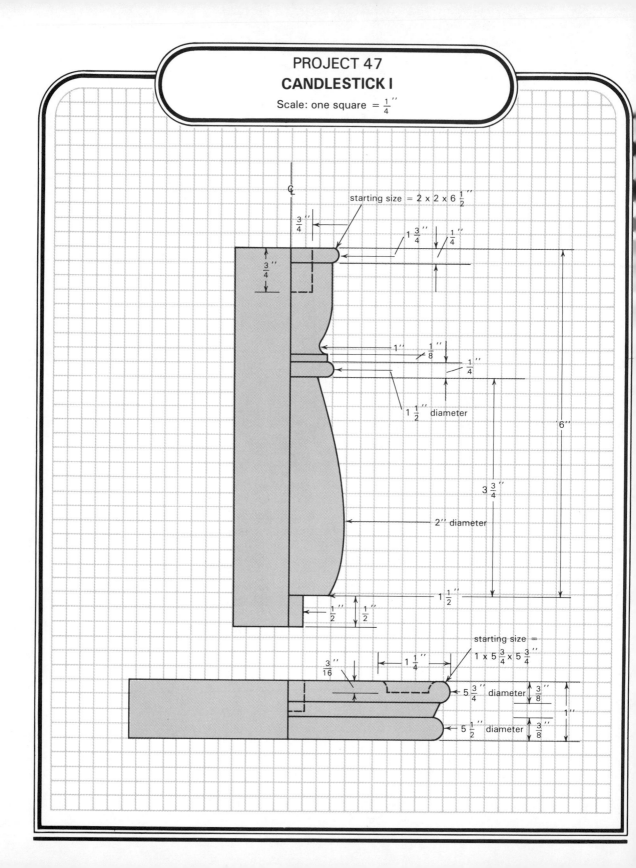

# Candlestick II

This project starts with a piece of $6 \times 6$ that you saw to make $4\frac{1}{2}$ inches square. Cut the corners to produce the octagon shown in the drawing detail. Shaping can be done with the stock mounted on a faceplate or held between centers. If you choose the latter method, shape as much of the $\frac{1}{4}$-inch-deep candle recess as you can while the piece is in the lathe. The small section that remains—the area against which the tailstock center must bear—can be shaved off with a chisel.

We wanted a somewhat antique effect, so we didn't do a super sanding job. After a base coat of sealer, we did a couple of applications of gold paint. And that's all. The results seemed very suitable for a Christmas Candlestick.

**317**

**Proj. 48.** The wood isn't exotic; the finish is gold paint. To form the candle, keep bending outer areas back as the flame melts the center section.

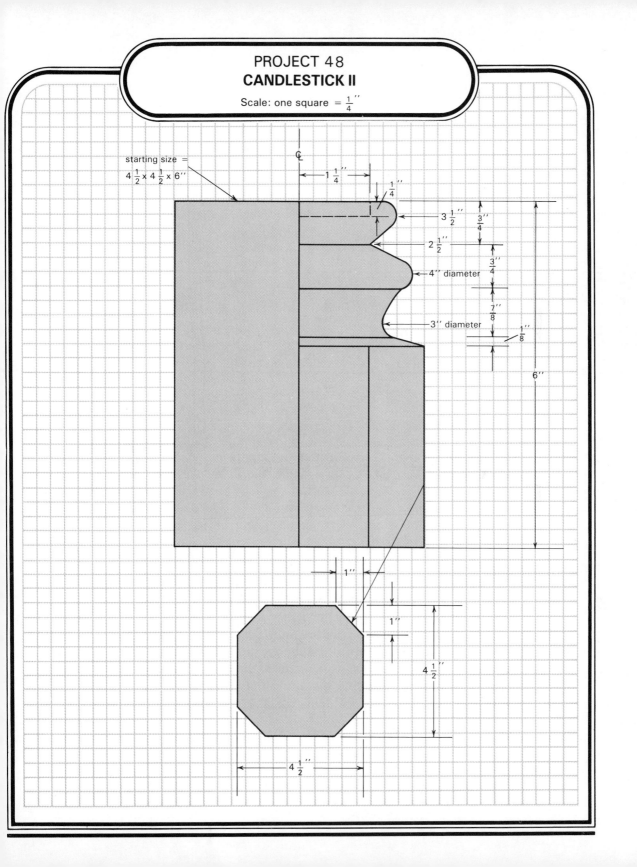

# PROJECT 48
## CANDLESTICK II

Scale: one square = $\frac{1}{4}''$

starting size = $4\frac{1}{2} \times 4\frac{1}{2} \times 6''$

$1\frac{1}{4}''$

$\frac{1}{4}''$

$3\frac{1}{2}''$

$\frac{3}{4}''$

$2\frac{1}{2}''$

$\frac{3}{4}''$

4'' diameter

$\frac{7}{8}''$

3'' diameter

$\frac{1}{8}''$

6''

1''

1''

$4\frac{1}{2}''$

$4\frac{1}{2}''$

# Candlestick III

The material used for this project—a scrap piece of $4 \times 4$ construction-grade lumber—usually isn't considered suitable for turning. But the effect visualized—a much-used, ancient, household item—did come off. It wasn't just the shape of the piece that did it, but the texture that appeared when we wire-brushed the project after it had been turned.

Fir lumber lends itself to wire brushing because it has areas of hard and soft grain. That helps produce the unique surface texture of the method. The texturing can be done by forcing the work against a wire brush turning in a drill press or by gripping the work in a vise and working on it with a wire brush chucked in a portable drill. The texturing should be subtle—

**Proj. 49.** You can find the base stock for projects like this at almost any house construction site—just a length of 4 × 4 construction-grade fir. The texture results from working over the wood with a wire brush. Allow candle drippings to stay on the project, or drip wax deliberately using a second candle to achieve a well-used look.

as if it were caused by years of handling. Be sure to wear safety goggles when doing wire-brush work. Loose wires become harmful projectiles.

Make the candle spike with an 8d nail. Clip off the head and then drive it into the project through a pilot hole. The candle socket is made by reshaping a metal cap from a large aerosol can. Attach the socket to the project with a couple of $\frac{1}{2}$-inch, *panhead* sheet-metal screws.

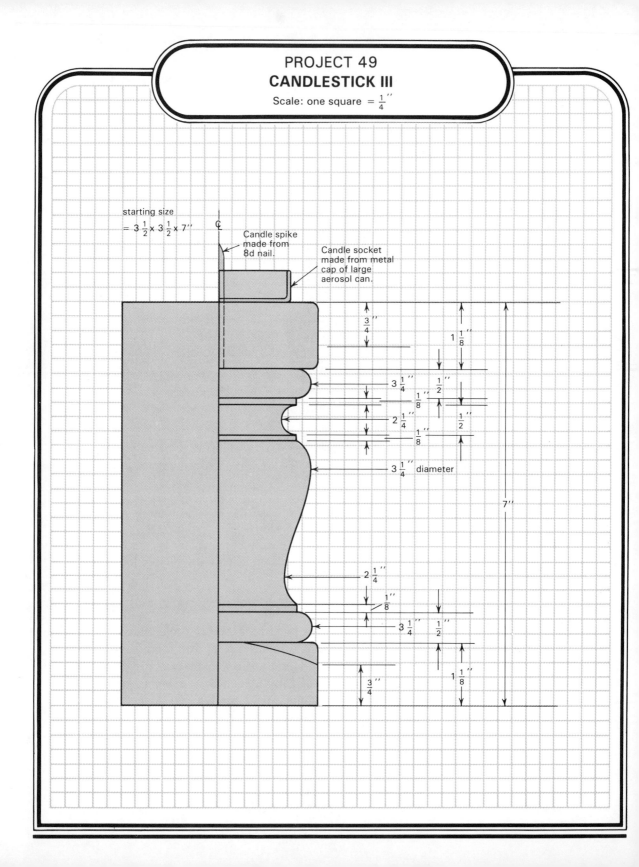

# PROJECT 49
# CANDLESTICK III

Scale: one square $= \frac{1}{4}''$

starting size
$= 3\frac{1}{2} \times 3\frac{1}{2} \times 7''$

Candle spike
made from
8d nail.

Candle socket
made from metal
cap of large
aerosol can.

$\frac{3}{4}''$

$1\frac{1}{8}''$

$3\frac{1}{4}''$

$\frac{1}{2}''$

$\frac{1}{8}''$

$2\frac{1}{4}''$

$\frac{1}{2}''$

$\frac{1}{8}''$

$3\frac{1}{4}''$ diameter

$7''$

$2\frac{1}{4}''$

$\frac{1}{8}''$

$3\frac{1}{4}''$     $\frac{1}{2}''$

$\frac{3}{4}''$

$1\frac{1}{8}''$

# Candlestick IV

This is the kind of project that appeals simply because it doesn't abide by the rules that say lathe projects should be symmetrical and sleek and glistening. You have to scrounge for the material: 4- to 5-inch-diameter pieces of fallen limbs (with bark still attached) from such trees as walnut, oak, apricot, or apple. The pieces you cull can have knots or worm holes —the blemishes are regarded as decorative details.

The lathe turning required is minimal; it's just a matter of shaping the top and bottom ends of the stock. Drill the hole for the candle before you place the raw stock on a small faceplate or screwcenter.

**Proj. 50.** Projects like this have appeal and can be made with "scrap wood" salvaged from fallen limbs of various trees. You can leave the bark on for effect.

After shaping, do a minimal amount of sanding on the turned areas, and clean the bark area. This can be done with light touches of a soft wire brush. A couple of coats of sealer is enough of a finish.

# PROJECT 50
## CANDLESTICK IV

Scale: one square $= \frac{1}{4}''$

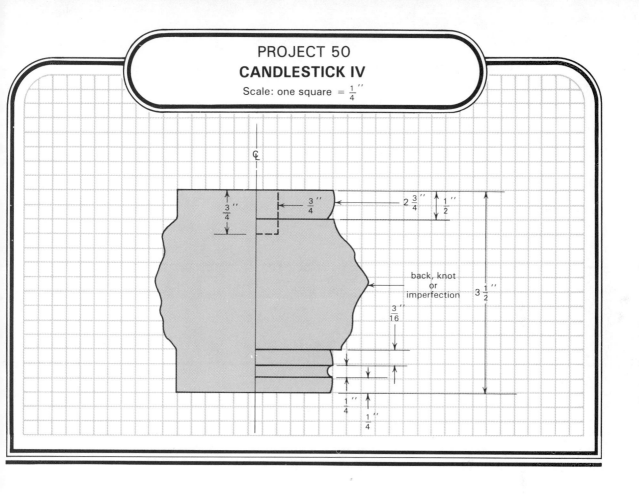

# Nut Bowl

This is typical of lathe projects that have an inlaid appearance because the turning block is made by gluing together pieces of contrasting wood. Technically, the wood species should have similar density and porosity. But in practice, choices are often based on personal preference, wood availability, and cost. Many times, the light-colored wood is maple or birch, and the dark wood is mahogany or walnut. A good many laminated lathe projects have been successfully done by combining such different woods as redwood and pine.

Whatever the material, a good gluing job is essential. Coat both mating surfaces with glue and hold the assembly under clamp pressure until you are sure the glue is dry. Cut the block to a bit more than diameter size before mounting it on a faceplate. This will be easy to do on a band saw. If you

**Proj. 51.** Inlaid projects result when you combine contrasting woods to form the base block for turning. The projects can be the size suggested in the drawing, or they can be larger or even shallower—the technique is the same. A good prior gluing job is critical.

lack such equipment, you can get good results by making straight cuts across corners with a handsaw.

The bulk of the shaping on this kind of work will be done with a roundnose chisel and a scraping action. When you are about at the final form, switch to a squarenose chisel for smoothing. Sand with progressively finer grits of paper until the wood is satiny smooth.

A conventional finish is okay if the project will be used to hold nuts or similar edibles. If this project, or any of its type, is planned for use as a salad bowl, then finish with mineral oil or the special Salad Bowl Finish discussed on page 63.

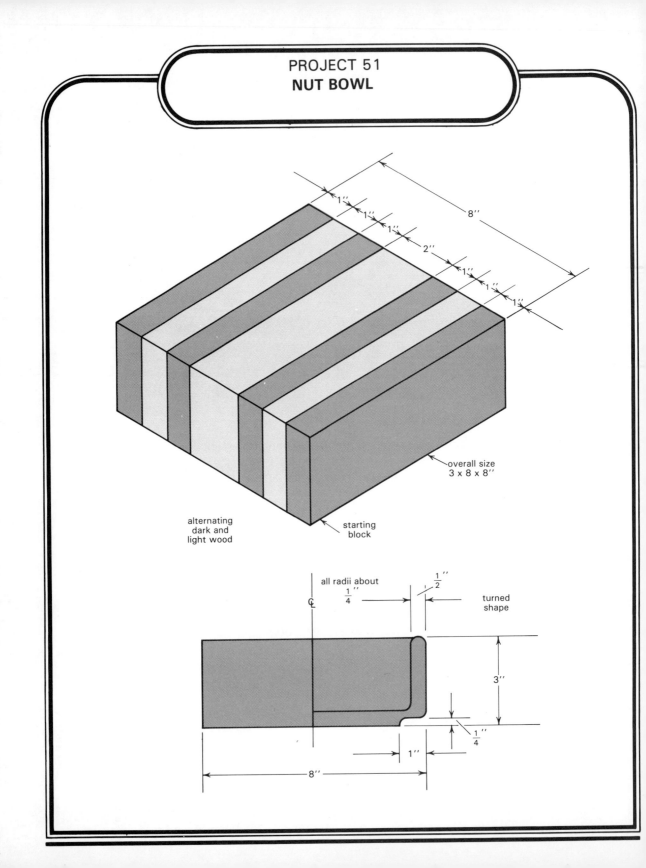

# PROJECT 51
## NUT BOWL

1''
1''
1''
2''
1''
1''
8''

overall size
3 x 8 x 8''

alternating
dark and
light wood

starting
block

all radii about
$\frac{1}{4}$''

$\frac{1}{2}$''

turned
shape

3''

$\frac{1}{4}$''

1''

8''

# A COLLECTION OF TABLES

# Scrapwood End Table

This is a way to use up odds and ends of lumber and plywood to produce a practical household accessory. We used leftover strips of various types of plywood, some of them with a hardboard veneer, but there are other ways to go. Use just lumber, combine lumber with plywood or, if you wish, buy lumber of your choice especially for the project. As the photos show, a scrapwood assembly can be finished with just sealer for a novelty effect, or finished so no one can tell what throwaways were used.

If you prefer a clear finish, the Scrapwood Table will look something like this.

First, size the materials to produce the 18 pieces needed for the slab. These can be assembled with glue and suitable clamps, if you have them, or by following this procedure: Coat the mating surfaces of two pieces with

Most people wouldn't believe that the materials used here were once headed for the fireplace.

glue and then bond them by driving a half dozen or so 4d box nails. Work the same way to add other strips but switch to 6d nails. Attach the last strips with 6d *finishing* nails so that you can set and conceal them with wood

**Scrapwood End Table**

## MATERIALS LIST

| Part No. | Name | Pieces | Size | Material |
|---|---|---|---|---|
| 1 | slab pcs. | 18 | $\frac{3}{4} \times 1\frac{1}{2} \times 30''$ | plywood or lumber |
| 2 | legs | 4 | $\frac{3}{4} \times 3 \times 16\frac{1}{2}''$ | " |
| 3 | handles | 2 | $\frac{3}{4} \times 1 \times 11''$ | " |
| 4 | rails | 2 | $\frac{3}{4} \times 1\frac{1}{4} \times 12''$ | " |
| 5 | reinforcement | 4 | $\frac{5}{8}''$ wide w/$1\frac{1}{2}''$ legs | angle iron |

dough. Position nails in alternate strips to spread holding power and to avoid hitting nails already in place.

Next, cut four pieces for the legs, but do not shape them until you have formed the dadoes and notches. You can, if you wish, work as shown in Detail A in the drawing to form the notches after the legs have been tapered. Make the rails and handles and attach them to the legs with glue and 6d finishing nails. Shape the handles and the outside corners of the legs as shown in the drawing details.

Before going further, sand the slab and the leg assemblies well. Check all edges for voids and fill any that you find with wood dough.

Attach the leg assemblies to the slab with glue and 6d finishing nails, and add the metal angle reinforcements.

If you like a novelty effect, finish the project with several applications of sealer, sanding between coats. A final coat of varnish or clear polyurethane is optional.

A more formal appearance will result if you work this way: Use a product such as Duratite's Water Putty, mixing the white powder with water so you have a thick, paintlike consistency. Apply this liberally by brush and then sand the coating smooth after it has dried. Now you can apply a stain of your choice, working as you would on any other project. We brushed on dark walnut and then wiped off excess with a lint-free cloth, allowing some "extra" to stay around joint areas. Another light sanding and then an application of polyurethane clear finish and the job was done.

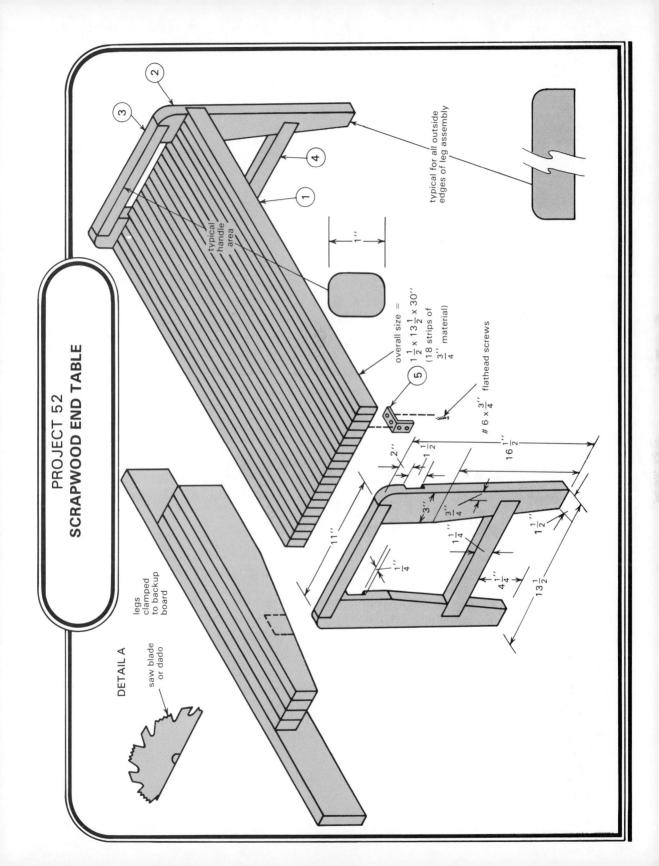

# PROJECT 52
## SCRAPWOOD END TABLE

typical for all outside
edges of leg assembly

typical handle area

1″

overall size =
$1\frac{1}{2} \times 13\frac{1}{2} \times 30$″
(18 strips of
$\frac{3}{4}$″ material)

# 6 × $\frac{3}{4}$″ flathead screws

2″

1½

16½″

3″

$\frac{3}{4}$

11″

1¼

1½

1″

½

¼

$4\frac{1}{4}$″

$13\frac{1}{2}$

DETAIL A

legs clamped
to backup
board

saw blade
or dado

# Butcherblock End Table

We chose to work with a good grade of kiln-dried knotty pine to make this end table, but you can opt for another material—maple or birch, or an even more exotic species such as walnut or mahogany. Perhaps your decision will be based on what materials are already on hand.

Start the project by cutting the pieces required for the slab. Note that tne four end pieces are shorter than the others to accommodate the legs. Slab assembly can be accomplished with glue and clamps or by following the

The chances are that you can get material for the Butcherblock End Table by checking through your scrap bin. Knotty pine was used here, but maple or birch, or even mahogany or walnut is suitable.

## project 53
### Butcherblock End Table

# MATERIALS LIST

| Part No. | Name | Pieces | Size | Material |
|---|---|---|---|---|
| 1 | slab pcs. | 20 | $\frac{3}{4} \times 2 \times 18''$ | lumber |
| 2 | end pcs. | 4 | $\frac{3}{4} \times 2 \times 14''$ | " |
| 3 | legs | 8 | $\frac{3}{4} \times 2 \times 18''$ | " |
| | | or 4 | $1\frac{1}{2} \times 2 \times 18''$ | " |
| 4 | ties | 4 | $\frac{5}{8} \times 5''$ | dowel |

"clamp-less" technique that was described for the Scrapwood End Table (Project 52).

Make the legs by gluing together pieces of $\frac{3}{4}$-inch material or by sawing larger stock so that it will have a $1\frac{1}{2} \times 2$-inch cross section. Mark the location of the dowel hole in one leg. Drill a pilot hole and then use the piece as a template to mark hole locations in the other legs.

It's best to attach the legs to the slab before opening the holes for the dowel ties to full size. Coat mating areas with glue, and then hold the legs in place with bar clamps or by wrapping a length of strong cord around the perimeter of the assembly and tightening the cord as if it were a tourniquet.

When the glue is dry, drill the $\frac{5}{8}$-inch holes through the legs and into the slab. The depth of the hole should be a bit more than 5 inches. Use a sliver of wood to coat the inside of the hole with glue and then tap in the dowels. Allow the last $\frac{1}{16}$ inch or so to project so the tie can be sanded flush. The dowel you use can match or contrast with the table's main material.

The project calls for a clear finish. First use a sealer, sand, and then apply a coat of clear polyurethane.

# PROJECT 53
## BUTCHERBLOCK END TABLE

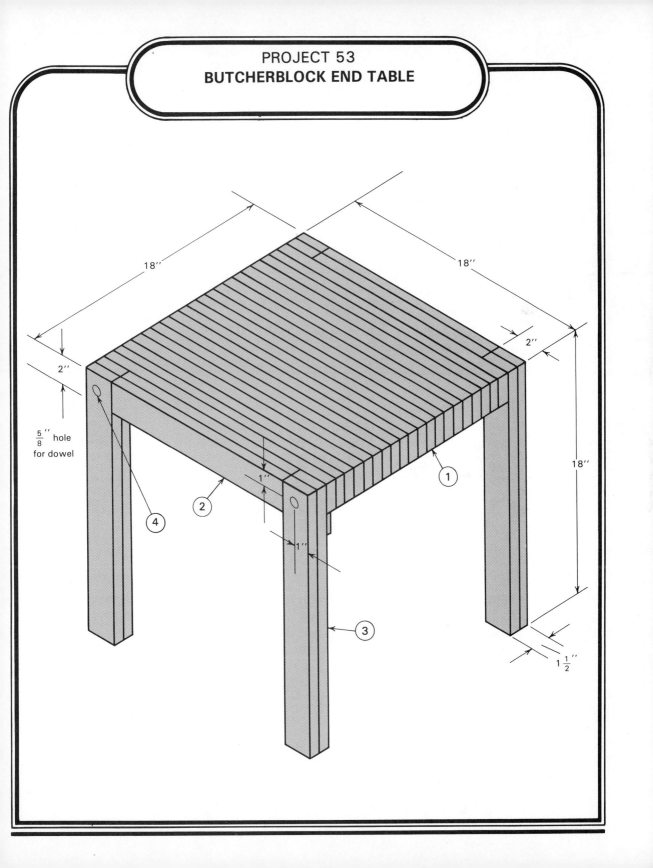

18''

18''

2''

2''

18''

$\frac{5}{8}''$ hole
for dowel

1''

1''

$1\frac{1}{2}''$

1

2

3

4

# Glass Top Coffee Table

This project requires some careful joinery, but it's well within the scope of anyone who doesn't mind taking time to do precise cutting and careful assembling. Like any project, it can be made with hand tools. But procedures will be easier if you can work on a table saw and have bar clamps for assembly work.

You'll need good hardwood. Use a wood like maple, birch, or white oak

This table can have the plate-glass top, as shown, or a top of other materials discussed at the end of the text.

## project 54
### Glass Top Coffee Table

## MATERIALS LIST

| Part No. | Name | Pieces | Size | Material |
|---|---|---|---|---|
| 1 | legs | 8 | $1\frac{1}{2} \times 4 \times 16''$ | hardwood lumber |
| 2 | rails | 4 | $1\frac{1}{2} \times 4 \times 22''$ | " |
| 3 | ties | 16 | $\frac{1}{2}''$ dia. $\times 2''$ | dowel |
| 4 | cleats | 4 | $\frac{3}{4} \times \frac{3}{4} \times 27''$ | hardwood lumber |
| 5 | top | 1 | $\frac{1}{2} \times 27 \times 27''$ | plate glass* |

*The text tells about substitute materials.

if you want a light, natural finish. Work with something like walnut or mahogany if you want a darker appearance.

Start by cutting pieces for the legs and the rails to the sizes shown in the materials list. Cut one edge of each leg piece to 45 degrees. It's best here to test the table-saw setup by making a trial cut in scrap wood. Then you'll know the angle is correct before you shape the good stock. Assemble the leg pieces by coating mating surfaces with glue and holding them together with 6d finishing nails. If you enjoy joinery, it won't be hard to cut narrow grooves in the surface of the bevels to allow a spline to reinforce the joint.

Work very carefully when you lay out the locations for the dowel holes in the legs and the rails. The holes will be easier to form if you work on a drill press. But they can be accurately done with a portable electric drill or a brace and bit. Drill the holes just a bit deeper than 1 inch. Commercial dowels are available with chamfered ends that are spirally grooved to allow excess glue to escape from the hole. If you make your own dowels, chamfer the ends and use a dovetail saw or similar tool to cut two or three shallow, lengthwise grooves in the dowels.

Use a sliver of wood to coat the inside of the holes in the legs with glue, and then tap the dowels into place. Now coat mating surfaces and the inside

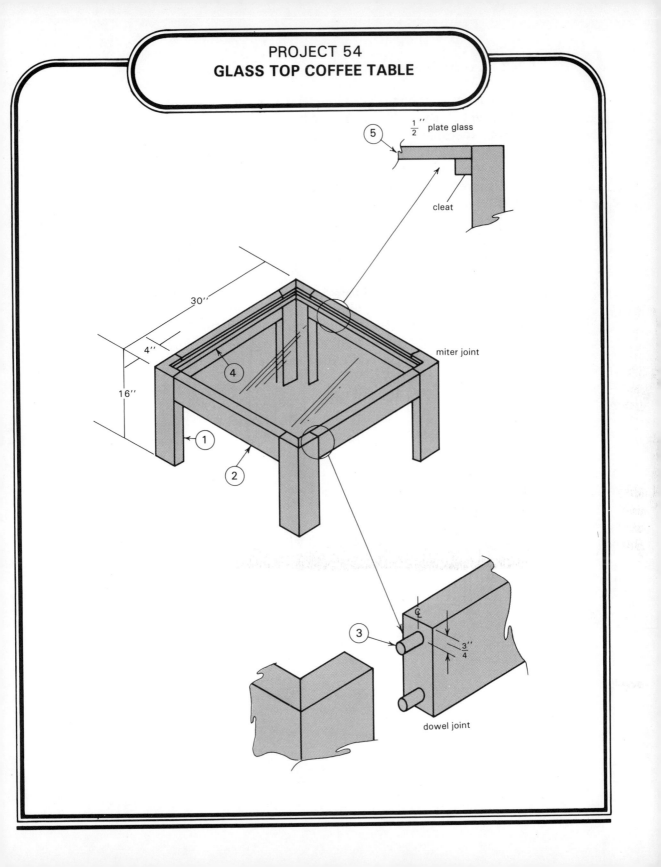

# PROJECT 54
# GLASS TOP COFFEE TABLE

$\frac{1}{2}''$ plate glass

5

cleat

30''

4''

16''

4

miter joint

1

2

3

$\frac{3''}{4}$

dowel joint

of the holes in the rails with glue and join the leg assemblies to the rails. This will be easy to do if you have bar clamps or a band clamp. Otherwise, use the tourniquet rope trick—loop strong cord around the assembly and then twist tightly with a strip of wood. Use pieces of heavy cardboard under the cord at the corners to avoid marring the wood. Allow the glue to dry overnight before removing whatever you have used to secure the assembly.

The final construction step is to attach the cleats for the glass top. Don't precut these to exact size. Instead, start with too-long pieces and trim them to exact length as you install them. Hold the cleats in place with glue and 6d finishing nails.

When you order the plate glass, be sure its length and width will be about $\frac{1}{8}$ inch less than the actual dimensions of the area the glass must fit. If you prefer not to have a see-through top, you can substitute a $\frac{1}{2}$-inch-thick piece of plywood covered with a plastic laminate of your choice. You can also use a piece of plywood with a surface veneer that matches the wood of the table's frame.

# Coffee Table plus Seats

The table and seats are a neat and practical ensemble, but you can choose to make either. The table can stand on its own; the seats will be handy when you have overflow guests.

The intended use can affect your choices of material. If you want formal projects, work with a fancy hardwood plywood like walnut, mahogany, or maple. If the project will be used in a place such as a child's room where it might be abused, a paintable plywood like pine or top-grade fir and a table surface veneered with a tough plastic laminate make sense.

**343**

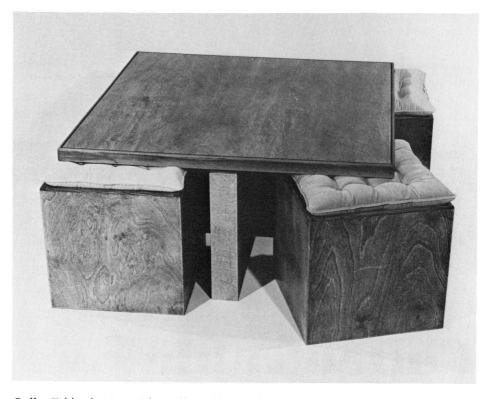

Coffee Table plus Seats. The coffee table and the seats make an attractive and practical ensemble. The seats are sized to fit into the corners made by the table's understructure for storage until needed.

Start by cutting the table top to exact size and then covering its edges with matching strips of wood that are rabbeted, as shown in the drawing detail. It's best to start with pieces that are longer than you need, so they can be trimmed to exact size as they are applied. Make the attachment with glue and three or four 4d finishing nails through each piece.

Next, cut the pieces that will form the cruciform cleat assembly (parts 3 and 4) to which the pedestals will be attached. Very carefully mark the location of the cleats on the underside of the top—the cross shape should divide the top into four equal squares—and then attach the parts with glue and 7d box nails. The glue alone will do the job; the nails are used mostly to keep the pieces positioned and secure until the glue dries.

Consider before cutting the pedestal parts to size that the drawing shows the end pieces miter-jointed to the sides. This is fine, but you can choose to use a butt joint if you make the ends of lumber instead of plywood. If you do use lumber, reduce the $15\frac{1}{4}$-inch dimension of part 6 by $\frac{3}{4}$ inch.

Start assembly by joining the pedestal sides at the inside corners. A butt joint, reinforced with glue and 6d box nails, is okay. This will give you four L-shape assemblies that you then make into the complete pedestal structure by adding the end pieces.

Attach the completed pedestal to the top cross-shape cleats with glue and 6d finishing nails. The final step is to form the bottom brace, which you can do by working with individual pieces or by cutting the cross shape from one piece of $2\times12\times12$-inch stock. Attach the brace with glue and 6d finishing nails, or just hold it in place with clamps until the glue dries.

## SEATS

These are just boxes, but they do call for careful work because of the miter joint used at each corner. The best procedure is to cut all the pieces you need for the box sides and the cleats. Attach the cleats with glue and 5d box nails to one side at each corner of the box structure. The cleats will provide helpful support when you add the remaining sides to close in the boxes. Use glue and 4d finishing nails to connect the sides, but drive the nails into the mitered joint, not the cleats.

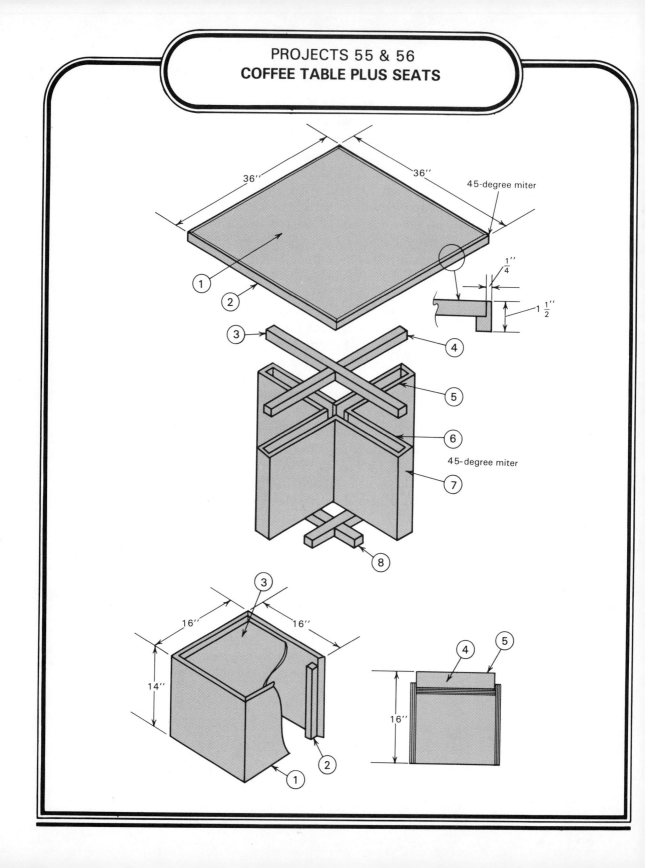

# PROJECTS 55 & 56
## COFFEE TABLE PLUS SEATS

36''

36''

45-degree miter

①

②

$\frac{1''}{4}$

$1\frac{1}{2}''$

③

④

⑤

⑥

45-degree miter

⑦

⑧

③

16''

16''

14''

②

①

④

⑤

16''

### projects 55 and 56
### Coffee Table plus Seats

# MATERIALS LIST

| Part No. | Name | Pieces | Size | Material |
|---|---|---|---|---|
| 1 | top | 1 | $\frac{3}{4} \times 35\frac{1}{2} \times 35\frac{1}{2}''$ | plywood |
| 2 | trim | 4 | $\frac{3}{4} \times 1\frac{1}{2} \times 36''$ | lumber (to match top) |
| 3 | cleat | 1 | $1\frac{1}{2} \times 1\frac{1}{2} \times 32''$ | lumber |
| 4 | cleats | 2 | $1\frac{1}{2} \times 1\frac{1}{2} \times 15\frac{1}{4}''$ | " |
| 5 | pedestal sides | 4 | $\frac{3}{4} \times 16 \times 17\frac{1}{4}''$ | plywood (to match top) |
| 6 | pedestal sides | 4 | $\frac{3}{4} \times 15\frac{1}{4} \times 17\frac{1}{4}''$ | " |
| 7 | pedestal ends | 4 | $\frac{3}{4} \times 3 \times 17\frac{1}{4}''$ | " |
| 8 | brace | (May be cut as individual pieces or as an integral unit from a piece of $1\frac{1}{2} \times 12 \times 12''$ lumber.) | | |

| | | Seats | | |
|---|---|---|---|---|
| 1 | box sides | 16 | $\frac{3}{4} \times 14 \times 16''$ | plywood |
| 2 | cleats | 16 | $1 \times 1 \times 13\frac{1}{4}''$ | lumber |
| 3 | tops | 4 | $\frac{3}{4} \times 14\frac{1}{2} \times 14\frac{1}{2}''$ | plywood |
| 4 | pads | 4 | $2 \times 16 \times 16''$ | foam rubber |
| 5 | covers | 4 | 24" square pieces | material of your choice |

Cut the top pieces to size and add them to the assembly. These rest on the top end of the cleats and are attached with glue and 6d finishing nails. You can also add a couple of 6d finishing nails through each side into the edge of the top.

The pads are 2-inch-thick pieces of cloth–or plastic–covered foam rubber. One way to work is to cover the foam rubber, being very careful how you fold the corners, and to hold the material in place with tape on the underside. Then install the pad with contact cement. Another way is to add the covering after the rubber is in place. Fold the edges of the cover and attach them to the sides of the seat with decorative upholstery tacks.

A third way is to make or buy cushions 2 inches thick and 16 inches square and simply set them into place. Or attach them with tufting buttons, large, decorative buttons that are secured with strong twine needled through the cushion. In this case, small holes for the twine must be drilled through the top of the seat. Pull the twine tight after passing it through the hole in the seat, and then knot it around a short piece of dowel.

# Butcherblock Kitchen Table

The butcherblock table is functional and sturdy, and will be a lot more useful than conventional light-duty cutting boards to anyone interested in the culinary arts. Professional units are usually of maple or birch. You can opt for such material or choose easier-to-work, more economical pine. Projects like this have also been done with straight-grain fir—a tough and handsome material. Whatever wood you work with must be clear and kiln-dried.

If you begin construction of this table intending to offer it as a gift, you may in the end decide to keep it.

The best procedure is to begin by cutting all parts to the sizes shown in the materials list. Since the actual width and thickness of all parts is $1\frac{1}{2} \times 3\frac{1}{2}$ inches, you can buy standard $2 \times 4$'s; so the starting chore amounts to no more than sawing parts to length. One point, though: the $2 \times 4$'s will have slightly rounded corners, so they should be sawed or planed to create a true flat on one edge. Do this on one edge of the slab pieces and the legs. The other parts can be treated in similar fashion, or you can live with them as they are.

Do a careful layout on one of the slab pieces to mark the location of the holes needed for the threaded rod. Drill pilot holes through the piece and then use it as a template to mark hole locations in other parts. Remember that the legs also must be drilled for the rods. Enlarge the holes to about $\frac{9}{16}$ inch. This is oversize, so that the rods will be easy to insert and there will be some leeway when you align the slab parts.

The holes in the two end pieces are counterbored, so that washers and nuts can be set below the surface of the wood. Judge the diameter of the counterbore by the size of the washer. The depth of the counterbore will depend on whether you wish to conceal the rods with wood plugs. Either way, form the counterbores in the two pieces before you drill through them for the rod.

Next step is to cut the dadoes required in the legs and the rails. You can quickly form them using a dado assembly on a table saw, or you can shape them by hand by first making the shoulder cuts with a backsaw and then using a chisel to clean out the waste. Accomplish all the detail work before starting assembly. Make a trial run by putting pieces together without glue to test for accuracy.

The final step is to coat mating surfaces with glue while you assemble them. Start by inserting the rods through one of the slab's end pieces, and then add others as you coat them with glue. Be sure to insert the legs in correct positions. Tighten up on the nuts a bit at a time, making sure that the top edges of the slab pieces are flush with each other. Check with a square to see that the legs are perpendicular to the slab. Some haste is required here so that the glue doesn't set before you apply pressure. Working with a glue that has a long set time will help. Bar clamps are useful here.

## project 57
### Butcherblock Kitchen Table

# MATERIALS LIST

| Part No. | Name | Pieces | Size | Material |
|---|---|---|---|---|
| 1 | slab pcs. | 14 | $1\frac{1}{2} \times 3\frac{1}{2} \times 24''$ | lumber |
| | | 2 | $1\frac{1}{2} \times 3\frac{1}{2} \times 17''$ | " |
| 2 | legs | 4 | $1\frac{1}{2} \times 3\frac{1}{2} \times 30''$ | " |
| 3 | rails | 2 | $1\frac{1}{2} \times 3\frac{1}{2} \times 20''$ | " |
| 4 | stretcher | 1 | $1\frac{1}{2} \times 3\frac{1}{2} \times 16\frac{1}{2}''$ | " |

Also needed: three pieces of $\frac{1}{2}''$-diameter threaded steel rod, about 24" long, with 6 washers and 6 nuts.

If you use them, tighten the nuts *after* clamp pressure has been applied. Use a damp, lint-free cloth to remove all excess glue.

You can add the rails and stretcher by using only glue, or you can reinforce them with screws driven through counterbored holes which can then be filled with wood plugs. Bar clamps or a band clamp will make the attachment of the last pieces easier, but if you lack such equipment, use the tourniquet trick. Make a loop of strong rope around the parts and then use a stick to twist the loop tightly.

Finishing, after sanding, can be done with the special "Salad Bowl Finish" discussed on page 63, or with several applications of mineral oil. Allow each application to soak in before adding more. Wipe off excess oil with a lint-free cloth after the final coating. The oil treatment can be repeated periodically after the project is in use.

# PROJECT 57
## BUTCHERBLOCK KITCHEN TABLE

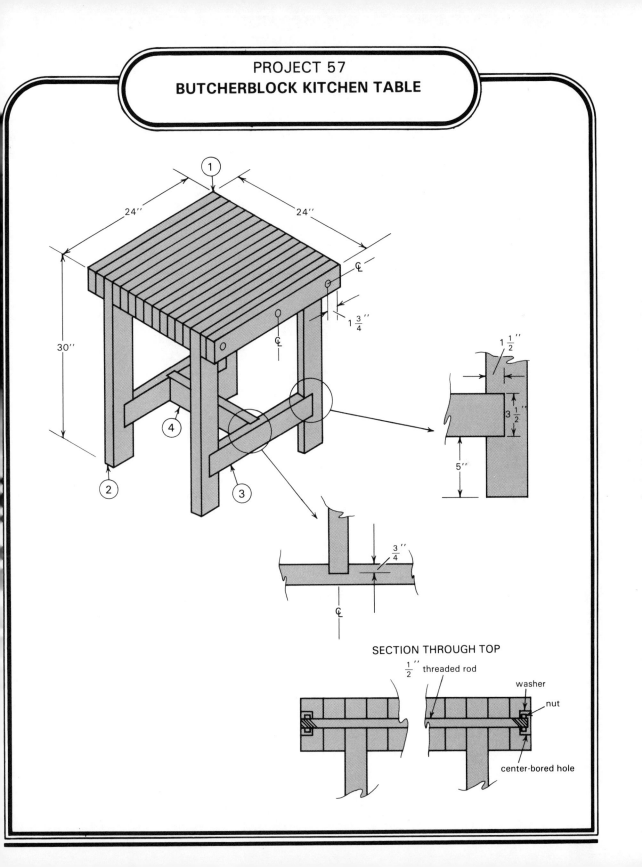

SECTION THROUGH TOP

# A TRIO OF CAMPY TABLE LAMPS

## projects 58-60

**Lamps
from One-Gallon
Oil Tin.
Two Cookie Tins.
Metal Waste Basket.**

The slang word "camp" has many meanings. It is used here in the sense that applies to items that are tremendously popular simply because they are a departure from the accepted norm or, to put it formally, that have "perversely sophisticated appeal."

Anyway, the projects are fun to make and use, will be appreciated by any recipient, are very saleable, and in the practical sense, can be made with containers that are usually discarded. The containers used are just examples. Many other items are suitable—large cookie tins, tea canisters, and so on. If the item you choose isn't large enough for the purpose, stack several of them.

## IN GENERAL

Most containers aren't heavy enough to be used as is for lamp bases. To add stability, place about a 1-inch-thick layer of *dry* sand in the container. Keep the sand in place by topping it with a suitable-size piece of $\frac{1}{2}$-inch-thick plywood, and then sealing the joint between wood and container walls with small pieces of duct tape.

The hole you drill for the lamp cord should be grommeted so the cord can't be damaged by sharp edges. Grommets, which are simply forced into place, are available in various sizes at electrical supply stores. Those shown here are made for a $\frac{1}{4}$-inch hole. Container walls are quite thin. When you form the hole, start with a very small bit, and then gradually enlarge the hole to full size. Use a file or sandpaper to remove any burrs.

All the necessary metal parts—threaded tube, nuts and washers, harps, and so on—are standard bits and pieces used in lamp-making or repairing. They are available in hobby supply stores and do-it-yourself centers. Sockets are available for single- or triple-wattage bulbs. The shades are purchased items. When you shop, take the base with you so that you can judge proportion and appearance before buying.

Cut the top from the tin by using a conventional can opener, and remove any burrs or sharp edges with a file. Wash the container with warm water and detergent, and after drying it, use it as a template to draw the outline of the top closure piece. Cut this very carefully for a tight fit, and drill the center hole for the threaded tube. Insert the tube and lock it in place with top and bottom nuts. The projection of the tube at the top should be about $\frac{3}{8}$ inch.

Place the sand and the grommet in the container and thread the cord into place before tapping the top piece into position. Secure the top with two sheet-metal screws driven through each side of the container. The screws are small enough and the metal is thin enough to let you form starting holes with an awl. Then add the harp base and socket. Harps vary in length. You can choose one to suit the shade you want—they all lock into a standard harp base.

Paint the top piece to match the predominant color on the base.

**Proj. 58.** The lamp base is made from a salvaged olive oil container. Use care when forming the top closure piece. Size so snugly that it must be tapped into place.

# PROJECT 58
## LAMP FROM ONE-GALLON OIL TIN

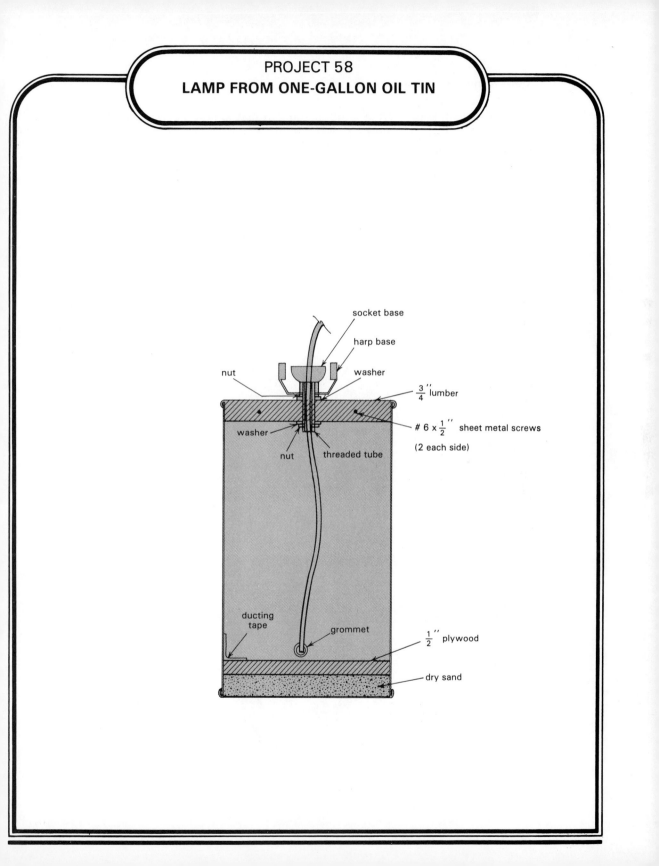

The drawing shows an assembly you can use to stack tins. First cut two pieces of $\frac{1}{2}$-inch-thick plywood that will fit snugly in the containers. Hold them in place in the container lids, and form the holes for the threaded tubes. Attach the top container to the lid of the bottom unit with the threaded tube and top and bottom nuts.

Once the sand and the grommet are in place, thread the lamp cord into position and then secure the top unit's position by driving one sheet-metal screw through each side of the bottom container. The screw should pass through the lid and container and into the plywood. If you wish, you can drive a couple of the same size screws through the bottom of the top tin.

Secure the second piece of plywood to the top lid by using the threaded tube, washers, and nuts, and then put the assembly in place, securing its position by driving two more screws.

**Proj. 59.** This lamp base was made by stacking two same-size cookie tins. The drawing shows how the parts are secured.

# PROJECT 59
# LAMP FROM TWO COOKIE TINS

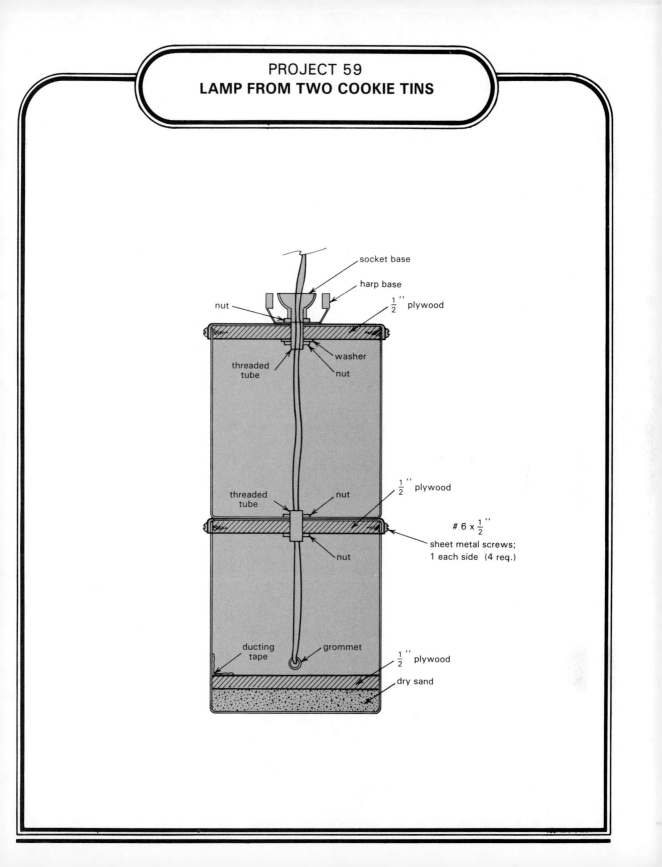

The container used here is a piece of pop-art in itself. Ours duplicates an old-time peanut butter tin, but there are others that simulate soup and beer cans and similar items. A money-saving tip here—hardware stores may sell the cans at much lower cost than highbrow stationery stores will.

Make the top closure piece by first cutting a disc of $\frac{3}{4}$-inch-thick plywood to fit tightly in the container. Next, cut a disc of $\frac{1}{4}$-inch-thick tempered hardboard with a diameter 1 inch greater than the container's. Drill center holes through each piece for the threaded tube, and after coating mating areas with glue, put the pieces together by adding the threaded tube and the top and bottom washers and nuts. It's a good idea to add a few small clamps about the perimeter.

Add the sand and install the grommet, and after threading the lamp cord into position, tap the top assembly into place and secure it with two screws.

Sand the perimeter of the hardboard so that it is nicely rounded, and apply a coat of sealer. You can finish with varnish or something similar, or simply polish with several applications of hard paste wax.

**Proj. 60.** This lamp base was made from a waste basket that is pop art in itself. Similar containers are copies of soup cans, beer cans, and the like.

# PROJECT 60
## LAMP FROM METAL WASTE BASKET

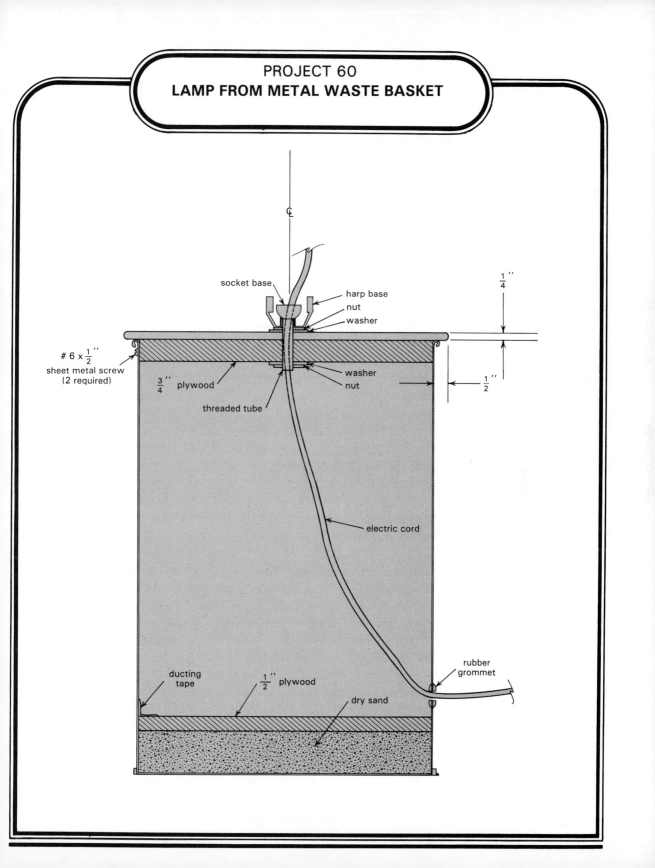

socket base

harp base

nut

washer

$\frac{1}{4}$''

# 6 x $\frac{1}{2}$''
sheet metal screw
(2 required)

washer

nut

$\frac{3}{4}$'' plywood

threaded tube

$\frac{1}{2}$''

electric cord

rubber grommet

ducting tape

$\frac{1}{2}$'' plywood

dry sand

# MORE FURNITURE

# Bathroom Bench

This bench provides a place for a magazine or book, a dish of special soap, a bottle of lotion—whatever you might want near you while soaking in a hot tub. Also, it's convenient afterwards, for sitting while you dry off.

For this project, you'll need lumber. For example, you'll need clear pine if you choose to paint the project, or a hardwood such as mahogany, walnut, or birch if you want a natural finish.

Start the project by cutting the top to size and then forming the two end pieces. The bevel on the edgings can be cut with a saw or shaped with a plane. Assemble the pieces with glue and 6d finishing nails. It's wise on this

You don't often think of making furniture for the bathroom, but this neat little bench is handy for holding tub-side items and for sitting on while drying.

## project 61
### Bathroom Bench
# MATERIALS LIST

| Part No. | Name | Pieces | Size | Material |
|---|---|---|---|---|
| 1 | top | 1 | $\frac{3}{4} \times 10 \times 14\frac{1}{2}$" | lumber |
| 2 | edging | 2 | $\frac{3}{4} \times 2 \times 10$" | " |
| 3 | base | 1 | $\frac{3}{4} \times 10 \times 16$" | " |
| 4 | legs | 4 | $\frac{3}{4} \times 5 \times 12\frac{1}{2}$" | " |

project to use a waterproof or, at least, a highly moisture-resistant adhesive.

Cut the base to size and shape its ends as shown in the drawing detail. Here, too, the bevels can be formed by sawing or planing. Use sandpaper to round off sharp corners.

Each leg consists of two pieces which are joined to form a 90 degree angle. The joint can be a miter, as the drawing shows, but you can get by with a butt joint; the connection will not be very visible. In either case, use glue and finishing nails to assemble the pieces—4d nails for a miter, 6d nails for a butt joint.

Put together the four components with glue and 6d finishing nails. Be sure to go over all edges and surfaces with fine sandpaper before applying a finish. The project should not have any sharp corners, so round off all edges with sandpaper.

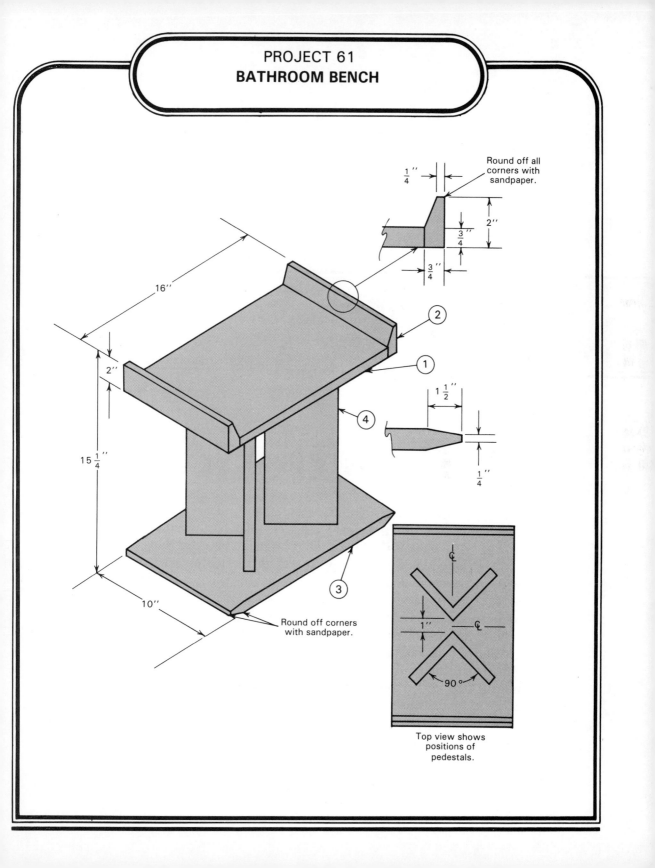

# PROJECT 61
## BATHROOM BENCH

Round off all corners with sandpaper.

$\frac{1}{4}''$

2''

$\frac{3}{4}''$

$\frac{3}{4}''$

16''

2''

$15\frac{1}{4}''$

10''

$1\frac{1}{2}''$

$\frac{1}{4}''$

① ② ③ ④

Round off corners with sandpaper.

1''

90°

Top view shows positions of pedestals.

# Child's Desk

This desk can also serve adults as a kitchen "office," a hobby workbench, a telephone desk. All the parts are $\frac{3}{4}$-inch-thick hardwood plywood except for the leg assemblies, which should be made of a matching lumber.

Start construction by cutting to size all the pieces needed for the top structure. Cut the dadoes that are required in the ends and in the top and bottom pieces. Each end is dadoed for the top (part 4); the top and bottom parts are dadoed for the divider (part 5).

Next put together the bottom, the back, and the two end pieces. These are all butt-jointed, secured with glue and 6d finishing nails.

Now cut the parts that are needed for the legs and bases, and form the mortise-and-tenon joints used to connect the pieces. Anyone with a drill press and mortising chisels will not need guidance here. If you lack power

The Child's Desk is a good homework or hobby aid, but it can serve other functions. The top shelf shown in this photo is optional. You can add it by gluing and nailing with 6d finishing nails.

equipment (or necessary accessories), you can form mortises by drilling a series of overlapping $\frac{1}{2}$-inch-diameter holes and then cleaning out the waste with a chisel. Form the tenon by sawing, either on a table saw or by hand with a backsaw. Size the tenon for a slip fit. It should be snug, but not so tight that you must use considerable force to insert it. An alternate method of assembly is to do an *end-lap joint.* Cut a $\frac{3}{4}$-inch-deep, $3\frac{1}{2}$-inch-wide dado in the base pieces, and a $\frac{3}{4}$-inch-deep by $3\frac{1}{2}$-inch-long rabbet in the legs. The cut parts will mate and have flush surfaces. If you make the end-lap joints, increase the length of the leg pieces accordingly. Form the top end of the legs by sawing what is essentially a very wide rabbet.

Attach the leg assemblies to the semi-assembled top case with glue and by driving flathead wood screws from the inside of the end pieces. Use two screws for each leg, locating them so they will not be visible when the writing surface (part 4) is added.

Coat the dadoes for the end, top, and bottom parts with glue, and then slip into place the top (part 4) and the divider (part 5). The joints between these components can be reinforced with 6d finishing nails.

You can cover exposed plywood edges with commercial wood tape. Some tapes have an applied adhesive that makes a permanent bond when the tape is pressed on with an ordinary household iron. Other tapes require that the attachment be done with contact cement. In either case, you should be able to find a tape that matches the veneer of the plywood used for the project. Another way to cover edges is to cut $\frac{1}{8}$- to $\frac{1}{4}$-inch-thick strips of wood that you then apply to the exposed plywood edges with glue and brads.

The optional, plastic laminate cover for the top of the writing surface can be attached with contact cement.

A thorough sanding job is, of course, the first step toward a good finish. Make sure flat surfaces are smooth; round sharp corners with sandpaper. Apply a liberal coat of sealer, and after twenty minutes or so, wipe off any excess with a lint-free cloth. A couple of coats of clear polyurethane finish should complete the job. A light sanding between applications of final finish is a good idea.

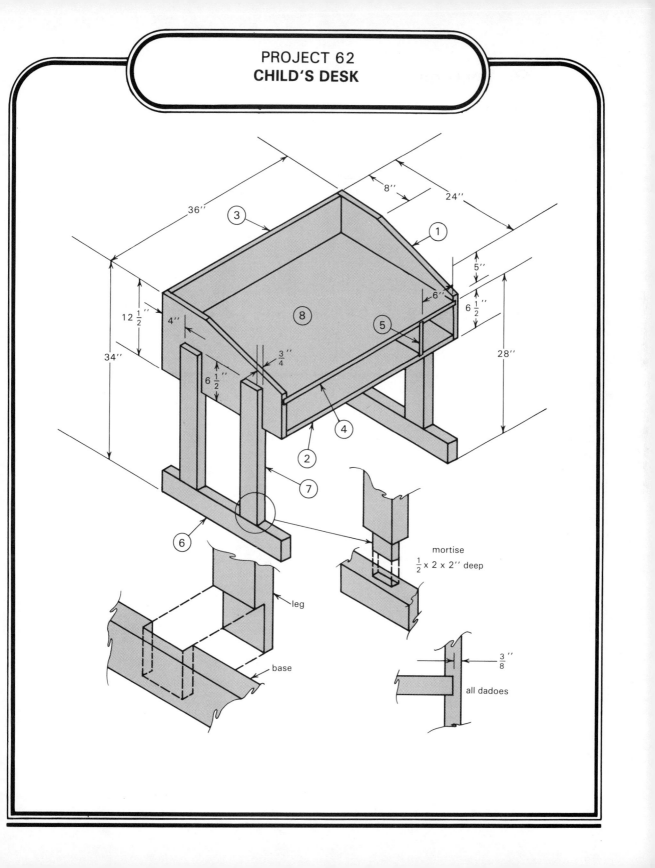

# PROJECT 62
## CHILD'S DESK

36''

8''

24''

③

①

5''

6''

6 ½

12 ½''

4''

⑧

⑤

28''

34''

¾''

6 ½''

④

②

⑦

⑥

mortise
½ x 2 x 2'' deep

leg

base

⅜''

all dadoes

**project 62**
**Child's Desk**

## MATERIALS LIST

| Part No. | Name | Pieces | Size | Material |
|---|---|---|---|---|
| 1 | ends | 2 | $\frac{3}{4} \times 12\frac{1}{2} \times 24''$ | hardwood plywood |
| 2 | bottom | 1 | $\frac{3}{4} \times 23\frac{1}{4} \times 34\frac{1}{2}''$ | " |
| 3 | back | 1 | $\frac{3}{4} \times 12\frac{1}{2} \times 34\frac{1}{2}''$ | " |
| 4 | top | 1 | $\frac{3}{4} \times 23\frac{1}{4} \times 35\frac{1}{4}''$ | " |
| 5 | divider | 1 | $\frac{3}{4} \times 5\frac{3}{4} \times 23\frac{1}{4}''$ | " |
| 6 | base | 2 | $1\frac{1}{2} \times 3\frac{1}{2} \times 24''$ | lumber |
| 7 | legs | 4 | $1\frac{1}{2} \times 3\frac{1}{2} \times 26\frac{1}{2}''$ | " |
| 8 | cover (optional) | 1 | $23\frac{1}{4} \times 34\frac{1}{2}''$ | plastic laminate |

# Corner Bric-a-Brac Shelf

Many people have small relics, travel mementos, little handcrafted projects they like to display; so a shelf like this one is nice to make for the home, to sell, or for gift giving. The version shown can stand on a piece of furniture or hang on a wall in a corner of a room. If you wish, the project can be a standing unit—just add more shelves and make longer posts.

**371**

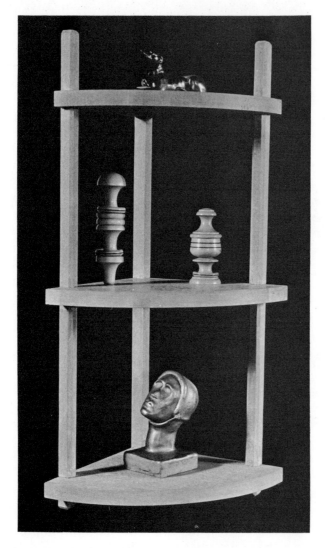

Our Corner Bric-a-Brac Shelf is all mahogany with a matte natural finish. You can achieve a completely different look by, say, using clear pine and painting it in bright colors.

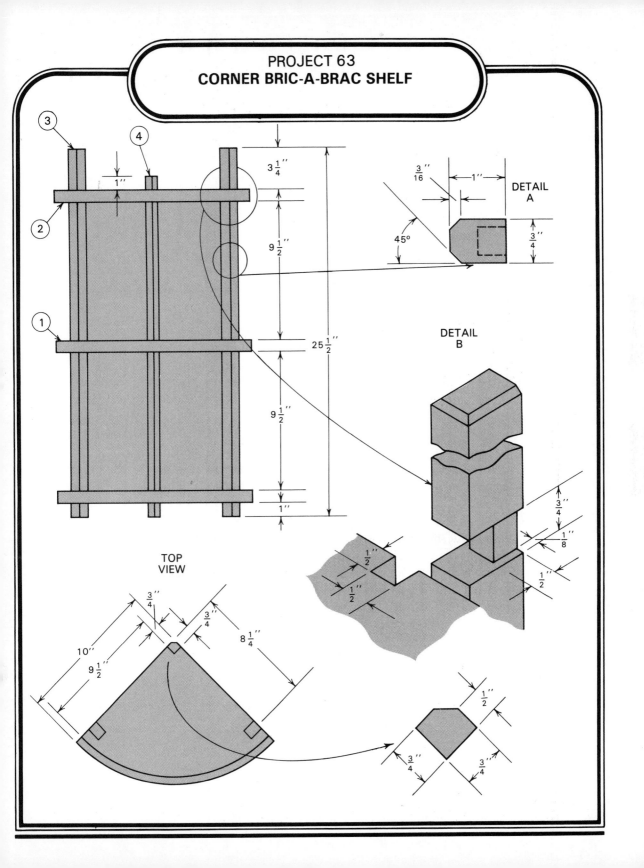

# PROJECT 63
## CORNER BRIC-A-BRAC SHELF

DETAIL
A

DETAIL
B

TOP
VIEW

## project 63
### Corner Bric-a-Brac Shelf

## MATERIALS LIST

| Part No. | Name | Pieces | Size | Material |
|---|---|---|---|---|
| 1 | shelf | 2 | $\frac{3}{4} \times 10 \times 10''$ | lumber |
| 2 | shelf (top) | 1 | $\frac{3}{4} \times 9\frac{1}{2} \times 9\frac{1}{2}''$ | " |
| 3 | posts | 2 | $\frac{3}{4} \times 1 \times 25\frac{1}{2}''$ | " |
| 4 | post (back) | 1 | $\frac{3}{4} \times \frac{3}{4} \times 23\frac{1}{4}''$ | " |

First cut the shelf pieces—including the top one, which has a smaller radius—to overall size. Mark one piece for the back corner notch and the two notches required for the longer posts. Make a pad of the parts either by gripping them in a vise or by holding them with clamps. Form the notches by using a dado setup on a table saw or by hand with a backsaw to make the shoulder cuts and then chiseling out the waste. Form the curved front edge either by sawing parts individually or by working on a pad assembly.

Cut the posts to overall size, and chamfer the front edges of the longer ones as shown in Detail A. Mark the layout on the two longer posts for the notches that will receive the shelves (Detail B). These notches can be formed on a table saw or by hand with a backsaw and chisels.

Assemble the parts with glue and by driving 6d finishing nails from the back surfaces of the posts into the shelves.

There is an alternative method of assembly. Size the notches (for the long posts) in the shelves to suit the cross-sectional dimensions of the posts. Then you can skip the notching shown in Detail B and simply attach the posts to the shelves with glue and toenailing from the back of the posts into the shelves.

# The Cube

Basically the cube project is a system of structural boxes that are functional, attractive, and have almost unlimited uses. A few units can utilize space in a corner. Two sets, composed of two units each, can be spanned with a shelf to make a desk. You can build enough of them to cover a wall or create a divider. The advantage of such a modular system is that, although a particular arrangement will appear as a permanent installation, it can be quickly and easily reformed to serve another purpose or as a change of decor.

As the drawings show, there are construction options as well. Mitered corners reinforced with splines are the most sophisticated approach, and not difficult to do if power equipment is available. Butt joints are the easiest to build, and will be strong enough when they are reinforced with glue and

**375**

# MATERIALS LIST

Each cube, if assembled with mitered joints and a $\frac{3}{4}''$-inset back, requires:
  Frame—4 pieces of $\frac{3}{4} \times 14 \times 14''$ plywood
  Back—1 piece of $\frac{3}{4} \times 12\frac{1}{2} \times 12\frac{1}{2}''$ plywood
If a rabbet joint is used, two of the frame pieces should be $\frac{3}{4} \times 13\frac{1}{2} \times 14''$.
If a butt joint is used, two of the frame pieces should be $\frac{3}{4} \times 12\frac{1}{2} \times 14''$.
A $\frac{1}{4}''$-thick back, inset in rabbet cuts (Detail E), should be $\frac{1}{4} \times 13\frac{1}{2} \times 13\frac{1}{2}''$.
A shelf, if used, should be $\frac{3}{4} \times 13\frac{1}{4}''$ long. Its width depends on other factors (see text).

8d finishing nails. The $\frac{3}{4}$-inch-thick inset back will provide considerable bracing to a butt joint construction. A note here: Regardless of whether you use fancy or plain joints, plywood edges will be exposed. This isn't necessarily an eyesore if you use cabinet-grade plywood or plan on painting the cubes. Anyway, you can conceal edges by applying readily available wood tape.

Material choices vary from hardwood plywoods finished in natural tones to more economical plywoods that can be painted. Painting can be simple, with all units the same color; or, in a more daring approach, units can be done in bright, contrasting colors.

If you choose to make some cubes with shelves, remember that the units are designed to be used vertically or horizontally, so the shelves should be centered. The width of the shelf is affected by the way the cube is put together. For one thing, the depth of shelf must be reduced by the thickness of the piece you use for the back. If you plan a door, then the shelf must be further reduced by the door's thickness.

Doors can be hung on mortised hinges or, if decor permits, with small, surface-mounted butt hinges. One example of places where butt hinges can be effective: white cubes with black hardware. Door pulls can be commercial items (metal or wood) or you can just bore a 1-inch-diameter finger hole. Either way, be sure the pull is centered between the top and bottom edges of the door. This way, cubes with doors can be inverted; then you can elect whether the door will swing to the left or the right.

Be sure to "dress" door sizes; that is, reduce length and width dimensions

The Cube project consists of modular boxes that can be stacked for a variety of uses. Adaptations are easy, whether for a different function or merely for a visual change.

just enough so that the door will function without binding. Use a conventional magnetic catch to hold the door in closed position.

My cubes are 14 inches square. If you like, you can make a few that are 28 inches long to make arranging even more flexible.

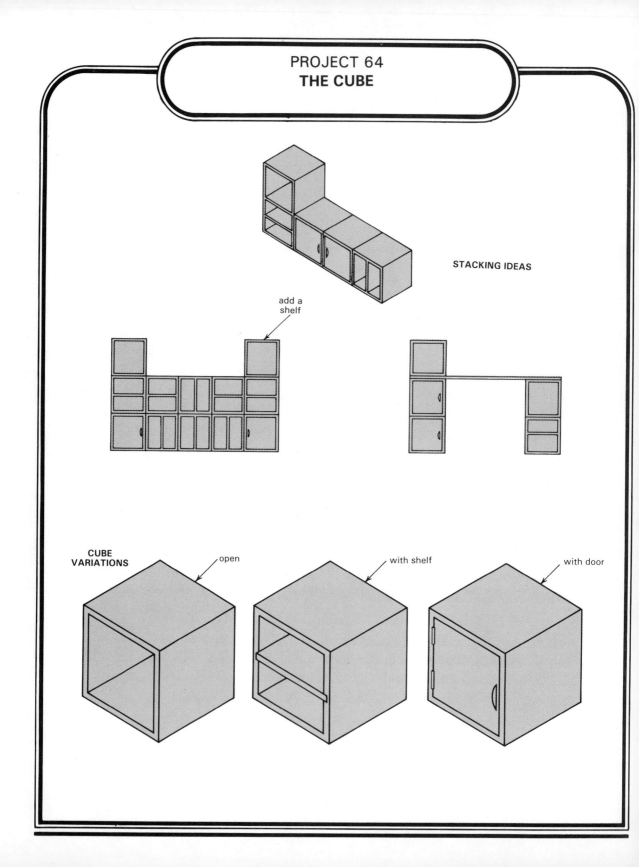

# PROJECT 64
## THE CUBE

**STACKING IDEAS**

add a
shelf

**CUBE VARIATIONS**

open

with shelf

with door

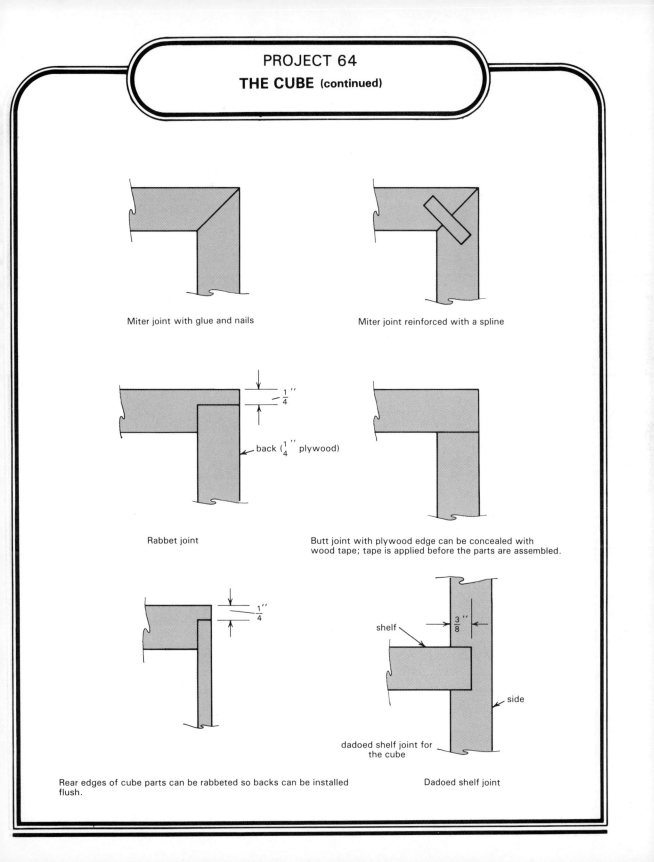

Miter joint with glue and nails

Miter joint reinforced with a spline

$\frac{1}{4}$″

back ($\frac{1}{4}$″ plywood)

Rabbet joint

Butt joint with plywood edge can be concealed with wood tape; tape is applied before the parts are assembled.

$\frac{1}{4}$″

shelf

$\frac{3}{8}$″

side

dadoed shelf joint for the cube

Rear edges of cube parts can be rabbeted so backs can be installed flush.

Dadoed shelf joint

# Magazine Stand

The Magazine Stand is patterned after a blacksmith's tool carrier, although this project is not an actual reproduction. Heavy tools were stored in the bottom tray while smaller items like nails were held in the top tray, which also served as a carrying handle.

The first step is to size the two pieces for the bed. The plans call for two pieces here only because it is difficult to find lumber that is more than $11\frac{1}{4}$ inches wide. If you wish, you can substitute plywood to make a one-piece bed.

Next cut the two side pieces to size and attach them to the bed with glue and 6d finishing nails. If you have made the bed from two pieces of lumber, you now have two assemblies that form the bottom tray after the ends (part 3) are added. The sides and ends of the bottom tray can be used square or

The Magazine Stand is patterned after a blacksmith's tool carrier. Pine was used here, but other wood species, such as fir, look realistically old when burn-finished as described in the text.

## MATERIALS LIST

| Part No. | Name | Pieces | Size | Material |
|---|---|---|---|---|
| 1 | bed | 2 | $\frac{3}{4} \times 6\frac{1}{4} \times 16''$ | lumber |
| 2 | sides | 2 | $\frac{3}{4} \times 2\frac{3}{4} \times 16''$ | " |
| 3 | ends | 2 | $\frac{3}{4} \times 2\frac{3}{4} \times 14''$ | " |
| 4 | feet | 4 | $1\frac{1}{2} \times 1\frac{1}{2} \times 3\frac{1}{2}''$ | " |
| 5 | verticals | 2 | $\frac{1}{2} \times 3\frac{1}{2} \times 13\frac{1}{2}''$ | " |
| 6 | tray base | 1 | $\frac{1}{2} \times 4\frac{1}{2} \times 14\frac{1}{2}''$ | " |
| 7 | tray edge sides | 2 | $\frac{3}{8} \times 1\frac{1}{2} \times 14\frac{1}{2}''$ | " |
| 8 | tray edge ends | 2 | $\frac{3}{8} \times 1\frac{1}{2} \times 5\frac{1}{4}''$ | " |

you can bevel the outside surfaces to produce the tapered look seen in the photograph. The beveling can be accomplished with either a saw or a plane.

Make the feet and attach them to the bed with glue and 6d finishing nails driven from the top surface. Now cut the verticals and put them into place with glue and 4d nails. These parts can have straight sides or they can be partially shaped.

Cut the top tray base to size, and add to it the side and end pieces with glue and $\frac{3}{4}$-inch-long brads. Attach the assembled top tray to the vertical pieces with glue and 6d finishing nails.

Here is how to finish the project for the "old" look which seems appropriate: First, work over the entire project with coarse sandpaper, rounding edges in a nonuniform manner so that the project will appear to be much used and timeworn. Next, work with fine sandpaper or steel wool so that edges and surfaces will be satiny smooth. Then use a propane torch to char the wood. You'll find that soft-grain areas will take on an attractive, darker hue. Use fine sandpaper to remove residue, wipe off dust with a brush or cloth, and then apply a coat of sealer. The final step is to apply satin-texture, clear polyurethane.

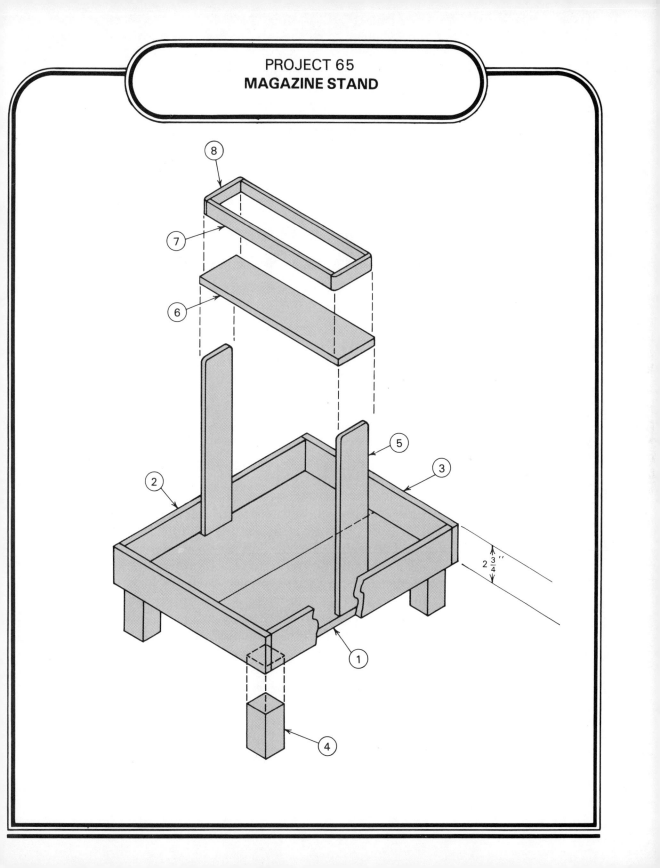

# PROJECT 65
## MAGAZINE STAND

# OUTDOOR PLANT CONTAINERS

There are probably as many shapes and sizes of commercial and home-made plant containers, or planters, as they are often called, as there are species of flowers and vegetables. But they all have particular construction traits in common. They should be sturdy to stay together outdoors, tight enough for excess moisture to escape through drainage holes and not through joints, and made so that the wood will be protected from the hazards of soil contact.

Some woods have a degree of natural immunity against rot and insect damage; for example, redwood and cedar. But any wood can be protected; so you're not limited to these particular species when building containers for plants. Two precautions you can take, even if the wood is redwood or cedar, are to line the inside of the container with sheet plastic and to paint soil-contact areas with liquid asphaltum.

Materials you can work with include lumber, exterior grades of plywood, and plywood house siding which is available in various wood species and different surface textures. Thus, choices can be affected by what material is readily available or by a desire for an effect that suits a particular environment. For example, you can choose a plywood siding that matches the house.

Exterior surfaces of containers can be protected with sealers, finished clear, left to weather, or painted—there are many options.

The construction of plant containers deserves as much attention as any project. A simple box with nailed butt joints will soon fall apart. Its durability can be drastically improved merely by adding a *waterproof* glue—not a *water-resistant* glue—in the joints.

Good work results when you cut carefully, use the right glue, and make sure to use aluminum or galvanized fasteners. A good precaution is to seal the inside joint lines with a caulking compound.

Good drainage is important if for no other reason than the fact that trapped, excess moisture will damage plants. You can provide good drainage by drilling $\frac{3}{8}$- or $\frac{1}{2}$-inch holes through the bottom of the container. Space the holes about 5 or 6 inches apart and cover them with small pieces of plastic, aluminum, or copper insect screening so soil won't fall through. If you install a solid plastic liner, drill the drainage holes before placing the liner. Slit the plastic over each hole before placing the screening.

Another precaution: Place a layer of small stones in the bottom of the container before filling with soil. This will allow excess water to flow to the drainage holes. Don't completely fill containers with soil. Allow about 1 inch of space from the surface of the soil to the top of the container. This makes it easier to water and will prevent the soil from spilling over.

# Tiered Planter

Cut the four pieces needed for the bottom frame to length, and then form the 45-degree angle cut needed at each end. Form a $\frac{5}{8}$-inch-deep, $\frac{3}{4}$-inch-wide rabbet in the bottom edge of each frame piece and assemble the four parts with glue and 8d finishing nails. Cut the bottom to size and install it with glue and 6d nails.

Next cut four pieces for the feet and attach them to the underside of the base with glue and 3d box or common nails. The last steps are to cut and put together the four pieces of the inside frame and to attach the assembly to the base with glue, driving 8d box nails up from the bottom of the base.

The project can be put together with butt joints instead of miter and rabbet cuts, but it will be necessary to adjust part sizes accordingly.

The Tiered Planter will look its best if you put low-growing plants in the bottom tier and a taller, flowering plant in the top area. Container designs of this type are good for growing strawberries.

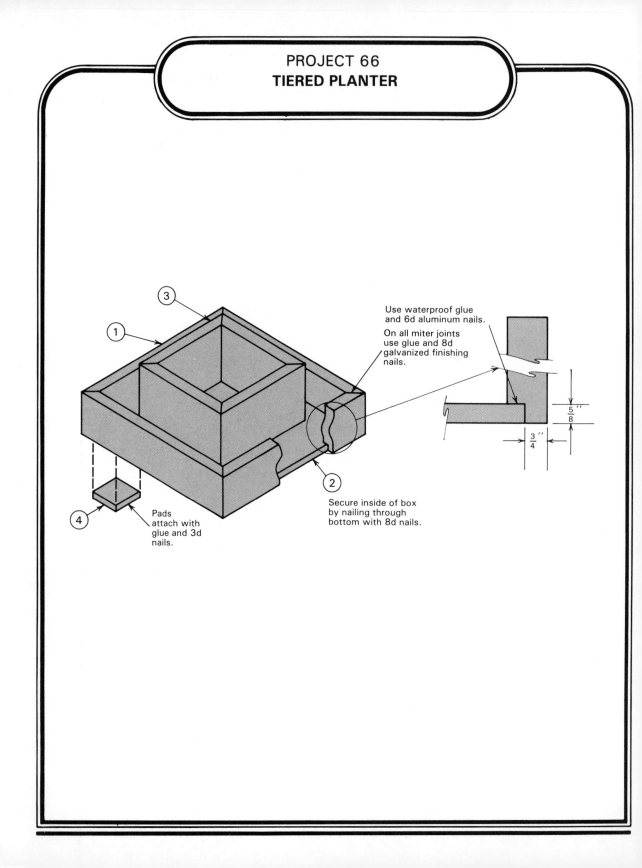

Use waterproof glue
and 6d aluminum nails.

On all miter joints
use glue and 8d
galvanized finishing
nails.

$\frac{5}{8}''$

$\frac{3}{4}''$

Secure inside of box
by nailing through
bottom with 8d nails.

Pads
attach with
glue and 3d
nails.

**project 66**
**Tiered Planter**

# MATERIALS LIST

| Part No. | Name | Pieces | Size | Material |
|----------|------|--------|------|----------|
| 1 | bottom frame | 4 | $1\frac{1}{2} \times 6 \times 24''$ | lumber |
| 2 | base | 1 | $\frac{5}{8} \times 22\frac{1}{2} \times 22\frac{1}{2}''$ | exterior-grade plywood |
| 3 | inside frame | 4 | $1\frac{1}{2} \times 10 \times 14''$ | lumber |
| 4 | pads (feet) | 4 | $\frac{5}{8} \times 4 \times 4''$ | exterior-grade plywood or lumber |

# Skyscraper Planter

This project consists of three separate containers which are most effective when used as a group. The pieces differ only in height; so the construction procedure is the same for each one.

First cut the four side pieces and the four cleats. Use glue and 5d galvanized box nails to attach the cleats to what will be opposite sides of the container. Position the cleats to extend 1 inch below the bottom of the project.

Add the remaining sides, again using glue but this time fastening with 4d galvanized finishing nails driven through the miter cuts.

The Skyscraper Planters can be used individually in separate settings, but they are most striking when grouped. Consider using plants that will cascade over planter edges.

**project 67**

**Skyscraper Planter**

# MATERIALS LIST

| Part No. | Name | Pieces | Size | Material |
|----------|------|--------|------|----------|
| | | | **PIECE A** | |
| 1 | sides | 4 | $\frac{3}{4} \times 10 \times 12''$ | exterior-grade plywood |
| 2 | cleats | 4 | $1 \times 1 \times 12''$ | lumber |
| 3 | bottom | 1 | $\frac{3}{4} \times 8\frac{1}{2} \times 8\frac{1}{2}''$ | exterior-grade plywood |
| | | | **PIECE B** | |
| 1 | sides | 4 | $\frac{3}{4} \times 10 \times 16''$ | exterior-grade plywood |
| 2 | cleats | 4 | $1 \times 1 \times 16''$ | lumber |
| 3 | bottom | 1 | $\frac{3}{4} \times 8\frac{1}{2} \times 8\frac{1}{2}''$ | exterior-grade plywood |
| | | | **PIECE C** | |
| 1 | sides | 4 | $\frac{3}{4} \times 10 \times 20''$ | exterior-grade plywood |
| 2 | cleats | 4 | $1 \times 1 \times 20''$ | lumber |
| 3 | bottom | 1 | $\frac{3}{4} \times 8\frac{1}{2} \times 8\frac{1}{2}''$ | exterior-grade plywood |

The last step is to cut the bottom to fit, notching each corner to accommodate the cleats, and installing it with glue and two 8d finishing nails through each side. The bottom is set flush with the lower edge of the sides.

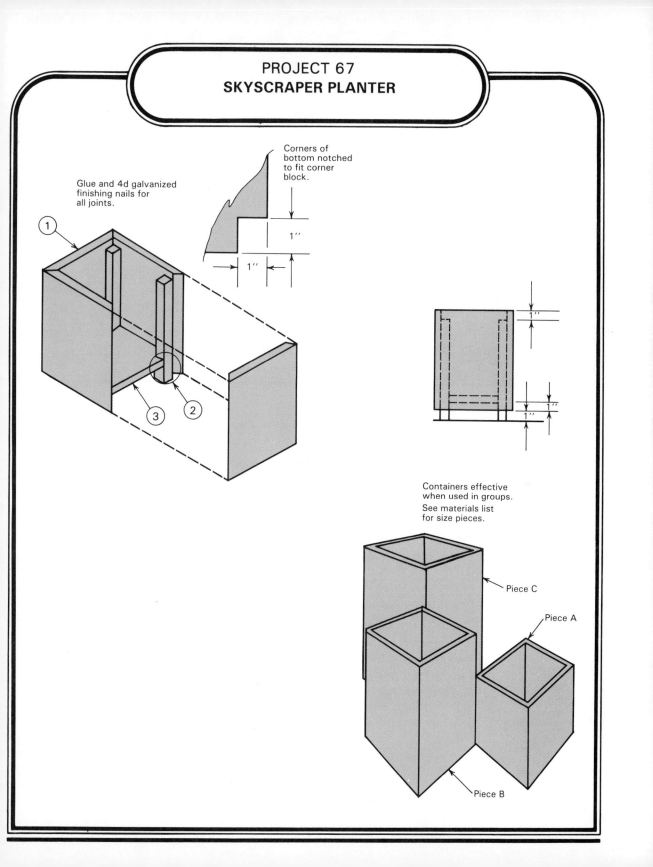

# PROJECT 67
# SKYSCRAPER PLANTER

Corners of
bottom notched
to fit corner
block.

1''

1''

Glue and 4d galvanized
finishing nails for
all joints.

① ② ③

1''

1''

1''

Containers effective
when used in groups.
See materials list
for size pieces.

Piece C

Piece A

Piece B

# Large Planter

There are two ways you can form the corners: Join two pieces of stock with a miter joint, or saw $3\frac{1}{2}$-inch-square material so that what remains will be a one-piece corner. The section that is cut out will still be usable on some other project.

Next cut the sides and ends. Attach the ends to corners with glue and 4d galvanized box nails driven from the inside. Then use the same attachment procedure to add the sides.

Cut the two pieces required for the bottom, and put them in place with glue and 8d galvanized finishing nails that you drive from outside surfaces. Be sure to install the bottom so the casters will project at least $\frac{1}{4}$ inch below the bottom of the container.

The Large Planter can be used for a shrub or a dwarf tree. The casters allow you to move the planter easily.

## project 68
### Large Planter

## MATERIALS LIST

| Part No. | Name | Pieces | Size | Material |
|----------|------|--------|------|----------|
| 1 | corners | 8 | $1 \times 3\frac{1}{2} \times 18''$ | lumber |
|   |   | or 4 | $3\frac{1}{2} \times 3\frac{1}{2} \times 18''$ | " |
| 2 | sides | 2 | $\frac{5}{8} \times 18 \times 24''$ | exterior-grade plywood |
| 3 | ends | 2 | $\frac{5}{8} \times 16 \times 18''$ | " |
| 4 | bottom | 2 | $1\frac{1}{2} \times 8 \times 22\frac{3}{4}''$ | lumber |
| 5 | frame sides | 2 | $\frac{5}{8} \times 2\frac{1}{2} \times 27\frac{3}{4}''$ | lumber or exterior-grade plywood |
| 6 | frame ends | 2 | $\frac{5}{8} \times 2\frac{1}{2} \times 21''$ | " |

Also need four swivel-type plate casters with 2" wheels.

The last step is to add the top frame. To start, cut these pieces a bit longer than necessary so you can trim them to exact length as you add them to the project. Attach with glue and 4d galvanized box nails.

# PROJECT 68
## LARGE PLANTER

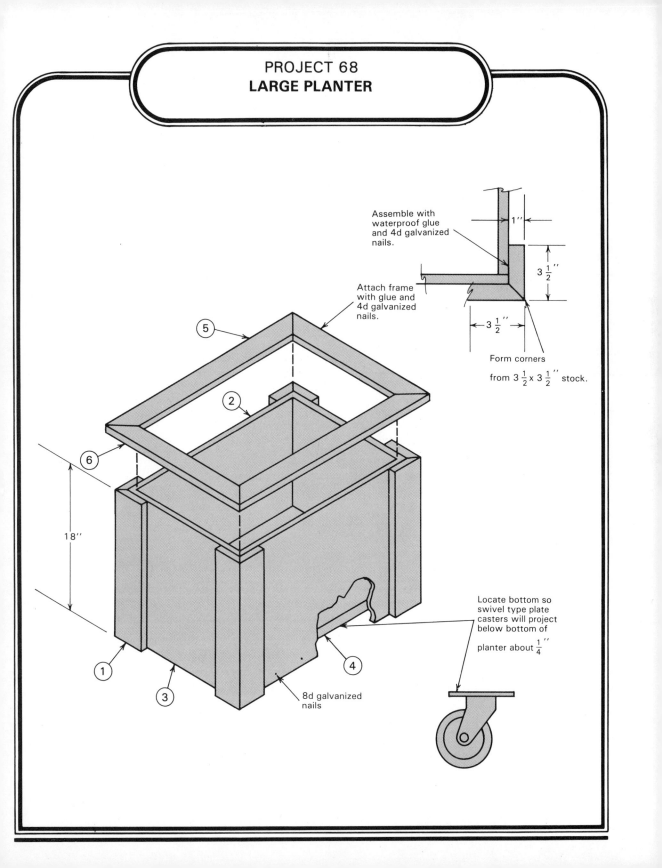

Assemble with waterproof glue and 4d galvanized nails.

1″

$3\frac{1}{2}″$

$3\frac{1}{2}″$

Form corners from $3\frac{1}{2} \times 3\frac{1}{2}″$ stock.

Attach frame with glue and 4d galvanized nails.

⑤

②

⑥

18″

①

③

④

8d galvanized nails

Locate bottom so swivel type plate casters will project below bottom of planter about $\frac{1}{4}″$

# Flower Pot Tree

The Flower Pot Tree is a unique and attractive stand for displaying plants. It can be placed permanently in the ground or made with a base so that you can use it anywhere, even in the house. Design options include supports, so pots can hang from chains; or shelves so pots can just sit.

For in-ground placement, you can use a pressure-treated post, or choose any species like pine, fir, redwood, or cedar—so long as the soil/concrete contact areas are treated with a preservative. Do this even if you work with redwood or cedar, which have a degree of natural resistance against decay and insect damage.

There are many ways to build the Flower Pot Tree. It's a good idea to know in advance the type of plants and the sizes of the pots you wish to display.

How much spacing you use between the supports or shelves will depend on the size of the pots and the type of plants you will display. A permanent installation for pots which will hang from a chain can be taller than the six feet suggested. Seven or even eight feet above grade is not out of line and can be very dramatic.

Study the drawings carefully before you start. Use a waterproof glue in all joints in addition to the aluminum or galvanized nails that are called for. Holes for supports should be sized to provide a tight fit. If you use large dowels, be sure to coat them with a sealer before putting them in place. Aluminum tubing will work okay, and holds up well outdoors. Materials such as pipe or steel rod will rust, and should be treated with a protective spray finish. They can, of course, be painted. A wrought-iron black paint is a good choice. Also protect any chain that is used, unless the chain is galvanized, and you are satisfied with its appearance.

Wood parts can be painted. Or you can opt for a natural appearance, by applying several coats of an exterior-type sealer.

# PROJECT 69
# FLOWER POT TREE

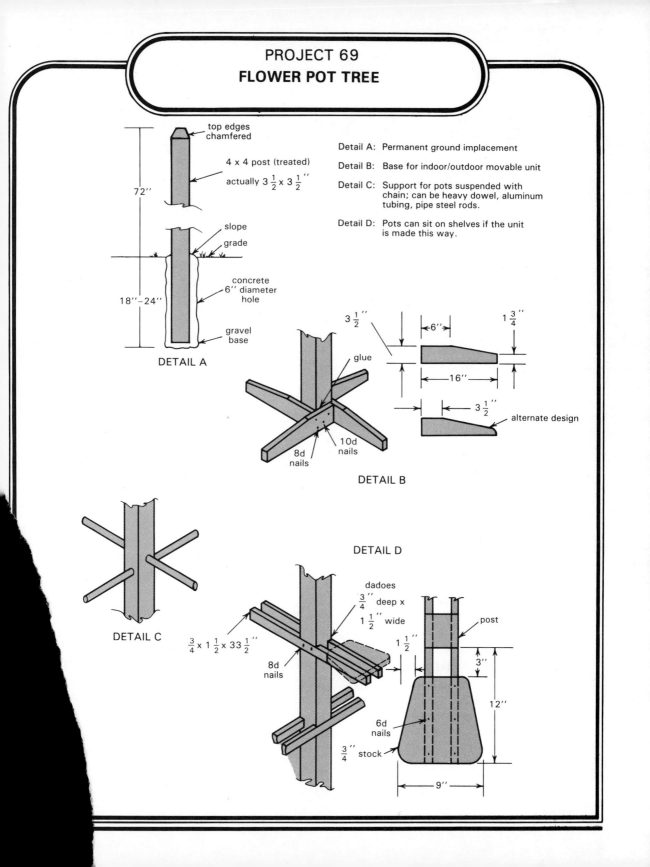

top edges chamfered

4 x 4 post (treated)

actually $3\frac{1}{2}$ x $3\frac{1}{2}$ ''

72''

slope

grade

concrete 6'' diameter hole

18''–24''

gravel base

DETAIL A

Detail A: Permanent ground implacement

Detail B: Base for indoor/outdoor movable unit

Detail C: Support for pots suspended with chain; can be heavy dowel, aluminum tubing, pipe steel rods.

Detail D: Pots can sit on shelves if the unit is made this way.

$3\frac{1}{2}$ ''

6''

$1\frac{3}{4}$ ''

16''

$3\frac{1}{2}$ ''

alternate design

glue

10d nails

8d nails

DETAIL B

DETAIL C

DETAIL D

$\frac{3}{4}$ x $1\frac{1}{2}$ x $33\frac{1}{2}$ ''

8d nails

dadoes $\frac{3}{4}$ '' deep x $1\frac{1}{2}$ '' wide

post

$1\frac{1}{2}$

3''

12''

6d nails

$\frac{3}{4}$ '' stock

9''

# FOUND WHIMSEYS

# Crested Bird

Walk through any gift shop and you will see natural wood forms somewhat modified by craftspeople. They're fun to make, nice to get paid for, and great as gifts. The general idea is to depart from the norm, to creatively visualize nature's throwaways as mementos with new significance.

Project 70 was a limb with a large knot or growth with a junction above that where another branch had ingrown. The weathering-away of the bark in several places highlighted the form's animal vitality. Sometimes these pieces resemble animal forms. Sometimes they seem to have a life of their own. I don't use any finish on them at all—and just give them a simple bas

**402**

How did this figure come to be? Nature did it all. All you need do with pieces like this is mount them on a base.